COVERT CONDITIONING

Edited by

Dennis Upper
Veteran's Administration Hospital, Brockton

Joseph R. Cautela
Boston College

Pergamon Press
New York • Oxford • Toronto • Sydney • Frankfurt • Paris

Pergamon Press Offices:

U.S.A. Pergamon Press Inc., Maxwell House, Fairview Park, Elmsford, New York 10523, U.S.A.

U.K. Pergamon Press Ltd., Headington Hill Hall, Oxford OX3 0BW, England

CANADA Pergamon of Canada Ltd., 150 Consumers Road, Willowdale, Ontario M2J 1P9, Canada

AUSTRALIA Pergamon Press (Aust) Pty. Ltd., P O Box 544, Potts Point, NSW 2011, Australia

FRANCE Pergamon Press SARL, 24 rue des Ecoles, 75240 Paris, Cedex 05, France

FEDERAL REPUBLIC OF GERMANY Pergamon Press GmbH, 6242 Kronberg/Taunus, Pferdstrasse 1, Federal Republic of Germany

Library of Congress Cataloging in Publication Data

Main entry under title:

Covert conditioning.

(Pergamon general psychology series)
Includes index.
1. Behavior therapy. 2. Conditional response.
I. Upper, Dennis, 1942- II. Cautela,
Joseph R.
RC489.B4C68 1979 616.8'914 79-61
ISBN 0-08-023347-3
ISBN 0-08-023346-5 pbk.

Printed in the United States of America

Table of Contents

Preface

Although more than 250 studies utilizing or investigating covert conditioning procedures have appeared in the psychological literature since 1966, to date there has been no central source of information about the six basic covert conditioning procedures, the rationale underlying their use, and their potential application (either singly or in combination) to a variety of clinical problems. The present volume brings together a representative sample of articles from the rapidly-growing covert conditioning literature in an attempt to meet the need for such a central source.

In selecting articles for publication in this volume, the editors have endeavored to include (a) articles which describe the most representative use in clinical practice of each procedure, (b) experimental analogue studies, (c) reports of promising breakthroughs in the application of covert conditioning techniques to new clinical problems, and (d) articles which, as a group, cover a broad range of target behaviors, clinical settings, and client populations.

Section I of the book covers the theoretical background of covert conditioning and presents evidence to support its basic underlying assumptions. Each of the next six sections introduces one of the major covert conditioning techniques (covert sensitization, covert reinforcement, covert negative reinforcement, covert extinction, covert modeling, covert response cost), presents experimental analogue evidence (if available) of its efficacy, and describes the use of that procedure in treating a number of clinical target behaviors. The chapters in the final section—Section VIII —describe the clinical application of combinations of covert conditioning techniques to a variety of problems.

The editors wish to extend their thanks and appreciation to the authors and publishers of these articles for permitting them to be included here; to the people at Pergamon Press who aided in the book's production; and to our families, friends, and professional colleagues for their support, advice, and encouragement.

Dennis Upper
Joseph R. Cautela

SECTION I
THEORETICAL
BACKGROUND

Chapter 1
Covert Conditioning: Assumptions and Procedures*
Joseph R. Cautela

Summary—The paper discusses the assumptions and procedures of six covert conditioning techniques that include: covert positive reinforcement, covert negative reinforcement, covert sensitization, covert extinction, covert response cost, and covert modeling. Extensive research evidence is cited and the current trends in this area are briefly noted.

A number of recent publications indicate a trend toward the development of procedures which manipulate imagery to modify covert and overt behavior. Wolpe legitimized the investigation of covert processes within a behavioristic framework through the assumption that if a client is led to imagine particular events in an office or consulting room, then overt and covert behavior would change outside of the therapy session in a predictable manner (1958). Since Wolpe's initial contribution, a number of investigators have developed techniques to modify behavior which involve the manipulation of covert events.

One group of investigators such as Bandura (1969), Cautela (1973), Homme (1965), and Stampfl and Levis (1967), stay within the learning theory framework in their conceptualization of the role of covert events in the control of behavior. Another group of investigators subscribe to cognitive behavior modification: they focus on the importance of covert events in behavior modification but do not conceptualize these events in a learning theory framework. Investigators in this category include Davison and Wilson (1973), Lazarus (1971), Mahoney (1974), and Meichenbaum (1973, 1974). Investiga-

---

*Reprinted with permission from the *Journal of Mental Imagery*, 1, 1977, 53-64 © Brandon House, Inc.

tions within a learning theory framework are apt to hold the homogeneity assumption, i.e., covert events obey the same laws as overt events. They also assume that covert and overt events interact to influence each other. The cognitive behavior modifiers generally do not accept the homogeneity assumption but accept the interaction effect. As probably is clear from the above, the practitioners of covert conditioning procedures belong to the first group and accept both the homogeneity and the interaction assumptions. Covert conditioning also assumes that these events are best conceptualized within the operant framework. The covert conditioning procedures and the operant conditioning and social learning analogues are presented in Table 1.

GENERAL DESCRIPTION OF ALL PROCEDURES

Following a behavioral analysis, therapists present a general rationale for the use of covert conditioning procedures. A typical rationale is presented below:

Your undesired behaviors occur primarily because they are being maintained by the environment. The environment has many ways of influencing you. People in the environment may be rewarding, punishing, or ignoring you, and thereby maintaining a particular behavior. Your observation of what other people do and what happens to them also affects your behavior. These are just a few examples. By changing how the environment influences you, we can change your behavior. If you are rewarded for a desirable behavior, the desired behavior will increase. If you are punished for an undesired behavior, it will decrease. I shall teach you techniques in which you imagine yourself or another person performing a particular behavior, and then you imagine the appropriate consequence. When you imagine your scene, it is important that you involve all your senses. If you are walking through the woods, imagine that you can feel the wind on your face, hear branches rubbing against one another, see the rays of sun filtering through the leaves, and smell the earth. Experience the movements in your body. The most critical part of your imagining is that you feel that you are actually experiencing the event rather than just seeing yourself.

The client is then asked to imagine a scene in order to demonstrate his imagery ability. He is asked to raise his right index finger when the scene is clear. Inquiry is made concerning the scene's clarity and emotive capacities. If the client's imagery is deemed adequate, he is asked to imagine the scene by himself. If a client experiences difficulty in imagining in general, or in any sense modality in particular, appropriate imagery training is given.

The therapist then adds the behavior to be changed to the imagery sequence. If the client wishes to become more assertive, for example, the therapist describes a scene in which the client is asserting himself properly. He requests the client to signal when this experience is clear. He then instructs the client to reinforce himself with the previously practiced scene. At the end of the sequence and every forthcoming sequence, the therapist inquires into the clarity of possibly other dimensions of the behavior-consequence sequence. The therapist then instructs the client to complete the entire sequence on his own. There are many possible themes and variations of therapist-client imagining. The most commonly used sequence is a series of twenty complemen-

Table 1.1 Operant, Social Learning, and Covert Conditioning Procedures

Operant Procedures	Covert Conditioning Procedures
Positive Reinforcement	*Covert Positive Reinforcement*
The increase in response probability occurring when a stimulus follows a response	The increase in response probablity occurring when an imagined stimulus follows an imagined or actual response.
Negative Reinforcement	*Covert Negative Reinforcement*
The increase in response probability occurring when an aversive stimulus is terminated by a response.	The increase in response probability occurring when an imagined, aversive stimulus is terminated by an imagined or actual response.
Punishment	*Covert Sensitization*
The decrease in response probability occurring when an aversive stimulus follows a response.	The decrease in response probability occurring when an imagined aversive stimulus follows an actual or imagined response.
Extinction	*Covert Extinction*
The decrease in response probability occurring when the stimulus which formerly increased the response does not follow the response.	The decrease in response probability occurring when an imagined stimulus which formerly increased the response does not follow the actual or imagined response.
Response Cost	*Covert Response*
The decrease in response probability occurring when a stimulus which is a reinforcer does not follow the response.	The decrease in response probability occurring when an imagined stimulus which is a reinforcer does not follow the actual or imagined response.
Social Learning Procedures	Covert Conditioning Procedures
Modeling	*Covert Modeling*
The learning of new responses or the changing of existing responses by watching others and the consequences.	The learning of new responses or the changing of existing responses by imagining watching others or oneself and by imagining the consequences.

tary trials where the therapist describes a scene and the client then covertly models the same scene.

Covert Positive Reinforcement

Covert positive reinforcement (CPR) (Cautela, 1970a) is a technique in which the person rewards himself in imagination for the desired behavior in real life or in imagination (see Table 1). CPR is used with both approach and avoidance behaviors which the client wishes to change. While the procedure is similar in some respects to systematic desensitization, it differs from and extends beyond desensitization. Unlike desensitization, it does not require relaxation or a hierarchy, and it is conceptualized as an operant procedure in which a covert reinforcer will increase response probability. It extends beyond desensitization; for, it can be used with both avoidance and approach behaviors.

As usual, the client is given a full explanation of the use of the procedure. Thus, the degree of his cooperation is improved. Furthermore, the more information the client possesses the more generalization is likely to occur.

Initially, the therapist describes a reinforcer chosen from the Reinforcement Survey Schedule or another source. For example:

You are lying on the beach on a hot summer day. Concentrate on all the details around you. Notice all the sensations. Feel the hot sun beating down on you and the warmth from the blanket. Smell the refreshing air. Watch the waves come rolling up onto the beach. Be aware of how good your body feels now that you are swimming through the water.

The client is asked to indicate how vivid and how pleasant the scene was. He is instructed to imagine this scene whenever the therapist says "reinforcement." The therapist then describes the client engaged in the feared but desired behavior or avoiding the inappropriate behavior. The client is told to signal as soon as this scene is clear. Upon the signal, the therapist says "reinforcement" and allows 10-15 seconds for the client to enjoy the reinforcer. The therapist then again checks for clarity of imagery and proceeds to describe the client engaged in sequences of behavior-reinforcement-behavior- reinforcement. For example, a therapist who is working with a client to increase social activities might choose to employ the following scenes:

Imagine that you are sitting at home wishing you had the nerve to ask John, a man you recently met and would like to get to know, out for a drink. You decide to call him up. As soon as this is clear, signal. (Client signals). Reinforcement. (Pause). Was your reinforcing scene clear? (Client responds). All right, let's continue. You walk over to the phone, start dialing, and take a deep breath to relax. Raise your finger when this is clear. (Client signals). Reinforcement. (Pause). You finish dialing, hear the phone ring, and hear John say, "Hello." You say, "Hi, John this is . . . I thought it might be fun to finish our conversation of the other evening and was wondering if you could come over for a drink Thursday night." Signal when this is clear. (Client signals). Reinforcement. You hear John say, "Sure, I'd really like to do that." (Client signals). Reinforcement.

The therapist then requests that the client imagine the same sequence of behaviors and reinforcements to himself. He stresses the importance of clear imagery and a feeling of ease and confidence while doing the behaviors.

A preponderance of experimental evidence indicates that CPR is effective in modifying behavior (Ascher, 1973; Blanchard & Draper, 1973; Cautela, Steffen, & Wish, 1972; Cautela, Walsh, & Wish, 1971; Epstein & Peterson,

1973; Flannery, 1972; Guidry & Randolph, 1974; Krop, Calhoon, & Verrier, 1971; Krop, Messinger, & Reiner, in press; Krop, Perez, & Beaudion, 1973; Ladouceur, 1974; Manno & Marston, 1972; Marshall, Boutilier, & Minnes, 1974; Marshall, Strawbridge, & Keltner, 1972; Tondo & Cautela, 1974; Wisocki, 1973). Other evidence is more equivocal (Ladouceur, 1974; Marshall, Strawbridge, & Keltner, 1972).

Covert Negative Reinforcement

Covert negative reinforcement (CNR) (Cautela, 1970b) is analogous to operant negative reinforcement (ONR). The response to be increased terminates an aversive stimulus. This termination of the aversive stimulus by the desired behavior has the effect of increasing the desired behavior. In the same way that fastening one's seat belt is encouraged by the termination of the buzzing, so walking into a feared meeting is fostered by imagining the end of something far more aversive.

This procedure is used as a final alternative when the client has not responded positively to a covert reinforcement or a covert modeling procedure. These procedures may fail, if the client has few reinforcers: he cannot even visualize anything pleasant; or he may be so afraid that he cannot bring himself to imagine someone else performing the feared behavior.

There are several points to be made concerning the choice of the aversive stimulus: (1) it must elicit fear, (2) it must be clear, (3) it must be one which the client can terminate immediately, otherwise, backward classical conditioning of the already feared behavior and another very aversive stimulus may occur. Nausea should probably not be used because the nauseous feeling may linger (Ashem & Donner, 1968). The possibility that the clients will become further sensitized to his aversive stimulus has not been borne out. On the contrary, it has been found that he appears to become accustomed to it. This phenomenon may be explained by several different hypotheses. First, habituation may be occurring merely because of repeated exposure to the feared stimulus. Secondly, the client's control over the aversive stimulus's onset and offset may lessen its aversiveness. Thirdly, the pairing of the aversive stimulus and the subsequent adaptive response may also minimize its aversiveness.

Two examples of CNR scenes follow. In the first case, the client is afraid to go into his office. His aversive stimulus is snakes.

Imagine that you have fallen into a pit of snakes. There are rattlesnakes, copperheads, and a boa constrictor. You move back to avoid a copperhead and step on a rattlesnake. The rattlesnake is hissing and about to bite. Shift. Imagine that you are walking into your office feeling calm and confident.

In the second case, the behavior to be increased is sexual activity with women. The aversive stimulus is exposure to criticism.

Imagine that you are at work and your boss is criticizing you for a job done poorly. Shift. Imagine that you are lying in bed with a woman and that she is gently rubbing your back.

In all cases, it is important that when the therapist says "shift," the client terminate the aversive scene and switch to the behavior to be increased.

At first glance, it may appear that CNR is not the appropriate analogue to ONR, since the therapist is prompting the response, the results, and the elimination of aversive stimulation. However, when the client practices CNR scenes himself, then he is making the response that terminates the noxious stimulation. The use of CNR by the client is appropriately analogous to ONR.

Experimental evidence suggests that CNR is an effective procedure to use. Two analogue studies present evidence that CNR increases performance (Ascher & Cautela, 1972; Marshall, Boutilier, & Minnes, 1974), and that it is as effective as desensitization and a combination of COR and relaxation (Marshall, Boutilier, & Minnes, 1974). A third study suggests that it can be used to enhance people's opinions of the elderly (Cautela & Wisocki, 1969). However, some equivocal results have also been reported.

Covert Sensitization

Originally covert sensitization (CS) was not conceptualized within the operant framework (Cautela, 1967). However, later it was conceived as a punishment procedure within that framework (see Table 1). A highly aversive imaginal consequence, previously rated by the client as noxious, is made contingent upon a maladaptive approach behavior. This stimulus may be relevant or irrelevant to the problem. Vomiting has been the most frequently used covert aversive consequence; other common stimuli are worms, rats, spiders, and maggots. The maladaptive approach behaviors typically treated by covert sensitization are: obesity, alcoholism, smoking, sexual problems, and drug abuse.

Prior to the beginning of the CS procedure, the client is given an explanation for the use of this technique. The complexity of the rationale varies with the client's level of sophistication. Basically, the client is told that CS is an aversive conditioning or punishment procedure; that the reason it is being used is to decrease the probability of the identified problem behavior; and that he will imagine an aversive consequence soon after imagining the maladaptive behavior.

The initial scene is then described to the client. For example, a scene concerning the treatment of obesity might have the following format:

You are sitting in your favorite chair, feeling rather bored. You decide to go to the kitchen to see what there is to eat. You notice last night's leftover dessert. Just as you reach for the fork, you experience a queasy feeling in your stomach. You pick up the fork and you feel hot and cold flashes. Just as you sink the fork into the pie bitter particles come into your mouth. You cut into the pie and vomit comes gushing up into your throat and spews all over the pie, the table, and your clothes. You look at the pie and it is covered with soft, spongy mucous material. The blueberries look like sores sticking out of the slimy matter. Looking at it makes you feel even sicker and vomit pours out of both your mouth and nose. You feel wretched and humiliated. You turn away, notice the sunlight flowing through the window, smell a fresh breeze, and immediately begin to feel better.

The client is then asked to rate the clarity and emotiveness of the scene. If he has recreated it clearly and experienced disgust, he is asked to imagine the same scene by himself. Scenes are created for specific food stimuli, locations, times etc., to enhance their effectiveness in dealing with specific problems. Self-control or relief scenes are also added and alternate with aversive scenes. An escape scene might take this form:

You are sitting in your favorite chair and decide to have a snack. Just as you decide to eat, you feel queasy in your stomach. You say to yourself, "I am not going to eat." As soon as you decide not to eat, you feel fine and are proud you resisted temptation and exercised self-control.

The literature on CS indicates that, in general, it is an effective procedure. The data indicate that CS is more effective with some behaviors than with others. The most promising area for the use of CS appears to be sexual disorders: all studies report CS to be highly effective (Barlow, Agras, Leitenberg, Callahan, & Moore, 1972; Barlow, Leitenberg, & Agras, 1969; Maletzsky, 1974; Maletzsky & George, 1973), even when the opposite expectation is induced (Barlow et al., 1972).

In the area of smoking, CS combined with other procedures, such as those used to decrease anxiety, appears to be effective (Gerson & Lanyon 1972); Wagner & Bragg, 1970). It also is at least as effective as other self-control procedures (Lawson & May, 1970; Sipich, Russel, & Tobias, 1974; Wisocki & Rooney, 1974). The evidence for alcoholism and obesity is less consistent. Some studies suggest that CS can decrease drinking (Ashem & Donner, 1968; Fleiger & Zingle, 1973); another (Blanchard, Libet, & Young, 1973) reports negative results. Several studies suggest that CS is as efficacious or more so than other procedures to lose weight (Foreyt & Hagen, 1973; Harris, 1969; Janda & Rimm, 1972; Manno & Marston, 1972; Murray & Harrington, 1972;). However, two studies show that little weight was actually lost (Foreyt & Hagen, 1973; Lick & Bootzin, 1971).

Covert Extinction

In covert extinction (CE) (Cautela, 1971), the client imagines that he is engaging in his particular problem behavior but that he is not receiving any of the usual environmental or social reinforcements for it. CE can be used with maladaptive approach and avoidance behaviors. The smoker provides an example of the maladaptive approach behavior. He may imagine that he is inhaling a cigarette but that he cannot smell anything, cannot feel the smoke in his body, cannot discern any nicotine in the cigarette, and does not feel relaxed. The scene is appropriately embellished by the therapist: he stresses the absence of sensations in any sense modality, of feeling, thinking or behaving reinforcers. An example of a maladaptive avoidance behavior is a child's fear of going to school. It imagines that it will play with its mother, but the mother makes plans to be out of the house all day and that there is absolutely nothing to do. For both the approach or avoidance behavior, CE is generally used when the environmental stimuli are conditioning the behavior at a higher rate than are the procedures in use, or when individuals who are maintaining the behavior will not or cannot cooperate in the use of extinction.

There are three difficulties in using either overt or covert extinction. Two of these difficulties are ones about which the client should be forewarned. He should be told, that he is likely to feel resentful when the reinforcement usually accompanying his actions is no longer present. But to ease this problem, he can be assured that the resentment is natural, that it can be decreased by CPR, and that it will fade in time. Secondly, the client should be warned that the behavior to be extinguished is likely to increase for a brief period. A brief discussion of studies showing an extinction affect may be helpful to make the client understand the burst of responding prior to the decrease. The third difficulty is the common refusal on the part of the client to realize that he is rewarding his maladaptive behaviors, or to believe that he is performing the behavior to get attention. Therefore, the therapist should be prepared to provide a convincing rationale.

There is one experimental study (Ascher & Cautela, 1974) and some uncontrolled data (Gotestam & Melin, 1974) that suggest that CE is a viable procedure. In a 3 × 2 factorial study, Ascher and Cautela compared CE, anticipated extinction, and noninstruction under both overt reinforcement and no overt reinforcement. The study showed that CE was effective whether or not overt reinforcement was present. In the Gotestam and Melin study, four amphetamine addicts undergoing CE reported no physiological arousal when they illegally injected themselves with the drugs. In a 9-month follow-up two of the four were still not using drugs.

Covert Response Cost

Covert response cost (CRC) (Cautela, in press) is the removal of an imagined positive reinforcer contingent upon an actual or, more commonly, an imagined response. CRC is similar to CS: both are aversive conditioning procedures used to decrease response probability. In CS, however, an aversive stimulus is added to the scene; in CRC, a positive stimulus is subtracted. CS is used with maladaptive approach behaviors, but CRC can be used with both approach and avoidance behaviors.

Overt response cost literature suggests that the procedure does not have the side effects of escape (Phillips, Phillips, Fixsen, & Wolf, 1971) or of disruptive behavior associated with punishment. Cautela (in press) reports that some clients claim a greater conditioned emotional response with CRC than with CS.

There is merit in using the CRC concomitantly with CS. The utilization of two different procedures to decrease behavior(s) may prevent boredom or habituation; some alternation of CS and CRC scenes may render the clients more alert and more apt to do homework. Furthermore, the use of two procedures may preclude habituation to one aversive stimulus.

The choice of the positive reinforcer to be removed is made from a Response Cost Survey Schedule (Cautela, in press). This is a Likert-type scale which asks the client to rate the extent of aversion he would feel upon losing any particular item on a 1-5 scale. An example of the use of CRC for drinking behavior follows (Cautela, in press).

As you walk into the house after work, you say to yourself, "I think I'll start off with a belt" (Client signals for clarity). Shift. Imagine your new car is smashed against a tree. The entire right side is caved in. You wonder how long you will be without your car. You think of the reduced value of the car not compensated by the insurance. (Client signals for clarity). Imagine that you are walking toward the liquor cabinet to pour yourself a straight shot before your wife knows that you are home. (Signal). Shift. Imagine the smashed car scene. Now imagine that you are opening the bottle and raising it to your lips.

Two caveats are in order. The therapist should monitor the client's anxiety levels when using CRC with an avoidance problem, to insure that his general arousal level is not heightened. When dealing with approach problems, the therapists should ensure that the client immediately shifts from the undesirable behavior to CRC scenes. The immediacy of the aversiveness is more effective than delayed response cost.

Both overt and covert response costs are relatively untried procedures. Nevertheless, there are two experiments pointing to the efficacy of CRC. Tondo, Lane, and Gill (1975) using an ABCD design, found that CRC reduced both bites and sips of the targeted eating response. In a group design, Scott and Jackson (1975) compared CRC, COR and a control group on test anxiety. They found that the text anxiety of Ss in CRC and COR groups was reduced significantly more than that of the Ss in the control group.

Covert Modeling

Covert modeling (CM) (Cautela, in press) is based on its overt equivalent, and involves the learning of new behaviors or altering of existing behaviors by, in imagination, watching people's behaviors and the consequences that befall them. Overt modeling itself is usually regarded as a social learning phenomenon. It is said to work via two processes (Bandura, 1969); contiguity and mediation. However, modeling behavior can also be conceptualized as an operant learned in infancy and then reinforced on an intermittent schedule (Cautela, in press).

CM can be used with any type of behavior problem, both by itself or in combination with other procedures. There are two particular advantanges in using CM. First, with an individual reporting excessive fear or difficulty in employing one of the other procedures, CM can be used as a shaping procedure in which he first watches someone else perform the behavior, then watches himself perform the behavior, then imagines performing the behavior, and finally actually performs the behavior. Secondly, with a client who is becoming bored with other procedures or who is reporting difficulty using them, CM is a useful alternative.

The client is given a rationale including anecdotal and experimental evidence backing up the point that people can learn by watching other people, and, more specifically, by watching them in imagination. Thereafter, the general use of the procedure is similar to other covert conditioning techniques. An example of CM used with a woman who was afraid to speak in a group of people follows:

Imagine that you are sitting in a lecture watching a woman of your age and looks. She is standing in front of the class and appears calm and relaxed. She is smiling and makes friendly comments to the students. A student asks a question and she listens intently, she then pauses to think of an answer, and responds in a relaxed, nondefensive way. The class ends and you notice a student walk up to her and tell her that he really enjoyed the class, particularly her manner of answering questions in a calm, articulate manner.

There is much experimental evidence which suggests that CM is an effective technique (Cautela, Flannery, & Hanley, 1974; Kazdin, 1973a, 1973b, 1974a, 1974b). It has been found to be as effective as overt modeling on most dependent measures (Cautela, Flannery & Hanley, 1974). The addition of COR to a CM procedure seems to enhance its effectiveness (Kazdin, 1973b). A coping model is more effective than a mastery model (Kazdin, 1973a, 1974a, 1974b). Multiple models are more effective than single models (Kazdin, 1974a).

CURRENT TRENDS

Currently the investigations concerning covert conditioning focus on the process studies which are designed to determine the viable factors in covert conditioning. For example, are the effects of covert reinforcement upon anxious behavior due to reciprocal inhibition? Are the effects of covert sensitization due to suggestion, demand characteristics? Currently we are expanding the use of covert conditioning to additional populations such as children and the mentally retarded. Also we are employing covert conditioning in the modification of organic dysfunction, e.g., pain and epilepsy.

REFERENCES

Ascher, L.M. An analog study of covert positive reinforcement. In R.D. Rubin, J.P. Brady and J.R. Henderson (Eds.) *Advances in behavior therapy* , Vol. 4. Proceedings of the Fifth Conference of the Association for Advancement of Behavior Therapy. New York: Academic Press, 1973.

Ascher, L.M., & Cautela, J.R. Covert negative reinforcement: An experimental test. *Journal of Behavior Therapy and Experimental Psychiatry*, 1972, 3, 1-5.

Ascher, L.M., & Cautela, J.R. An experimental study of covert extinction. *Journal of Behavior Therapy and Experimental Psychiatry*, 1974, 5, 233-238.

Ashem, B., & Donner, L. Covert sensitization with alcoholics: A controlled replication. *Behavior Research and Therapy*, 1968, 6, 7-12.

Bandura, A. *Principles of behavior modification*. New York: Holt, Rinehart and Winston, 1969

Barlow, D.H., Agras, W.S., Leitenberg, H., Callahan, E.J., & Moore, R.C. The contribution of therapeutic instruction to covert sensitization. *Behavior Research and Therapy*, 1972, *10* , 411- 415.

Barlow, D.H., Leitenberg, H., & Agras, W.S. The experimental control of sexual deviation through manipulation of the noxious scene in covert sensitization. *Journal of Abnormal Psychology*, 1969, *14* , 596-601.

Blanchard, E.B., & Draper, D.O. Treatment of a rodent phobia by covert reinforcement: A single subject experiment. *Behavior Therapy, 1973, 4*, 559-564.

Blanchard, E.B., Libet, J.M., & Young, L.D. Apneic aversion and covert sensitization in the treatment of a hydrocarbon inhalation addiction: A case study. *Journal of Behavior Therapy and Experimental Psychiatry*, 1973, *4*, 383-387.

Cautela, J.R., Covert sensitization. *Psychological Reports*, 1967, 20, 459-468.

Cautela, J.R., Covert reinforcement. *Behavior Therapy*, 1970, *1*, 33-50.(a)

Cautela, J.R. Covert negative reinforcement. *Journal of Behavior Therapy and Experimental Psychiatry*, 1970, 1, 273-378.(b)

Cautela, J.R. Covert extinction. *Behavior Therapy*, 1971, 2, 192-200.

Cautela, J.R. Covert processes and behavior modification. *Journal of Nervous and Mental Disease*, 1973, *157*, 27-36.

Cautela, J.R. Covert modeling. In press.

Cautela, J.R., Flannery, R.B. Jr., & Hanley, S. Covert modeling: An experimental test. Behavior Therapy, 1974, 5, 494-502.

Cautela, J.R., Steffen, J., & Wish, P. Covert reinforcement: An experimental test. Unpublished manuscript. Boston College, 1972.

Cautela, J.R., Walsh, K.J., & Wish P.A. The use of covert reinforcement in the modification of attitudes toward the mentally retarded. *Journal of Psychology*, 1971, *77*, 257-260.

Cautela, J.R., & Wisocki, P. The use of imagery in the modification of attitudes toward the elderly: A preliminary report. *Journal of Psychology*, 1969, *73*, 193.199.

Davison, G.C., & Wilson, G.T. Processes of fear-reduction in systematic desensitization: Cognitive and social reinforcement factors in humans. *Behavior Therapy,* 1973, *4*, 1-21.

Epstein, L.H., & Peterson, G.L. Differential conditioning using covert stimuli. *Behavior Therapy*, 1973, *4*, 1-21.

Flannery, R.B. A laboratory analogue of two covert reinforcement procedures. *Journal of Behavior Therapy and Experimental Psychiatry*, 1972, *3*, 171-177.

Fleiger, D.L., & Zingle, H.W. Covert sensitization treatment with alcoholics. *Canadian Counselor*, 1973, *7*, 269-277.

Foreyt, J.P., & Hagen, R.L. Covert sensitization: Conditioning or suggestion? *Journal of Abnormal Psychology*, 1973, *82*, 17-23.

Gerson, P., & Lanyon, R.I. Modification of smoking behavior with aversion-desensitization procedure. *Journal of Consulting and Clinical Psychology*, 1972, *38*, 399-402.

Gotestam, K., & Melin, L. Covert extinction of amphetamine addition. *Behavior Therapy*, 1974, 5, 90-92.

Guidry, L.S., & Randolph, D.L. Covert reinforcement in the treatment of test anxiety. *Journal of Counseling Psychology*, 1974, *21*, 260- 264.

Harris, M.B. Self-directed program for weight control: A pilot study. *Journal of Abnormal Psychology*, 1964, *74*, 263-270.

Homme, L.E. Perspectives in psychology: XXIV Control of coverants, the operants of the mind. *Psychological Record*, 1965, *15*, 501-511.

Janda, L.H., & Rimm, D.C. Covert sensitization in the treatment of obesity. *Journal of Abnormal Psychology*, 1972, *80*, 37-42.

Kazdin, A.E. Covert modeling and the reduction of avoidance behavior. *Journal of Abnormal Psychology*, 1973, *81*, 87-95. (a)

Kazdin, A.E. Effects of covert modeling and reinforcement on assertive behavior. *Proceedings of the 81st Annual Convention of the American Psychological Association, Montreal, Canada*, 1973, *8*, 537-538.(b)

Kazdin, A.E. Covert modeling, model similarity and reduction of avoidance behavior. *Behavior Therapy*, 1974, *5*, 325-340.(a)

Kazdin, A.E. Effects of covert modeling and model reinforcement on assertive behavior. *Journal of Abnormal Psychology*, 1974, *83*, 240-252.(b)

Krop, H., Calhoon, B., & Verrier, R. Modification of the "self-concept" of emotionally disturbed children by covert reinforcement. *Behavior Therapy*, 1971, *2*, 200-204.

Krop, H., Messinger, J., & Reiner, C. Increasing eye contact by covert reinforcement. *Interpersonal Development*, in press.

Krop, H., Perez, F., & Beaudoin, C. Modification of "Self- concept" of psychiatric patients by covert reinforcement. In R.D. Rubin, J.P. Brady, & J.D. Henderson (Eds.), *Advances in Behavior Therapy*, Vol. 4. Proceedings of the Fifth Conference of the association for the Advancement of Behavior Therapy. New York: Academic Press, 1973.

Ladouceur, R. An experimental test of the learning paradigm of covert positive reinforcement in deconditioning anxiety. *Journal of Behavior Therapy and Experimental Psychiatry*, 1974, 5, 3-6.

Lawson, D.M., & May, R.B. Three procedures for the extinction of smoking behavior. *Psychological Record*, 1970, *20*, 151- 157.

Lazarus, A.A. *Behavior therapy and beyond*. New York: McGraw-Hill, 1971.

Lick, J., & Bootzin, R. Covert sensitization for the treatment of obesity. Paper presented to the Midwestern Psychological Association. Detroit, 1971.

Mahoney, M.J. *Cognition and behavior modification*. Cambridge, Mass.: Ballinger Publishing Co., 1974.

Maletzsky, B.M. Assisted covert sensitization in the treatment of exhibitionism. *Journal of Consulting and Clinical Psychology*, 1974, 42, 34-40.

Maletzsky, B.M., & George, F.S. The treatment of homosexuality by "assisted" covert sensitization. *Behavior Research and Therapy*, 1973, *11*, *655-657*.

Manno, B., & Marston, A.R. Weight reduction as a function of negative reinforcement. *Behavior Research and Therapy*, 1972, *10*, 201-207.

Marshall, W.L., Boutilier, J., & Minnes, P. The modification of phobic behavior by covert reinforcement. *Behavior Therapy*, 1974, 5, 469-480.

Marshall, W.L., Strawbridge, H., & Keltner, A. The role of mental relaxation in experimental desensitization. *Behavior Research and Therapy*, 1972, *10*, 355-366.

Meichenbaum, D. Cognitive factors in behavior modification: Modifying what clients say to themselves. In C.M. Franks and G.T. Wilson (Eds.), *Annual review of behavior therapy, theory, and practice, Vol. 1*. New York: Brunner-Mazel, 1973.

Meichenbaum, D. *Cognitive behavior modification*. Morristown, New Jersey: General Learning Press, 1974.

Murray, D.C., & Harrington, L.G. Covert aversive sensitization in the treatment of obesity. *Psychological Reports*, 1972, *30*, 560.

Phillips, E.L., Phillips, E.A., Fixen, D.L., & Wolf, M.M. Achievement place: Modification of the behavior of predelinquent boys within a token economy. *Journal of Applied Behavior Analysis*, 1971, *4*, 45-59.

Scott, D., & Jackson, W. Experimental test of covert response cost with a comparison to covert reinforcement for the treatment of test anxiety. Unpublished manuscript, Boston College, 1975.

Sipich, J.F., Russell, R.K., & Tobias, L.L. A comparison of covert sensitization and "nonspecific" treatment in the modification of smoking behavior. *Journal of Behavior Therapy and Experimental Psychiatry*, 1974, *5*, 201-203.

Stampfl, T., & Levis, D.J. Essentials of implosive therapy: A learning theory based psychodynamic behavioral therapy. *Journal of Abnormal Psychology*, 1967, *72*, 496-503.

Tondo, T.R., & Cautela, J.R. Assessment of imagery in covert reinforcement. *Psychological Reports*, 1974, *34*, 1271-1280.

Tondo, T.R., Lane, J.R., & Gill, K. Jr. Suppression of specific eating behaviors by covert response cost: An experimental analysis. *Psychological Record*, 1975, *25*, 187-196.

Wagner, M.K., & Bragg, A. Comparing behavior modification approaches to habit decrement-smoking. *Journal of Consulting and Clinical Psychology*, 1970, *34*, 258-263.

Wisocki, P.A. A covert reinforcement program for the treatment of test anxiety: Brief report. *Behavior Therapy*, 1973, *4*, 264-266.

Wisocki, P.A., & Rooney, E.J. A comparison of thought stopping and covert sensitization techniques in the treatment of smoking: A brief report. *Psychological Record*, 1974, 24, 191-192.

Wolpe, J. *Psychotherapy by reciprocal inhibition*. California: Stanford University Press, 1958.

Chapter 2
Covert Conditioning: A Theoretical Analysis*
Joseph R. Cautela and Mary Grace Baron

Summary — There appears to be a consensus that an investigation of covert events is necessary for a complete study of human behavior. Covert conditioning involves the manipulation of covert events. Three assumptions of covert conditioning (homogeneity, interaction, and learning) are presented together with a theoretical analysis and supportive evidence.

RECENT HISTORY OF COVERT PROCESSES IN PSYCHOLOGY

Conventional behaviorism (Watson, 1925; Stevens, 1939) inadvertently promoted the viewpoint that the world of human behavior is divided into public and private events (Koch, 1964). It was assumed that, in a scientific account of human behavior, unobservable private events (such as thoughts, feelings, images) are anathema. Watson (1919, p. viii) explained the conspicuous absence of traditional mentalistic concepts in his works:

These terms are in good repute, but I have found that I can get along without them . . . I frankly do not know what they mean, nor do I believe any one else can use them consistently.

He retained concepts such as thinking and attention only because he could carefully redefine them in terms of observable events. Watson (1919, p. 14) classified human responses using the following categories: (a) *explicit habit*

---

*Reprinted with permission from *Behavior Modification*, 1977, *1*, 351-368. © Sage Publications, Inc. 1977.

responses, e.g., violin playing, talking; (b) *implicit habit responses,* e.g., thinking, general body language habits, bodily sets or attitudes which are not easily observable by instrumentation or experimental aid (these are systems of conditional reflexes in various glands and unstriped muscles); (c) *explicit hereditary responses,* which include man's observable instinctive and emotional responses, e.g., love, rage; (d) *implicit hereditary responses,* e.g., ductless gland secretions, circulation systems and other biological responses which can be seen with the aid of instrumentation. He cautioned that responses of the second category (implicit habit responses) can become too easily neglected in discussion. Psychology should "bury subjective subject matter," wrote Watson (1925), but psychology should also not forget or exclude those behaviors which, because of their implicit nature, are difficult to observe.

American learning theorists such as Guthrie (1935), Skinner (1938), Hull (1934), and Spence (1956), in accepting the behaviorist dictum, found it more convenient to study only animal behavior, which apparently is influenced less by mediational (nonobservable) processes. The learning theorists assumed that studying a relatively simple organism (that is, one influenced by fewer variables) would provide the foundation for the study of more complex human behavior. In Russia, before the publication of Watson's (1913) work, Pavlov (as cited in a later translation in 1927) had already applied an objective approach to the study of cortical functioning by experimenting with animals under highly controlled conditions.

Some present-day behaviorists (Bandura, 1969, p. 586; Day, 1969; Skinner, 1953, 1963; Terrace, 1971) deny a dichotomous view of human behavior and espouse a radically different behaviorism which is characterized by systematic inclusion of private events in the experimental analysis of behavior. This departure from conventional behaviorism was triggered perhaps as an attempt to account for the discrepancies between the results of animal and human conditioning studies, or perhaps because some interesting complex human behaviors have demanded experimental attention. The radical behaviorists are in agreement that a unified account of nature awaits a science of human behavior which explains both public and private phenomena (Skinner, 1953, p. 258).

The general approach of radical behaviorists has been to assume a functional equivalence between overt (public) and covert (private) events (Day, 1969). This functional similarity means that covert events operate in an environment in a manner similar to overt events. In other words, events which are part of the observable environment and events which are unobservable, or private, have equal status in the explanation and control of human behavior.

A number of behaviorists have made theoretical statements supporting the functional equivalence of overt and covert events. Skinner (1953, p. 257) has written that an integrated view of nature cannot ignore the universe within an organism's skin. When studying private events, Skinner says, "We need not suppose that events which take place within an organism's skin have any special properties for that reason.'' A private event may be distinguishable by its limited accessibility, or perhaps even by its diminished strength, but certainly not by its structure or nature. Homme (1965) concludes that the inaccessibility of private events has deterred scientists from producing a technology of private events, but that nature does not really care who is manipulating the independent variables of which behavior is a function, even if that is the organism itself. Homme advises that modern behaviorism should not be bogged down with describing the topography of private behaviors, but rather should make direct attempts to control the frequency of private events.

Terrace (1971) analyzes seemingly nonbehavioristic, private concepts (such as ''awareness'') as conditioned behavior which owes its existence to a history of differential rewards mediated by other people. Ferster (1973) encourages a functional analysis of abstract descriptions (e.g., ''depression'') which are generally regarded as the domain of clinical psychology. Ferster (1973, p. 869) writes, ''The aspects of mental life believed heretofore to be inaccessible to objective descriptions can now be uncovered by recording the functional relation between the objectively observed components of a patient's performance.''

Though the preceding statements were all made by operant investigators, there is still a dearth of systematic experimentation by operant investigators into the area of covert behaviors. No systematic method or complete theoretical structure has yet been proposed for the continued scientific investigation of covert processes. The purpose of this paper is to present a rationale for the assumptions of covert conditioning along with relevant empirical evidence.

CLASSIFICATION AND INVESTIGATION OF BEHAVIORAL PROCESSES

Behavioral processes can be classified into three categories:

(1) overt processes;

(2) covert psychological responses, which include (a) thinking, or talking to oneself, (b) imaging, or making responses similar to those that are made to particular external stimuli when these stimuli are not present, and (c) feeling, or reproducing sensations (bodily cues) which one learns (via the verbal community) to apply to certain inferred responses (e.g., pain);

(3) covert physiological responses of body systems, organs, cells of which one is unaware, or responses of which one is aware, but which are not observable to others.

Some covert physiological processes are more potentially amenable to overt examination. Physiological apparatus can "amplify" a covert physiological response to bring it to a point of easy recognition. Covert psychological responses (e.g., imagery) are assumed to be occurring concomitantly with a physiological event (e.g., increased heart rate accompanying the image of a phobic object). Some covert events (e.g., thoughts) can best be made public through language mediation.

One could study categories of behavioral processes (overt and covert) separately, giving no consideration to their interaction or correspondence. One could also study the influence of one category on another. Furthermore, one may assume that different laws govern the activity of different categories (an assumption of discontinuity) or that the same laws operate on each category (an assumption of continuity). Also, one may assume a learning model to describe and explain these processes or assume some ot her model (e.g., the cognitive or psychodynamic) to guide investigations.

BEHAVIOR MODIFICATION AND PRIVATE EVENTS

In explaining private events, some behavior modifiers hold a learning-continuity assumption. These include Wolpe (1958), Cautela (1971a), Stampfl (1967), and Homme (1965). Another group of theorists call themselves cognitive behavior modifiers. These include Meichenbaum (1974), Lazarus (1971), Mahoney (1974), and Davison (1975). Among the learning theorists, there are those who operate within a respondent learning model (e.g., Wolpe), others whose orientation is operant (e.g., Homme, Cautela), and others who are exponents of Mowrer's two-factor theory (e.g., Stampfl). The cognitive behavior modifiers do not have a general theory, but conceptualize the existence of internal activities such as talking to self, problem-solving, and imagery, which mediate overt responses. Generally, those who hold a learning model also make an assumption of continuity between public and private events. The covert conditioning model described below assumes the continuity of overt and covert events, an interaction between these events, and examines these events within a learning (operant) framework.

COVERT CONDITIONING

The term "covert conditioning" (Cautela, 1976a) refers to a set of imagery-based procedures which alter response frequency by the manipulation of consequences. Analogous to the overt operant procedures which reduce response frequency (i.e., punishment, extinction, and response cost) are the techniques of covert sensitization (Cautela, 1966, 1967), covert extinction (Cautela, 1971b), and covert response cost (Cautela, (1976c). Covert positive reinforcement (Cautela, 1970b) and covert negative reinforcement (Cautela, 1970a) both increase response frequency. Bandura's (1969) work on modeling and observational learning provides the basis for another covert conditioning technique: covert modeling (Cautela, 1976b). Cautela places this technique within the operant model, although Bandura (1969) views modeling as an outgrowth of a contiguity-mediational model.

Procedurally, in each of the covert conditioning techniques a person is asked to imagine a response to be modified and then is asked to immediately imagine a consequence. In clinical use, covert conditioning generally means that both the responses to be modified and the consequence are presented in imagination. Experimental investigations of the covert conditioning procedures have presented the response to be increased both overtly and in imagination. The consequence, however, is always presented in imagination.

Assumptions Underlying Covert Conditioning

The covert conditioning procedures are based on three main assumptions.

1. *Homogeneity*. There is a continuity, or homogeneity between overt and covert behaviors. This assumption has variously been labeled the continuity assumption (Mahoney, 1974) or the assumption of functional equivalence (Day, 1969). We prefer the term "homogeneity," since "continuity" implies different substantive categories of response, and "equivalence" implies a separateness or distinction between overt and covert events. If there is homogeneity between overt and covert behaviors, then empirically derived conclusions about overt phenomena can be transferred to covert phenomena.

Covert and overt processes share similar importance and similar properties in explaining, maintaining, and modifying behavior. However, covert conditioning does not make the assumption that covert responses correspond to the real work any more than do overt responses; that is, covert conditioning does not assume that our sense modalities register photocopies of the real world.

2. *Interaction*. There is an interaction between overt and covert events. That is, when an individual makes covert responses, whether at the prompting of another individual (e.g., a therapist) or other stimulus events, these responses can influence overt and covert behavior in a manner similar to overt behaviors. Similarly, overt events can influence covert behavior. This assumption does not, of course, deny that sometimes covert events occur concomitantly with overt events and that sometimes covert events involve mere labeling of current overt events. Furthermore, when we conceptualize overt and covert behaviors or physiological and psychological behaviors as different

levels of activity, it is only for convenience of analysis, since the terms covert or psychological actually refer to a particular set of physiological events. Therefore, when we speak of covert or psychological events influencing overt or physiological events, we are not referring to purely covert events influencing physiological events. Rather, we are talking about a particular class of physiological events influencing another class of physiological events. In other words, the covert conditioning assumptions are not positing the same laws as governing qualitatively different classes of events.

3. *Learning*. Covert and overt events are similarly governed by laws of learning. We have focused on learning phenomena to illustrate the assumed identity between overt and covert events as there are substantial parametric data to both stimulate comparative analysis of covert and overt phenomena and provide further hypotheses for investigation. This learning theory approach has been criticized on the grounds that generalizations from one species of organism to another are not applicable because of unique biological constraints. One must remember, however, that there are ample data on learning in humans and that the assumption of homogeneity between the two classes of behavior (overt and covert) need only be applied to human behavior.

Evaluation of the Assumptions of Covert Conditioning

A theory can never be proven or disproven in an absolute sense, but evidence can influence the investigator to either accept the theory as it is, accept it in part, or deny it in total. The validity of either the homogeneity or nonhomogeneity assumptions can, thus, never be demonstrated with absolute certainty. Evidence can, however, influence one's confidence in the validity of either assumption.

In evaluation of a theory, the criteria for its acceptance include (1) degree of parsimony, (2) internal consistency, (3) derivation of fruitful hypotheses, and (4) supporting evidence for the hypotheses. The homogeneity assumption, with the imposition of a learning model, appears more parsimonious than the nonhomogeneity assumption since it involves fewer assumptions. The assumptions of covert conditioning have internal consistency (i.e., the assumptions do not contradict each other). A number of hypotheses (the covert conditioning techniques and hypothesis of the influence of learning variables on a number of covert behaviors such as dreaming and imagery) have been derived from the homogeneity/learning assumption.

The importance of espousing a homogeneity or nonhomogeneity assumption about covert events is more than a philosophical quibble or pure academic question. An investigator's position on this issue determines the type of methods used in therapy, as well as the research strategy and the variables studied in both experimental and nonexperimental settings. Certainly, the covert conditioning procedures would not have been derived had not homogeneity been assumed within a learning/operant model.

Evidence is presented elsewhere (Cautela, 1973) concerning the efficacy of the covert conditioning procedures derived from a homogeneity/learning model. These studies demonstrating the efficacy of covert conditioning and desensitization (Paul, 1969; Wolpe, 1958) in the treatment of behavior disorders give supportive evidence for the interaction hypothesis. The behavioral studies cited in this paper further support this assumption by showing the influence of overt events on covert events and covert events on overt events. Presented below are some data bearing on the equivalence of overt and covert events and behavioral studies supporting the learning assumption.

PHYSIOLOGICAL STUDIES

One way to show the similarity of overt and covert behavior is to make covert responses and stimuli "more observable" with concomitant physiological measures.

Miller (1935) obtained similar galvanic skin responses (GSR) while subjects performed related overt and covert responses. He presented to his subjects the symbols "T" and "4" in random order. "T" was always followed by electric shock, while "4" was never followed by shock. The subjects said each symbol aloud at each presentation. After a series of trials, subjects showed a large GSR to the presentation of the "T" (shock) and a small GSR to "4" (no shock). Subjects were then presented with a series of dots and told to say "4" to the first one, "T" to the second, "4" to the third, and so on. Finally, they were instructed to think "4" to the third, and so on. Finally, they were instructed to think "4" and "T" instead of saying them aloud when the dots were presented. Both saying and thinking "T" elicited a large GSR, and saying and thinking "4" elicited a small GSR. In this experiment the cue value of saying and thinking a word seems functionally equivalent, i.e., able to produce a similar response.

Cohen (1967) demonstrated the elicitation of an EEG wave form, the contingent negative variation (CNV), using both overt stimuli (light flashes, sound tones) and covert stimuli (words). John (1967), in a discussion of the parameters known to influence EEG-evoked potential wave form, cited evidence to demonstrate that different geometric patterns (e.g., a square and a circle) elicit evoked potentials of different form. He further referred to unpublished work in which researchers have observed that wave shapes resembling those normally evoked by presentation of a particular geometric form can be obtained in response to illumination of an empty visual field if the person *imagines* that the same form is present in the field (John, 1967, pp. 410-411).

Schwartz and Higgins (1971) recorded the heart rate of 17 subjects as they prepared to make both overt (key press) and covert (silently thinking the word "stop") responses. Their data show a reliable and similar preparatory cardiac response with both overt and covert responses. They also reported that the specific form of the cardiac response to the overt and covert modes was similarly affected by a task variable (instructions to respond slowly or rapidly). The preceding studies (1) support the homogeneity of overt and covert events in three different physiological responses, (2) strongly imply that the "actual (observable) activation of musculature and its efferent outflow resulting in *overt* behavior is not a necessary prerequisite for autonomic responding" (Schwartz and Higgins, 1971, p. 1145), (3) provide a record of the time of occurrence (and other possible topographic indices, e.g., latency, duration, and so on) of a covert event, (4) strengthen a hypothesis of homogeneity between overt and covert parameters (such as the instructions given in the Schwartz and Higgins study). On the whole, these studies present preliminary steps in the elaboration of covert events both as stimulus and as response.

BEHAVIORAL STUDIES

Procedurally, the following studies demonstrate the homogeneity of overt and covert events and support our interaction and learning assumptions by either comparing the effects of (1) related or (2) equated overt and covert events (independent variables) on an overt event (dependent variable), or (3) manipulating the parameters of a covert event and comparing the effects with known results of the same manipulation on an overt event.

Two experiments by Mahoney, Thoresen, and Danaher (1972) which also support the covert conditioning assumptions differ from the general procedural pattern of the studies cited here in that they measure the effects of overt events (external reward and punishment) on selected covert events (associative methods used in noun-pair recall). In the first experiment, a baseline was established for each subject's "free" use of each of a number of associative methods (repetition, sentence generation, imagery, or other methods). In a subsequent reinforcement phase, subjects who had reported a low rate of imagery use were then reinforced with dimes whenever they reported using imagery; subjects who had reported a high rate of imagery were reinforced with dimes whenever they reported using repetition. A consequent reversal phase involved reinforcement for reporting associative responses opposite to those which had just previously been reinforced. A final phase reinstated the conditions of the initial reinforcement phase. The ABCB design (baseline, reinforcement, reversal, and return to reinforcement) showed very clearly that whenever imagery was reinforced it was increased, and when repetition was reinforced imagery decreased. A second experiment, using the same design, demonstrated the effects of punishment (monetary loss) on covert associative responses. In this case, whenever imagery was punished it decreased, and when repetition was punished imagery increased.

Two studies report comparable behavioral changes produced by functionally related (but not equivalent) overt and covert independent variables. Krop, Calhoun, and Verrier (1971) reported that covert reinforcement (during which a subject reinforced himself with an idiosyncratically pleasing image on signal) and overt reinforcement (the subject was reinforced with a token) given after positive self-descriptive statements changed self-concept in the positive direction. Only the change produced by covert reinforcement was significant, however.

Callahan and Leitenberg (1973) compared aversion therapies based on covert sensitization (imagined aversive event following images of sexual behavior) with contingent shock (physical aversive event following penile erection to slides of sexually deviant material). They found no clear difference between techniques on the dependent measure of penile circumference change. Subjective reports of decreased sexual arousal were greater with covert sensitization. These two studies not only support the functional equivalence of overt and covert events, but also suggest that, in some situations (e.g., when subjective measures are used), a covert event may even be more effective as a reinforcing or punishing stimulus.

The following three studies were designed so that the independent variable conditions were topographically (i.e., duration, number of trials, characteristics of the experimental situation, and so on) as similar as possible, with the exception that in one condition a covert or imagined component was substituted for an overt component. Weiner (1965) observed the key-pressing of two subjects during 30 one-hour sessions on FI 10'' under conditions of both actual cost (i.e., point loss on a counter) and imagined loss (verbal instructions to imagine point loss on counter). Compared to baseline (no cost responding), both conditions suppressed responding, although the cumulative curves of the imagined cost condition show less consistent responding (i.e., more jagged curve). Unfortunately, the real and imagined cost conditions in this study were not counter-balanced to exclude the possible enhancing effects of real cost trials on the following imagined cost trials. Tondo (1974) also used a within-subject design to compare the effects of the presentation of "real" point reinforcers versus instructions to "imagine" the same point reinforcement contingent upon a certain class of interresponse times (IRTs) for a key-pressing task. Both the real and the imagined reinforcement conditions were equally effective (compared to a feedback only condition) in significantly increasing the frequency of the target responses. Tondo found no treatment order effects. Cautela, Flannery, and Hanley (1974) presented evidence of comparative effectiveness of covert modeling and overt modeling in increasing approach behavior to a previously feared item (rat). One strong point of this study was the extent to which model and process variables were equated in the overt and covert conditions. For example, the same model was observed by one group and imagined by the other. Also, observational and imagined scenes were equivalent in length (two minutes) and number (six).

The argument for the similarity of overt and covert events is strengthened by a set of studies which show equivalent effects of a number of variables (reinforcement and punishment, quality and quantity of reinforcement, reinforcement satiation, overlearning, and model characteristics) on both overt and covert events.

The ability of an imagined consequence to increase or decrease response rate has been demonstrated by Epstein and Peterson (1973). Following baseline measures of subjects' choices of numbers from 0 to 100, they were signaled to generate pleasant imagery after certain number choices and unpleasant imagery after other number choices. Subsequently, subjects made significantly fewer choices of numbers which had been followed by unpleasant imagery and more choices of numbers which were previously followed by pleasant imagery.

The amount (i.e., quantity or quality) of an imagined positive consequence differentially affects learning in a manner similar to an actual positive reinforcement. Ascher (1973) conducted a covert reinforcement analog study using a target response of pronoun usage. He reported more conditioning and greater resistance to extinction with greater (30 rather than 10) quantity of covert reinforcement trials. Similarly, Ascher (1970) varied the number of trials (again 10 or 30) in a acquisition of lever-pulling task. Performances during extinction trials presented overtly (i.e., continued lever-pulling produced no reinfocement) and covertly (subjects asked to imagine lever-pulling with no result) were equivalent.

A low or neutral quality imagined reinforcer has been used in some studies (Ascher and Cautela, 1972; Cautela, Walsh, and Wish, 1971) as a control condition for a high quality reinforcer. These studies have uniformly found that highly pleasant imagined reinforcers are superior to a low or neutral quality imagine in increasing response frequency.

More systematically, Baron (1975) examined the effects of quality (high or low pleasure ratings) and duration (5 or 15 seconds) of imagined reinforcement on subjects' relative response rate (i.e., proportion of responses) on each key of a two-choice key-pressing task. A VI 10''-10'' schedule of reinforcement programmed delivery of signals for imaging. One group of subjects (quality group) was signaled to alternately imagine a highly pleasurable and a less pleasurable image. Another group (duration group) imaged a highly pleasurable scene for 5 or 15 seconds alternately. Subjects in the quality group made a significantly greater number of key-presses on the key which produced a signal for a highly pleasurable image than on the key which signaled the less pleasurable image. Also, the distribution of key-presses matched their relative ratings of the quality of the two images. That is, if a high quality image was rated as twice as pleasurable as a low quality image, the subjects made twice as many key-presses on the key which signaled the high quality image than on the key which signaled the low quality image. Subjects in the duration condition showed no significant difference in rate of responding over the two keys. These results are in line with data from studies with animals (Baum, 1974; Herrnstein, 1970; Hollard & Davison, 1971; Schmitt, 1974; Todorov, 1973) and humans (Baum, 1973; Cohen, 1974; Nevin, 1969; Schroeder & Holland, 1969) on the matching of response rate to relative rate of reinforcement.

Tondo and Cautela (1974) conducted a post hoc analysis of data generated in a covert reinforcement study (on the relation between high and low imagery ability and subsequent COR effects) and found that in COR, an image's pleasantness ratings decreased as the frequency of use of the COR image increased. This finding substantiated the satiation effects commonly found with increased use of an overt reinforcer.

Goguen (1973) studied the effects of overlearning of covert conditioning (covert reinforcement and covert sensitization) on maintaining the extinction of smoking behavior. At six-weeks, three-months, and six-months follow-up, those subjects who received six additional covert conditioning trials after they stopped smoking had significantly lower reacquisition rates than a control group who received convert conditioning only until they stopped smoking.

Similarities in parametric variations in overt and covert modeling has been studied extensively by Kazdin. He demonstrated that, as predicted from the literature on overt modeling (Bandura, 1969), varying such model characterizatics as age and sex (Kazdin, 1974a), whether the model uses "coping" or "mastery" strategies to solve a problem (Kazdin, 1974b), and presenting favorable consequences to the model's behavior and using multiple versus single models (Kazdin, 1975a, 1975b) all enhance the effects of covert modeling.

On the whole, the physiological and behavioral studies cited above give evidence for a unified explanatory model of human behavior which includes both overt and covert events. We have supplied some empirical evidence for the assumptions of covert conditioning. However, as previously mentioned, "facts" do not prove or disprove a theory. It is the authors' contention that the rationale for and the evidence related to the covert conditioning model should strengthen confidence in the heuristic value of the model.

REFERENCES

Ascher, L. M. *Covert extinction: An experimental test*. Unpublished data, 1970. (Available from author at Eastern Pennsylvania Psychiatric Institute, Philadelphia, Pennsylvania.).

Ascher, L. M. An experimental analog study of covert positive reinforcement. In R. D. Rubin, J. P. Brady, & J. D. Henderson (Eds.), *Advances in behavior therapy* (Vol.4). New York: Academic Press, 1973.

Ascher, L. M., & Cautela, J. R. Covert negative reinforcement: An experimental test. *Journal of Behavior Therapy and Experimental Psychiatry*, 1972, 3, 1-5.

Bandura, A. *Principles of behavior modification*, New York: Holt, Rinehart, & Winston, 1969.

Baron, M. G. The operant analysis of imagery: Parameters of covert reinforcement. (Doctoral dissertation, Boston College, 1975). *Dissertation Abstracts International*, 1975, 36, 1496-B. (University Microfilm No. 75-20, 696)

Baum, W. H. Personal communication, January 10, 1973.

Baum, W. H. Choice in free-ranging wild pigeons. *Science*, 1974, 185, 78-79.

Callahan, E., & Leitenberg, H., Aversion therapy for sexual deviation: Contingent shock and covert sensitization. *Journal of Abnormal Psychology*, 1973, 81,60-73.

Cautela, J. R. Treatment of compulsive behavior by covert sensitization. *Psychological Record*, 1966, 16, 33-41.

Cautela, J. R. Covert sensitization. *Psychological Reports*, 1967, 20, 459-468.

Cautela, J. R. Covert negative reinforcement. *Behavior Therapy and Experimental Psychiatry*, 1970, 1, 273-278.(a)

Cautela, J. R. Covert reinforcement. *Behavior Therapy*, 1970, 1, 33-50. (b)

Cautela, J. R. Covert conditioning. In A. Jacobs & L. Sachs (eds.), *Psychology of private events*. New York: Academic Press, 1971. (a)

Cautela, J. R. Covert extinction. *Behavior Therapy*, 1971, 2, 192-200. (b)

Cautela, J. R. Covert processes. *Journal of Nervous and Mental Diseases*, 1973, 157, 27-36.

Cautela, J. R. Covert conditioning. *Mental Imagery*, 1976. (a)

Cautela, J. R. Covert modeling. *Journal of Behavior Therapy and Experimental Psychiatry*, 1976. (b)

Cautela, J. R. Covert response cost. *Psychotherapy: Theory, Research, & Practice*, 1976. (c)

Cautela, J. R., Flannery, R. B., & Hanley, S. Covert modeling: An experimental test. *Behavior Therapy*, 1974, 4, 494-502.

Cautela, J. R., Walsh, K., & Wish, P. The use of covert reinforcement of attitudes in the modification of attitudes toward the mentally retarded. *Journal of Psychology*, 1971, 77, 257-260.

Cohen, J. The interaction of responses in the brain to semantic stimuli. *Psychophysicology*, 1967, 2, 187-196.

Cohen, M. Unpublished data. Harvard University, 1974.

Davison, G. Personal communication. 1975.

Day, W. F. Radical behaviorism in reconciliation with phenomenology. *Journal of Experimental Analysis of Behavior*, 1969, 12, 315-328.

Epstein, L. H., & Peterson, G. L. Differential conditioning using covert stimuli. *Behavior Therapy*, 1973, 4, 96-99.

Ferster, C. B. A functional analysis of depression. *American Psychologist*, 1973, 28, 857-870.

Goguen, L. *Effects of over-learning on covert conditioning*. Unpublished doctoral dissertation, University of Mouncton, 1973.

Guthrie, E. R. *The psychology of learning*. New York: Harper, 1935.

Herrnstein, R. J. On the law of effect. *Journal of the Experimental Analysis of Behavior*, 1970, 13, 243-266.

Hollard, V., & Davidson, M. C. Preference for qualitatively different reinforcers. *Journal of the Experimental Analysis of Behavior*, 1971, 16, 375-380.

Homme, L. E. Perspectives in psychology: XXIV. Control of coverants, the operants of the mind. *Psychological Record*, 1965, 15, 501-511.

Hull, C. L. *Principles of behavior,* New York: Appleton, 1943.

John, E. R. *Mechanisms of memory*. New York: Academic Press, 1967.

Kazdin, A. E. Comparative effects of some variations of covert modeling. *Journal of Behavior Therapy and Experimental Psychiatry*, 1974, 5, 225-231. (a)

Kazdin, A. E. Covert modeling, model similarity, and reduction of avoidance behavior. *Behavior Therapy*, 1974, 5, 325-340. (b)

Kazdin, A. E. Covert modeling, imagery assessment, and assertive behavior. *Journal of Consulting and Clinical Psychology*, 1975, 43, 716-724. (a)

Kazdin, A. E. Effects of covert modeling, multiple models and model reinforcement on assertive behavior. *Behavior Therapy*, 1975. (b)

Koch, S. Psychology and emerging concepts of knowledge as unitary. In T. W. Wann (Ed.), *Behaviorism and phenomenology*. Chicago: University of Chicago Press, 1964.

Krop, H., Calhoun, B., & Verrier, R. Modification of the "self-concept" of emotionally disturbed children by covert reinforcement. *Behavior Therapy*, 1971, 2, 201-204.

Lazarus, A. A. *Behavior therapy and beyond*. New York: McGraw-Hill, 1971.

Mahoney, M. J. *Cognition and behavior modification*. Cambridge, Mass.: Ballinger, 1974.

Mahoney, M. J., Thoresen, C. E., & Danaher, B. G. Covert behavior modification: An experimental analogue. *Journal of Behavior Therapy and Experimental Psychiatry*, 1972, 3, 7-14.

Meichenbaum, D. *Cognitive behavior modification*. Morristown, N.J.: General Learning Press, 1974.

Miller, N. E. *The influence of past experience upon the transfer of subsequent training*. Unpublished doctoral dissertation, Yale University, 1935.

Nevin, J. A. Signal detection theory and operant behavior. Review of D. M. Green & J. A. Swets' *Signal detection theory and psychophysics*. *Journal of the Experimental Analysis of Behavior*, 1969, 12, 475-480.

Pavlov, I. P. [*Conditioned reflexes: An investigation of the physiological activity of the cerebral cortex*.] Translated by G. V. Anrep. London and New York: Oxford University Press, 1927.

Paul, G. L. Outcome of systematic desensitization. II. Controlled investigations of individual treatment, technique variations, and current status. In C. M. Franks (Ed.), *Behavior therapy: Appraisal and status*. New York: McGraw-Hill, 1969.

Schmitt, D. R. Effects of reinforcement rate and reinforcement magnitude on choice behavior in humans. *Journal of the Experimental Analysis of Behavior*, 1974, 21, 409-420.

Schroeder, S. R., & Holland, J. G. Reinforcement of eye movement with concurrent schedules. *Journal of the Experimental Analysis of Behavior,*, 1969, 12, 847-903.

Schwartz, G. E., & Higgins, J. D. Cardiac activity preparatory to overt and covert behavior. *Science*, 1971, 173, 1114-1146.

Skinner, B. F. *The behavior of organisms*. New York: Macmillan, 1938.

Skinner, B. F. *Science and human behavior*. New York: Macmillan, 1953.

Skinner, B. F. Behaviorism at fifty. *Science*, 1963, 140, 951-958.

Spence, K. W. *Behavior theory and conditioning*. New Haven, Conn.: Yale University Press, 1956.

Stampfl, T. G. Implosive therapy, Part I: The theory. In S. G. Armitage (Ed.), *Behavioral modification techniques and the treatment of emotional disorders*. Battle Creek, Mich.: V. A. Publications, 1967.

Stevens, S. S. Psychology and the science. *Psychological Bulletin*, 1939, 36, 221-263.

Terrace, H. S. *Awareness as viewed by conventional and by radical behaviorism*. Paper presented at the meeting of the American Psychological Association, Washington, D.C., 1971.

Todorov, J. C. Interaction of frequency and magnitude of reinforcement on concurrent performances. *Journal of the Experimental Analysis of Behavior*, 1973, 19, 451-458.

Tondo, T. R. *The effects of real vs. "imagined" (covert) reinforcement of specific interresponse times*. Unpublished doctoral dissertation, University of Mississippi, 1974.

Tondo, T. R., & Cautela, J. R. Assessment of imagery in covert reinforcement. *Psychological Reports*, 1974, 34, 1271-1280.

Watson, J. B. Psychology as the behaviorist views it. *Psychological Review*, 1913, 20, 158-177.

Watson, J. B. *Psychology from the standpoint of behaviorist*. Philadelphia: Lippincott, 1919.

Watson, J. B. *Behaviorism*. New York: Horton, 1925.

Weiner, H. Real and imagined cost effects upon human fixed-interval responding. *Psychological Reports*, 1965, 17, 659-662.

Wolpe, J. *Psychotherapy by reciprocal inhibition*. Stanford, Calif.: Stanford University Press, 1958.

SECTION II
COVERT SENSITIZATION

Chapter 3
Covert Sensitization*†
Joseph R. Cautela

Summary — A new treatment for maladaptive approach behavior (''covert sensitization'') is described. The term ''covert'' is used because neither the undesirable stimulus nor the aversive stimulus is actually presented. These stimuli are presented in imagination only. The word ''sensitization'' is used because the purpose of the procedure is to build up an avoidance response to the undesirable stimulus. A description and rationale for covert sensitization is presented. Treatment of alcoholism, obesity, homosexuality, and delinquent behavior by covert sensitization is also described.

From a behavioral standpoint, maladaptive behavior can be divided into maladaptive avoidance responses and maladaptive approach responses. Maladaptive avoidance responses, such as phobias, fear of failure, fear of criticism, have been treated effectively by reciprocal inhibition procedures developed by Joseph Wolpe (1958). These procedures include desensitization, assertive training, and the use of sexual responses. Other methods of dealing with the anxiety components of this type of response involve thought stopping and aversion-relief therapy.

The treatment of such maladaptive approach responses as obsession, compulsion, homosexuality, drinking, and stealing has employed aversive stimulation in the reduction and/or elimination of the frequency of the faulty approach behavior. In the usual technique of aversive stimulation, shock is presented contiguously with a socially undesirable stimulus (e.g., a picture of a homosexual is flashed on a screen at the same time a shock is delivered to the feet (Thorpe, Schmidt, & Castell, 1963) or shock is administered in the presence of a fetish object (Marks, Rachman, & Gilder, 1965).

---

*Reprinted with permission of author and publisher from *Psychological Reports*, 1967, *20*, 459-468.

†Paper presented to DeJarnette State Sanitorium and Blue Ridge Psychology Club on October 7, 1966.

Recently, I have developed a new procedure for treating maladaptive approach behavior (Cautela, 1966). This procedure is labeled ''covert sensitization.'' It is called ''covert'' because neither the undesirable stimulus nor the aversive stimulus is actually presented. These stimuli are presented in imagination only. The word ''sensitization'' is used because the purpose of the procedure is to build up an avoidance response to the undesirable stimulus.

DESCRIPTION OF PROCEDURE

The patient is taught to relax in the same manner as used in the desensitization procedure (Wolpe, 1958, pp. 139-155). He is asked to raise his index finger when he can relax completely without any tension. This usually takes no more than three or four sessions. When the patient is able to relax completely, he is told that he is unable to stop drinking in excess (or eating, or whatever is the problem to be treated) because it is a strong learned habit which now gives him a great amount of pleasure. He is also told that the way to eliminate his problem is to associate the pleasurable object with an unpleasant stimulus. The patient is then asked (while relaxed with his eyes closed) to visualize very clearly the pleasurable object (e.g., food, liquor, homosexual). When he can do this, he is told to raise his index finger. After he signals, he is told to next visualize that he is about to take the object (commit the compulsive act). If the object is liquor, for instance, he is asked to visualize himself looking at the glass with the alcoholic beverage in it. Then he is to visualize a sequence of events: holding the glass in his hand, bringing it up to his lips, having the glass touch his lips. When he imagines this latter scene, he is told to imagine that he begins to feel sick to his stomach. In imagination, he begins to vomit. The vomit goes all over the floor, the drink, his companions and himself. He is then asked to visualize the whole scene by himself and to raise his finger when he can picture it and actually feel nauseous when he had the intention of drinking, gradually getting sicker as he touches the glass, raises it, etc.

A feeling of relief is provided in scenes when he turns away from the pleasurable object. He is told to imagine that as he rushes outside into the fresh clean air, or home to a clean, invigorating shower, or whenever he is tempted to drink and refuses to do it, the feeling of nausea goes away and he no longer feels ill.

After several practice trials in the therapist's office, the patient is instructed to continue treatment on his own twice a day by means of ''homework'' assignments which are 10 to 20 repetitions of the trials experienced in the office. He is also carefully instructed to imagine immediately that he has just vomited on his drink whenever he is tempted to drink, or about to order one, or about to ingest it. Patients report that treatment is quite effective whenever it is followed conscientiously. As therapy progresses, the use of this procedure as a self-control technique usually continues, and the patients are able to monitor their behavior very well. It is important to note that, when anxiety is an essential part of the maladaptive response, desensitization is also utilized.

Theoretical Basis

Since the individual is asked to imagine an aversive situation as soon as he has thought of drinking or is about to drink, this is a punishment procedure. An aversive stimulus is made to follow the response to be reduced. Evidence indicates that punishment is quite effective in reducing the frequency of responses and that this reduction can be long lasting or permanent (Kushner & Sandler, 1966). Certain conditions should be carefully arranged to produce a decrease in resonse frequency. The noxious stimulus should be contiguous with that response. The response should have a history of positive reinforcement (e.g., drinking). The aversive stimulus should be presented on a continuous basis, at least initially, after which a partial schedule can be presented. The level of punishment should be clearly noxious but not so intense as to immobilize the organism.

Since the patient is usually told that the nausea and vomiting behavior decreases and he feels better as soon as he turns away from the undesirable object (e.g., beer, food, homosexual), this is analogous to an escape procedure which occurs when a particular behavior terminates the presentation of a noxious stimulus. Eventually, avoidance behavior occurs, as evidenced by the fact that the patients report they no longer have the urge or the temptation for the particular stimulus. The cues which have been previously associated with the noxious stimulation of nausea and vomiting now have become discriminatory stimuli for avoidance behavior (Hall, 1966, p. 212).

TREATMENT OF SPECIFIC MALADAPTIVE APPROACH RESPONSES

Treatment of Alcoholic Problems

Besides the usual brief history taken in all behavior therapy cases, special attention is paid to certain characteristics of the client's drinking behavior. With the use of a specially constructed questionnaire and interviews, the following factors are determined: (1) history of the drinking problem, (2) frequency of present drinking behavior, (3) where S usually does his drinking, (4) what S drinks, and (5) antecedent conditions that are followed by drinking behavior.

A client may, for example, do most of his drinking in a bar room and may usually drink straight whiskey and sometimes beer. The covert sensitization sessions will then consist of scenes in which the client is about to drink whiskey in a bar room. If he drinks alone at home, scenes concerning the home will also have to be included. Essentially we try to cover all the applicable kinds of drinking and all the places where the particular drinking behavior occurs.

A practical problem still exists concerning whether to proceed first with the kind of drinking he does most often in the most usual situations or to begin covert sensitization with the type of drinking and its situations which occur the least often. For the most part, I have used the first method. The primary advantage of the second method, however, is the provision of some measure of success since it involves the least amount of habit strength and will make the client more eager to continue treatment. A description of the procedure is as follows:

You are walking into a bar. You decide to have a glass of beer. You are now walking toward the bar. As you are approaching the bar you have a funny feeling in the pit of your stomach. Your stomach feels all queasy and nauseous. Some liquid comes up your throat and it is very sour. You try to swallow it back down, but as you do this, food particles start coming up your throat to your mouth. You are now reaching the bar and you order a beer. As the bartender is pouring the beer, puke comes up into your mouth. You try to keep your mouth closed and swallow it down. You reach for the glass of beer to wash it down. As soon as your hand touches the glass, you can't hold it down any longer. You have to open your mouth and you puke. It goes all over your hand, all over the glass and the beer. You can see it floating around in the beer. Snots and mucous come out of your nose. Your shirt and pants are all full of vomit. The bartender has some on his shirt. You notice people looking at you. You get sick again and you vomit some more and more. You turn away from the beer and immediately you start to feel better. As you run out of the bar room, you start to feel better and better. When you get out into clean fresh air you feel wonderful. You go home and clean yourself up.

An important characteristic of the covert sensitization procedure is that its effects are very specific. If one treats for aversion to beer, there will be very little generalization to wine and whiskey. Avoidance to wine and whiskey must be treated separately. Sometimes I combine a covert sensitization trial for wine, beer and whiskey by having the client see a glass of wine, a glass of beer, and a glass of whiskey on a table. As in the manner described above, he is told that he is sick and he vomits over all three beverages.

Treatment of Obesity

Approach. The client is requested to write down everything he eats or drinks from session to session. Other details of his eating behavior are determined in a manner similar to that used in treating an alcoholic patient. A questionnaire has also been constructed for this purpose. Covert sensitization sessions are not begun until two or three weeks have passed, in order to obtain some kind of baseline in terms of the eating habits. The therapist is especially concerned with four factors when he reads over the client's eating behavior of the previous week: (1) nature of the food, (2) when he eats (with special concern for eating between meals), (3) how much he eats, and (4) where he eats.

At first covert sensitization is applied to sweets of all types, especially to foods with heavy carbohydrate content, and then to between-meal eating. The amount of food is usually the prime concern after the kinds of food and the time of eating has been considered. If the therapist finds that the patient is eating too much apple pie or pastry for dessert, for instance, he can proceed in the following manner:

> I want you to imagine you've just had your main meal and you are about to eat your dessert, which is apple pie. As you are about to reach for the fork, you get a funny feeling in the pit of your stomach. You start to feel queasy, nauseous and sick all over. As you touch the fork, you can feel food particles inching up your throat. You're just about to vomit. As you put the fork into the pie, the food comes up into your mouth. You try to keep your mouth closed because you are afraid that you'll spit the food out all over the place. You bring the piece of pie to your mouth. As you're about to open your mouth, you puke; you vomit all over your hands, the fork, over the pie. It goes all over the table over the other peoples' food. Your eyes are watering. Snot and mucous are all over your mouth and nose. Your hands feel sticky. There is an awful smell. As you look at this mess you just can't help but vomit again and again until just watery stuff is coming out. Everybody is looking at you with shocked expressions. You turn away from the food and immediately start to feel better. You run out of the room, and as you run out, you feel better and better. You wash and clean yourself up, and it feels wonderful.

In addition to the scenes (about ten per session) in which the patient gives in to the temptation and vomits, scenes in which the patient is initially tempted and then decides not to eat the food are also included in equal number. An example of such a scene is as follows:

> You've just finished eating your meal and you decide to have dessert. As soon as you make that decision, you start to get that funny feeling in the pit of your stomach. You say, "Oh, oh; oh no; I won't eat the dessert." Then you immediately feel calm and comfortable.

Homework. The patient is asked to repeat the scenes presented during the therapy session twice a day until the next therapeutic session. He is also asked to imagine he is vomiting on a particular food whenever he is tempted to eat it. For instance, if he is tempted to eat potato salad, he is told immediately to imagine that the potato salad has vomit all over it.

Some general comments on the treatment of obesity. A physical examination, including an investigation of thyroid activity and metabolic rate, is required of all patients prior to treatment. Each week they are asked about their general health and well being in order to ensure that no physical harm is being done.

The patients are weighed at the beginning of each session. If there is indication that eating food is a mechanism of anxiety reduction, the patient is also treated to reduce the sources of anxiety.

After they have lost 15 pounds, the patients are often asked to perform simple neck and arm exercises to avoid loose skin in these regions. They are also encouraged to walk as much as possible. After the patient has reached the weight desired, as determined by height-weight charts taking the body frame into consideration, the same eating habits which have occurred during the past two or three weeks are encouraged. *S* continues to be monitored in therapeutic sessions for another month. He is then asked to keep track of his own eating habits, and he is taught when and how to apply covert sensitization to himself whenever he finds he is nearing the maximum weight assigned to him. If he finds that he can't do this on his own, he can call the therapist for a "booster" session. This happens rarely, however. Most of the patients are able to control their weight very well. The patients report that they still enjoy the food they eat.

Of all the syndromes treated, covert sensitization seems to be most effective in dealing with the problems of obesity. This treatment is also very specific in its effects.

Treatment of Homosexuality

In the treatment of the behavior disorders indicated above, the task of the therapist is to somehow break the relationship between the stimulus (alcohol or food) and the response (drinking or eating). In the case of homosexuality, the stimulus is an individual of the same sex who elicits a response of sexual approach behavior. The therapist then attempts to identify individual characteristics which are sexually attractive and under what conditions. For example, some individuals prefer obese sexual objects, some prefer short, young, or intellectual ones.

Description of procedure. The following instructions may be given:

I want you to imagine that you are in a room with X. He is completely naked. As you approach him you notice he has sores and scabs all over his body, with some kind of fluid oozing from them. A terrible foul stench comes from his body. The odor is so strong it makes you sick. You can feel food particles coming up your throat. You can't help yourself and you vomit all over the place, all over the floor, on your hands and clothes. And now that even makes you sicker and you vomit again and again all over everything. You turn away and then you start to feel better. You try to get out of the room, but the door seems to be locked. The smell is still strong, but you try desperately to get out. You kick at the door frantically until it finally opens and you run out into the nice clean air. It smells wonderful. You go home and shower and you feel so clean.

One essentially builds up a hierarchy of the desirable sexual objects and the available contacts of likely sexual stimulation. Covert sensitization is applied to all items in the hierarchy, with the most desirable sexual object usually being treated first.

Scenes are also presented in which the patient sees pictures of homosexuals and vomits on them. Homework similar to that given in the treatment of the other disorders is given in this case as well. The homosexual patient is also told that if he sees someone and becomes sexually attracted to him or whenever he starts to have a sexual fantasy about an undesirable sexual object, he is immediately to imagine that the object is full of sores and scabs and he vomits on the object.

Examples. This method has been only recently applied to homosexuals. I have treated two cases; one case has been treated at Temple Medical School.

One of my cases was a delinquent in a training school. According to his reports and those of the staff and of other boys in the training school, he has not engaged in homosexual behavior since the termination of covert sensitization treatment and has now been released from the training school.

My second case was a member of the Armed Forces. This individual's behavior was primarily vicarious. All his sexual fantasies, with and without masturbation, were homosexual in nature. This behavior has been reduced to about four temptations a week which last about a second. This case is still in the process of treatment.

In the Temple Medical School case, it has been four months since the last therapeutic session, and the patient has not engaged in any homosexual behavior to date, according to his own reports and those of his wife. He is continuing with the homework.

All in all, the preliminary results are promising, although much work still remains to be done in this area.

Treatment of Juvenile Offenders

Since March of this year (1966), I have been using behavior therapy procedures in individual and group settings with juvenile offenders at the Rhode Island Medical Center. My preliminary guess, based on his experience, is that the usual behavior therapy procedures, such as relaxation, desensitization, and Thought Stopping, can be effective in the treatment of juvenile offenders. I have also used covert sensitization where applicable. In one case, it was used in the treatment of homosexuality as I reported above. Currently under treatment is a boy with a severe alcoholic problem. His juvenile offenses have always occurred while he was drinking. Covert sensitization seems to be quite effective with this boy. He is allowed to go home on weekends. Reports from him and his mother indicate that his drinking has been drastically reduced on these weekends at home when previously he used to drink himself into a two-day stupor.

I have also treated stealing behavior (car stealing and breaking and entering offenses). Car stealing is one of the most frequent offenses of juvenile offenders. In the treatment of this type of behavior, the boy is asked what cars he prefers to steal and under what conditions. A hierarchy is then constructed from that information. A typical scene is as follows:

You are walking down a street. You notice a real sharp sports car. You walk toward it with the idea of stealing it. As you're walking toward it you start to get a funny feeling in your stomach. You feel sick to your stomach and you have a slight pain in your gut. As you keep walking, you really start to feel sick, and food starts coming up in your mouth. You're just about to reach for the handle of the door and you can't hold it any longer. You vomit all over your hand, the car door, the upholstery inside, all over your clothes. The smell starts to get to you and you keep puking from it. It's all over the place. It's dripping from your mouth. You turn around and run away and then you start to feel better.

I've also treated some cases of glue sniffing in a similar manner. My main surprise in working with juvenile offenders is that most of them will cooperate well with the behavior therapy procedures. Group relaxation also seems usable without too much difficulty.

EXPERIMENTAL DATA

In behavior therapy our procedures are usually derived from the results of controlled laboratory studies. We also try to test the validity of our techniques by appropriate experimentation.

Donner and Ashem,* at the New Jersey Neuro-psychiatric Institute in Princeton, attempted an experimental test of the efficacy of covert sensitization in the treatment of institutionalized alcoholics. Preliminary data indicate that 3 out of 4 of the non-treated controls resumed drinking after a 6-mo. follow-up. Only 2 out of 7 of the covert sensitization group resumed drinking after a 6-mo. follow-up. All treated Ss received 9 sessions. These data are only preliminary, since more Ss remain to be followed-up. Investigators are waiting for the 6-mo. period to be completed.

In this study, one S had to be eliminated after some training sessions because the mere mention of alcohol made him actually vomit. This is important to note because the treatment of covert sensitization should be explicitly applied to the individual's *desire* to drink alcohol, not just to the alcohol itself. All of the covert sensitization Ss were also given relaxation training. Study is needed to determine whether relaxation is necessary for effective treatment; I have used it to help develop clear imagery.

Forward and backward covert sensitization groups were included in the study. In the backward covert sensitization group, individuals were asked to imagine vomiting before they took the alcohol. No differences were found between the backward and forward conditioning covert sensitization groups. One can easily hypothesize that the backward conditioning group was not truly backward conditioned, since the nausea could still be present from a previous trial.

Another study, using aversive electric stimulation (MacCulloch, *et al.,* 1966), has reported no success in the treatment of four cases of alcoholism. These results are somewhat puzzling since, using the same procedure, they were able to successfully treat homosexuals (MacCulloch, *et al.,* 1965). There are a number of possible procedural differences that either individually or

---

*L. Donner, & B. Ashem. Unpublished research data from a study at the Neuro-psychiatric Institute in Princeton, New Jersey, 1966.

collectively might account for the efficacy of covert sensitization as compared to the use of electrical stimulation as an aversive stimulus in the treatment of alcoholism. One of the crucial procedural differences is that in covert sensitization the patients are taught to apply the procedure to themselves outside of the office situation in a prescribed manner. Patients are usually told to practice the procedure 10 to 20 times a day. Also, they are told to apply the procedure any time they have a temptation to drink. This assigned "homework" accomplishes three important behavioral effects. In the first place, more conditioning trials are used (there are more reinforcements). Secondly, the patient now has a procedure under *his* control that can be applied whenever the temptation actually occurs. So a lot of *in vivo* conditioning occurs when an individual is tempted in particular situations. Thirdly, according to reports by patients, just knowing they have a procedure they can use whenever they need it, reduces the over-all anxiety level. Another difference between the procedures is that the aversive stimulus used in covert sensitization (vomiting) has stimulus and response properties that have probably been presented quite often when the patient has been drinking. With the covert sensitization procedure, we are using a behavior that has already accompanied the stimulus to drink and the response of drinking. We have some conditioning trials even before we start our formal treatment procedure.

A major difference between procedures that has yet to be explored systematically is the difference in effect of presenting the aversive stimulus in imagination or in actuality. In *a priori* speculation, one would assume that the actual presentation of the aversive stimulus would be more effective than the imaginary presentation of the stimulus, since in the actual presentation of the stimulus there is more control over the intensity and occurrence of the aversive stimulus. Also, the actual presentation of the stimulus probably results in greater perceived pain.

Perhaps none of the above differences in procedure is responsible for the apparent difference in results when using covert sensitization as compared to electrical stimulation. Perhaps MacCulloch, *et al.*'s (1966) procedure simply needs modification for effective results. For example, the interval between the CS and the US can be varied; or the number of conditioning trials per session can be an important factor; also the intensity of the electrical stimulation used may not be the most appropriate.

Covert sensitization, as I have used it, is a relatively new procedure. But, of course, the use of aversive simulation to overcome faulty approach behavior is not new. I have applied my procedure to a wide variety of behaviors and the technique looks quite promising. One of the reasons for its effectiveness is probably the sense of control the individual feels over his own behavior. So far, the treatment of obesity appears to show the greatest promise in terms of probability of remission and number of sessions required for change. Treatment of alcoholic problems appears the most difficult in terms of prognosis and number of treatment sessions necessary. There are two factors that could account for this. (1) The habit strength for the alcoholic responding is much higher because of the large number of reinforcements possible within a given day. The number of homosexual contacts one can make, or the number of times a car can be stolen are relatively small by comparison. (2) The drive-reducing properties of alcohol are quite strong because of the physiological effect alcohol has on the nervous system. So even though one could argue that, if you count every mouthful of food as a reinforcement, it is possible to have as many reinforcers in a given day as are possible with drinking, it is unlikely that food as a rule has the strong reducing properties of alcohol.

More controlled studies are needed in this area, such as the one carried out by the Neuro-psychiatric Institute.

REFERENCES

Cautela, J. R. Treatment of compulsive behavior by covert sensitization. *Psychol. Rec.,* 1966, 16, 33-41.

Hall, J. F. *The psychology of learning.* Philadelphia: Lippincott, 1966.

Kushner, M., & Sandler, J. Aversion therapy and the concept of punishment. *Behav. Res. Ther.,* 1966, 4, 179-186.

MacCulloch, M.J., Feldman, M.P., Orford, J.F., & MacCulloch, M.L. Anticipatory avoidance learning in the treatment of alcoholism: a record of therapeutic failure. *Behav. Res. Ther.,* 1966, 4, 187-196.

MacCulloch, M.J., Feldman, M.P., & Pinschof, J.M. The application of anticipatory avoidance learning to the treatment of homosexuality: avoidance response latencies and pulse rate changes. *Behav. Res. Ther.,* 1965, 3, 21-44.

Marks, I. M., Rachman, S., & Gelder, M. G. Methods for the assessment of aversion treatment in fetishism with masochism. *Behav. Res. Ther.,* 1965, 3, 253-258.

Thorpe, J. G., Schmidt, E., & Castell, D. A comparison of positive and negative (aversive) conditioning in the treatment of homosexuality. *Behav. Res. Ther.,* 1963, 1, 357-362.

Wolpe, J. *Psychotherapy by reciprocal inhibition.* Stanford: Stanford Univer. Press, 1958.

Chapter 4

Experimental Control of Sexual Deviation Through Manipulation of the Noxious Scene in Covert Sensitization*†

David H. Barlow, Harold Leitenberg, and W. Stewart Agras

Summary — Pedophilic behavior in one *S* and homosexual behavior in another *S* were decreased, increased, and once again decreased by introducing, removing, and reintroducing the noxious scene in covert sensitization, a form of aversion therapy. The results indicated that verbal description of the nauseous scene was an effective aversive stimulus, and that pairing this scene with scenes of the undesired behavior was responsible for declines in deviant sexual behavior during covert sensitization.

The treatment of sexual deviation by aversion therapy has recently become more popular (Feldman, 1966). All studies reported to date, however, are either uncontrolled single case reports or uncontrolled group outcome studies.

*Reprinted with permission from the *Journal of Abnormal Psychology*, 1969, *74*, 597-601. ©The American Psychological Association 1969.

†This study was supported in part by United States Public Health Service Clinical Research Center Grant FR-109 and National Institute of Mental Health Grant MH-13651. Part of the data was presented at the meeting of the Eastern Psychological Association, Washington, D. C., April 1968.

It is not possible to determine from such data whether the reported success is due to the conditioning techniqure or to another of the myriad of variables present either singly or in combination in the therapeutic situation.

The usual way to isolate relevant treatment variables is the group comparison in which a control group experiences the same treatment as an experimental group with the exception of the independent variable. Group differences are then ascribed to the independent variable. An alternative method used in this study is to demonstrate experimental control in individual cases. One way of doing this is to sequentially vary some aspect of treatment while measuring associated changes in a well-specified, clinically relevant behavior (cf. Agras, Leitenberg, & Barlow, 1968; Leitenberg, Agras, Thomson, & Wright, 1968; Wolf, Birnbrauer, Williams, & Lawler, 1965).

In this experiment the aversion therapy studied was covert sensitization (Cautela, 1966). In this procedure, descriptions of extremely noxious scenes are paired with scenes of the undesired behavior. Uncontrolled case studies suggest that covert sensitization may modify sexual deviation. Cautela (1967) treated two homosexuals with this method resulting in reports by the patients of decreases in homosexual behavior, while Davison (1968) treated a case of long-standing sadistic fantasies with a combination of covert sensitization and positive conditioning to heterosexual stimuli and achieved a remission. Other case studies include Kolvin's (1967) successful treatment of a fetish.

The crucial procedure in covert sensitization is thought to be the pairing of verbal descriptions of a noxious scene with descrptions of scenes involving the undesired behavior. This notion was tested in the present study in two cases of sexual deviation by first pairing the two scenes, then removing the noxious scene while holding other variables constant, and finally pairing the scenes once more. If the pairing procedure is critical to therapeutic success, then any improvement should be reversed or stopped when the noxious scene is removed.

METHOD

Subjects

The S_1 was a 25-yr.-old married male who reported a 13-yr. history of pedophilic experiences ranging from fantasies to several instances of sexual contact. He came for treatment after the solicitation of a neighbor's 9-yr.-old daughter was discovered. The neighbor, rather than report him to the police, insisted that he seek psychiatric help. Sexual relations with his wife averaged twice a month.

The S_2 was a 32-yr.-old married male who reported a 14-yr. history of homosexual experiences averaging about three contacts per week, usually in public toilets. He recently had fallen in love with a ''boyfriend,'' which was threatening his marriage and which motivated him to seek treatment. Sexual relations with his wife, although prevalent early in the marriage, had been virtually nonexistent for the previous 3 yrs.

Measures

A hierarchy of sexually arousing scenes was constructed. For S_1 the hierarchy contained 45 scenes involving small girls. For example, the top item in the hierarchy was, "You are alone in a room with a very sexy looking 10-year-old girl with long blond hair." One of the least arousing items was, "While driving in your car you can see a small, thin, six-year-old girl walking down the street." For S_2 the hierarchy contained 27 scenes involving males. The top scene in this hierarchy pictured a "30-year-old, well-built, good-looking fellow, dressed neatly and standing in a large rest room." At the other end of the hierarchy was "an older, sloppily-dressed fellow" in the same location. Five scenes involving the boyfriend were added to these 27 items. The five scenes ranged from sexual contact to talking with him on the telephone. Thus, the total number of items was 32.

Base-line procedures were then instituted for five sessions, during which three measures were taken: First, Ss kept a small notebook in which they recorded each time that they were sexually aroused, for S_1 by the sight of an immature girl, and for S_2 by the sight of a mature male. The S_1, as an out-patient, recorded these events daily. Due to the distance of his home from the treatment center, S_2 remained in the hospital during the week and returned home on weekends. He was, therefore, instructed to visit one of the local bars 4 nights a week for 1–2 hr., during which time he recorded incidents of sexual arousal.

Second, the hierarchy scenes were typed on individual cards. For S_1 the 45 cards were divided into five packs of 9 cards each, chosen in such a way that each pack contained an equally arousing set of scenes. The 32 cards of S_2 were not divided. The S_1 then was given one of the packs, while S_2 was given the whole set. On every experimental day each S was asked to enter a separate room where he could sort each of the cards into one of five envelopes marked 0–4. He was told,

The numbers on the envelopes represent amount of sexual arousal, 0 equals no arousal, 1 equals a little arousal, 2 a fair amount, 3 much, and 4 very much arousal. I would like you to read the description of each scene and place a card in the envelope which comes closest to how arousing the scene is to you at this moment.

If he then put one card in the Number 4 envelope and one in the Number 3 envelope, his score to that point would be 7.

Third, galvanic skin responses (GSRs) were recorded from a Grass polygraph (Model 7) with silver, silver-chloride, palmar and wrist electrodes to six selected scenes from the hierarchy of each S. The same six scenes were used throughout the experiment. The S was relaxed and then asked to close his eyes and imagine the scene as clearly as possible. GSR deflection was measured as change in log conductance that was averaged for the six scenes. This measure was taken during every session of the base line and before every second session during treatment.

Procedure

During the initial interview Ss were told,

We view this type of problem as a bad habit that has been picked up over the years and we are going to try to break that habit. We will be using some techniques that have been found effective in dealing with bad habits such as this one. However, no matter how successful, every treatment has its ups and owns so don't get discouraged.

This last sentence was designed to allay any fear of ultimate failure that might have arisen when extinction procedures were later introduced. The Ss were then trained in deep muscle relaxation following the method described by Jacobson (1938). The highest six items in S_1's hierarchy were chosen for sensitization. The S_1 was seen twice a week as an outpatient. Since S_2's major problem at the outset was an "overwhelming" attraction for his boyfriend, the five scenes describing the boyfirend were chosen for sensitization along with one scene concerning sexual contact with "pickups" in public toilets. The S_2 was seen 5 days a week as an inpatient, and from Experimental Day 12 on was generally seen twice a day.

In each session Ss were given relaxation instructions and presented with eight scenes. In four scenes S was described approaching the small girl (male), feeling nauseous and vomiting. For example, in one of the homosexual scenes, S_2 was described approaching his boyfriend's apartment.

As you get closer to the door you notice a queasy feeling in the pit of the stomach. You open the door and see Bill lying on the bed naked and you can sense that puke is filling up your stomach and forcing its way up to your throat. You walk over to Bill and you can see him clearly, as you reach out for him you can taste the puke, bitter and sticky and acidy on your tongue, you start gagging and retching and chunks of vomit are coming out of your mouth and nose, dropping onto your shirt and all over Bill's skin.

The description of the nauseous scene was usually expanded and lasted for 30 to 60 sec. In the remaining four scenes S would be described approaching the small girl (male) and beginning to feel nauseous. At that point he would turn, start walking away from the scene, and immediately feel relieved and relaxed. The scenes were presented randomly. The sexually arousing scene was presented for approximately 10 sec., the nauseous scene for 30–60 sec., with an intertrial interval of 30 sec.

After 6 acquisition sessions consisting of 48 pairings for S_1, and 13 acquisition sessions consisting of 104 pairings for S_2, extinction was introduced.

The S was told, "For the next few sessions we are going to change the procedure a bit. We have found that this is the best course of action at this time. Remember to imagine only what I describe." Note that instructions during extinction suggest continued progress. The procedure during extinction consisted of presenting the sexually arousing scene for 10 sec., leaving the 30-sec. nauseous interval blank, and saying, "Stop imagining that," at the end of the interval. All other therapist behaviors remained constant.

After eight extinction sessions consisting of 64 scene presentations for each S, reacquisition was introduced. The design, then, consists of base-line measures; acquisition, in which sexually arousing scenes are paired with nauseous scenes; extinction, in which sexually arousing scenes are presented alone; and reacquisition.

RESULTS

Figure 1 plots the total score of the card sort for each experimental day and the total frequency of sexual arousal in blocks of 4 days surrounding each experimental day for S_1. These 4 days consisted of the 2 days before the session, the day of the session, and the day after the session.

During the base-line phase there was no treatment. The card sort remained stable during this period while reports of pedophilic urges steadily rose.

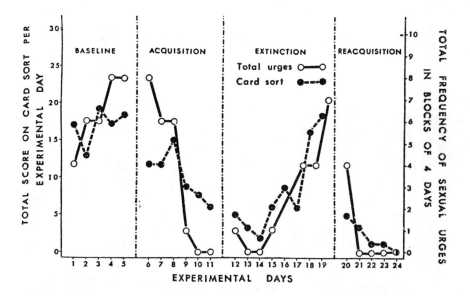

Fig. 4.1. Total score on card sort per experimental day and total frequency of pedophilic sexual urges in blocks of 4 days surrounding each experimental day. (Lower scores indicate less sexual arousal.)

Acquisition, in which the nauseous scene was paired with the sexually arousing scene, resulted in a sharp drop in both measures of inappropriate sexual
arousal. In extinction the nauseous scene was omitted, resulting in an increase
in both measures of sexual arousal.

The instruction preceding this extinction phase conveyed an expectancy of
therapeutic progress. This expectancy was verified when S said, toward the
end of extinction, "I know you're doing your best, but I guess I'm just not cut
out for this treatment." At this time S_1 became upset and depressed.

In reacquisition, the nauseous scene was reintroduced and measures of
sexual arousal dropped to zero. During this phase S_1 reported increased
heterosexual behavior.

GSR, analyzed as change in log conductance, was averaged over each of the
four experimental periods. The means (Ms) and standard deviations (SDs) in
μmhos are: base line, $M = 221$ and $SD = 141$; acquisition, $M = 27$ and $SD = 29$;
extinction, $M = 200$ and $SD = 92$; reacquisition, $M = 30$ and $SD = 23$.

Although there is a great deal of variability, it is clear that S_1's arousal rose
during extinction and declined during reacquisition.

Figure 2 plots the total score of the card sort on each experimental day for
S_2 and also the frequency of sexual arousal on each night out. For various
reasons S_2 was not able to go out each day that sessions were held. At one point
an illness prevented him from visiting the local bars for 4 consecutive nights
(Experimental Days 22-25). Therefore, points referring to frequency of sexual
arousal are plotted only on experimental days for which there are data.

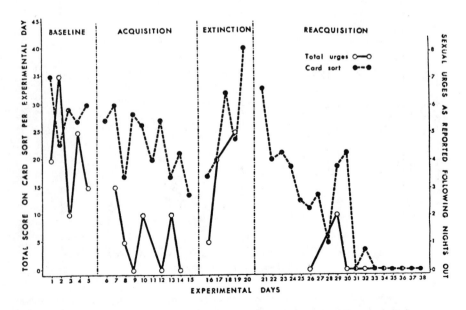

Fig. 4.2. Total score on card sort per experimental day and homosexual urges as reported
following nights out. (Lower scores indicate less sexual arousal.)

During the base-line phase both the card sort and reports of homosexual urges were relatively stable. The acquisition phase resulted in a drop in both measures of sexual arousal. In the course of extinction both measures rose sharply with the total score of the card sort rising above base-line levels.

During this phase S_2 also became depressed, and near the end of the period said: "This treatment isn't doing much good. I'm just as bad now as I was when I came in." At this time he engaged in his first homosexual affair since treatment began. Due to an illness of the therapist, there was a 9-day period between Experimental Days 20–22 during which S was only seen once (Day 21). Throughout this period S_2 generally refused to leave the hospital, even for the weekend, and remained quite depressed.

In reacquisition, measures of sexual arousal dropped to zero. All sessions beyond the twentieth session (Day 31) were self-administered. At this time, S_2 also reported increases in heterosexual behavior and acquisition of heterosexual fantasies.

Although mean magnitude of GSR declined sharply during acquisition, it did not recover during extinction and therefore could not be interpreted.

DISCUSSION

These findings demonstrate that pairing a noxious scene with a sexually arousing scene is a crucial procedure in covert sensitization. The effect of this pairing was separated from other psychotherapeutic variables such as therapeutic instructions, patient expectancies of improvement, and rapport between patient and therapist since these variables were still present during extinction when the noxious scene was removed, and yet behavior regressed.

The two noxious stimuli most often used in aversion therapy are emetic drugs (James, 1962) and more recently shock (Feldman & MacCulloch, 1965). This experiment demonstrates that an intensely imagined noxious scene can also act as an effective aversive stimulus. There would seem to be several advantages to using a noxious scene in clinical situations. First, the patient is less likely to refuse treatment because of the pain involved (Rachman, 1965). Second, it can be widely employed by many therapists, since it does not require drugs or apparatus.

Generally, there have been two therapeutic strategies in dealing with sexual deviations: decreasing deviant sexual behavior and increasing appropriate heterosexual behavior. This experiment indicates that covert sensitization alone is sufficient to decrease deviant behavior. More controlled research employing precise measures of heterosexuality is needed to determine what treatment variables are responsible for increases in heterosexual behavior. Further research is also necessary to ascertain whether reductions in deviant behavior resulting from covert sensitization would be maintained without continued treatment and careful attention to later sexual adjustment.

The present study does not completely overcome a measurement problem common to most psychotherapy research, namely, an excessive reliance on the patient's subjective reports of progress. Although there is evidence that GSR is a valid index of sexual arousal (Solyom & Beck, 1967; Wenger, Averill, & Smith, 1968), the remaining neasures are not behavioral in the sense of being publicly observable. While observable and objective behavioral measures have been devised for some neurotic (e.g., Leitenberg et al., 1968) and psychotic disorders (Ayllon & Azrin, 1965), it is more difficult in cases of sexual deviation where more than one person is involved. Recent studies in our laboratory and elsewhere (McConaghy, 1967), however, suggest that changes in penile volume to slides of inappropriate sexual objects, a measure originally devised by Freund (1963), may be useful in the measurement of sexual deviation.

REFERENCES

Agras, W. S., Leitenberg, H., & Barlow, D. H. Social reinforcement in the modification of agoraphobia. *Archives of General Psychiatry,* 1968, 19, 423–427.

Ayllon, T., & Azrin, N. H. The measurement and reinforcement of behavior of psychotics. *Journal of the Experimental Analysis of Behavior,* 1965, 8, 357–383.

Cautela, J. R. Treatment of compulsive behavior by covert sensitization. *Psychological Record,* 1966, 16, 33–41.

Cautela, J. R. Covert sensitization. *Psychological Reports,* 1967, 20, 459–468.

Davison, G. C. The elimination of a sadistic fantasy by a client-controlled counter-conditioning technique: A case study. *Journal of Abnormal Psychology,* 1968, 73, 84–90.

Feldman, M. P. Aversion therapy for setual deviations: A critical review. *Psychological Bulletin,* 1966, 65, 65–79.

Feldman, M. P., & MacCulloch, M. J. The application of anticipatory avoidance learning to the treatment of homosexuality. I. Theory, technique and preliminary results. *Behavior Research and Therapy,* 1965, 2, 165–183.

Freund, K. A laboratory method for diagnosing predominance of homo- or hetero-erotic interest in the male. *Behavior Research and Therapy,* 1963, 1, 85–93.

Jacobson, E. *Progressive relaxation.* Chicago: University of Chicago Press, 1938.

James, B. A case of homosexuality treated by aversion therapy. *British Medical Journal,* 1962, 1, 768–770.

Kolvin, I. "Aversive imagery" treatment in adolescents. *Behavior Research and Therapy,* 1967, 5, 245–248.

Leitenberg, H., Agras, W. S., Thomson, L. E., & Wright, D. E. Feedback in behavior modification: An experimental analysis in two phobic cases. *Journal of Applied Behavior Analysis,* 1968, 1, 131–137.

McConaghy, N. Penile volume change to moving pictures of male and female nudes in heterosexual and homosexual males. *Behavior Research and Therapy,* 1967, 5, 43–48.

Rachman, S. Aversion therapy: Chemical or electrical? *Behavior Research and Therapy,* 1965, 2, 289–299.

Solyom, L., & Beck, P. R. GSR assessment of aberrant sexual behavior. *International Journal of Neuropsychiatry,* 1967, 3, 52–59.

Wenger, M. A., Averill, J. A., & Smith, D. D. B. Autonomic activity during sexual arousal. *Psychophysiology,* 1968, 4, 468–478.

Wolf, M. M., Birnbrauer, J. S., Williams, T., & Lawler, J. A note on apparent extinction of vomiting behavior of a retarded child. In L. P. Ullmann & L. Krasner (Eds.), *Case studies in behavior modification.* New York: Holt, Rinehart & Winston, 1965.

Chapter 5
Treatment of Smoking by Covert Sensitization*
Joseph R. Cautela

Summary. — A detailed application of covert sensitization to smoking behavior is presented. Data are presented to indicate that the results of covert sensitization cannot be attributed to S's expectancies. The available evidence indicates that the technique is effective in modifying smoking behavior.

Recently, increasing attempts have been made to modify smoking behavior. Keutzer (1968) and Bernstein (1969) have presented evaluative reviews of studies concerned with this topic. In general, they concluded that most attempts to modify smoking behavior have enjoyed little success. However, there is some evidence that under certain circumstances aversion therapies have successfully decreased smoking activity.

Franks, Fried, and Ashem (1966) devised an apparatus which emits puffs of smoke in the face of a smoking S and provides a relief stimulus (a candy mint or a puff of fresh air) when S stops smoking. Resnick (1968) attempted to make smoking aversive by satiation. He employed three groups of Ss. One control group was asked to continue smoking at their normal rate. Another group was asked to double their consumption for a week, and a third group was asked to triple their cigarette smoking for 3 wk. A significant reduction was reported in the two satiated groups, but no change was reported in the control groups. Lublin (1969) also reports that satiation can produce an aversive response to cigarettes.

The imagining aversive conditioning technique of covert sensitization (Cautela, 1966, 1967) has also been used to modify smoking behavior. It is the purpose of this paper to describe the method of covert sensitization in the

---

*Reprinted with permission of author and publisher from *Psychological Reports*, 1970, 26, 415–420.

treatment of smoking behavior and present some studies in which covert sensitization has been utilized.

DESCRIPTION OF PROCEDURE

The general procedure of employing covert sensitization to treat maladaptive approach behaviors has been described in two previous papers (Cautela, 1966, 1967). In the covert sensitization procedure, the client is instructed to imagine he is about to engage in the maladaptive behavior. Then he is instructed to imagine that he is receiving a noxious stimulus (usually the feeling of nausea and vomiting). The procedure is labeled covert sensitization because both the behavior to be modified and the noxious stimulus are presented in imagination. The purpose of this procedure is to produce avoidance behavior. There is agreement among several investigators that imagery behavior is subject to the same principles as overt behavior and that the manipulation of imagery can affect overt behavior (Bandura, 1969, pp. 584–585; Cautela, 1969b; Franks, 1967; Kimble, 1961, p. 462). Concerning aversive imagery, Weiner (1965) found that both imagining aversive consequences and being presented with actual aversive consequences reduced response rate more than a condition involving no consequences.

In addition to the usual assessment procedures (Cautela, 1968), the client is given a smoking questionnaire (unpublished) designed to elicit information concerning smoking behavior: frequency of smoking, kinds of cigarettes smoked, places and conditions under which smoking occurs.

The client is told that smoking is a habit which gives pleasure and reduces tension, that smoking has been associated with many situations which tend to instigate smoking behavior, and that if he is made to associate something unpleasant with smoking, his desire to smoke will be decreased or eliminated. He is told to sit back in his chair, close his eyes and try to relax. He is then instructed as follows:

"I am going to ask you to imagine some scenes as vividly as you can. I don't want you to imagine that you are seeing yourself in these situations. I want you to imagine that you're actually in the situations. Do not only try to visualize the scenes but also try to feel, for example, the cigarette in your hand, or the back of the chair in which you are sitting. Try to use all your senses as though you are actually there. The scenes that I pick will be concerned with situations in which you are about to smoke. It is very important that you visualize the scenes as clearly as possible and try to actually feel what I describe to you even though it is unpleasant."

The following is a typical scene:

You are sitting at your desk in the office preparing your lectures for class. There is a pack of cigarettes to your right. While you are writing, you put down your pencil and start to reach for a cigarette. As soon as you start reaching for the cigarette, you get a nauseous feeling in your stomach. You begin to feel sick to your stomach, like you are about to vomit. You touch the package and bitter spit comes into your mouth. When you take the cigarette out of the pack, some pieces of food come into your throat. Now you feel sick and have stomach cramps. As you are about to put the cigarette in your mouth, you puke all over the cigarette, all over your hand, and all over the package of cigarettes. The cigarette in your hand is very soggy and full of green vomit. There is a stink coming from the vomit. Snots are coming from your nose. You hands feel all slimy and full of vomit. The whole desk is a mess. Your clothes are full of puke. You get up from your desk and turn away from the vomit and cigarettes. You immediately begin to feel better being away from the cigarettes. You go to the bathroom and wash up and feel great being away from the cigarettes.

After the scene is described to S, he is asked how clearly he visualized the scene and whether he felt some nausea and disgust. He is then asked to repeat the scene himself, trying to see the cigarettes as clearly as possible and trying to see and smell the vomit.

Other scenes are given in a similar manner concerning other places in which he smokes, e.g., if he takes a cigarette after coffee in the morning, a scene is described in which he is about to smoke but gets sick and vomits all over the table and the cigarette.

Alternating with an aversive scene is an escape or self-control scene. A typical self-control scene is:

You are at your desk working and you decide to smoke, and as soon as you decide to smoke you get this funny sick feeling at the pit of your stomach. You say to yourself, 'The hell with it; I'm not going to smoke!' As soon as you decide not to smoke you feel fine and proud that you resisted temptation.

The self-controlling response scenes make use of two procedures which have been found to increase response probability: (1) negative reinforcement (escape conditioning) (Mowrer, 1940) and (2) self-reinforcement (Kanfer & Marston, 1963).

At each therapy session, S is given 10 trials of vomiting alternating with 10 scenes of escape and self-control. At the end of each session, S is asked to practice the 20 scenes twice a day until the next session. Also he is instructed to say "Stop!" and imagine he is vomiting on a cigarette whenever he is tempted to smoke. At the beginning of each session, he is asked how mans times he practiced and how many cigarettes he has smoked.

If it is evident (as usually is the case) that anxiety is antecedent to smoking or tension results from nonsmoking, the client could also be desensitized to those situations in which he usually smokes. In practice then the drive component and motor component are being manipulated. If S finds that the tension is too much in certain situations where he usually smokes, he is told to relax in these situations. Relaxation is normally taught in the first sessions as a self-control procedure (Cautela, 1969a).

RESULTS

In clinical practice the procedure just outlined appears quite effective in the reduction and elimination of smoking behavior. The main problem in presenting anecdotal evidence for the efficacy of a clinical procedure is that the procedure is only one of a number of possible interacting variables that can influence outcome of treatment. In clinical practice, variables such as S's expectancy and the combination of covert sensitization with other procedures make it difficult to assess the contribution of covert sensitization to treatment effects.

Regarding the use of covert sensitization and the S's expectancy in outcome of treatment, Barlow, Leitenberg, and Agras have performed two studies. In one study (Barlow, Leitenberg, & Agras, 1969) they found that the degree of homosexual urges could be manipulated by introducing and withdrawing covert sensitization. No other procedure was explicitly utilized in combination with covert sensitization. In another study (Barlow, Agras, & Leitenberg, unpublished study[1]), they manipulated S's expectancy by giving instructions to the effort that relaxing alone would reduce urges and covert sensitization would increase urges for homosexual behavior. The results were contrary to the expectancies given to Ss. These results do not refute the possibility that expectancy or other factors are not important variables when combined with covert sensitization, but they do indicate the covert sensitization procedure itself can account for a large proportion of the outcome of treatment.

There have been some studies directly concerned with the effect of covert sensitization on smoking behavior. F. G. Mullen (personal communication, 1967) employed a control group, a group-treated covert sensitization group, and a group in which Ss were treated individually with covert sensitization. At the end of six sessions (½ hr. for each session), the control group went from 16.3 cigarettes a day to 15.4 a day. The two covert-sensitization groups went from a mean of 15.3 cigarettes a day to 3.6 cigarettes. The group-treatment of covert sensitization had a mean of 5.0 a day and the individually treated covert-sensitization Ss had a mean of 0.5 cigarettes a day. A 6-mo. follow-up showed that the control group had a mean of 17.1 cigarettes a day and the experimental groups had a mean of 10.1 a day. No member of the control group gave up smoking, but two members of experimental groups stopped smoking completely. Mullen reports that as early as the second session the majority of the experimental Ss commented that they no longer enjoyed the cigarettes they smoked. In view of the small number of sessions, the follow-up results are

---

[1]Barlow, D. H., Agras, W. S., & Leitenberg, H. The effect of instruction on the use of covert sensitization. (Unpublished study)

not surprising. The experiment should have employed a placebo group.

Viernstein[2] compared covert sensitization with educational-supportive and control groups in the modification of smoking behavior. Seven sessions were used and two therapists alternated weekly administration of the procedures. Ss subjected to covert sensitization smoked significantly ($p < .05$) fewer cigarettes at post-treatment and at a 5-wk. follow-up. She also reports that the covert sensitization Ss said that when they did smoke, they didn't enjoy the cigarette. It would have been interesting to see reports of a 6-mo. follow-up.

Wagner (1969) compared systematic desensiization alone, covert sensitization alone, relaxation alone, and a group in which systematic desensitization and covert sensitization were combined. He reports that at the end of the 30- and 90-day follow-ups, only the group with combined systematic desensitization-covert sensitization was smoking significantly less than the base rate. As a result of this study, Wagner and Bragg[3] developed a self-administering programmed recording of the systematic desensitization-covert sensitization procedure.

Implications

Evidence indicates that covert sensitization is effective in the modification of smoking behavior. When covert sensitization is combined with systematic desensitization and used as a self-control procedure, it appears more effective. Although the author has anecdotal evidence that the effects of covert sensitization can be long-lasting (i.e., at least a year), there is no experimental evidence which indicates the long-lasting effects of covert sensitization.

In empirical studies employing covert sensitization, it has been customary to employ a relatively small number of sessions. In clinical practice, the covert sensitization procedure is employed until the frequency of the maladaptive behavior such as smoking is reduced to zero. Then treatment is continued for a number of sessions. The continuation of the covert sensitization procedure after the response is eliminated is more apt to ensure less likelihood of reconditioning (Cautela, 1968; Pavlov, 1927, p. 57).

REFERENCES

Bandura, A. *Principles of behavior modification*. New York: Holt, Rinehart, & Winston, 1969.

Barlow, D. H., Leitenberg, H., & Agras, W. S. Experimental control of sexual

---

[2]Viernstein, L. K. Evaluation of therapeutic techniques of covert sensitization of smoking behavior. (Unpublished data, Queens College, Charlottesville, North Carolina, 1968)

[3]Wagner, M. K., & Bragg, R. A. Comparing behavior modification methods for habit decrement — smoking. (Unpublished data, V.A. Hospital, Salisbury, North Carolina, 1968)

deviation through manipulation of the noxious scene in covert sensitization. *Journal of Abnormal Psychology,* 1969, 5, 596–601.

Bernstein, D. A. Modification of smoking behavior: an evaluative review. *Psychological Bulletin,* 1969, 71, 418–440.

Cautela, J. R. Treatment of compulsive behavior by covert sensitization. *Psychological Record,* 1966, 16, 33–41.

Cautela, J. R. Covert sensitization. *Psychological Reports,* 1967, 20, 459–468.

Cautela, J. R. Behavior therapy and the need for behavioral assessment. *Psychotherapy: Theory, Research, and Practice,* 1968, 5, 175–179.

Cautela, J. R. Behavior therapy and self-control: techniques and implications. In C. Franks (Ed.), *The assessment and status of the behavior therapies and associated developments.* New York: McGraw-Hill, 1969. Pp. 323–340. (a)

Cautela, J. R. The use of imagery in behavior modification. In R. Rubin & C. Franks (Eds.), *Advances in behavior therapy, 1969.* New York: Academic Press, 1969, in press (b)

Franks, C, Reflections upon treatment of sexual disorders by the behavioral clinicians: an historical comparison with the treatment of the alcoholic. *Journal of Sex Research,* 1967, 3, 212–222.

Franks, C. Fried, R., & Ashem, B. An improved apparatus for aversive conditioning of cigarette smokers. *Behavior Research and Therapy,* 1966, 4, 301–308.

Kanfer, F. H., & Marston, A. R. Conditioning of self-reinforcement responses: an analogue to self-confidence training. *Psychological Reports,* 1963, 13, 63–70.

Keutzer, C. S. Behavior modification of smoking: the experimental investigation of diverse techniques. *Behavior Research and Therapy,* 1968, 6, 137–157.

Kimble, G. A. *Hilgard and Marquis' 'Conditioning and learning.'* New York: Appleton-Century-Crofts, 1961.

Lublin, I. Principles governing the choice of unconditioned stimulus in aversive conditioning. In R. Rubin & C. Franks (Eds.), *Advances in behavior therapy, 1968.* New York: Academic Press, 1969. Pp. 73–82.

Mowrer, O. H. An experimental analysis of "regression" with incidental observations on "reaction-formation." *Journal of Abnormal and Social Psychology,* 1940, 35, 56–87.

Pavlov, I. P. *Conditioned reflexes.* London: Oxford Univer. Press, 1927.

Resnick, J. H. The control of smoking behavior by stimulus satiation. *Behavior Research and Therapy,* 1968, 6, 113–114.

Wagner, M. K. A self-administered programmed recording for decreasing cigarette consumption. Paper presented at the Meeting of the Association for the Advancement of Behavior Therapy, San Francisco, August, 1968.

Weiner, H. Real and imagined cost effects upon human fixed-interval responding. *Psychological Reports,* 1965, 17, 659–662.

Chapter 6

The Treatment of a Nail-Biting Compulsion by Covert Sensitization in a Poorly Motivated Client*

Michael J. Paquin

Summary — A serious, long lasting nail-biting compulsion was successfully modified using covert sensitization in a female patient, despite a lack of motivation to change. Continued improvement was demonstrated at a 40 week follow-up. The significance of the case is enhanced by the use of objective, externally verified measures.

The present study demonstrates the effectiveness of covert sensitization in treating compulsive nail-biting in a person characterized by a lack of motivation for change. However, despite the high incidence of nail-biting (Coleman and McCalley, 1948), it has been one of the most difficult habits to modify (Azrin and Nunn, 1973) possibly because nail-biters appear to be sensitive to environmental controls (e.g. aversive comments) and thus bite their nails in solitude under reinforcing conditions (Bucher, 1968) which would tend to reduce motivation to change. The present case study has the advantage of including both an operational definition of patient motivation and an objective, easily verifiable measure of the target behavior (nail-biting), viz fingernail length.

*Reprinted with permission from the *Journal of Behavior Therapy and Experimental Psychiatry*, 1977, *8*, 181-183. © Pergamon Press.

CASE HISTORY

The case involved a 23-year-old female university student who could not control her compulsive nail-biting habit. Her unsightly, scarred fingers caused cross situational anxiety which impeded normal social interactions even with friends of the same sex.

The client had undergone, during the past 7 years, a series of unsuccessful treatment attempts, including familial and unguided self-control approaches, false nails, and valerian and iodine nail paints. She was frustrated at these failures and pessimistic about the possibility of gaining control of the habit when she approached an instructor soliciting volunteers for a "Behavior Modification Exercise" for graduate students and was given a description of the project. Several aspects of the information given to her are important *vis-a-vis* the client motivation component of therapy emphasized by Bucher (1968) and Azrin and Nunn (1973) in the treatment of nail-biting and other compulsions. The form stated, among other things, that "because students are not experts in the use of behavior modification techniques, but rather just beginning to learn these techniques, several important points must be made. The purpose of the exercise is to train the students not modify the behavior of the volunteers . . No guarantee of behavior change is made . . . The volunteer is free to withdraw from the exercise at any time for any reason." This may have had the serious side effect of reducing expectations for success and motivation for change, despite the intent, in her case, to provide *bona fide* therapeutic relief.

A behavioral analysis revealed that nail-biting was part of a behavioral chain which most often began by the client experiencing some form of anxiety, and which terminated in the reinforcing circumstances of relaxation and smoking a cigarette. Covert sensitization was deemed to be a means of substitution aversive consequences for this reinforcement, given that the unsightliness of the client's fingernails and the naturally-occuring, socially aversive consequences of nail-biting had become ineffective in controlling the compulsive habit ("I always want to finish the nail").

TREATMENT

Nail-biting was operationally defined as any hand movement which resulted in the finger tips coming in contact with the teeth for more than a few seconds, or more specifically when there was any chewing whatsoever, on the nails. A separate nail-biting incident was defined as occurring whenever contact with the teeth was broken and the hand moved away from the face, and then contact reestablished. The client kept hourly records on 3 × 5 in. cards of such nail-biting occurrences. Fingernail length was measured from the middle of the base of the fingernail, where it goes below the skin, to the top of the nail at the middle. Thus, the measure was the maximum length of each fingernail and represents a conservative indication of actual changes in nail-biting severity both in terms of frequency and intensity.

Covert sensitization has enjoyed some success in treating obsessions and compulsions (Daniels, 1974, Kazarian and Evans, 1977). The basis of the therapy followed Cautela's (1966, 1967) standard covert sensitization procedure. Twelve "deviant" scenes were constructed based upon the behavioral analysis conducted in the initial interviews. These scenes depicted the sequence of events terminating in nail-biting. They included a description of the setting (e.g. "the friend who used to play 'truthsies' with you is becoming quite frank with you, speaking bluntly about . . ."), the uncomfortable physiological experience and then the behaviors involved in nail-biting. The noxious scenes which followed were based upon Evans' (1975) Fear Inventory and a few scenes depicting situations which were still naturally aversive to her, such as the worsened appearance of her fingers after doing dishes. Six noxious scenes were used including Cautela's (1967) very lucid and sentient nausea scene.

Each stage of this imagery sequence was meticulously practiced separately, until the client could bring to mind, on her own, all of the relevant stimulus details. Typically 2 or 3 complete scene sequences were covered in a session. This was particularly important since the client was asked to practice the scenes covered during each session three times a night during the following week. She reported becoming sleepy when attempting to do more than three practice sessions a night.

The client overcame an initial difficulty of relaxing to verbal instructions and demonstrated a vivid imagination, often spontaneously adding details to the stimulus scenes. A total of seven covert sensitization treatments were given from the third to the ninth session, over a period of ten weeks. In three of these weeks she failed to keep scheduled appointments and failed to notify the therapist, reportedly due to forgetfulness. This pointed to ambivalent motivation, further indicated by several instances of failing adequately to practice the homework assignments. Six out of the thirteen (46%) self-monitoring and home practice exercises were either forgotten or not completed according to the client's own accounts. Spontaneous comments by the client corroborated this finding of low motivation. At the second session: she said "Wouldn't it be funny if I didn't want to change?" At the tenth session she admitted that as therapy progressed her feelings about the value of her time spent during therapy and homework exercises became more ambivalent because of academic pressures.

Despite this problem, covert sensitization significantly decreased the daily frequency of nail-biting and increased the length of all fingernails. During the baseline weeks immediately preceeding the first week of treatment the average length of all the fingernails was 7.6mm for both hands with a standard deviation (*S.D.*) of 1.5 for the left hand and 1.6 for the right.* During the last week of therapy the average length of the left hand nails had increased to 8.5mm (*S.D.* = 1.6) and to 9.1 (*S.D.* = 1.3) for the right hand. After a month follow-up this had increased to 9.4mm (*S.D.* = 1.6) and 10.1mm (*S.D.* = 1.3) respectively; a further follow-up 40 weeks after the first contact revealed average lengths of 11.6 and 12.2mm respectively, reflecting gains of more than 50% over baseline levels. The frequency of daily nail-biting also improved by the last week of therapy and continued to decrease in the follow-up weeks. During the baseline weeks the frequency of nail-biting was 10.14 times per day on the average (*S.D.* = 9.5). At the last week and at the first follow-up this had decreased to 6.4 (*S.D.* = 3.1) and 3.5 (*S.D.* = 3.4) respectively.

Concordant with the success of treatment, were the client's spontaneous and exuberant expressions of satisfaction at the follow-ups, especially with respect to the appearance of her nails. Although impossible to assess objectively *all* her nails were noticeably improved in quality as well as length; scar tissue was absent and the outer edge of the nails were relatively smooth rather than being uneven and rough from chewing. This was the most salient and important improvement for the client who reported that she no longer felt ashamed to display her hands publicly. This improvement generalized to interpersonal problems as well. She reported being more self confident and assertive in interpersonal situations that had previously been anxiety-provoking for her. In respect of this poorly motivated patient, the efficacy of covert sensitization in reducing nail-biting is impressive, showing once again that if learning procedures can be implemented the attitude of the patient is of relatively small importance.

REFERENCES

Azrin N. and Nunn R. (1973) Habit reversal: A method of eliminating nervous habits and tics, *Behav. Res. & Therapy* **11**, 619–629.
Bucher B. (1968) A pocket-portable shock device with application to nailbiting. *Behav. Res. & Therapy* **6**, 389–393.
Cautela J. R. (1966) Treatment of compulsive behavior by covert conditioning. *Psychol. Rev.* **16**, 33–41.

---

*Normative data regarding fingernail length is unavailable. However, the client's nails were all markedly shorter than usual, with no projecting portions. On several fingers scabs were visible from recent bleeding. The average fingernail length of the author, for a comparative example, is 12.2mm, measured at the middle of each nail. Many women possess and value nails, considerably longer (15-20 mm) than this. Since the normal rate of fingernail growth is slightly above 1 mm per month, the amount of improvement shown by the client represents considerable success in the control of compulsive nail-biting.

Cautela J. R. (1967) Covert sensitization, *Psychol. Rep.* **20**, 459–468.

Coleman J. and McCalley J. (1948) Nailbiting among college students, *J. abnorm. Psychol.* **43**, 517–525.

Daniels L. (1974) Rapid extinction of nailbiting by covert sensitization: A case study, *J. Behav. Ther. & Exp. Psychiat.* **5**, 91–92.

Evans D. R. (1975) *Evans' Fear Inventory.* Personal communication, Jan., 1975.

Kazarian S. S. (1975) *The Treatment of obsessional ruminations, a comparative study.* Doctoral dissertation, Psychology dept., U. of Western Ontario, London, Canada, N6A5C2.

Kazarian S. S. and Evans D. R. (1977) Modification of obsessional ruminations: a comparative study, *Can. J. Behav. Sci* **9**, 91–100.

Chapter 7
Covert Sensitization Treatment of Exhibitionism*
Ronald C. Hughes

Summary — Covert sensitization using nausea as the aversive stimulus was successfully applied in the treatment of a case with a twenty year history of exhibitionism. The behavior was eliminated and the client remained symptom free at one month, one year and three year follow-up. The method of alternating escape and avoidance scenes during treatment sessions and the rationale for not assigning "homework" is briefly described.

The treatment of exhibitionism, first described and named by Charles Laseque (1877), is rarely reported in the literature although the disorder may account for 25 to 35% of all reported sexual offenses (Ellis and Brancale, 1956; Mohr, Turner, and Jerry, (1964). This may be due to the low rate of exhibitionists submitting to treatment.

Bond and Hutchinson (1960) and Evans (1968) described the use of chemical and electrical aversion therapy in the treatment of exhibitionists. Cautela (1971) reported on the use of covert sensitization in the treatment of various sexual deviations including exhibitionism. However, to date there has been no detailed account of the use of covert sensitization in the treatment of exhibitionism. The following report attempts to supply this.

CASE HISTORY

The client was a 27-year-old unmarried male in his senior year of college. He

---

*Reprinted with permission from the *Journal of Behavior Therapy and Experimental Psychiatry*, 1977, 8, 177–179. © Pergamon Press.

requested outpatient treatment in a mental health clinic after a recent episode of exhibitionism. During the initial interview in April, 1973, he said he had been exposing himself for nearly 20 years. He had never been arrested, even though he had exposed himself four or five times a month for the past five years.

A detailed history of his exhibitionistic behavior was taken, less to determine the cause than to identify the stimulus conditions likely to precede the undesirable behavior. The stimulus conditions included: time of day; setting; and the mood of the client before exposing himself. Relevant characteristics of the female audience included age, race, build, dress and reaction. On every occasion, the client would drive home immediately after exposing himself, and relive the incident in detail while masturbating, timing his orgasm to the moment his audience noticed his penis. The sight of young girls walking in isolated areas had become a discriminative stimulus for the chain of responses commonly known as exhibitionism.

After an explanation of the rationale, procedure and possible discomfort associated with covert sensitization, the client consented to treatment.

TREATMENT

The client was given a 20 min demonstration of deep muscle relaxation. He was asked to keep a daily record of several behaviors and return in two weeks for his first treatment session. The behaviors he was to note included: number of times he exposed himself; number of urges to expose himself; masturbation with exhibitionistic fantasies; masturbation with fantasies of intercourse; and intercourse. He completed a Minnesota Multiphasic Personality Intentory (MMPI) and showed markedly elevated scores on scales 9, 4, and 8.

Treatment sessions followed the general format described by Cautela (1967; Cautela and Wisocki, 1971) using nausea as the aversive stimulus. The scenes were presented in two forms; escape and avoidance. In the former, the client was asked to imagine that he engaged in the act of exhibitionism, became deathly nauseous, and as he escaped from the act of exposing himself he became relaxed and refreshed. During avoidance scenes the client was asked to imagine himself becoming strongly nauseous at a time when he was tempted to expose himself; but as he avoided exposing himself he would begin to feel refreshed and tranquil. The avoidance scenes were used to produce an aversion to items early in the stimulus-response chain. Only escape scenes were presented at the first session. Avoidance scenes were interspersed randomly during the final four sessions. Thirteen escape scenes and nine avoidance scenes were presented during the five treatment sessions. Treatment was terminated after eight weeks, on the understanding that the client would return for further treatment as needed. An MMPI was administered at the final session.

RESULTS AND DISCUSSION

Stomach contractions were readily apparent, as was flushing and grimacing during the sessions of covert sensitization. Escape scenes were given ratings of 80 to 100 on a 100 point "Subjective anxiety scale" (Wolpe, 1969, pp. 116), while avoidance scenes were given a rating of 30 to 40.

Sexual intercourse and masturbation with fantasies of intercourse showed the greatest variability among the client's behaviors, ranging from zero to eight times a week. Exposing himself, as well as urges to do so became drastically reduced during baseline and treatment periods. He did not expose himself during baseline and during treatment only once — in the fifth week. The urge to expose himself occurred three and four times respectively during the two weeks of the baseline period, and he had two fleeting thoughts of exhibiting each week during the treatment period. During an equivalent period before treatment, he would have exposed himself at least eight to ten times.

The client did not masturbate to exhibitionistic fantasies during either baseline or treatment. He was explicitly instructed not to do so at the first treatment session because of the finding that masturbation to deviant fantasy tends to increase the probability of sexually deviant behavior (McGuire et al., 1965; Evans, 1968).

All scores on the post-treatment MMPI were significantly reduced and within normal limits. A t test for comparison of change (McNemar, 1969) was performed and with nine degrees of freedom, was significant beyond the 0.02 level.

After the first aversion session the client said that nausea had always been extremely unpleasant to him and that he strongly experienced the nausea suggested at the sessions. Likewise, the nausea reduction scenes were experienced as very refreshing. The client reported that when out of necessity he drove in the areas where he had previously sought to exhibit himself he now kept his eyes straight ahead and felt as though he should not be there.

At a follow-up interview one month after termination, the client had not exposed himself. He had not practiced the "homework" scenes as had been suggested because his urges were fleeting, and he felt that the imagined scenes would focus his attention on the undesired thoughts. He was seen for an hour one year and again three years after treatment. Each time he reported that he had not exposed himself since last contacted.

REFERENCES

Bond I. and Hutchinson H. (1960) Application of reciprocal inhibition therapy to exhibitionism, *Canad. Med. Assoc. J.* **83**, 23–25.
Cautela J. R. (1967) Covert sensitization, *Psychol. Reports* **20**, 459–468.

Cautela J. R. and Wisocki P. (1971) Covert sensitization for the treatment of sexual deviations, *Psychol. Record* **21**, 37–48.

Ellis A. and Brancale R. (1956) *The Psychology of Sex Offenders*, Thomas, Springfield, IL.

Evans D. R. (1968) Masturbatory fantasy and sexual deviation, *Behavior Res. & Therapy* **6**, 17-20.

Laseque E. C. (1877) Les exhibitionistes, *L'Union Medicale*, troisieme serie.

McGuire R., Carlisle J. and Young B. (1965) Sexual deviation as conditioned behavior, *Behavior Res. & Therapy* **2**, 185–190.

McNemar Q. (1969) *Psychological Statistics*, Wiley, New York.

Mohr J. W., Turner R. E. and Jerry M. D. (1964) *Pedophillia and Exhibitionism*, University of Toronto Press, Toronto.

Wolpe J. (1969) *The Practice of Behavior Therapy*, Pergamon Press, Oxford.

SECTION III
COVERT REINFORCEMENT

Chapter 8
Covert Reinforcement*†
Joseph R. Cautela

Summary — A new procedure for behavior modification is described. The author designates the procedure as covert reinforcement. The term "covert" is used because the response and reinforcing stimulus are presented in imagination. The word "reinforcement" is employed because the purpose of the procedure is to increase response probability.

A rationale for use of the procedure is given in learning theory terms. The details of the procedure are derived from empirical data of learning studies.

Examples of the actual application of covert reinforcement to various maladaptive behaviors are presented.

An experiment performed by the author and his associates which supports the assumption that reinforcement presented in imagination can increase response probability is described.

In this paper the term "reinforcement" refers to any stimulus which increases the probability of a response when it is presented contiguously with or immediately after the response. When this same stimulus is withdrawn, response probability is decreased.

A reinforcing stimulus may be presented in three ways:

1. It may be presented externally and transmitted to the central nervous system via external receptors, e.g., food, music, smiling, praise, etc.

2. It may be presented by direct stimulation of the central nervous system, bypassing the external receptors. This method is exemplified by the work of Olds (1956).

3. It may be presented by instructing the patient to initiate mediational

---

*Reprinted with permission from *Behavior Therapy,* 1970, *1*, 33–50. © Academic Press, Inc. 1970.

†This paper is based in part on papers presented at Dejarnette State Hospital, Stanton, Virginia, on January 15, 1969, and Brandeis University, Waltham, Massachusetts, on April 22, 1969. The author expresses his appreciation to Miss Patricia Wisocki for her suggestions and careful reading of the manuscript.

processes such as thinking or imagery. (We will prescind here from the problem of imageless thought.) It is assumed in this paper that stimuli which act as representatives of external stimuli (imagery) can be, under certain conditions, functionally equivalent to the stimuli presented by the other two methods of presenting reinforcing stimuli. This assumption of functional equivalence between external stimuli and covert stimuli has support from a number of sources.

Some investigators operating within a learning theory framework assume that the same principles which influence overt behavior can be applied to covert behavior as well. Pavlov assumed that the second-signaling system, which includes words, abstract ideas, and images, obeys the same laws as the first signaling system (1955, p. 285). This same view concerning the functional similarity of external and internal stimuli was alluded to briefly by Guthrie in his discussion of intention and maintaining stimuli (1935, pp. 205–206). Hull (1952) in his later theorizing assigned a great deal of importance to the fractional antedating reaction (^{r}g) and its stimulus correlate (Sg). He expressed the idea that the ^{r}g-Sg relationship would lead to further knowledge of covert processes such as planning, foresight, expectation, purpose, etc. (p. 350). Hull assumed, of course, that the same principles governing overt responses would govern covert processes. More recently, from within the operant paradigm, Homme (1965) expressed the conviction that "operants of the mind" obey the same laws as observable operants.

A crucial assumption of this paper is that the manipulation of covert processes can influence overt processes in a predictable manner. There is some support for such an assumption. Kimble (1961, p. 462) holds that the fact that thoughts are capable of providing cues means that, theoretically, they can provide the same conditions for the control of behavior as environmental events do. More recently this assumption has been made explicit by Franks (1967) in a statement that conditioning to fantasy situations should be readily acquired and generalized quickly to reality levels. In the covert reinforcement procedure described in this paper both the response and reinforcing stimulus presented in imagination are made as similar as possible to the external response and stimulus. It is assumed that on the basis of stimulus-response generalization there will be a transfer to conditioning from imagination. Though this assumption remains to be experimentally verified, there is ample evidence that both stimulus and response generalization occur. Kimble presents a table of 17 studies demonstrating stimulus generalization involving different species including humans (1961, pp. 329–330). Williams (1941), Arnold (1945), and Antonitis (1951) present experimental data for response generalization.

Investigators in behavior therapy are providing evidence that manipulation of imagery and other covert processes can effectively modify maladaptive behavior. Studies by Wolpe (1958), Lang (1964), Paul (1966), and Davison (1965) support the assumption that desensitization based on relaxation can modify maladaptive avoidance responses. Stampfl and Levis' (1966) work on implosive therapy shows promise in this regard. The author's own interest in the use of imagery to modify maladaptive behavior was expressed publicly in two previous papers (Cautela, 1966, 1967). In these papers, a procedure was described for the treatment of maladaptive approach behaviors such as alcoholism, homosexuality, overeating, and excessive smoking. In this procedure the patient is asked to imagine that he becomes nauseated and vomits as he is about to obtain the undesirable stimulus, e.g., take a drink. The undesirable stimulus is also presented in imagination. Since both the conditioned stimulus and the aversive stimulus are presented in imagination and since the purpose of the procedure is to build up an avoidance response to an undesirable stimulus, the procedure was labeled covert sensitization. Since the publcation of the two papers, a number of studies (Stuart, 1967; Ashem & Donner, 1968; Barlow, Leitenberg & Agras, (1968; Mullen, 1968; Viernstein, 1968) have provided empirical validation that covert sensitization is effective in the modification of maladaptive approach behavior.

The successful use of such procedures in imagination has recently led the author to speculate on the possibility of presenting a reinforcing stimulus in imagination in order to influence behavior in a manner similar to the external presentation of reinforcing stimuli. In other words, it is assumed that the functional relationship between behavior and a reinforcing stimulus presented in imagination is similar to the functional relationship between behavior and a reinforcing stimulus externally presented.

It is the purpose of this paper to describe that technique and suggest application of it to various forms of maladaptive behavior. This procedure is labeled covert reinforcement. The term ''covert'' is used because both the response and the reinforcing stimulus are presented in imagination. The term ''reinforcement'' is used to indicate that the purpose of the procedure is to increase response probability. The labeling of the procedure as covert reinforcement (COR) permits one to utilize information gained from the empirical studies investigating the parameters of reinforcement to maximize the effectiveness of the procedure. In describing the procedure it will be demonstrated how covert reinforcement has been applied in line with reinforcement principles. The description of the method in this paper has been limited to the modification of maladaptive behavior, but in principle is applicable to all behavior influenced by learning.

GENERAL DESCRIPTION OF METHOD

Discovery of Possible Reinforcers

After it has been determined from the usual behavioral analysis of a patient (Cautela, 1968) that covert reinforcement is indicated, the first step in the procedure is to discover possible reinforcing stimuli. For this goal three possible sources are utilized:

(a) The main source of identifying reinforcing stimuli is the Reinforcement Survey Schedule (RSS) (Cautela & Kastenbaum, 1967) which is administered routinely as part of the behavioral analysis.

The RSS is composed of 54 major items and is divided into four primary sections: (1) reinforcers which can be presented in palpable, facsimile, or imaginary form; (2) reinforcers which can be presented only in facsimile or imaginary form; (3) situational contexts which may be reinforcing; and (4) a survey of frequently occurring daily behaviors. In the first three sections the respondent is asked to rate each item on a 5-point scale according to the degree to which he feels enjoyment or pleasure for it. The points on the scale are the following: not at all, a little, a fair amount, much, very much.

After the patient has completed the Reinforcement Survey Schedule, the items to which he attached "very much" responses are rank ordered by him, ranging from the least pleasurable to the most pleasurable items. The first three items so ranked are then tested for possible presentation as reinforcing stimuli. The procedure of using the patient's high preference items for reinforcing stimuli is based on experimental data which indicate that the quality of reinforcement influences the effectiveness of a reinforcer (Guttman, 1963; Hutt, 1954). In general, the more preferred stimuli are the more effective reinforcers.

In order to test the item for its reinforcing qualities, the patient is asked to close his eyes and imagine receiving the stimulus, e.g., if the item selected is rock and roll music, the patient is instructed in the following manner:

Choose your favorite rock and roll song — one that you know quite well — and try to imagine you can really hear it. As soon as you feel you can really hear it clearly, signal me by raising your index finger.

After the patient signals, the therapist inquiries about the clarity of the stimulus. If he affirms that the stimulus was imagined clearly, the trial is repeated and the same question is asked.

The item is included for use as a reinforcing stimulus if the following criteria are met:

1. The patient perceives it as highly desirable, pleasurable, or enjoyable.

2. The patient is able to obtain a clear image of the stimulus. According to Hull the more similar the generalized stimulus or response to the original stimulus or response, in terms of JNDs, the greater the generalized effective habit strength (Hull, 1943, p. 199). This postulate is highly substantiated by the data presented by Kimble (1961, pp. 329–330).

3. The patient is able to obtain the image almost immediately after its presentation, i.e., within 5 sec. Data from many experiments indicate the

closer the reinforcement to the response in time the greater the influence on response rate (Kimble, 1961, p. 140).

(*b*) The second method of determining possible reinforcing stimuli is by asking the patient to suggest other events or items not on the Reinforcement Survey Schedule which would be pleasurable for him. (One female subject reported that winning $25,000 in a contest would be very pleasant for her.)

(*c*) Further information about possible reinforcing stimuli can be derived from case histories, relatives, friends, and ward personnel (if the patient is institutionalized). This source of information is utilized primarily with patients who report few pleasures in life and label few or no items in the "very much" column of the Reinforcement Survey Schedule.

The first two procedures of obtaining reinforcers are usually quite adequate for most patients.

It is important to have a number of possible reinforcers available for each patient so that satiation will not occur. Ayllon and Azrin (1968, pp. 119–120) found that if a reinforcer is used too frequently, it can lose its effectiveness. For this reason the reinforcers are often varied, even within the same session.

Description of Procedure

When COR is used it is not necessary to formally teach the patient to relax, nor is it necessary to construct a hierarchy as in the desensitization procedure.

Where desensitization is used to modify maladaptive avoidance behavior and covert sensitization is employed to modify maladaptive approach behavior, the COR procedure can be used to modify both maladaptive avoidance and approach behavior.

Before describing the COR procedure for different maladaptive behaviors, a typical example of the application of the technique is presented below.

A male subject treated for homosexuality, who had lost sexual urges toward males by the use of covert sensitization, was reluctant to call a girl for a date. He claimed he was nervous and sometimes even forgot our instructions about calling a particular girl he knew well. He was then instructed as follows:

In a minute I am going to ask you to try and relax and close your eyes. Then I will describe a scene to you. When you can imagine the scene as clearly as possible, raise your right index finger. I will then say the word 'reinforcement.' As soon as I say the word 'reinforcement' try to imagine the reinforcing scene we practiced before — the one about your swimming on a hot day, feeling the refreshing water, and feeling wonderful. As soon as the reinforcing scene is clear, raise your right index finger. Do you understand the instructions? Remember to try to imagine everything as vividly as possible, as if you were really there. All right, now close your eyes and try to relax.

After the patient has closed his eyes and appears comfortable, the therapist presents a scene such as this one:

I want you to imagine that you are home in the kitchen and you say to yourself, 'I think I'll call Jane for a date,' When you have that scene clearly, raise your finger. (As soon as he raises his finger to signal clear imagery, the experimenter says, 'Reinforcement.') Was the delivery of the reinforcement clear? All right, let's continue. After you've decided to call Jane, you walk toward the phone and you start dialing. Raise your finger when this is clear. ('Reinforcement.') All right, now you have finished dialing. Jane answers. You say, 'Hello' and ask her if she is free Saturday night and tell her that you would like to take her out. Raise your finger when this is clear. ('Reinforcement.') Now do the whole procedure yourself. Imagine you decide to call. Deliver a reinforcement to yourself, then imagine you are dialing, then deliver a reinforcement to yourself. Then imagine you are asking for a date and again deliver a reinforcement to yourself. When you are all finished, raise your right index finger. Now take your time. Make sure you get clear imagery. You can see the kitchen. You can see and feel the phone, etc. Also try to imagine that you are comfortable and confident while you are in the kitchen going through the procedure. All right. Start.

After the finger is raised, the therapist asks the following questions: ''Was everything clear?'' ''Did you have any trouble?'' And then asks him to try it again. After the patient has practiced the entire sequence, he is told to practice twice a day at home, doing the procedure two times each practice session. He is urged to try to actually make the call and when he is about to call, he is told to deliver the reinforcements to himself at the same places he did in imagination.

THE USE OF COVERT REINFORCEMENT IN THE TREATMENT OF VARIOUS MALADAPTIVE BEHAVIORS

In all the cases presented, the procedure and its purposes as presented earlier in this paper were fully explained to the patient along with its rationale. Data by Ayllon and Azrin (1964) indicate that instructions on the relationship between the response and reinforcement are more effective with patients than the use of reinforcement alone. Ferster (1953) states that the use of instructions in relationship to reinforcement procedures is in accord with the theory of operant conditioning.

After the presentation of the case examples, more specific details on the technique based on reinforcement procedures will be discussed.

Avoidance Behaviors

In maladaptive avoidance behaviors, antagonistic approach responses are reinforced. As stated previously, it is not necessary to construct a hierarchy; instead the logical sequence of approach behavior is reinforced. An example is presented below to illustrate the procedure as applied to avoidance behaviors.

A doctoral candidate who had flunked his doctoral qualifying examinations three times was referred for treatment because of extreme test anxiety. In 3 months he was to be given his last chance to pass his examination. He was considered an excellent student as indicated by his grades on papers, semester examinations, and oral discussion. He also reported that when he studied, he would become anxious and could not concentrate. The following procedure was utilized:

Close your eyes and try to relax. I want you to imagine you are sitting down to study and you feel fine. You are confident and you are relaxed. I know you may be anxious here but try to imagine that when you are about to study you are calm and relaxed, as if you were acting a part. Start. (When the S raises his finger, the therapist delivers the word, 'Reinforcement' which in this case signals the image of skiing down a mountain feeling exhilarated.) Practice this twice a day and just before you study.

Now let's work on the examination situation. It is the day of the examination and you feel confident. ('Reinforcement.') You are entering the building in which the exam is going to be given. ('Reinforcement.') You remember that in all these scenes you are to try to feel confident. Now you enter the building and go into the classroom. ('Reinforcement.') You sit down and kid around with another student who is taking the exam. ('Reinforcement.') The proctor comes in with the exam. You feel good; you know you are ready. ('Reinforcement.') The proctor hands out the exam. ('Reinforcement.') You read the questions and you feel you can answer all of them. ('Reinforcement.')

Now let's do that again. This time you look the questions over and you are not sure about one question, but you say, 'Oh well, I can still pass the exam if I flunk this one question.' ('Reinforcement.') All right, this time you look over the exam, and you can see two questions about which you are in doubt, and you say, 'Well, I can still pass this exam if I take my time and relax.' ('Reinforcement.')

He was then given the usual instructions about doing the whole scene and practicing at home. He was also told to vary the reinforcing stimulus, e.g., another scene was reciving his doctoral degree at graduation. As the sessions continued, he reported that he felt more relaxed while studying and was able to keep up with his study schedule. After ten sessions, including behavioral analysis and a discussion of study habits and his future, he took the doctoral examination; he reported he was confident and relaxed, and that he passed the exam.

The COR procedure has also been employed successfully with the gamut of phobias such as public speaking, being alone, fear of distance from home, getting dirty, etc.

Obsessive-Compulsive Behavior

The COR technique was used successfully with several cases of obsessive-compulsive behavior.

In one case described by Wisocki (1969) a young mother reported that she felt compelled to fold clothes over and over again, three or four times, until there were no wrinkles in them. Then she would put each item in a drawer, stack it neatly, and spend the next 15 min straightening out the clothes, refolding them again and again. She found herself spending hours on a task that ordinarily required 20 min; and had gotten to the point where she dreaded washing clothes because it meant she would have to fold them.

In treatment she was told to imagine that she was folding each item of clothing once and putting it aside. When she signalled that this scene was clear, the therapist said, "Reinforcement" and she immediately imagined that she was sipping sweet tea. Gradually she was told to imagine that as she folded something once, there was a slight wrinkle in it, but that she just shrugged and said. "It doesn't really matter." The therapist, upon the signal that the scene was clear, again said, "Reinforcement" and she imagined her reinforcing stimulus. This sequence was continued through various scenes in which she folded clothes quickly, was unmindful of wrinkles, put them in the drawer, and walked away without returning to refold them. She now reports that she can do every behavior for which she was reinforced and feel comfortable.

The COR procedure apparently was successfully applied to the behavior of a male patient who felt compelled to constantly check the gas jets, the locks on the car doors, and the water faucets.

If the thoughts are precursors to the behavior, we may combine thought-stopping with COR. For example, a female patient felt that if she expressed resentment toward someone, their dead ancestors would punish her. She was instructed to say "Stop" when the thought occurred, and she was reinforced for thinking that the idea of dead ancestors haunting someone was foolish.

In all compulsive behaviors, the patient is reinforced for not repeating the behavior although it is necessary to start with repeating the behavior a few times and then gradually decreasing it to one trial. This choice depends upon the duration of the compulsive behavior and the amount of anxiety it generates.

Maladaptive Approach Behavior

The author's usual treatment procedure for maladaptive approach behavior such as homosexuality (Cautela & Wisocki, 1969) and alcoholism (Cautela, in press) has been to combine covert sensitization with other procedures such as thought-stopping, relaxation as a self-control procedure, and desensitization. Covert sensitization has been used to treat consumatory behavior itself, e.g., the patient imagines he is getting sick and is about to vomit as he is about to drink, engage in homosexual behavior, steal, or overeat (Cautela, 1967). The treatment procedure is accelerated if COR is employed, and sometimes it is not even necessary to employ formal desensitization.

After employing the usual covert sensitization procedure in which a patient (a homosexual) is told that he is becoming sick and vomits as he is about to approach a male nude for homosexual behavior, he is instructed in the following manner: "As you turn away from the guy, you immediately start to feel better." ('Reinforcement.') He signals when the scene is clear and the therapist says, "You walk away." ('Reinforcement.') "You say to yourself, 'What the hell, am I crazy to do something so disgusting?' " ('Reinforcement.')

COR is also used a great deal in treating the homosexual's approach behavior toward females. Various sexual scenes are presented in which he feels confident, performs well with, and is complimented by the girl. Of course, he is reinforced in successive steps. He is also reinforced for positively scanning girls, e.g., "I want you to imagine you see a luscious looking girl on the street, and you say to yourself, 'Oh boy, I'd love to feel her soft skin against my body.' " ('Reinforcement.') "Then think to yourself, 'I can have more fun with girls in sex than with men if I try hard.' " ('Reinforcement.')

Similar procedures have also been employed with alcoholics, obesity problems, and assaultive behaviors of juvenile offenders (Cautela, 1969).

Increasing Thought Response Probabilities

Working within the operant paradigm, Homme (1965) has made use of the Premack hypothesis (Premack, 1959) to increase the probability of desirable thoughts or statements about oneself. Essentially the Premack hypothesis states that if there are two responses with different probabilities of occurrence, the response with the higher probability can be used to increase the occurrence of the lower probability response. In this procedure a verbal contract is made between the therapist and the patient so that the response of higher probability is contingent upon the occurrence of the response of lower probability.

It appears that COR may also be effective in increasing the probability of particular thought processes. For example, a male patient who had severe anxiety about being sexually adequate with girls was told to think particular thoughts contrary to his fears, such as: "I can satisfy girls as much as any other fellow," after which he imagined his reinforcing stimulus. A female with a fear of an apparent allergy to breezes was told: "I want you to say to yourself, 'If a breeze touches me, so what?' " ('Reinforcement.') A male who felt he had to leave his place of employment for fear of making mistakes was instructed: "Now say to yourself, 'If I made a mistake, so what? Everyone makes mistakes.' " ('Reinforcement.') A female patient who felt depressed and alone was told to think, "Life is not hopeless; it's what you put into it that counts." ('Reinforcement.') It appears that after much practice and homework, the thought becomes part of the belief system of the client.

Covert Reinforcement as a Self-Control Procedure

COR can be used as a self-control procedure in a number of ways. Clients who are taught relaxation as a self-control procedure (Cautela, 1969) are instructed to relax before they enter an anxiety-provoking situation, during an anxiety-provoking situation, and after an anxiety-provoking situation. If they report that they did not follow through on the instructions about relaxation, they are given scenes in which they are covertly reinforced for making a relaxed response (e.g., taking a deep breath and relaxing the muscles) as they are about to enter an anxiety-provoking situation. In such a case, the client has been exposed, in imagination, to an anxiety-provoking situation; has relaxed in imagination; and has reinforced himself for it. This procedure appears effective in increasing the probability that in real life situations, the client will use the relaxation response as a self-control technique. One striking observation of such syndromes as pervasive anxiety, depression, and antisocial behavior is that the client is not able to, or does not, initiate self-controlling responses. When he has made responses in a desired direction, they have been followed by either aversive consequences or very little reinforcing consequences. Some experimental evidence by Seligman and others (Seligman & Maier, 1967; Seligman, Maier, & Geer, 1968; Seligman, 1968, 1969) has bearing on this point. In Seligman's paradigm, when a dog is exposed to unavoidable electric shock and is then placed in an escape situation, it usually makes no attempt to escape and, in fact, appears to have given up. Instead, it continues to accept the shock. Dogs who receive this treatment differ markedly from other dogs who have not been placed in an escapable shock situation prior to escape training and who readily learn the escape procedure. Seligman's assumption (1969) is that the animals in the unavoidable shock situation learn helplessness since their responses do not alter environmental contingencies. He expresses hope that these laboratory studies will suggest functional analogies that may be useful in curing and preventing the "helplessness" response pattern.

Patients who have been taught and make use of self-control procedures make verbal responses and exhibit behavior asserting the fact that just knowing they have available appropriate responses reduces anxiety and makes them feel more confident and secure (Cautela, 1969). Other investigators report similar findings concerning self-control. Rehm and Marston (1968) report a reduction in social anxiety and an increase in social adaptation as a result of self-reinforcement.

Further Details on Procedure

At the present time this procedure is employed with every patient seen by the author. It has become the author's main approach and is supplemented by other standard behavior therapy procedures. For example, if a client is having some difficulty asserting himself, he is given scenes in which he is asserting himself and is covertly reinforced for that behavior. In each session, the patient is given five to ten trials on each response to be increased. The patients are given homework assignments in which they are told to practice the procedure once or twice a day, depending on the patient's motivation, the strength of the response to be changed, and the immediate necessity to change the response (e.g., responses antagonistic to suicidal thoughts). The therapist has to be careful in choosing the proper reinforcement. Patients differ on clarity of imagery depending upon the sensory modality employed. Some patients can vividly imagine that they are eating certain foods; other clients who may report great pleasure in eating certain foods are unable to feel the taste of the food in their mouths when asked to imagine it.

PARAMETERS OF COVERT REINFORCEMENT

As mentioned previously, the labeling of this procedure as covert reinforcement makes available to us the general body of knowledge concerning reinforcement. Such knowledge can be utilized to maximize the efficacy of covert reinforcement. In the application of the covert reinforcement procedures, we have attempted to control five parameters that investigators agree influence reinforcement (Kimble, 1961, pp. 137–166). They are the following:
1. the number of reinforcements
2. intertrial interval
3. immediacy of reinforcement
4. schedules of reinforcement
5. drive state.

The Number of Reinforcements

There is agreement among both S-R and operant workers that the strength of conditioning increases as a function of the number of reinforcements (Pavlov, 1927, pp. 22–31; Hull, 1943, p. 327; Skinner, 1938, pp. 87, 91). Therefore, we give as many trials as possible of COR in the consulting room.

Intertrial Interval

In order to avoid inhibition of reinforcement (Pavlov, 1927, p. 239) and too rapid a growth of inhibitory potential (Hull, 1943, p. 360), an attempt is made to distribute the trials in the consulting room (e.g., a few in the beginning and a few at the end of the session) and at least a minute between individual trials. The patients are also instructed to practice at different times during the day, allowing at least a minute between trials.

Immediacy of Reinforcement

As previously mentioned, evidence of many kinds (Kimble, 1961, p. 165) indicates that responses which are followed immediately by a reward are learned more rapidly than responses for which the reward is delayed. As a result patients are instructed to switch immediately to the reinforcing scene when the therapist says, ''Reinforcement.'' The patient is carefully watched for his signal which indicates that he has imagined the image clearly in order for the therapist to say ''Reinforcement'' as soon as the finger is raised.

Schedules of Reinforcement

The goal of the COR procedure is to achieve a high rate of responding and increase resistance to extinction. Operant literature (Lewis, 1960) has amassed many data demonstrating that partial reinforcement leads to higher response rates and greater resistance to extinction than 100% reinforcement. In comparison with interval schedules, ratio schedules usually produce higher response rates. In applying COR, a 100% reinforcement schedule is used at first, i.e., reinforcement after every scene. After there is some evidence that the desired responses are being increased, the ratio of reinforcement is increased in successive steps. First, there is reinforcement for the initial response in the usual manner. On the next trial, however, the patient is instructed to imagine the desired response and this time to erase the image when instructed to do so, rather than reinforcing it. After a minute, he is to imagine the thought once more, and this time it is reinforced. This procedure is then repeated with reinforcement coming only after the third, then fourth, then fifth presentation of the desired response, so that the last schedule is one reinforcement to every five scenes. This last step in the procedure could be diagrammed as follows: scene — one minute rest — scene — one minute rest — scene — one minute rest — scene — one minute rest — scene — delivery of reinforcement. The patient is asked to follow this procedure on his own outside the office. When the response seems well-established, a one-to-five ratio is used exclusively just before termination of treatment of that particular maladaptive behavior.

Drive State

Operant investigators also manipulate deprivational states to increase the effectiveness of reinforcers (Teitelbaum, 1966). Although this variable is difficult to manipulate in the clinical setting, attempts have been made to do so, e.g., if a client is using an eating response as a reinforcing stimulus, he is encouraged to practice before meals; if he is using a swimming scene as a reinforcer, he is asked to practice when he feels especially hot. A client using a sexual response as a reinforcer is asked to practice when the urge is particularly high. (For obvious reasons this reinforcing scene sometimes has to be monitored closely.) One client whose reinforcing scene was one in which she was lying on a beach in the sun relaxing, practiced the scene whenever she felt tired. (She was cautioned not to practice when she was extremely tired so that the clarity of the imagery would not be diminished.).

Possible Problems That May Arise in the Use of Covert Reinforcement

1. Poor Imagery. Occasionally some clients claim that they have very poor imagery. This can be overcome either by imagery training or by examining the clarity of imagery in all the sense modalities. The therapist should be very careful to describe the scenes used in COR in as much detail as possible, including as many sense modalities as possible to increase the probability of transfer to the real situation.

2. Lack of Practice Outside the Office. Usually this can be overcome somewhat by applying the COR procedure itself to scenes of practicing outside the office.

3. Anxiety and Covert Sensitization. Some clients who are being treated for maladaptive avoidance behavior report that although they are beginning to approach the feared object, they still experience some anxiety in doing so. It is explained that the anxiety will usually extinguish because the avoidance response is not reinforced in that the anticipated danger does not occur. Also with these patients, a special effort is made to have them imagine that they feel comfortable and happy while they are imagining the scene to be reinforced. In practice, by the time treatment is terminated, the patients seldom report the least amount of anxiety.

4. Possible Spontaneous Recovery or Reconditioning After Treatment. The usual procedure is to produce overlearning by continuing treatment for at least six sessions after the maladaptive behavior has been eliminated (Cautela, 1968). The patient is also carefully instructed to reapply the procedure if he observes that the maladaptive behavior is beginning to recur.

COMPARISON OF COVERT REINFORCEMENT AND EMOTIVE IMAGERY

As previously indicated, other investigators have used induced imagery for behavior modification. Wolpe has stressed the lack of arousal in his desensitization procedure (1958), while Stampfl and Levis' (1966) has induced high arousal states in imagination. Cautela (1966, 1967) utilized arousal imagery such as nausea and vomiting. Lazarus and Abramovitz (1962) have employed pleasant, exciting scenes in story form to overcome children's fears. Their procedure is to build a hierarchy of the feared objects or situations and present items of the hierarchy in story form while presenting pleasurable images (e.g., the presence of a hero who evokes pleasurable and exciting feelings). Although COR is similar to emotive imagery in that both procedures make use of pleasant stimuli, they differ in a number of respects. In COR it is not necessary to build a hierarchy. In COR very brief pleasant scenes are used. COR is used to modify a wider variety of maladaptive behavior than phobic responses. The COR procedure is conceptualized within a reinforcement paradigm rather than a counterconditioning paradigm. Conceptually COR uses the reinforcement paradigm to guide the procedures with a body of well-establish principles. The author feels that the COR procedure, as conceptualized and described here, do not justify the possible assertion that COR can be equated with emotive imagery. Furthermore, COR has the advantage of being able to be used as a self-control procedure and may also act as *in vivo* reinforcement.

RESULTS OF COVERT REINFORCEMENT

The author's confidence that COR is a very powerful tool for behavior modification is due to a number of reasons:

1. The application of other behavior modification procedures such as desensitization based on relaxation, implosive therapy, and covert sensitization have received experimental confirmation of their efficiency in the modification of maladaptive behaviors.

2. There is nothing in the writings of learning theorists such as Pavlov, Hull, and Guthrie to contradict the effective use of imagery in behavior modification.

3. The procedure has produced desired changes in a variety of behaviors. Often, in fact, when other behavior modification procedures have been slow to bring about results, or have been ineffective, the use of the COR procedure produces the desired behavior. Also, when the COR procedure is used exclusively, the results seem to be achieved in less time with less effort.

Anecdotal evidence is not sufficient proof of the efficacy of the procedure. It is the author's hope that this present paper will generate attempts to apply the COR procedure in behavior modification, to generate new hypotheses, and to promote careful, controlled research for its scientific test. Cautela, Steffan, and Wish (1969) have already completed a basic research study on the effect of covert reinforcement on a task of size estimation. A brief summary of the study will provide an example of the kind of basic research which can be derived from the concept of covert reinforcement.

Subjects were shown slides of circles and asked to estimate the diameter of each circle. Baselines of mean estimates were established for each subject. Some subjects were given COR after either underestimating or overestimating diameter size. (No subject was reinforced for both over- and underestimation.) This group was compared with other groups who were *(a)* not given COR; *b)* given noncontingent COR (COR was presented in a predetermined manner, not dependent on subjects' responses); *(c)* a group which received the word "Reinforcement" after an over- or underestimation; *(d)* a group asked to imagine neutral scenes after an over- or underestimation. The results of the experiment indicate that subjects in the group given contingent COR gave more over- or underestimations than any other group. The Duncan Multiple Range Test comparing the COR group with every other group revealed a significant difference well beyond the .01 level for every group but (c). For the (c) group the comparison was significant at the .05 level.

The results strongly support the hypothesis that reinforcement in imagination can increase response probability.

REFERENCES

Antonitis, J. J. Response variability in the white rat during conditioning, extinction, and reconditioning. *Journal of Experimental Psychology,* 1951, **42**, 273–281.

Arnold, W. J. An exploratory investigation of primary response generalization. *Journal of Comparative Psychology, 1945,* **38**, 87–102.

Ashem, B., & Donner, L. Covert sensitization with alcoholics: A controlled replication. *Behavior Research and Therapy,* 1968, **6**, 7–12.

Ayllon, T., & Azrin, N. H. Reinforcement and instruction with mental patients. *Journal of Experimental Analysis of Behavior,* 1964, **7**, 327–331.

Ayllon, T., & Azrin, N. *The token economy.* New York: Appleton-Century-Crofts, 1968.

Barlow, D. H., Leitenberg, H., & Agras, W. S. Preliminary report of the experimental control of sexual deviation by manipulation of the US in covert sensitization. Paper read at the Eastern Psychological Association, Washington, D. C., 1968.

Cautela, J. R. Treatment of compulsive behavior by covert sensitization *Psychological Record,* 1966, **16**, 33–41.

Cautela, J. R. Covert sensitization. *Psychological Reports,* 1967, **20**, 459–468.

Cautela, J. R. Behavior therapy and the need for behavioral assessment. *Psychotherapy: Theory, Research, and Practice,* 1968, **5**, 175–179.

Cautela, J. R. Behavior therapy and self-control: Techniques and implications. In C. M. Franks (Ed.), *Behavior therapy: Appraisal and status.* New York: McGraw-Hill, 1969. Pp. 323–340.

Cautela, J. R. The treatment of alcoholism by covert sensitization. *Psychotherapy: Theory, Research, and Practice,* in press.

Cautela, J. R., & Kastenbaum, R. A reinforcement survey schedule for use in therapy, training, and research. *Psychological Reports,* 1967, **20**, 1115–1130.

Cautela, J. R., Steffan, J., & Wish, P. Covert reinforcement: An experimental test. Unpublished data, Boston College, 1969.

Cautela, J. R., & Wisocki, P. A. The use of male and female therapists in the treatment of homosexual behavior. In C. M. Franks & D. Rubin (Eds.), *Advances in behavior therapy.* New York: Academic Press, 1968. Pp. 165–174.

Davison, G. C. The influence of systematic desensitization, relaxation, and graded exposure to imaginal aversive stimuli on the modification of phobic behavior. Unpublished doctoral dissertation, Stanford University, 1965.

Ferster, C. B. The use of the free operant response in the analysis of behavior. *Psychological Bulletin,* 1953, **50**, 263–274.

Franks, C. M. Reflections upon the treatment of sexual disorders by the behavioral clinician: An historical comparison with the treatment of the alcoholic. *Journal of Sex Research,* 1967, **3**, 212–222.

Guthrie, E. R. *The psychology of learning.* New York: Harper, 1935.

Guttman, N. Operant conditioning, extinction, and periodic reinforcement in relation to concentration of sucrose used as a reinforcing agent. *Journal of Experimental Psychology,* 1953, **46**, 213–224.

Homme, L. E. Perspectives in psychology. XXIV. Control of coverants, the operants of the mind. *Psychological Record,* 1965, **15**, 501–511.

Hull, C. L. *Principles of behavior.* New York: Appleton-Century-Crofts, 1943.

Hull, C. L. *A behavior system.* New Haven: Yale University Press, 1952.

Hutt, P. J. Rate of frequency as a function of quality and quantity of food reward. *Journal of Comparative Physiological Psychology,* 1954, **47**, 235–239.

Kimble, G. A. *Hilgard and Marquis' Conditioning and learning.* New York: Appleton-Century-Crofts, 1961.

Lang, P. J. Experimental studies of desensitization psychotherapy. In J. Wolpe, A. Salter, & L. Reyna (Eds.), *The conditioning therapies.* New York: Holt, Rinehart, & Winston, 1964, Pp. 38–53.

Lazarus, A. A., & Ambramovitz, A. The use of "emotive imagery" in the treatment of children's phobias. *Journal of Mental Science,* 1962, **108**, 191–95.

Lewis, D. J. Partial reinforcement: A selective review of the literature since 1950. *Psychological Bulletin,* 1960, **57**, 1–28.

Mullen, F. G. The effect of covert sensitization on smoking behavior. Unpublished study, Queens College, Charlottesville, North Carolina, 1968.

Olds, J. Pleasure centers in the brain. *Scientific American,* 1956, **195**, 105–116.

Paul, G. L. *Insight vs. desensitization in psychotherapy.* Stanford: Stanford University Press, 1966.

Pavlov, I. P. *Conditioned reflexes.* Translated by G. V. Anrep. London: Oxford University Press, 1927.

Pavlov, I. P. *Selected works.* Translated by S. Belsky. J. Gibbons (Ed.), Moscow: Foreign Languages Publishing House, 1955.

Premack, D. Toward empirical behavior laws: I. Positive reinforcement. *Psychological Review,* 1959, **66**, 219–233.

Rehm, L., & Marston, A. Reduction of social anxiety through modification of self-reinforcement: An investigative therapy technique. *Journal of Consulting and Clinical Psychology,* 1968, **32**, 565–574.

Seligman, M. E. Chronic fear produced by unpredictable electric shock. *Journal of Comparative and Physiological Psychology,* 1968, **66**, 401–411.

Seligman, M. E. For helplessness: Can we immunize the weak? *Psychology Today,* June, 1969, 42–44.

Seligman, M. E., & Maier, S. F. Failure to escape traumatic shock. *Journal of Experimental Psychology,* 1967, **74**, 1–9.

Seligman, M. E. Maier, S.F., & Geer, J. H. Alleviation of learned helplessness in the dog. *Journal of Experimental Psychology,* 1968, **73**, 256–262.

Skinner, B. F. *The behavior of organisms: An experimental analysis.* New York: Appleton-Century, 1938.

Stampfl, T. G., & Levis, D. J. Implosive therapy: The theory, the subhuman analogue, the strategy and the technique. In *Possible use of conditioning therapy with chronic schizophrenia*. Battle Creek, Michigan: U. S. Publications, 1966. Pp. 12–21.

Stuart, R. B. Behavioral control of over-eating. *Behavior Research and Therapy,* 1967, **5**, 357–365.

Teitelbaum, P. The use of operant methods in the assessment and control of motivational states. In W. K. Honig (Ed.), *Operant behavior: Areas of research and application*. New York: Appleton-Century-Crofts, 1966. Pp. 565–608.

Viernstein, L. Evaluation of therapeutic techniques of covert sensitization. Unpublished data. Queens College, Charlottesville, North Carolina, 1968.

Williams, S. B. Transfer of reinforcement in the rat as a function of habit strength. *Journal of Comparative Psychology,* 1941, **31**, 281–296.

Wisocki, P. A. The use of covert sensitization and covert reinforcement in the treatment of obsessive-compulsive behavior: A new approach Unpublished Study. Boston College, Chestnut Hill, Massachusetts, 1969.

Wolpe, J. *Psychotherapy by reciprocal inhibition*. Stanford: Stanford University Press, 1958.

Chapter 9

A Laboratory Analogue of Two Covert Reinforcement Procedures*†

Raymond B. Flannery, Jr.

Summary — Covert reinforcement was experimentally investigated for its effectiveness in reducing a specific fear. In addition, fear reduction was compared in two groups both treated by covert reinforcement, in one using the actual fear stimulus, in the other the imagined fear stimulus. On four behavioral and subjective measures both treatment groups showed significantly more fear reduction than did an attention-control group. These findings are consistent with previous research findings which used other behavior modification techniques. A comparison of the procedure with systematic desensitization is presented, and the implications for research and clinical practice discussed.

Behavior therapy is a discipline rooted in experimental methodology (Paul, 1969; Wolpe, 1958; Yates, 1970). The clinical practice is influenced by on-going laboratory analogue research on a technique and its specific components. Systematic desensitization (Wolpe, 1958), based on respondent conditioning, is an excellent example of this (Cooke, 1966; Davison, 1968; Lang

---

*Reprinted with permission from the *Journal of Behavior Therapy and Experimental Psychiatry*, 1972, *3*, 171-177. ©Pergamon Press.

†This paper is based on a portion of a doctoral dissertation submitted to the Department of Psychology, University of Windsor, in partial fulfilment of the requirements for the Ph.D. degree. The author wishes to thank Doctors W. Balance, W. Bringmann, J. Cohen, R. Daly, N. Holland, G. Namikus, members of the doctoral committee, and Dr. J. R. Cautela, external examiner.

and Lazovik, 1963; Paul, 1966). Recently, Bucher and Lovaas (1970) have cited the need for a control group paradigm to augment the traditional ABA baseline approach in evaluating operant conditioning treatment effects. The present analogue addresses itself to this need in experimentally investigating the efficacy of a newly introduced operant procedure, covert reinforcement (Cautela, 1970).

Covert reinforcement (Cautela, 1970) is an operant procedure which presents the reinforcing stimulus in imagination. Typically the first step in this method is to find possible reinforcers. There are several ways in which this can be done, of which the most convenient is the Reinforcement Survey Schedule (Cautela and Kastenbaum, 1967). This survey obtains information on the situations and objects which are strongly rewarding to a particular individual. The imagined reproductions of these are referred to as "reinforcing scenes" by Cautela (1970). It is important that the individual be taught to imagine these scenes with a good deal of clarity and vividness. When he has learned this, he is instructed to pair the reinforcing scene with the word "reinforcement". Subsequently, when the individual emits the response to be increased the therapist says the word "reinforcement" and the client shifts to imagining the reinforcing scene.

The development of this procedure enables Cautela (1970) to incorporate experimental data from operant research on shaping procedures, positive reinforcement, delay, partial reinforcement, and interstimulus interval. Cautela has assumed two learning principles as the basis of this procedure. The first is the functional equivalence of imagined stimuli which under certain conditions act as representatives of external stimuli. Skinner (1953) maintained that covert events obey the same laws of contingency as overt processes. Homme (1965) has taken the same position more recently. Further support for this assumption has been summarized by Kimble (1961).

The second important assumption has been that the covert processes can influence overt processes in a predictable manner. In the field of behavior modification it has been shown that covert events can affect overt maladaptive behavior using systematic desensitization (Barlow *et al.*, 1969; Lang and Lazovik, 1963, Lazarus, 1963; Paul, 1966), covert sensitization (Anant, 1966; Cautela, 1966, 1967; Stuart, 1967), and implosive therapy (Stampfl and Levis, 1967).

A recent experiment by Cautela, Steffen and Wish (1970) tested the procedure of covert reinforcement to determine if reinforcement presented in imagination can be used for shaping overt responses. The responses to be altered were over- or underestimation of the diameter of six circles. The results indicated that the covert reinforcement groups showed significantly greater increases in errors of size estimation when reinforced for such errors. In addition, Cautela (1970) has presented several clinical cases in which covert reinforcement methods were successfully employed. For example, a young mother was relieved of a compulsion to fold clothes. Finally, a study of attitude change toward the mentally retarded (Cautela, Walsh and Wish, 1970) indicated that subjects who were taught to imagine a mentally retarded person and then reinforced covertly, reported subsequently more positive attitudes towards the mentally retarded.

These initial studies of covert reinforcement have supported its effectiveness in modifying overt behavior. However, the potential usefulness of covert reinforcement for the reduction of specific human fear has thus far rested on clinical evidence (Cautela, 1969, 1970), and there remained the need for a controlled laboratory investigation of the problem.

The controlled experiment presented here utilized covert reinforcement (Cautela, 1970) for the reduction of specific focal fear; but introduced the fear-evoking stimuli *in vivo*. In systematic desensitization (Wolpe, 1958), the fear stimulus can be presented in imagination, or *in vivo;* and both methods of presentation have been reported to be efficacious (Yates, 1970, p. 141). Previous analogues of systematic desensitization comparing both methods of presentation (Barlow *et al.*, 1969; Cooke, 1966; Garfield *et al.*, 1967) have suggested that the presentation of the actual fear stimulus was somewhat the more effective. A secondary purpose of this study was to explore whether these findings would be replicated in an analogue based on an operant procedure.

METHOD

Subjects

Forty-five female student nurses comprised the experimental population. They were selected in two steps.

First, a preliminary survey was administered during class to two large sections of nursing students. Those who reported strong aversion to laboratory rats were asked to approach, stroke, and hold an uncaged rat in a laboratory. Additionally, they completed the Fear Intensity Scale and the Fear Survey Schedule in an office adjoining the laboratory. Of the students who completed all these procedures, 45 were chosen who indicated sufficient fear on the three behavioral and two self-report measures. (The varying criteria are discussed below.) The subjects were randomized into two treatment groups and one control group, all groups being equated with respect to age and level of educational attainment. Each subject was paid $5.00 for her efforts.

Measures

(1) **Behavioral measures.** A white laboratory rat roaming about freely on a 1 ft² platform on top of a 4 ft high wooden stand was used throughout the experiment as the fear-evoking stimulus. This phobic stimulus was chosen for reasons similar to De Moor's (1970) that is, the ease of control, a rat-phobic

population, and the basic ethical consideration that the stimulus object was not central to the subjects normal daily functioning. The experimenter and the subjects wore heavy duty leather gloves with 4-in. nylon cuffs at all times in handling the animal. Like Davison (1968) the experimenter always stood two feet away in the pre- and post-tests so that there would be no vicarious extinction or counterconditioning (Wolpe, 1958, p. 198).

Three different behavioral measures were administered. The *approach* measure consisted of 10 1-ft increments which were crossed when a subject moved towards the animal platform. The point at which the subject stopped was recorded. The *stroke* measure consisted of the subject touching the rat and stroking its back twice. A subject was given credit for *hold,* the last behavioral measure, if she was able to pick up and hold the object for 3 min. The last two measures were scored in a dichotomous fashion on the basis of "yes" or "no". These three behavioral measures were not assumed to be necessarily correlated in every subject — in keeping with the observations of Lang (1969). For example, individuals will at times force themselves to approach phobic objects though experiencing varying degrees of fear.

(2) **Subjective measures.** The *Fear Intensity Scale* was a seven point scale similar to one originally used by Lang and Lazovik (1963). It ranged from "no fear" (1) to "very intense fear" (7), and served in the present study to indicate the intensity of the subject's fear of the laboratory rat. A second measure was the *Fear Survey Schedule* (Wolpe and Lang, 1964), which was employed to assess a wide range of fear arousing stimuli. In contrast with clinical findings (Wolpe, 1958), previous experimental studies of systematic desensitization (Cooke, 1966; Garfield *et al.,* 1967) reported no reduction in general fear when one specific fear was reduced in the laboratory. One question was whether the same would apply in changing one specific fear by an operant procedure.

Procedure

Pre-treatment stage. Each rat-aversion subject completed the fear survey schedule in an office and then went to the laboratory. There, she was asked to perform three different behavioral responses: approach a rat, stroke it twice, and hold it for 3 min. Finally, still in the presence of the animal she completed the fear intensity scale.

The subjects ranged on the approach measure from no approach at all to 5 ft of approach (the threshold of the laboratory door). Three subjects did attempt to stroke the rat twice. Each had stopped at the threshold of the laboratory and then upon request had forced themselves to run quickly towards the animal. Each had run from the phobic stimulus after contact, visibly shaken, had reported intense feelings of fear, and spontaneously stated a desire never to return to the laboratory. They were nevertheless included to study the factorial complexity of fear (Lang, 1969). None of the remaining 42 subjects would stroke or hold the rat.

On the fear intensity scale, the subjects ranged from moderate (4) fear to very intense (7) fear. The mean for each group was strong (5) fear. The fear survey schedule was scored according to Wolpe and Lang (1964), and the mean for each group was 181.

Since these pre-test data were similar to previous research (Barlow et al., 1969; Willis, 1968) these subjects were considered suitable for the present study.

The final part of the pre-treatment stage involved one hour of training individually for each of the 45 subjects in the necessary procedures for covert reinforcement (Cautela, 1970). Each subject was asked to complete the Reinforcement Survey Schedule (Cautela and Kastenbaum, 1967), and to choose three of the most meaningful reinforcers. These would serve as the subject's reinforcing scenes for the experiment. The remainder of the session was spent in training for vividness and clarity of each of the three scenes; the subject beginning by imagining the reinforcing scene for 30 sec and then pairing it with the word "reinforcement." The last step consisted of pairing combinations of three neutral images (a leaf floating on water, sunny sky on a clear day, panorama of trees changing color in the Fall) with the three reinforcing scenes when the subject heard the experimenter say the word "reinforcement." This was done to insure that the subject understood the basic covert reinforcement procedure, i.e., having emitted the appropriate neutral image, she was reinforced by one imagined scene. Each neutral image and each reinforcing stimulus was presented for 30 sec. Each intertrial interval was 60 sec.

Treatment stage. During this phase, the subject was seen for three 55-min sessions within a 7-day period. Each session started with a 10-min practice session in the covert reinforcement. In the *in vivo* treatment group (T_1) each subject was immediately taken to the laboratory, and placed 10 ft away from the platform with the experimental animal. The experimenter then instructed the subject to concentrate on the actual environment, while he read to her the first step of a 13 step hierarchy in the laboratory environment. The subject was further instructed to close her eyes upon hearing the experimenter say the word "reinforcement," and to imagine her reinforcing scene for 30 sec. She was then given the choice of either remaining where she was and repeating the same hierarchy step, or, of moving one foot closer to the animal platform the next hierarchy step. She indicated her choice by saying either, "I choose to move forward to the next hierarchy step" or "I choose to repeat this hierarchy step." She was reinforced by the experimenter for the behavior chosen.

The sequence of presentation of the hierarchy, reinforcement with imagined rewarding scenes, and movement in the direction of the actual fear object was then continued by each subject for the remainder of each of three experimental sessions. Any subject who reached the last step of the hierarchy where she would stroke and hold the animal was asked once more to complete the fear intensity index.

The same procedures were followed in the case of the subjects exposed to the fear stimulus in imagination only (T_2), with one exception. They were asked to carry out all the activities in imagination. The hierarchy steps to be imagined were the same as those read by the experimenter to the T_1 subjects. The subject was asked to imagine the first step of the hierarchy (10 ft from the animal) as the experimenter read it to her. When she heard the word "reinforcement," she shifted to her reinforcing scene. As with the T_1 group, each subject was then offered a choice of hierarchy steps, and indicated her choice by the appropriate verbal statement. Each time she imagined the chosen hierarchy step she was reinforced.

The attention control group (C_1) was given a brief practice session in covert reinforcement at each session. Following this, the remainder of each session was spent discussing her fear of laboratory rats.

Post-treatment stage. At the end of her third and last experimental session, each subject was subjected once more to the three behavioral tests — approach, stroke, hold — and given the fear intensity scale in the laboratory. The Fear Survey Schedule was repeated in the office.

RESULTS

Behavioral Indices

As seen in Table 1, both treatment groups showed decreases in fear toward the actual fear stimulus (the rat) after the treatment as indicated by the approach, stroke, and hold measures — that is, subjects approached the rat more closely after treatment, and more subjects stroked the rat and held it after treatment than before. No appreciable change in these measures was observed in the attention control group. The *in vivo* treatment group (T_1) showed a greater decrease in fear than the group presented with the fear stimulus in imagination (T_2).

A repeated analysis of variance for the approach measure, and nonparametric tests for the stroke and hold measures were carried out to determine the significance of the observed differences. Significant main and interaction effects for the approach measure beyond the $0 \cdot 001$ critical level were found for groups ($F = 14 \cdot 68$; $df = 2/42$), the repeated factor (pre- and post-treatment) ($F = 167 \cdot 89$; $df = 1/42$) and the double interaction ($F = 31 \cdot 26$; $df = 2/42$). As in the rest of the study, individual comparisons were carried out by the more conservative *post hoc* Newman-Keuls procedure. Each treatment group approached significantly nearer to the fear stimulus ($p < 0 \cdot 01$). The

Table 9.1. Mean number of feet approached to fear stimulus and mean scores on the self report fear measures for pre- and post-treatment (SD in parentheses)

Measures	Groups					
	T_1		T_2		C	
	Pre-Treatment	Post Treatment	Pre-Treatment	Post Treatment	Pre-Treatment	Post Treatment
Approach	4	10	4	9	4	5
	(1•99)	(0•00)	(1•99)	(0•77)	(1•99)	(2•04)
Fear Intensity	5	2	5	4	5	5
Scale	(0•82)	(1•71)	(0•82)	(1•45)	(0•82)	(0•77)
Fear Survey	181	167	181	178	181	176
Schedule	(28•43)	(27•49)	(36•02)	(36•34)	(20•73)	(26•61)

control group did not change significantly. It should be noted that all groups had been equated on initial approach. No significant differences were found between the two treatment groups.

For the two other behavioral measures, stroke and hold, nonparametric tests measuring the number of subjects reducing their fear were carried out. To measure within group changes, McNemar's Test was used (Siegel, 1956). All groups at first displayed the same fear or inability to stroke and hold the animal. In T_1, 14 subjects changed from not being able to stroke the animal to stroking it. The one subject who initially stroked the rat continued to do so. This change was significant ($X^2 = 12•07$; $df = 1, p < 0•001$). Similarly, 11 of these subjects held the rat who had refused to do so previously. Four subjects continued to refuse to hold the animal. This increase in the number of subjects reducing their fear was also significant ($X^2 = 7•14$; $df = 1, p < 0•01$). In the T_2 group, reduction of fear was seen only for the stroke measure. One subject stroked the animal both before and after treatment, seven subjects refused to do so at either time, and seven subjects who had initially refused to stroke the animal did so after treatment. The number of subjects changing to stroking the rat almost reached significance (observed $X^2 = 3•5$; $df = 1$, expected $X^2 = 3•84$ for 0•05 critical level). Only one T_2 subject would hold the rat after treatment. In the control group, there was no increase in the number of subjects able to stroke or hold the rat. In fact, the one subject who had initially stroked the rat refused to do so after treatment.

Fisher exact probabilities tests (Siegel, 1956) were carried out to compare the differences between groups for fear reduction on the stroke and hold measures. Significantly more T_1 subjects decreased their unwillingness to stroke or hold the rat than control subjects ($p < 0•005$). On both measures, significantly more T_1 than T_2 subjects changed their initial unwillingness to stroke and hold the rat ($p < 0•05$). It should be noted that the hold measure as a fear indicator only showed fear reduction in the T_1 group.

Table 9.2. Number of subjects who stroked and held fear stimulus on pre-treatment and post-treatment conditions

Measures	Groups					
	T₁		T₂		C	
	Pre-Treatment	Post-Treatment	Pre-Treatment	Post-Treatment	Pre-Treatment	Post-Treatment
Stroke	1	15	1	8	1	0
Hold	0	11	0	1	0	0

Subjective Measures

The results of the two self-report measures are shown in Table 1. There were slight decreases in the fear intensity scale and fear survey schedule in both treatment groups. Only on the fear survey schedule did the control group show any decrease.

A repeated measures analysis of variance for the Fear Intensity Scale and a repeated measures analysis of variance for the Fear Survey Schedule were carried out to determine the significance of the observed differences. Significant main and interaction effects for the Fear Intensity Scale beyond the $0 \cdot 001$ critical level were found for groups ($F = 11 \cdot 77$; $df = 2/42$), the repeated factor (pre- and post-treatment scores) ($F = 35 \cdot 49$; $df = 1/42$), and the double interaction ($F = 15 \cdot 55$; $df = 2/42$). Individual comparisons of this parametric data were carried out by the Newman-Keuls procedure. Each treatment group showed significantly decreased subjective fear to the actual fear stimulus ($p < 0 \cdot 01$). The control group did not change significantly. Each treatment group significantly decreased its subjective fear intensity to the animal more than the control group ($p < 0 \cdot 01$). The T₁ group showed significantly greater reduction in intensity of fear than the T₂ group ($p < 0 \cdot 01$).

The second self-report measure was the fear survey schedule. Again, a repeated measures analysis of variance showed no significant main or interaction effects for groups ($F = 0 \cdot 169$; $df = 2/42$), the repeated factor (pre- and post-treatment scores) ($F = 3 \cdot 02$; $df = 1/42$), or the double interaction ($F = 2 \cdot 35$; $df = 2/42$).

DISCUSSION

Both treatment groups showed significant reductions of fear on four of the five measures in the study, the exception being the Fear Survey Schedule. The results are in agreement with several previous investigations (Lang, 1969;

Paul, 1966; Wolpe, 1958) which have shown adaptive changes of focused fears when a respondent conditioning paradigm of psychotherapy is used. They also confirm the effectiveness of covert processes in changing overt fears (Cautela, 1966; Cooke, 1966; Garfield *et al.*, 1967; Lang and Lazovik, 1963; Paul, 1966; Wolpe, 1958). It was also concluded that the use of imagery in an operant paradigm — the covert reinforcement procedure (Cautela, 1970) — is about as effective as the use of imagery in systematic desensitization (Wolpe, 1958). The covert reinforcement procedure also provides a way of evaluating the results of operant conditioning in addition to the traditional ABA baseline procedure (Bucher and Lovaas, 1970).

The group presented with the actual fear stimulus showed greater fear reduction than the group presented with the imaginary stimulus. This was true on all measures except the Fear Survey Schedule. It is possible that this may be due to the perceptual vividness of the actual object.

Ten of the 12 subjects who held the animal indicated that the animal was now a pet they wished to keep. The rat was no longer a negative or neutral stimulus, but something positive. At times it is clinically important not only to remove the fear but to enhance approach behavior such as in the case of interpersonal behavior between marital partners, or parent and child.

That there were no significant differences on the Fear Survey Schedule for any of the groups in this operant procedure is consistent with reported laboratory research for respondent techniques (Cooke, 1966; Garfield *et al.*, 1967). Changing one focal fear in the laboratory does not lead to a general reduction in fear. This study dealt with a focal fear in normal college students in only three treatment sessions.

One issue which has both experimental and clinical importance is that of transfer of training from the office or laboratory to daily functioning. The present study included transfer data not reported here because the transfer situation was judged to be too similar to the laboratory to be a real test of transfer. It is suggested that subjects treated with the actual fear stimulus would perform better in a highly similar setting than those treated with the fear stimulus in imagination, but that the latter would exhibit more transfer in a highly dissimilar environment. Should the findings of an actual experiment support the hypothesis, the clinician might then choose the method of presentation according to the generality of the client's presenting problem. For example, the therapist would present the actual fear stimulus if the client were afraid of German shepherd dogs only, but present it in imagination if there were anxiety to dogs in general.

REFERENCES

Anant S. S. (1966) The treatment of alcoholics by a verbal aversion technique: A case report, *Manas* **13**, 79-86.

Barlow D., Leitenberg H., Agras W. and Wincze J. (1969) The transfer gap in systematic desensitization: An analogue study, *Behav. Res. & Therapy* **7**, 191-196.

Bucher B. and Lovaas O. (1970) Operant procedures in behavior modification with children, *Learning Approaches to Therapeutic Behavior Change* (Edited by Levis D.), Aldine, Chicago.

Cautela J. (1966) Treatment of compulsive behavior by covert sensitization, *Psychol. Rec.* **16**, 33-41.

Cautela J. (1967) Covert sensitization, *Psychol. Rep.* **20**, 459-468.

Cautela J. (1969) *The Use of Imagery in Behavior Modification*. Paper presented at the Association for the Advancement of Behavior Therapy, San Francisco, September.

Cautela J. (1970) Covert reinforcement, *Behav. Therapy* **1**, 33-50.

Cautela J. and Kastenbaum R. (1967) A reinforcement survey schedule for use in therapy, training, and research, *Psychol. Rep.* **20**, 1115-1130.

Cautela J., Steffen J. and Wish P. (1970) *An Experimental Test of Covert Reinforcement*. Paper presented at the American Psychological Association, Miami, Florida (Mimeographed).

Cautela J., Walsh K. and Wish P. (1970) The use of covert reinforcement in the modification of attitudes towards the mentally retarded, *J. Psychol.* (in press).

Cooke G. (1966) The efficacy of two desensitization procedures: An analogue study, *Behav. Res. & Therapy* **4**, 17-24.

Davison G. (1965) Relative contributions of differential relaxation and graded exposure to the *in vivo* desensitization of a neurotic fear, *Proceedings of the 73rd Annual Convention of the American Psychological Association*, American Psychological Association, Washington, D.C.

Davison G. (1968) Systematic desensitization as a counterconditioning process, *J. Abnorm. Psychol.* **73**, 91-99.

De Moor W. (1970) Systematic desensitization versus prolonged high intensity stimulation (flooding), *J. Behav. Ther. & Exp. Psychiat.* **1**, 45-52.

Eysenck H. (1970) Behavior therapy and its critics, *J. Behav. Ther. & Exp. Psychiat.* **1**, 5-15.

Garfield Z., Darriun P., Singer B. and McBrearty J. (1967) Effects of *in vivo* training on experimental desensitization of a phobia, *Psychol. Rep.* **20**, 515-519.

Homme L. (1965) Control of coverants, the operants of the mind, *Psychol. Rec.* **15**, 501-511.

Kimble G. (1961) *Hilgard and Marquis' Conditioning and Learning*, Appleton-Century-Crofts, New York.

Lang P. (1969) The mechanics of desensitization and the laboratory study of human fear, *Behavior Therapy: Appraisal and Status* (Edited by Franks C.), McGraw-Hill, New York.

Lang P. and Lazovik A. (1963) Experimental desensitization of a phobia, *J. abnorm. soc. Psychol.* **66**, 519-525.

Lazarus A. (1963) The results of behavior therapy in 126 cases of severe neurosis, *Behav. Res. & Therapy* **1**, 69-79.

Paul G. (1966) *Insight vs. Desensitization in Psychotherapy*, Stanford University Press, Stanford, Calif.

Paul G. (1969) Outcome of systematic desensitization. II: Controlled investigation of individual treatment, technique variations, and current status, *Behavior Therapy: Appraisal and Status* (Edited by Franks C.), McGraw-Hill, New York.

Rachman S. (1966) Studies in desensitization—II: Flooding, *Behav. Res. & Therapy* **4**, 1-6.

Siegel M. (1965) *Nonparametric Statistics for the Behavioral Sciences*, McGraw-Hill, New York.

Skinner B. (1953) *Science and Human Behavior*, Macmillan, New York.

Stampfl T. and Levis D. (1967) Implosive therapy: The theory, the subhuman analogue, the strategy, and the technique, *Possible Use of Conditioning Therapy with the Chronic Schizophrenic*, U.S. Publications, Battle Creek, Michigan.

Stuart R. (1967) Behavior control of overeating, *Behav. Res. & Therapy* **5**, 357-365.

Willis R. (1968) *A study of the comparative effectiveness of systematic desensitization and implosive therapy*. Unpublished doctoral dissertation, University of Tennessee.

Wolpe J. (1958) *Psychotherapy by Reciprocal Inhibition*, Stanford University Press, Stanford, Calif.

Wolpe J. and Flood J. (1970) The effect of relaxation on the galvanic skin response to repeated phobic stimuli in ascending order, *J. Behav. Ther. & Exp. Psychiat.* **1**, 195-200.

Wolpe J. and Lang P. (1964) A fear survey schedule for use in behavior therapy, *Behav. Res. & Therapy*, **2**, 27-30.

Wolpe J. (1969) *The Practice of Behavior Therapy*, Pergamon Press, New York.

Yates A. (1970) *Behavior Therapy*, John Wiley, New York.

Chapter 10

Group Systematic Desensitization versus Covert Positive Reinforcement in the Reduction of Test Anxiety*†

Marion P. Kostka and John P. Galassi

Summary — The study compared modified versions of systematic desensitization and covert positive reinforcement to a no-treatment control condition in the reduction of test anxiety. Both experimental groups received eight treatment sessions, and the systematic desensitization group received two additional sessions devoted to relaxation training. The two treatments were comparable and generally superior to the control group in pretest-posttest and pretest-follow-up changes as measured by the Suinn Test Anxiety Behavior Scale and the Achievement Anxiety Test. On an anagrams performance test, the covert reinforcement and control groups were superior to the desensitization group. No significant differences occurred in subjectively experienced anxiety during the performance test.

Test anxiety disrupts the capacity of a student to concentrate, think, and remember, and it is accompanied by tension, restlessness, and in some, muscular contractions. Test anxiety is commonly experienced by college

*Reprinted with permission from the *Journal of Counseling Psychology*, 1974, *21*, 464-468. ©The American Psychological Association 1974.

†This study is based on the first author's doctoral dissertation submitted to West Virginia University.

students (Donner & Guerney, 1969; Eysenck & Rachman, 1965; Johnson & Sechrest, 1968).

A variety of approaches ranging from insight-oriented counseling to behavioral techniques such as implosion, attentional training, systematic desensitization, and covert positive reinforcement have been used in the treatment of this problem. The most successful of these approaches has been systematic desensitization. At least 15 experimental studies (Kostka, 1973) have reported successful reduction of test anxiety using this procedure.

Despite its effectiveness, systematic desensitization does have limitations. The need for a hierarchical arrangement of anxiety-arousing stimuli complicates the application of this procedure to a group. In addition, instruction in deep muscle relaxation is time consuming, and accurate hierarchy construction requires clinical expertise.

In contrast, covert positive reinforcement, a recently developed therapeutic procedure (Cautela, 1970), requires neither a hierarchical arrangement of stimuli nor relaxation training. The procedure is predicated on the assumption that any behavior that can be influenced overtly by operant conditioning also can be influenced covertly by that procedure. If a student imagines making nonanxious responses in a test situation and these responses are followed repeatedly by the imagination of reinforcing stimuli, then the future probability of nonanxious responses in actual test situations will increase. Because neither deep muscle relaxation nor a hierarchical arrangement of stimuli is needed, covert positive reinforcement offers the advantage of a time saving over systematic desensitization, as well as considerable flexibility in application. Although it is a new technique, research documenting the effectiveness of covert positive reinforcement is accumulating (Flannery, 1970; Wisocki, 1973).

The purpose of this study was to compare the effectiveness of covert positive reinforcement and of systematic desensitization with a no-treatment control condition in the reduction of test anxiety. The two procedures were modified slightly to make them more comparable and to apply them in a group setting. We hypothesized that (a) both treatments would be more effective than a no-treatment control in reducing test anxiety, and (b) both experimental groups would report less anxiety and perform better in a test situation following treatment than the control group.

METHOD

Subjects

Fifteen students who identified themselves as test anxious were assigned randomly to two experimental groups, 8 to covert positive reinforcement and 7 to systematic desensitization. Of these, 11 subsequently completed the program, 6 in the covert reinforcement group and 5 in the systematic desensitization group.

A no-treatment control group of 12 subjects was drawn from two psychology classes. The control subjects achieved pretest scores on the Suinn Test Anxiety Behavior Scale (Suinn, 1969) and the Achievement Anxiety Test (Alpert & Haber, 1960) comparable to the scores of the experimental subjects.

Procedure

All subjects were administered the Suinn Test Anxiety Behavior Scale and the Achievement Anxiety Test before and after treatment and at a five-month follow-up period. At posttesting, a timed anagrams performance test was administered to the subjects. Subjects also reported their level of felt anxiety during the performance test on the Subjective Units of Disturbance Scale (Wolpe, 1969). Professionals conducted both treatments. They followed a written procedure manual and alternated leading groups in order to control for extraneous trainer variables.

Treatments

Subjects in the systematic desensitization group received one-hour treatment sessions twice a week for a five-week period. The first two sessions consisted of an explanation of the treatment rationale and training in deep muscle relaxation. During the next eight sessions, test-related scenes drawn from a 24-item standard hierarchy were presented in imagination and paired with deep muscle relaxation. The criteria for successful completion of a scene was two 10-second presentations without a signal of anxiety from any group member. Finally, the subjects were asked to practice imagining the scenes at home during the interval between sessions.

The covert positive reinforcement group received eight one-hour sessions conducted in a group setting. The treatment rationale was presented in the initial session. During each session, subjects imagined responding without anxiety to three test-related scenes. Each scene was presented three times, followed by imagination of a reinforcing stimulus. Reinforcing stimuli were selected based on subjects' responses to the Reinforcement Survey Schedule (Cautela & Kastenbaum, 1967). Although not presented in a hierarchical order, the test-related scenes either were drawn from or were constructed to be similar to the scenes imagined by the systematic desensitization group. Home practice also was required of subjects in this group.

Thus the two treatments were comparable in the number of scenes imagined, the content of the scenes, and the amount of home practice. They differed in the number of treatment sessions because the systematic desensitization group received two additional sessions for training in deep muscle relaxation.

Instruments

The Suinn Test Anxiety Behavior Scale (Suinn, 1969) is composed of 50 items that describe test-related scenes. Scores on the scale correlate positively with number of errors in course examinations and negatively with final course grades. The Achievement Anxiety Test (Alpert & Haber, 1960) consists of 19 items. Nine of these items measure facilitating test anxiety, and the remaining 10 items measure debilitating anxiety.

At the posttest, a timed anagrams test was administered to all subjects under anxiety-arousing instructions. The purpose of the test was to provide a behavioral measure of the effects of the treatments. The anagrams were drawn from Sargent (1940, pp. 12-15) and were administered by a confederate.

After completing the anagrams test, the subjects rated their anxiety levels on a modified Subjective Unit of Disturbance Scale of 1-100. The subjects were instructed that 1 represents how they felt during an average day and that they should rate their anxiety during the performance test in relation to this baseline.

Statistical Analyses

Pretest-posttest and pretest-follow-up change scores were computed for all subjects on the Suinn Test Anxiety Behavior Scale and on both subscales of the Achievement Anxiety Test. These data were subjected to one-way analyses of variance and Duncan's new multiple-range tests for nearly equal numbers. Pottest anagrams scores and Subjective Unit of Disturbance Scale scores also were subjected to these analyses. The .05 level of significance was adopted.

RESULTS

Analyses of variance and Duncan's new multiple-range tests were performed on pretest scores on the three test anxiety measures. Significant differences ($p < .05$) between the groups were found only on the debilitating portion of the Achievement Anxiety Test. Control subjects were less test anxious than were the experimental subjects on this measure.

Table 1 presents the results of analyses on the pretest-posttest change scores. All groups recorded decreases in test anxiety from pretesting to posttesting on the Suinn Test Anxiety Behavior Scale. However, only the decrease achieved by the systematic desensitization group significantly ($p < .05$) exceeded that attained by the control group. The covert positive reinforcement group did not differ from either the control or the systematic desensitization groups. The decrease in debilitating anxiety of both experimental groups was significantly greater ($p < .05$) than that of the control group. No differences between the experimental groups were significant.

Even though the level of facilitating anxiety increased for both treatment

Table 10.1 Means, Standard Deviations, and Duncan's New Multiple-Range Test on Pretesting–Posttesting Difference Scores for Dependent Variables

	Group		
Dependent variable	Control ($n = 12$)	Covert positive reinforcement ($n = 6$)	Systematic desensitization ($n = 5$)
Suinn Test Anxiety Behavior Scale			
SD	28.849	17.889	12.178
M	20.417	35.000	51.600
Debilitating Achievement Anxiety Test			
SD	4.509	6.804	3.782
M	.833	7.500	8.600

	Control	Systematic desensitization ($n = 5$)	Covert positive reinforcement ($n = 6$)
Facilitating Achievement Anxiety Test			
SD	2.747	1.140	4.262
M	.500	−1.400*	−3.167*

Note. Means not underscored by the same line are significantly different ($p <.05$).
*Negative scores indicate gains in facilitating anxiety from pretests to posttests.

groups from pretesting to posttesting, only the increase attained by the covert positive reinforcement group significantly exceeded ($p < .05$) that of the control group. No significant differences were found between the treatment groups.

The results of the anagrams performance test are presented in Table 2. The covert positive reinforcement and control groups unscrambled significantly ($p < .05$) more anagrams than the systematic desensitization group. The performance of the control and covert groups did not differ significantly. Table 2 also indicates no significant differences between the levels of felt anxiety (Subjective Units of Disturbance Scale scores) experienced by the three groups during this performance test.

Table 3 reports the results of analyses of the change score data from pretesting to follow-up testing. Scores of the Suinn Test Anxiety Behavior Scale decreased for the covert positive reinforcement group over the

Table 10.2 Means, Standard Deviations, and Duncan's New
Multiple-Range Test on Dependent Variable in the Posttest
Performance Situation

| | Group | | |
| | Control | Covert positive reinforcement | Systematic desensitization |
Dependent variable	(n = 12)	(n = 6)	(n = 5)
Number of anagrams correct			
SD	3.119	2.429	2.550
M	10.500	11.500	7.000
Subjective Units of Disturbance Scale score			
SD	15.877	27.644	20.736
M	44.583	60.833	54.000

Note. Means not underscored by the same line are significantly different (p <.05).

five-month period between posttesting and follow-up testing. On the other
hand, the systematic desensitization group maintained its previous (pretest-
posttest) level of improvement. As a result, both experimental groups
achieved significantly greater (pre-testing-follow-up testing) decreases (p <
.05) in test anxiety than did the no-treatment control group. No differences
between the experimental groups were significant.

The decreases in debilitating anxiety by both treatment groups from pretesting to posttesting not only were maintained but also were improved at follow-
up testing (Table 3). The experimental groups differed significantly (p < .05)
from the control group but not from each other in level of pretesting-follow-up
decreases in debilitating anxiety.

Although the levels of facilitating anxiety of the experimental groups increased between posttesting and follow-up, no significant differences were
found between the pretesting-follow-up facilitating anxiety scores of the three
groups. This was due to the fact that the control group recouped the losses in
facilitating anxiety which had occurred from pretesting to posttesting and
increased their levels of facilitating anxiety during the interval between posttesting and follow-up.

DISCUSSION

Covert positive reinforcement was as effective as systematic desensitization
and superior to a no-treatment control group in the reduction of test anxiety

Table 10.3 Means, Standard Deviations, and Duncan's New
Multiple-Range Test on Pretesting–Follow-up Difference Scores
for Dependent Variables

		Group	
		Covert positive	Systematic
	Control	reinforcement	desensitization
Dependent variable	(n = 12)	(n = 6)	(n = 5)
Suinn Test Anxiety Behavior Scale			
SD	22.645	18.468	13.554
M	22.583	50.333	51.800
Debilitating Achievement Anxiety Test			
SD	3.696	4.665	3.114
M	.250	12.167	11.200
Facilitating Achievement Anxiety Test			
SD	3.204	5.231	2.950
M	−1.417	−5.833*	−3.200*

Note. Means not underscored by the same line are significantly different ($p < .05$).

*Negative scores indicate gains in facilitating anxiety from pretests to follow-up tests.

among college students. Moreover, covert positive reinforcement required
two fewer sessions (no relaxation training) and did not use a hierarchical
arrangement of anxiety-arousing stimuli. The effectiveness of the two treatments was demonstrated by pretesting-posttesting and pretesting-follow-up
change scores on the Suinn Test Anxiety Behavior Scale and the Achievement
Anxiety Test.

The failure of the two experimental groups to achieve significantly greater
gains (pretesting-follow-up) in facilitating anxiety as compared to the control
group is a finding that has been reported in earlier studies (Johnson & Sechrest,
1968; Mitchell & Ingham, 1970; Prochaska, 1971). Perhaps the effects of
covert positive reinforcement and systematic desensitization are limited to the
reduction of debilitating anxiety.

The failure to find differences on the Subjective Unit of Disturbance Scale
as well as the unexpected differences in anagram performance may be attributed in part to differential testing conditions. The experimental groups were
administered the anagram test in the treatment room immediately following
their last session, but the control subjects were tested in a large classroom. As a
result, the latter were not close to either the confederate tester or the mechani-

cal timer. Thus, differential amounts of anxiety may have been generated by the two test situations. An explanation for the poorer anagram performance by the systematic desensitization subjects is not readily apparent.

Because both treatments were effective in reducing test anxiety, future research should investigate which target behaviors and subject characteristics respond most readily to each approach.

REFERENCES

Alpert, R., & Haber, R. N. Anxiety in academic achievement situations. *Journal of Abnormal and Social Psychology,* 1960, **61,** 207-215.

Cautela, J. R. Covert reinforcement. *Behavior Therapy,* 1970, **1,** 33-50.

Cautela, J. R., & Kastenbaum, R. A Reinforcement survey schedule for use in therapy, training, and research. *Psychological Reports,* 1967, **20,** 115-130.

Donner, L., & Guerney, B. Automated group desensitization for test anxiety. *Behavior Research and Therapy,* 1969, **7,** 1-13.

Eysenck, H., & Rachman, S. *The causes and cures of neurosis,* London: Routledge & Kegan Paul, 1965.

Flannery, R. An investigation of differential effectiveness of office vs. in vivo therapy of a simple phobia: An outcome study. Unpublished doctoral dissertation, University of Windsor, 1970.

Johnson, S., & Sechrest, L. Comparison of desensitization and progressive relaxation in treating test anxiety. *Journal of Consulting and Clinical Psyshology, 1968,* **32,** 280-286.

Kostka, M. P. The effectiveness of group systematic desensitization vs. covert positive reinforcement as utilized by paraprofessionals in the reduction of test anxiety in college students. Unpublished doctoral dissertation, West Virginia University, 1973.

Mitchell, K. R., & Ingham, R. J. The effects of general anxiety on group desensitization of test anxiety. *Behavior Research and Therapy,* 1970, **8,** 69-78.

Prochaska, J. O. Symptom and dynamic cues in the implosive treatment of test anxiety. *Journal of Abnormal Psychology,* 1971, **77,** 133-142.

Sargent, S. S. Thinking processes at various levels of difficulty. *Archives of Psychology,* 1940, No. 249.

Suinn, R. The STABS, a measure of test-anxiety for behavior therapy: Normative data. *Behavior Research and Therapy,* 1969, **7,** 335-339.

Wisocki, P. A. A covert reinforcement program for the treatment of test anxiety: Brief report. *Behavior Therapy,* 1973, **4,** 264-266.

Wolpe, J. *The practice of behavior therapy.* New York: Pergamon Press, 1969.

Chapter 11

Treatment of a Rodent Phobia by Covert Reinforcement: A Single Subject Experiment*

Edward B. Blanchard and Douglas O. Draper

Summary — The efficacy of Cautela's covert reinforcement treatment procedure was tested in a single subject experiment with a clinically disabling phobia. The experiment confirmed the overall efficacy of the procedure; however, imaginal reinforcement following imaginal exposure was not necessary for improvement in approach behavior. On several other, more global self-report measures of fear, the imaginal reinforcement was found to be either facilitative or necessary to improvement.

In 1970, Cautela described a new behavioral technique for treating phobias and other neurotic disorders: covert reinformcement (COR). The essential aspects of this technique were that the patient was instructed to imagine a graduated series of approach responses to the feared object of situation; each imagined approach response was followed by an imaginal reinforcement, cued by the therapist's saying the word "reinforcement." The latter were developed specifically for the patient based on his report of events which were highly pleasant. The rationale for the procedure was based on the operant conditioning principle that the likelihood of a response's recurring is increased when it is followed by a reinforceing event. Cautela (1970) presented anecdotal evidence for the efficacy of this procedure with patients suffering from

*Reprinted with permission from *Behavior Therapy*, 1973, *4*, 559-564. © Academic Press, Inc. 1973.

phobias, obsessive-compulsive neuroses, and homosexuality. Several leading authorities (Agras, 1972; Marks, 1972; Rachman, 1972) have speculated that exposure to the feared object may be the crucial aspect of all behavioral treatments of phobias. In the single subject experiment described below, the following of imaginal exposure by imaginal reinforcement was manipulated while several different dependent variables were measured.

METHOD

Case History

The patient was a 20-year-old female student at a college in a nearby town. She was referred by one of her teachers after the following incident: she had become visibly upset and had to leave class crying when there was a discussion of mice.

Other indications of the intensity of the phobia were that the patient, a psychology major, reported that she deliberately cut several classes in which live demonstrations of a rat in a Skinner box were made in class. She also reported discomfort in reading about studies involving rats and had to cover pictures of rodents in her textbook in order to read them. Her fear of rodents extended to rats, mice, hamsters, and guinea pigs and was of such intensity that she avoided pet shops and conversations in which these animals were discussed.

The problem was made more salient because the patient had a very strong interest in attending graduate school in psychology. Her expressed goal for treatment was to become comfortable enough around rodents that she could complete courses in experimental psychology.

Treatment Conditions

The first treatment condition consisted of three 1-hr sessions over the course of two weeks, during which there was a detailed exploration of the history of the patient's disorder. In these sessions, the therapist was very supportive and attempted to give the patient some insight into her disorder.

The second condition consisted of six 30-min sessions of COR at the rate of three per week. The format followed was that described by Cautela (1970) and summarized at the first of this paper. A tape recording of instructions for COR was given to the patient to facilitate her practice at home.

The third condition was a control for the effects of the imaginal reinforcement through following the same procedure as above except that the imaginal reinforcement following imagined approach responses was omitted. A new tape was recorded for this phase. Three ½-hr sessions of this covert exposure were given, introduced to the patient by the rationale that she was doing so well that the reinforcement could be omitted. The fourth condition was a return to the original COR procedure for three more 30-min sessions to complete the experimental analysis.

A second control condition during whifh no treatment took place was included for one week to assess the effects of the passage of time and various nonspecific life events of the patient. The final (sixth) treatment condition consisted of two 45-min sessions of participant modeling (PM). This procedure, which consists of having the therapist model fearless approach behavior and then encourage the patient to engage in live, rather than imaginal, approach behavior, has been noted to be highly effective and efficient in small animal phobias (Bandura, Blanchard, & Ritter, 1969; Blanchard, 1970). At this point, treatment was terminated as a result both of the patient's having achieved the level of fearlessness she desired and of the school year's end.

Dependent Variables

All of the assessment procedures were conducted by a second experimenter,* who played no other part in the experiment and who was blind to treatment conditions. Assessment sessions were held once per week on the same day of the week throughout all treatment phases of the experiment and also at a 6-week follow-up.

Approach behavior. The principal dependent variable was approach behavior to a very large (18 in. from nose to tip of tail) live, laboratory rat, which was housed in a glass cage with a wire mesh top which could be securely fastened. The items used in the approach behavior test (ABT) were adopted from several previously used hierarchies.

Physiological arousal. The patient's heart rate (HR) was measured by counting pulse rate several times during the assessment sessions: first, as a baseline, before the patient began the ABT; then at the point of maximum approach behavior at the first test; and finally at the point of maximum approach behavior during each ABT. The increase in HR from baseline to the other measurement points was the dependent variable.

Psychological arousal. At each point that HR was measured, the patient was also asked to rate how fearful, tense, and anxious she was at that moment on a scale ranging from 0 to 10.

General fear of rats. The patient was asked to indicate how afraid of rats

* The authors express their thanks to Larry Young for conducting the assessment sessions of this experiment.

in general she was by marking on a scale from 0 to 10 both before the ABT and again after it. The average of the two ratings was the dependent variable.

Attitudes towards rats. The final measure taken was of the patient's attitudes towards rats. This was measured by having the patient rate the term "laboratory rats" on six semantic differential scales. This measure was also taken both before and after the ABT and the average of the two ratings used.

Self report of fantasy. The patient was asked informally about rats by the therapist. Mention of "nightmares" or bad dreams about rats were scored plus, while no mention was scored minus.

RESULTS AND DISCUSSION

In order best to show the effects of the various treatment conditions on all of the dependent variables, the results for all of the dependent variables are plotted in Fig. 1 as a function of time in each treatment condition.

The most important index of improvement, especially from the point of view of the behavior therapist, is change in overt behavior. Referring to the first part of Fig. 1, one can see that there was a greater rate of increase in approach during the COR than during the insight-oriented psychotherapy sessions. This is shown by the change in shape of the cumulative curve.

The removal of the imaginal reinforcement from the COR procedure in condition 3 did not lead to a decrease in the slope of the approach behavior curve. Instead, this dependent variable continued to show improvement. Reinstatement of imaginal reinforcement led to a further increase in the slope. In the second control phase (condition 5), during which no treatment was performed, there was a decrease in slope of the approach curve. Finally, there was another increase in slope of the curve, indicating a further increase in approach behavior, as a result of the PM.

The measure of physiological arousal during the ABT, i.e., increase in HR from pre-ABT to maximum approach behavior for that session, showed a decrease in arousal after the first condition and a further decrease as a result of COR. Interestingly, there was an increase in arousal (condition 3) over that experienced in the COR phase when the imaginal reinforcement was removed, followed by a decrease when reinforcement was reinstated, and a further decrease as a result of the PM treatment.

For psychological arousal during the ABT, a somewhat different pattern of results was obtained: there was a decrease in affective arousal as a result of the brief psychotherapy. There was a further decrease during COR. No further decreases were observed until after the PM; for ratings made at the point of maximum approach behavior after the first COR treatment, however, there was a slight increase in arousal during the first control phase when the imaginal reinforcement was removed from the COR procedure.

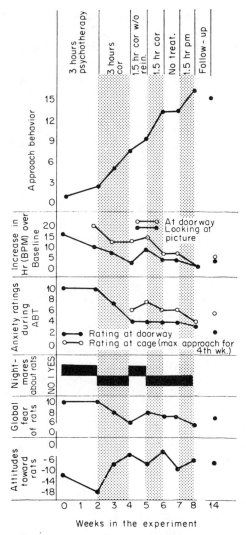

Fig. 11.1. Changes in all dependent variables as a function of condition of the experiment.

The self report measures show different patterns. There was no decrease in general fear of rats as a result of condition 1. The initial use of COR led to a decrease which was partially reversed during the control phase of condition 3. This dependent variable remained constant during the second control phase (no treatment in condition 5) and decreased further as a result of PM.

Attitudes toward rats became more negative as a result of the brief psychotherapy treatment. Administration of COR led to a positive change in attitude. This was followed by a slight decrease during the first control phase. Further improvement was found after the reinstitution of the full COR treatment. After that, attitudes became more negative during the no treatment phase (condition 5) and again improved slightly during the PM treatment. During both condition 1 and condition 3 (COR without reinforcement), the patient spontaneously reported having bad dreams about rats, and even nightmares, which awakened her. She further reported an absence of these dreams during the two COR treatment phases. When questioned about this matter during conditions 5 and 6, she reported no return of the disturbing fantasy material.

As can be seen in Fig. 1, at a follow-up assessment session, 6 weeks after the conclusion of treatment, all of the gains noted at the conclusion of treatment were still present with the possible exception of attitudes which had shown a slight decline. A telephone follow-up assessment session (4½ months post treatment) revealed the patient to be doing well with no recurrence of any fears of rats or other rodents.

As to whether the improvement was due to imaginal reinforcement following imaginal exposure to the feared object, or to the latter alone, the results are mixed: removal of the reinforcement led to no decrease in the rate of improvement in approach behavior. On all of the other dependent variables, particularly the more global self report measures, removal of the reinforcement led to a cessation of improvement or even to a reversal. Thus, while the imaginal reinforcement may not be necessary for improvement, it is certainly facilitative, especially in the sense that the patient finds the treatment procedure less unpleasant and is thus willing to stay in treatment.

This discrepancy between changes in approach behavior and changes in other dependent variables during control conditions in which an active element of a procedure is omitted has been noted previously. In a study of the effects of relaxation in systematic desensitization, Agras, Leitenberg, Barlow, Curtis, Edwards, & Wright (1971) found that removal of relaxation led to no decrease in the rate of improvement as measured by approach behavior but a noticeable decrease in self report measures.

REFERENCES

Agras, W. S. *Behavior modification: Principles and clinical applications*. Boston: Little, Brown & Co., 1972. Pp. 151–153.

Agras, W. S., Leitenberg, H., Barlow, D. H., Curtis, N., Edwards, J., & Wright, D. Relaxation in systematic desensitization. *Archives of General Psychiatry*, 1971, **25**, 511–514.

Bandura, A., Blanchard, E. B., & Ritter, B. G. The relative efficacy of desensitization and modeling approaches for inducing behavioral, affective, and attitudinal changes. *Journal of Personality and Social Psychology*, 1969, **13**, 173–199.

Blanchard, E. B. The relative contributions of modeling, informational influences, and physical contact in the elimination of phobic behavior. *Journal of Abnormal Psychology*, 1970, **76**, 55–61.

Cautela, J. R. Covert reinforcement. *Behavior Therapy,* 1970, **1**, 33–50.

Marks, I. M. Flooding (implosion) and allied treatments. In W. S. Agras (Ed.), *Behavior modification: Principles and clinical applications.* Boston: Little, Brown & Co., 1972. Pp. 154–155.

Rachman, S. Clinical applications of observational learning, imitation and modeling. *Behavior Therapy,* 1972, **3**, 379–397.

Chapter 12

Covert Reinforcement: Two Studies and a Comment*

John J. Steffen†

Summary — Two studies are reported: the first extends the generality of covert reinforcement; the second poses a question about the processes that underlie behavior change with this procedure. Exp. 1, conducted with 50 male hospitalized psychiatric patients, indicated that covert reinforcement produced a significant change in plural-noun responding on a word naming task. Exp. 2, using the same experimental design, with 25 male and 25 female college students, showed significant change only for male subjects. While some support has been produced for the efficacy of covert reinforcement, a question is raised concerning the value of an operant model for explaining behavioral change via covert reinforcement.

The usefulness of covert reinforcement as a behavior therapy technique has now been reasonably documented through case reports (Cautela, 1970; Cautela & Baron, 1973) and controlled experiments (Flannery, 1972; Wisocki, 1973). However, questions remain concerning the generality of this treatment beyond college students (Steffen, 1974), and the actual process(es) of behavior change underlying the treatment effects (Ladouceur, 1974; Mahoney, 1974). In this regard, the results of two experiments are presented: the first extends the use of covert reinforcement to hospitalized psychiatric patients; the second raises a question concerning presumed processes of change with such treatment.

---

*Reprinted with permission of author and publisher from *Psychological Reports*, 1977, *40*, 291-294.

†The author is grateful for the assistance of the patients, staff and administration of Lyons Veterans Hospital, Lyons, New Jersey in Exp. 1.

EXPERIMENT 1

Method

Subject. Subjects were 50 male patients drawn from the population of a psychiatric hospital who met the following three criteria: first a formal diagnosis of schizophrenia, chronic undifferentiated type; second, willingness and ability to participate in an experiment in the opinion of his ward nurse; and third, agree himself to participate. Subjects were from 22 to 57 yr. old ($M = 41.4$) and had been hospitalized from one to 27 yr. ($M = 10.0$). All subjects were receiving phenothiazine medication.

Procedure. Subjects were randomly assigned to one of five experimental groups. Subjects then met with the experimenters and were asked to complete the Reinforcement Survey Schedule (Cautela & Kastenbaum, 1967). They were then requested to say 200 words, one at a time. The only restriction to the word utterance was that they not name words which formed sentences (Greenspoon, 1955). For purposes of analysis, the 200 words were divided into four blocks of 50 words each. The five treatment conditions differed with respect to the additional instructions subjects were given. Subjects in the first group (no feedback) said the 200 words without interruption. Subjects in the second group (word alone) were told that the experimenter would say the word "scene" at certain times during the task. The experimenter said "scene" after each plural noun the subject emitted during the second and third blocks of 50 words. Subjects in the third group (random scene) were asked to select the item from the Reinforcement Survey Schedule which gave them the most pleasure. The experimenter then asked subject to imagine himself engaging in that activity whenever he said "scene." This pairing of the word "scene" with instructions to imagine the pleasant scene was repeated three times to ensure the subject understood the instructions. The subject was then requested to say the 200 words; the experimenter said "scene" 10 times, in the second and third blocks on a predetermined random basis. Subjects in Group 4 (least pleasurable scene) were asked to indicate the item that gave the least pleasure. This item was practiced and cued to the word "scene" as described in the Random Scene group. As subject said the 200 words, the experimenter used the cue word after each plural noun emitted in the second and third blocks. Subjects in Group 5 (Covert reinforcement) were treated similar to subjects in the random scene group with the exception that the experimenter said the cue word after each plural noun emitted in Blocks 2 and 3. All subjects were seen individually for approximately 1 hr.

Results

Subjects did not differ among groups in age ($F_{4,45} < 1.00, p > .05$) or length of hospitalization ($F_{4,45} < 1.00, p > .05$); nor did they initially differ from the frequency of plural nouns emitted in the first block ($F_{4,45} < 1.00, p > .05$).

The effect of the experimental manipulation was assessed on a change score computed by subtracting the number of plural nouns emitted in Block 1 from the number emitted in Block 4. Analysis showed that groups differed in this measure ($F_{4,45} = 5.82, p < .005$). A Duncan multiple-range test (Edwards, 1960) indicated that the covert reinforcement group differed from the others ($p < .01$), and the other groups did not differ from one another.

EXPERIMENT 2

Method

Subjects were 25 male and 25 female college students who were paid $3.00 for participation. The operations of Exp. 2 were identical to those of Exp. 1, with the exception that 5 male and 5 female subjects were assigned to each condition.

Results

Subjects did not differ in their frequency of plural-noun responses in the first block by group assignment ($F_{4,40} = 1.00, p > .05$), gender ($F_{1,40} < 1.00, p > .05$), or their interaction ($F_{4,40} = 1.02, p > .05$).

The same change score as used in Exp. 1 was the dependent measure for a two-way analysis of variance (treatment and gender). Both main effects for treatment ($F_{4,40} = 2.17, p > .05$) and gender ($F_{1,40} = 2.41, p > .05$) were not significant; the interaction, however, was significant ($F_{4,40} = 4.29, p < .01$). A Duncan multiple-range test indicated that only the male covert-reinforcement group was significantly different from the others ($p < .01$). The female covert-reinforcement group did not show a treatment effect.

DISCUSSION

Both experiments provide some general support of covert reinforcement as a viable behavior change technique. Results of these studies specifically indicated that covert reinforcement was superior to the control conditions in increasing plural-noun responding on the word-naming task. Each control condition provided a test of a competing hypothesis that could explain alternative sources of behavior change.

Exp. 1 is distinctive in that it provides evidence for the potential usefulness of covert reinforcement with hospitalized patients. Limitations on this experiment, however, preclude a strong acceptance of these findings. First, the target response bears slight similarity to clinically relevant target responses (Bernstein & Paul, 1971) that would be ordinarily considered in treating hospitalized patients. Second, although the experimental procedure was standardized, the experimenter was aware of the study's hypothesis. This should be controlled for in future research through a double-blind design.

Clear interpretation of the findings of Exp. 2 is difficult. The failure to find a significant change in plural-noun responding for female subjects is somewhat problematic for the assumption that an operant model provides adequate explanation of the process of change in covert reinforcement. Other researchers in posing this concern for fear-reduction studies of covert reinforcement have suggested that an extinction process underlies such behavioral change (Ladouceur, 1974; Marshall, Boutilier, and Minnes, 1974).

It is apparent that an operant-based model directing the study of covert events contributed to the relegitimization of cognitive phenomena within behavior therapy (Cautela, 1969; Homme, 1965). A model, however, is useful only to the extent that it can provide explanation and fruitful avenues of research. The results of Exp. 2 and of other researchers (e.g., Ladouceur, 1974; Marshall, *et al.*, 1974) suggest that an operant-based model of the processes of change in covert reinforcement may be inadequate. Several writers have suggested that a cognitive model may provide a better explanation of the processes of change (Bandura, 1969; Mahoney, 1974). The results of Exp. 2 highlight the potential importance of individual difference variables in contributing to the predictive power of a cognitive model of behavior change. Mischel (1973), in his reconceptualization of social learning theory, recommends inclusion of such individual difference and cognitive variables. Future research directed toward study of the processes of change in covert reinforcement would do well to systematically study both cognitive and non-cognitive attribute variables.

REFERENCES

Bandura, A. *Principles of behavior modification.* New York: Holt, Rinehart & Winston, 1969.

Bernstein, D., & Paul, G. L. Some comments on therapy analogue research with small animal "phobias." *Journal of Behavior Therapy and Experimental Psychiatry,* 1971, 2, 225-237.

Cautela, J. R. Covert reinforcement. *Behavior Therapy,* 1970, 1, 33-50.

Cautela, J. R., & Baron, M. G. Multifaceted behavior therapy of self-injurious behavior. *Journal of Behavior Therapy and Experimental Psychiatry,* 1973, 4, 125-131.

Cautela, J. R., & Kastenbaum, R. A reinforcement survey schedule for use in therapy, training and research. *Psychological Reports,* 1967, 20, 1115-1130.

Flannery, R. B. A laboratory analogue of two covert reinforcement procedures. *Journal of Behavior Therapy and Experimental Psychiatry,* 1972, 3, 171-177.

Greenspoon, J. The reinforcing effect of two spoken sounds on the frequency of two responses. *American Journal of Psychology*, 1955, 68, 409-416.

Homme, L. E. Perspectives in psychology: XXIV. Control of coverants, the operants of the mind. *Psychological Record*, 1965, 15, 501-511.

Ladouceur, R. An experimental test of the learning paradigm of covert positive reinforcement in deconditioning anxiety. *Journal of Behavior Therapy and Experimental Psychiatry*, 1974, 5, 3-6.

Mahoney, M. J. *Cognition and behavior modification*. Cambridge, MA: Ballinger, 1974.

Marshall, W. L., Boutilier, J., & Minnes, P. The modification of phobic behavior by covert reinforcement. *Behavior Therapy*, 1974, 5, 469-480.

Mischel, W. Towards a cognitive social learning reconceptualization of personality. *Psychological Review*, 1973, 80, 252-283.

Steffen, J. J. Covert reinforcement: some facts and fantasies. In G. Baron (Chair), Experimental analysis of covert reinforcement. Symposium presented at the meeting of the Association for Advancement of Behavior Therapy, Chicago, 1974.

Wisocki, P. A. A covert reinforcement program for the treatment of test anxiety: brief report. *Behavior Therapy*, 1973, 4, 263-266.

Chapter 13

Covert Positive Reinforcement Studies: Review, Critique, and Guidelines*†

Donald S. Scott and Anne K. Rosenstiel

Summary — The paper critically examines the experimental literature on covert positive reinforcement, including analogue tasks, attitude analogues, and clinical analogues. Methodological deficiencies across studies (e.g., variability in subjects' motivation and in experimenters' expertise, non-standardized outcome measures) are discussed, and suggestions for more systematized future research are presented.

Imagery has been employed in the clinical setting and the laboratory for a number of years. Wolpe's systematic desensitization (1958) was the first major technique systematically employing imagery in behavior modification. This technique has been extensively used to modify maladaptive avoidance behavior. Critical reviews of the literature on desensitization are published elsewhere (Bernstein & Paul, 1971; Paul, 1969a; 1969b).

Recently Cautela (1973) has developed a number of techniques which he calls covert conditioning. These techniques have been clinically employed to modify both maladaptive approach and maladaptive avoidance behavior. They

*Reprinted with permission from *Psychotherapy: Theory, Research and Practice*, 1975, *12*, 374-384.

†The authors wish to express their appreciation to Mary Grace Baron for her suggestions and careful reading of the manuscript.

have been successfully used in treating a number of seemingly intractable cases, such as heroin addiction (Steinfeld, Rautio, Egan & Rice, 1972; Wisocki, 1973b), intravenous amphetamine addiction (Gotestam & Melin, 1974), severe self-inurious behavior (Cautela & Baron, 1973), transsexualism (Barlow et al., 1973), obsessive-compulsive behavior (Wisocki, 1970, ago-raphobic behavior (Flannery, 1972b), and suicidal attempts (Jurgela, in press).

These techniques are labeled covert because both the response to be manipulated and the stimulus are presented to imagination (Cautela, 1973). There are five techniques which are analogous to the operant techniques developed in the laboratory. They are: covert positive reinforcement (Cautela, 1970a), covert negative reinforcement (Cautela, 1970b), covert sensitization (punishment) (Cautela, 1966; 1967), covert extinction (Cautela, 1971a) and covert modeling (Cautela, 1971b).

Cautela has based the covert conditioning techniques on two assumptions. First, covert events (thoughts, feelings and images) obey the same laws as overt events. Secondly, covert events, if applied systematically via instructions, can effectively control other covert and overt behavior in the same way as externally applied stimuli (Cautela, 1970c; 1973).

There have been a number of experimental studies on the covert conditioning techniques (Cautela, 1973). The purpose of this paper is to critically examine the experimental literature on one of these techniques, covert positive reinforcement (COR) and to make suggestions for more improved and systematized research. A discussion of the COR procedure will provide the background for a discussion of the literature.

THE COVERT REINFORCEMENT PROCEDURE

The purpose of covert reinforcement is to increase a response frequency by following it with a reinforcer. Both the response and the reinforcer are presented in imagination.

There are three steps involved in the application of COR (Cautela, 1970c). The first step involves the determination and selection of the response to be increased. Secondly, reinforcers must be selected and determined for use. The Reinforcement Survey Schedule (RSS) (Cautela & Kastenbaum, 1967) may be used for this purpose. A number of studies have shown that the RSS is both reliable (Keehn, Bloomfield & Hug, 1970; Kleinknecht, McCormick & Thorndike, 1971; 1973) and valid (Mermis, 1971). Reinforcers may also be determined from interviews with the subject and/or significant others, such as family and staff. Finally, the subject is asked "to imagine" the response to be increased followed by the previously determined reinforcer. Cautela (1973) describes "to imagine" as follows:

I am going to have you imagine certain scenes, and ask you to imagine you are really there. Try not to imagine that you are simply seeing what I describe; try to use your other senses as well. If in the scene you are sitting in a chair, try to imagine you can feel the chair against your body. If, for example, the scene involves being at a party, try to imagine you can hear people's voices, hear glasses tinkling, and even smell the liquor and food. Now remember, the main point is that you are actually there experiencing everything. You don't see yourself there, but are actually there.

COVERT REINFORCEMENT STUDIES

The focus of this paper is on the analysis of research design. There are 13 studies which have been divided into three general types of research: analogue tasks, attitude analogues, and clinical analogue studies.

Analogue Tasks

The target behaviors in these studies are less complex than those used in clinical studies. They are relatively simple and less generalizable to real life settings.

Cautela, Steffen & Wish (in press) showed subjects slides of circles and asked them to estimate the diameters. The mean estimation served as the baseline. There were five groups: (1) The COR group. Subjects imagined reinforcing scenes either after an under estimation of circle size as compared to their baseline or an over estimation. No subject was instructed to use COR for both an over and under estimation. (2) No scenes. (3) Non-contingent reinforcing scenes. (4) The experimenter said the word "reinforcement" after an over or under estimation of circle size. (5) "Neutral" contingent scene. "Neutral" was not defined. These last three groups controlled for the alternative hypothesis that something in the procedure itself, rather than the contingent reinforcing scene, produced a change in behavior. The COR group had a predicted change in circle size perception as compared to all groups except the word "reinforcement" alone group. This last group was significantly different from the no-scene group. The cricle size task has also been employed in a study by Tondo & Cautela (1974) examining some of the important variables in the COR procedure. This study is more appropriately discussed in the section on process studies below.

Steffen (1971) used contingent COR to study the Greenspoon effect. The subjects were hospitalized patients with a diagnosis of "schizophrenia, chronic undifferentiated type." Subjects said 200 words, one at a time. Results were analyzed in blocks of 50 words each. Experimental manipulation occurred only during blocks two and three. The experimental group imagined a scene contingent upon a plural noun. The four control groups were similar to Cautela, Steffan & Wish (in press) except that the word "scene" was substituted for the word "reinforcement" in group four.

Compared to block one, only the COR group emitted a significant greater number of plural nouns in block four. It is interesting to note that while simple "attention" um hum, etc. changed the frequency of the emission of certain word classes (Greenspoon, 1951), in this experiment attention, i.e., the word "scene" by itself did not significantly change the number of plural nouns emitted.

Krop, Messinger, & Reiner (in press) reinforced eye-contact on an anxiety arousing self disclosure questionnaire. During baseline, an interviewer asked the subject questions while he looked the subject in the eye. A hidden observer recorded the length of the subject's eye-contact. During the experimental session the COR group was instructed to imagine a "pleasant" scene following five or more seconds of eye-contact. The control groups were a contact control group and a non-contingent control group. The COR group was significantly different from both groups on a post treatment interview administered immediately after treatment, but not on a follow-up of one week.

Ascher (1973) tested three hypothesis: (1) An imagined reinforcer following an image of a pronoun would increase the probability that the subject would use that pronoun in a simple oral sentence, (2) the increase in pronoun selection would vary directly with the number of reinforcers, and (3) COR would extinguish in a manner similar to overt extinction.

Subjects were supplied an infinitive verb and were asked to construct a simple sentence. The dependent measure was the pronoun choice. The experiment consisted of a baseline for all groups, COR for two groups, and extinction for one of the COR groups.

The COR subjects were asked to imagine a pronoun and then a reinforcing scene. There were 50 pairings: 30 of one pronoun and 10 each of two other pronouns. To control for satiation subjects were instructed to use three reinforcing scenes. A control group imagined 50 reinforcing scenes. A control group imagined 50 reinforcing scenes and then 50 pronouns of 30, 10, and 10. A baseline only was taken on a fourth group. During extinction one COR group imagined the same three pronouns once without the reinforcing scenes.

The first two hypothesis were confirmed. The third was not. Although subjects used fewer tested pronouns, the baseline rate was not reinstated.

This is the only analogue task procedure which employed Cautela's definition of COR, i.e., a covert behavior followed by a covert reinforcer. In all other studies the response to be increased was overt.

Attitude Analogues

The dependent variables in these studies were self-reported attitudes toward others and one's self. One methodological problem common to these studies concerns whether the measured change occurs in the self-report, in the actual attitude, or in both. Can we say that reinforcing a response on a questionnaire results in an actual change or does it result in a change in the probability of a response unrelated to the attitude?

Cautela, Walsh, & Wish (1971) used COR to increase positive attitudes toward the "mentally retarded." Attitudes were measured by a questionnaire developed by the authors. The COR group subjects imagined a "mentally retarded" person, and then a "pleasant" scene. The control group subjects imagined a "mentally retarded" person only. Each group had one session to learn the scenes. They were then asked to practice the scenes at home. Subjects in both groups practiced an average of four times.

Three weeks later the questionnaire was readministered. Only the COR group had a significant increase in positive attitudes toward the "mentally retarded," as measured by the questionnaire.

Since the subjects were asked to imagine a "mentally retarded" person, one would hypothesize that there would only be an increase in the frequency of thinking about a "mentally retarded" person. The authors implied assumption was that the thinking frequency was somehow positively correlated with an attitude.

Two similar studies used COR to increase subjects' positive "self-concepts." The subjects were read statements from the Tennessee Department of Mental Health Self-Concept Scale (TDMH). The dependent measure was the subjects' response to the statements indicating a positive "self-concept." The first and third administration constituted the pre-post measures. The second administration was used in the experimental session.

In Krop, Calhoon, & Verrier (1971), the COR group imagined a reinforcing scene following an appropriate response. An overt reinforcement group received a token (subjects were already on a token system) and a gum drop. It is unclear why this group received two reinforcers and the COR group received only one. Nothing followed the responses of a control group. A noncontingent covert reinforcement group replaced the overt reinforcement group in Krop, Perez, & Beaudoin (1973).

In both studies only the COR group changed significantly from the first to the third administration of the TDMH. Change in the overt group in the first study did not reach significance. It seems that COR was more powerful than overt reinforcement. The two groups, however, received different reinforcers.

The authors state that both studies result in increased positive "self-concepts." Although the experiments were successful, the results may actually be an increase in certain responses to certain statements. Reinforcement may have simply strengthened a "yes" or "no" response, or just an agreement with the statement and not to a generalized "self-concept."

It is important to note, however, that both studies used institutionalized patients. Subjects in the first study were children with a mean age of 10.5 years and diagnosed as having certain behavior disorders. Male psychiatric patients were subjects in the second experiment. These populations were chosen because they were seen as deficient in positive "self-concepts."

Clinical Analogues

Three clinical analogue studies and one clinical case manipulated anxiety related avoidance behavior. A fourth clinical analogue study manipulated the maladaptive approach behavior of overeating.

Flannery (1972a) used rat phobic subjects. An in vivo treatment group started 10 feet from the rat. They covertly reinforced themselves, and then were given the choice of proceeding to the next step on a 13 step hierarchy or remaining at the same step. A second experimental group went through the same procedures except that the approach behavior was also in imagination. Subjects in both groups were instructed to cease imagining 30 seconds after the experimenter said the word "reinforcement." A third group served as an attention control.

A Behavioral Avoidance Test (BAT) and two subjective scales were used. According to Bernstein & Paul's (1971) criteria, a good BAT must include (1) instructions on how to handle the phobic stimulus, and (2) firm instructions to approach it. Although exact instructions were not included, subjects appear to have been firmly instructed to approach the phobic stimulus. Therefore, this BAT measurement appears to have met the second criterion, and the use of heavy duty gloves may have eliminated subjects unfamiliar with how to handle the rat. Only the two treatment groups changed significantly from pre-post measures. The in vivo approach group had a greater reduction in fear on one subjective scale.

Marshall, Boutilier, & Minnes (1974) compared COR, systematic desensitization (labelled experimental desensitization), and covert negative reinforcement (CNR), to three control groups.

Volunteer subjects with a fear of snakes were used as subjects. A 15 point BAT measure similar to Flannery's, and one subjective scale were used as measures. Subjects were given gloves and instructed to approach the snake until they felt uncomfortable, but not to force themselves to go further. This does not meet Bernstein & Paul's criteria for firm instructions.

All subjects in each group, except the no contact control, were administered treatment in groups of four. There were six groups: (1) Systematic desensitization, using scenes from the BAT. (2) COR. The scenes were presented in a randomized rather than hierarchial order. The COR procedure was altered, however, since subjects were also instructed to relax after imagining the approach behavior, but before imagining the reinforcer. To avoid satiation, subjects were instructed to alternate among four reinforcing scenes. (3) CNR as described by Cautela (1970). (4) Non-contingent COR. (5) Placebo control which consisted of a discussion of "strategies for coping with fears." (6) No contact control.

Results indicated that all three experimental groups showed greater improvement than control groups five and six. The desensitization and COR groups were equally effective, and when their results were combined and compared to the CNR group, the combined groups were more effective than the CNR on the BAT measure.

Wisocki (1973a) used COR to treat anxiety in a group setting. The experimental group listened to taped scenes of feeling calm and relaxed while in exam situations and doing well on the exam. A no contact group served as the control. The COR group only had a significant decrease in test anxiety.

All three of the experiments discussed above attempted to reduce anxiety. Ullmann & Krasner (1969) and Lang (1969) however, believe anxiety includes three general measurement methods: (1) physiological, (2) subjective, and (3) overt behavior. These three measures do not always correlate. Flannery and Marshall et al. used two methods. Wisocki, however, used only one: two anxiety scales. Bernstein & Paul's (1971) discussion of systematic desensitization analogue studies also seems applicable to the COR studies. They state:

A minimum requirement for any study in this area should be a demonstrable significant increase in anxiety, shown through direct multiple measurement of cognitive, physiological, and observable motoric behavior, as a result of the presence of the eliciting stimulus.

All three general methods of measurement were used for a single case design rat phobia (Blanchard & Draper, 1973). The client was a 20-year-old female college student with a "clinically disabling" phobia.

The experiment consisted of six phases: (1) "Psychotherapy" consisting of supportive and insightful history taking. (2) COR. The subject imagined a graduated series of approach behavior to the phobic stimulus followed by an imagined reinforcer. (3) Imagined approach behavior without the imagined reinforcer. (4) COR was reinstated. (5) No treatment for one week. (6) Participant modeling. During this phase, the experimenter modeled the approach behavior and encouraged the subject to do the same.

A second experimenter, blind to all treatment conditions, measured the six dependent variables. Measurements were taken once a week and at a six-week follow-up. The overt measurements, an approach behavior test and heart rate, were measured before the session and at the maximum approach point. There were four subjective measures.

Results of the approach behavior test indicated a greater improvement during the COR phase as compared to "psychotherapy." Without the imagined reinforcer, the approach behavior continued to increase, but the increase was not as great as in phase four when COR was reinstated. During the no treatment phase there was a decrease in the approach behavior whereas in participant modeling, there was an increase.

During phase three, three subjective measures included an attitude and global fear of rats, and an anxiety rating while near the cage of a live rat. The only measure that remained constant was the anxiety rating at the doorway of the room which housed the rat.

This clinical treatment lasted only two months and all measures showed a decided improvement. Results were maintained at a six-week follow-up and a four and a half month telephone interview. This study is a good clinical test of a clinical procedure.

Manno & Marston (1972) used COR to decrease the maladaptive approach behavior of overeating. All subjects wanted to lose a minimum of 15 pounds. Seven subjective rating scales, and actual weight, served as pre-post measures. The authors compared a group administered COR and a group administered covert sensitization (labelled negative covert reinforcement) to a contact control group. Both treatment groups did significantly better than the control, but they did not differ significantly from each other.

At a three month telephone follow-up all three groups had a further weight loss as compared to their weight at the end of treatment. The two treatment groups, however, had a greater weight loss compared to the control group. This study and Blanchard & Draper's (1973) study are the only two studies with long term follow-ups.

DISCUSSION OF COR STUDIES

General Considerations

Cautela has taken great pains in outlining in detail the clinical application of COR. However, nowhere in the literature is there an overall consideration of the experimental procedure. The following drawbacks of inter-experimental variability are discussed in an effort to help systematize future research.

Drawbacks in design. In the experiments reviewed in this paper, the instructions "to imagine" are not presented in a standard manner. This would make it easier to compare studies and more closely approximate the clinical situation as described by Cautela.

In all of these studies, the reinforcing stimuli are not quantified. For example, one of the items on the RSS is receiving praise. We have no indication in these experiments as to how much praise the subject might be receiving, by whom and under what circumstances. Also, Cautela et al. (in press) used the term "neutral" scene implying that the subject rated "not at all" pleasant on the RSS. However, an aversive scene could be so categorized. Not all experiments control for the duration of the scene or clarity of the scene. Most of these, however, control for the frequency of the reinforcing stimulus.

Subject motivation. Sources of motivation variability among subjects include differential reinforcement by the experimenter, self-selection into a study, and differences in sample characteristics (e.g., student vs. clinical). Many of the studies may fall plague to a criticism that may be leveled at studies both in and out of the behavior therapy discipline; that is, the subtle reinforcing and aversive feedback from the experimenter concerning the subject's own behavior which effects experiment outcome. In many of the experiments, the subjects were college students. Wisocki's (1973a) and Manno & Marston's (1972) subjects defined themselves as having maladaptive behaviors and volunteered to participate in the study to change that problem. Manno & Marston's (1972) subjects were willing to supply a $15 refundable deposit. The subject in the study done by Blanchard & Draper (1973) had a "clinically disabling" phobia. In the other studies, the subjects had no defined clinical problems, and may have participated for a variety of reasons which might include: being paid, meeting course requirements, and some might have participated out of curiosity. Bernstein & Paul's (1971) discussion of small animal phobias seems applicable here:

A college student, participating in an experiment conducted by a professor or other authority figure, is likely to be sensitive to and strongly influenced by social cues regarding appropriate behavior as they are communicated to him throughout the study.

Unfortunately, one strong index of this, the verbal instructions, has been deleted from most of the write-ups.

The two studies on positive "self-concepts" (Krop et al., 1971; Krop, Perez, & Beaudoin, (1973), and the study by Steffen (1971) are pioneering studies in the area of covert conditioning. The subjects were institutionalized, and some were diagnosed as chronic "schizophrenics." Some behavior therapists, including Wolpe (1970), believe that imagery techniques are not applicable to "schizophrenics and psychotics" since they are deficient in cognitive processes. The experimenters appear to have selected the subjects because they were available and were potentially cooperative. These studies at least suggest that there should be further investigation.

Subjects' expectancies. In three experiments (Cautela et al., in press; Cautela et al., 1971; Ascher, 1973), the subjects were asked if they knew the purpose of the experiment at the end of the experimental sessions. Only two of the 92 subjects in these three experiments could identify the purpose. In Cautela et al. (in press) and Cautela et al. (1971), the authors state, therefore, that the subjects did not behave in a way they thought would please the experimenter. However, Salzinger's (1969) review of the literature on verbal conditioning indicates that although the subject may not be aware of the contingencies, he may be responding to slight social cues regarding desired behavior. Ascher, however, refers to Dulaney (1961) who states that the subjects might have been aware of the purpose of their performance, and that this was not determined in the post-experimental interview. This involves a methodological problem. If subjects are not questioned thoroughly enough, then experimenters will not get the data on awareness. If subjects are questioned too thoroughly, experimenters may shape the subjects into the answer.

Generalization to non-experimental situations. Subjects in the study by Cautela et al. (1971) were asked to practice 21 times in 3 weeks. They practiced on the average of four times. Despite this poor cooperation, there was a significant behavior change. This may have occurred with so few trials because the behavior was not long standing with strong and complex histories of reinforcement. Clinical behaviors are generally more difficult to change. Generally therapists not only have to help change the maladaptive clinical behavior, but also teach incompatible responses to produce long term results with generalization. It is then that the question of the client's willingness to practice say 20 scenes per day becomes critical.

Experimenter variability. All studies, but especially analogue studies of clinical behaviors, require the experimenters to be well versed not only in the procedure itself, but also the small but important technical problems that arise furing the experiment. Otherwise, treatment may be biased. Most studies failed to describe the experimenter's characteristics, including his experience.

Measures. One of the assumptions in covert reinforcement is that the technique will result in a change in overt and covert behavior in a manner similar to a change in behavior from an overt reinforcing stimulus following an overt behavior. Studies should include measures of both covert and overt behavior. Only two studies do this (Flannery, 1972a; Blanchard & Draper, 1973). Many of the studies which measure covert behavior (thought, feeling, or image) need improved measures. Wisocki (1973a) is suggestive, but as the author notes, the single no contact group did not control for the non-specific effects of merely being treated or the subject and therapist characteristics. While Krop et al's (1971) experiment has fewer control difficulties, we cannot meaningfully compare the two groups. The two studies on "self-concept" (Krop et al., 1971; Krop, Perez & Beaudoin, 1973) need multiple measures. Flannery's (1972a) multiple measurements of covert behavior are generally in harmony with the overt behavior change. Blanchard & Draper's (1973) covert and overt measures were in harmony in all phases except the third.

Assumption testing. Aside from the issues of efficacy, Cautela has stressed the assumption that the technique can be subsumed under the operant conditioning paradigm and that covert events obey the same laws as overt events. These theoretical considerations need further exploration.

Problems would arise if the COR procedure was primarily an operant. Take, for example, test anxiety. If a subject imagines taking a test, but does not imagine being completely calm and relaxed, and there is some felt anxiety, then the feeling of being anxious might be reinforced. An alternative explanation is that reciprocal inhibition is a secondary property of reinforcement. In Flannery's study (1972a) COR may have served as a distraction as well as reinforcing approach behavior. These explanations are not applicable to some experiments, such as circle size perception, in which non-avoidance behaviors are manipulated.

Only one study (Krop et al., 1971) has tested Cautela's second assumption that covert events effectively control other covert and overt behavior in the same way as externally applied stimuli, While the covert procedure was more effective than the overt procedure, this was not the strongest test of the assumption since the reinforcers in the two groups were not equated in quantity and quality.

Variability of number of reinforcement trials. Since the number of reinforcers per subjects in three studies (Steffen, 1971; Krop et al., 1971; Krop, Messinger, & Reiner, in press) was dependent upon the idiosyncratic frequency of the behavior, not all subjects received the same number of COR trials. For four of the studies (Cautela, et al., in press; Krop, Messinger, & Reiner, in press; Krop, Perez, & Beaudoin, 1973; Steffan, 1971) a non-contingent reinforcement group imagined the reinforcement on the predetermined schedule. They may have occasionally reinforced a target behavior. One might look at this as a comparison of the relative frequency of reinforcement between the noncontingent group and the COR group. Compared to the no feedback control groups, however, the non-contingent groups did not differ in any of the studies. This critique does not hold true for the non-contingent control groups used by Ascher (1973) and Marshall et al. (1974), since the imagined reinforcement never followed the target behavior.

Extinction of COR. Blanchard & Draper (1973) state the reinforcer in the COR procedure, "may not be necessary for improvement, [but] it is certainly facilitative." This conclusion was based on the results of their control phase for the imagined reinforcer, where approach behavior increased when the subject just imagined the behavior but the increase was not as great as in COR. This phase appears to be more like an extinction phase rather than a test of the necessity of a reinforcer since an initial baseline of the imagined behavior without the reinforcement was not taken.

During the extinction phase, Ascher (1973) found that imagining the behavior to be increased alone did not increase the probability of the target behavior. Secondly, Ascher used only three extinction trials, after 50 COR trials, and had trends (although not statistically significant) toward a return to baseline.

One possible difference in the results is that the rodent phobia was a clinical case, and the subject had more self reinforcement trials outside the clinical setting prior to the extinction phase, and it was thus more difficult to extinguish. This phenomenon requires more study.

Non-correspondence between clinical and experimental definitions of COR. In his original and later description of COR, Cautela (1970c; 1973) has stated that *"both* the response and reinforcing stimulus are presented in imagination."* (Emphasis added.) The experiment by Cautela et al. (in press), the two studies on positive "self-concepts" (Krop et al., 1971; Krop, Perez, & Beaudoin, 1973), eye contact (Krop, Messinger, & Reiner, in press), Flannery's (1972a) first experimental group and Steffan's (1971) study does not technically fit the original COR definition. The behavior to be increased is overt and the reinforcing stimulus is presented in imagination. This does not mean to imply that the studies are hereby discredited. They immediately suggest very strong clinical procedures. Since in the experiments both covert and overt responses were used, we suggest that the definition of covert conditioning be expanded to include covert and overt behavior that is followed by a stimulus presented in imagination. Thus, there are two possible combinations of COR:

Covert behavior: covert stimulus

Overt behavior: covert stimulus

SUGGESTIONS FOR FURTHER RESEARCH

Experimental evidence on COR indicates that it is a successful method of modifying a wide variety of behaviors. Our suggestions for further research focus on (1) standardization of measurements, (2) standardization of design, and (3) process studies i.e., the analysis of effective variables of COR. The following suggestions seem applicable to COR, other covert conditioning techniques, and other behavior modification techniques.

Standardization of Measurements

Further studies in covert conditioning, as mentioned above, should have better measurements. Studies of anxiety should have multiple measures, including physiological, subjective and behavioral, as in Blanchard & Draper's study (1973). In terms of behavioral measures, the subject should be monitored in as close to the target behavior as possible. Paul's (1966) study on systematic desensitization of a speaking phobia could be used as a guideline.

Cautela (1970a; 1973) has defined covert behavior as a thought, feeling or image. Thus there are a number of different behaviors subsumed under the rubric of covert behavior. Covert events are even more elusive because we have no way of observing them. It seems necessary, therefore, that we use multiple measures of subjective reports. It also seems that we should have a measure other than a subjective measure of covert behavior. Research has indicated that there are physiological measures of some covert events, including sexual arousal and imagined aversive events (Barlow et al., 1969; Barlow et al., 1972). Schwartz & Higgins (1971) have shown that there are physiological measures of covert behavior, which are the same as a related overt behavior but of a less intensity. Van Egeren et al. (1971) have found that imagining threatening scenes produces autonomic arousal in direct proportion to the degree of subjective threat associated with the scenes.

Standardization of Design

Standardization of design would allow more meaningful comparisons of studies. Unless the variables listed below are treated as independent variables, we suggest the following standardizations.

Experimenter's characteristics. The experimenter should have previous clinical experience in using behavior modification techniques in general and the covert conditioning techniques specifically. Small, but nonetheless technical questions which arise during an experimental session must be handled smoothly by the experimenter. Otherwise, mishandling of the technical problems might bias subjects' subjective reports. Also, pseudo-treatment "placebo" groups seem to be particularly susceptible to mishandling, given the level of sophistication of many college students.

Instructions "to imagine." The instructions "to imagine" should be standardized. All should use Cautela's instructions presented above.

Imagery. Cautela (1970c; 1973) instructs the client to signal when the image of the behavior to be increased is clear. The client is immediately instructed to switch to the reinforcing scene. Prior to using a stimulus as a reinforcer, Cautela (1970c; 1973) asks the client to rate an imagined reinforcer both on clarity and pleasurableness (i.e., quality of reinforcement) on a zero to five scale. Zero indicates not at all and five indicates very much. Those stimuli rated on four to five both on clarity and pleasurableness are then employed. Secondly, the scene is only used if the reinforcer can be imagined within five seconds following a clear image of the response to be increased. Wisocki (1973a) used this criteria for her study. This follows from Cautela's assumption that overt and covert conditioning obey the same parameters of reinforcement (1970c; 1973). In overt reinforcement, the reinforcer is generally less effective if delayed (Kimble, 1971).

Reinforcement scene duration. Duration of the imagined reinforcer should be held constant. Subjects vary among themselves and from trial to trial with regard to the amount of time required to obtain a clear image. The duration should be measured from the time the subject signals that the image is clear. Subjects held the scene for five seconds in Ascher's study (1973) and for fifteen seconds in Tondo & Cautela (1974). These are limits which are both adequate and not fatiguing.

Intertrial interval. The time between conditioning trials should be controlled. Ascher (1973) had a ten second interval between trials. This seems to be an adequate interval.

Controls. Treatment of controls should be as similar to the experimental procedure as possible. In Flannery (1972a) and Krop, Perez & Beaudoin (1973), control groups were given COR training. Ascher (1973) included COR training in one control group.

Controls should believe that they are in an experimental group and participating in a legitimate procedure. We suggest experimenters hand each subject at the end of each experiment a written note stating: Psychological research generally includes a "real" group and a "pseudo" test group. Check which group you believe you were in: "real" group _____; "pseudo" group _____. While the results of this may be controversial, such public information (contingencies) would help the experimenters strive to treat all groups equally and decrease the possibility of subtle differential shaping by experimenter feedback to different groups. These points concerning the standardization of design, of course, should be empirically investigated. By treating the above as independent variables, we could then determine optimal scene duration, intertrial interval, and the best instructions to imagine.

Process Studies

The studies reviewed above suggest that COR is an effective procedure. Research should now examine what variables, in fact, are responsible for the change.

For example, studies by Barlow et al. (1969) and Barlow et al. (1973) using a single case study design, have shown that the important variable in covert sensitization is the pairing of the behavior to be decreased followed by the aversive scene, and the instructions of expected treatment outcome are not important.

One of the distinct advantages of the covert conditioning procedures in general and COR in particular is its apparent systematization. Clinicans have a wide variety of techniques applicable to many behavioral disorders. The assumption that the overt operant literature may be applicable to covert behavior is heuristically valuable for the researcher.

Other possible further areas of research, we suggest, would be to determine if the parameters of covert conditioning are in fact the same as the parameters of overt conditioning. We know that there are a number of other parameters of overt reinforcement. These include:

1. Intertrial Interval: Conditioning is more effective when there is an interval between conditioning trials. This is to avoid inhibition of reinforcement as Pavlov labeled it (1927) or reactive inhibition, as Hull (1943) conceived it.

2. Immediacy of Reinforcement: Reinforcement is more effective when administered immediately after the response is emitted than when it is delayed (Kimble, 1961).

3. Schedules of Reinforcement: Some schedules of reinforcement produce higher rates of responding than others. For example, differential reinforcement of high rates of responding schedule (DRH) produces a high rate of responding whereas a differential reinforcement of low rates of responding schedule (DRL) produces low rates (Reynolds, 1968).

4. Drive State: Data indicate that when an organism is in a deprived state such as hunger, a reinforcer such as food will have a greater effect on increasing response probability than if the organism is not in a deprived state (Kimble, 1961).

Two studies (Ascher, 1973; Blanchard & Draper, 1973) have studied extinction. Goguen (1973) studied the effects of overlearning on the treatment of smoking behavior using COR and covert sensitization. One group received six additional sessions of treatment after they had stopped smoking. Results of a six week, three month, and six month follow-up indicated that those who had overlearning "showed a significantly lower percentage of recuperation of their pre-experimental smoking level as compared to a control group of smokers who received covert conditioning until they stopped smoking without overlearning."

Baron (1974), using an overt response and a covert reinforcer, investigated some of the parameters of COR. Subjects key pressing was reinforced on a concurrent variable interval schedule. She used reinforcing scenes rated either highly pleasurable or of little pleasure as well as scenes of long and short duration (25 and 5 seconds). Results indicated a significant difference for when reinforcer quality was varied, but not for scene duration.

Parameters specific to the imagery techniques need further investigation. For example, studies examining the subject's imagery clarity have had differing results. Wisocki (1973a) and Baron (1974) both found a significant relationship between a change in behavior and clarity of imagery. Manno & Marston (1972) did not. More recently Tondo & Cautela (1974) used a circle size perception task with high imagery and low imagery experimental and control groups. High imagery-experimental subjects showed a significantly greater behavior change than either low imagery-experimental or high imagery-control subjects. However, there was no main effect for the COR groups.

Although some of the studies reviewed above do not have adequate controls, all have shown to be effective in modifying a number of behaviors. These behaviors include attitudes toward the "mentally retarded" (Cautela et al. 1971), certain behavioral tasks (Steffan, 1971; Ascher, 1973; Tondo & Cautela, 1974; Cautela et al., in press), behaviors where anxiety is the dependent variable (Blanchard & Draper, 1973; Flannery 1972a; Wisocki, 1973a; Marshall et al., 1974) and maladaptive approach behaviors (Manno &

Marston, 1972). These experiments have also shown that COR is effective in a group setting (Manno & Marston, 1972; Wisocki, 1973a; Marshall et al., 1974) and using single case experimental design (Blanchard & Draper, 1973). Although the subject population of most of the above studies were college students, the study by Steffen (1971) and Krop, Perez, & Beaudoin (1973) showed that COR can be effectively used to modify the behavior of psychiatric patients, while the study by Krop et al. (1971) was effective with children who had diagnosed behavioral disorders.

Given the breadth of experimental and clinical cases, which have all been shown to be effective, we feel that fruitful areas of further research in COR include (1) treating the proposed guidelines as independent variables, (2) testing Cautela's assumptions, and (3) determining what variables are important in treatment outcome.

REFERENCES

Ascher, L. M. An analog study of covert positive reinforcement. In R. D. Rubin, J. P. Brady & J. D. Henderson (Eds.), *Advances in behavior therapy* (Vol. 4). New York: Academic Press, 1973.

Barlow, D. H., Leitenberg, H., & Agras, W. S. Experimental control of sexual deviation through manipulation of the noxious scene in covert sensitization. *Journal of Abnormal Psychology,* 1969, **5,** 596-601.

Barlow, D. H., Leitenberg, H., Agras, W. S., Callahan, E. J., & Moore, R. C. The contribution of therapeutic instructions to covert sensitization. *Behaviour Research and Therapy,* 1972, **10,** 411-415.

Barlow, D. H., Reynolds, E. J., & Agras, W. S. Gender identity change in a transsexual. *Archives of General Psychiatry,* 1973, **28,** 569-576.

Baron, M. G. The experimental analyses of imagery: The parameters of covert reinforcement. Unpublished doctoral dissertation, Boston College, 1974.

Bernstein, D. A., & Paul, G. L. Some comments on therapy analogue research with small animal "phobias." *Journal of Behavior Therapy and Experimental Psychiatry,* 1971, **2,** 225-238.

Blanchard, E. G., & Draper, D. C. Treatment of a rodent phobia by covert reinforcement: A single subject experiment. *Behavior Therapy,* 1973, **4,** 559-564.

Cautela, J. R. Treatment of compulsive behavior by covert sensitization. *Psychological Record,* 1966, **16,** 33-41.

Cautela, J. R. Covert sensitization. *Psychological Reports,* 1967, **20,** 459-468.

Cautela, J. R. Covert conditioning. Paper presented at Conference of Private Events, University of West Virginia, Morgantown, West Virginia, April 1970. (a)

Cautela, J. R. Covert negative reinforcement. *Journal of Behavior Therapy and Experimental Psychiatry,* 1970, **1,** 273-278. (b)

Cautela, J. R. Covert reinforcement. *Behavior Therapy,* 1970, **2,** 192-200. (c)

Cautela, J. R. Covert extinction. *Behavior Therapy,* 1971, **2,** 192-200 (a)

Cautela, J. R. Covert modeling. Paper presented at the annual convention of the Association for Advancement of Behavior Therapy, Washington, D. C., September, 1971. (b)

Cautela, J. R. Covert processes and behavior modification. *The Journal of Nervous and Mental Disease*, 1973, **157**, 27-36.

Cautela, J. R., & Baron, M. G. Multifaceted behavior therapy of self-injurious behavior. *Journal of Behavior Therapy and Experimental Psychiatry*, 1973, **4**, 121-131.

Cautela, J. R., & Kastenbaum, R. A reinforcement survey schedule for use in therapy, training and research. *Psychological Reports*, 1967, **20**, 1115-1130.

Cautela, J. R., Steffen, J., & Wish, P. Covert reinforcement: An experimental test. *Journal of Clinical and Consulting Psychology*, in press.

Cautela, J. R., Walsh, K., & Wish, P. The use of covert reinforcement in the modification of attitudes towards the mentally retarded. *Journal of Psychology*, 1971, **77**, 257-260.

Dulaney, D. E., Jr. Hypothesis and habits in verbal "operant conditioning." *Journal of Abnormal and Social Psychology*, 1961, **63**, 261-263.

Flannery, R. B. A laboratory analogue of two covert reinforcement procedures. *Journal of Behavior Therapy and Experimental Psychiatry*, 1972, **3**, 171-177. (a)

Flannery, R. B. Covert conditioning in the behavioral treatment of an agraphobic. *Psychotherapy: Theory, Research, and Practice*, 1972, **9**, 217-220. (b)

Goguen, L. J. Effects of over-learning on covert conditioning. Unpublished doctoral dissertation, University of Montreal, Canada, 1973.

Gotestam, K. G., & Melin, G. H. Covert extinction of amphetamine addiction, *Behavior Therapy*, 1974, **5**, 90-92.

Hull, C. L. *Principles of behavior.* New York: Appleton-Century-Crofts, 1943.

Jurgela, A. The use of covert conditioning in the treatment of attempted suicide. *Journal of Behavior Therapy and Experimental Psychiatry*, in press.

Keehn, J. D., Bloomfield, F. F., & Hug, M. A. Uses of the reinforcement survey schedule with alcoholics. *Quarterly Journal of Studies on Alcohol*, 1970, **31**, 602-615.

Kimble, G. A. *Hilgard and Marquis' conditioning and learning.* New York: Appleton-Century-Crofts, 1961.

Kleinknecht, R. A., McCormick, C. E., & Thorndike, R. M. Stability of stated reinforcers as measured by the reinforcement survey schedule. *Behavior Therapy*, 1973, **3**, 407-413.

Krop, H., Calhoon, B., & Verrier, R. Modification of the "self-concept" of emotionally disturbed children by covert reinforcement. *Behavior Therapy*, 1971, **2**, 201-204.

Krop, H., Messinger, J., & Reiner, C. Increasing eye contact by covert reinforcement. *Interpersonal Development*, in press.

Krop, H., Perez, F., & Beaudoin, C. Modification of "self-concept" of psychiatric patients by covert reinforcement. In R. D. Rubin, J. P. Brady, & J. D. Henderson (Eds.), *Advancement in behavior therapy* (Vol. 4). New York: Academic Press, 1973.

Lang, P. J. The mechanics of desensitization and the laboratory study of human fear. In C. M. Franks (Ed.), *Behavior therapy: Appraisal and status.* New York: McGraw-Hill, 1969.

Manno, B., & Marston, A. Weight reduction as a function of negative covert reinforcement (sensitization) versus positive covert reinforcement. *Behavior Research and Therapy*, 1972, **10**, 201-207.

Marshall, W. L., Boutilier, J., & Minnes, P. The modification of phobic behavior by covert reinforcement. *Behavior Therapy*, 1974, **5**, 469-480.

Mermis, B. J. Self-report of reinforcers and looking time. Unpublished doctoral dissertation, University of Tennessee, 1971.

Paul, G. L. *Insight vs. desensitization in psychotherapy: an experiment in anxiety reduction.* Stanford, California: Stanford University Press, 1966.

Paul, G. L. Outcome of systematic desensitization I: Background procedures and uncontrolled reports of individual treatment. In C. M. Franks (Ed.), *Behavior Therapy: Appraisal and Status.* New York: McGraw-Hill, 1969. (a)

Paul, G. L. Outcome of systematic desensitization II: Controlled investigations of individual treatment, technique variations and current status. In C. M. Franks (Ed.), *Behavior therapy: Appraisal and status.* New York: McGraw-Hill, 1969. (b)

Pavlov, I. P. *Conditioned reflexes.* Translated by G. V. Anrep. London: Oxford University Press, 1927.

Reynolds, G. S. *A primer of operant conditioning.* Glenview, Ill.: Scott Foresman Inc., 1968.

Salzinger, K. The place of operant conditioning of verbal behavior in psychotherapy. In C. M. Franks (Ed.), *Behavior therapy: Appraisal and status.* New York: McGraw-Hill, 1969.

Schwartz, G. E., & Higgins, J. D. Cardiac activity preparatory to overt and covert behavior. *Science*, 1971, **173**, 1114-1146.

Steinfeld, G. J., Rautio, E. A., Egan, M., & Rice, A. H. The use of covert sensitization with narcotic addicts. (Further Comments) Unpublished manuscript, Federal Correctional Institution, Danbury, Conn., 1972.

Steffan, J. Covert reinforcement with schizophrenics. Paper presented at the annual convention of the Association for Advancement of Behavior Therapy, Washington, D. C., September, 1971.

Tondo, T. R., & Cautela, J. R. Assessment of imagery in covert reinforcement. *Psychological Reports*, 1974, **34**, 1271-1280.

Van Egeren, L. F., Feather, B. W., & Hein, P. L. Desensitization of phobias: Some psychophysiological propositions. *Psychophysiology*, 1971, **2**, 213-228.

Wisocki, P. A. Treatment of obsessive compulsive behavior by the application of covert sensitization and covert reinforcement: A case report. *Journal of Behavior Therapy and Experimental Psychiatry*, 1970, **1**, 233-239.

Wisocki, P. A. A covert reinforcement program for the treatment of test anxiety: Brief report. *Behavior Therapy*, 1973, **4**, 264-266. (a)

Wisocki, P. A. The successful treatment of heroin addiction by covert conditioning techniques. *Journal of Behavior Therapy and Experimental Psychiatry*, 1973, **4**, 55-61. (b)

Wolpe, J. *Psychotherapy by reciprocal inhibition.* Stanford: Stanford University Press, 1958.

Wolpe, J. The discontinuity of neurosis and schizophrenia. *Behavior Research and Therapy*, 1970, **8**, 179-188.

SECTION IV
COVERT NEGATIVE
REINFORCEMENT

Chapter 14
Covert Negative Reinforcement*†
Joseph R. Cautela

Summary — Covert Negative Reinforcement (CNR) is designed to increase the probability of a response by instructing a subject to imagine an aversive event and to terminate it by imagining the response to be increased. Examples of the applications of the procedure to maladaptive avoidance and approach behaviors are presented. The relation of the peocedure to the escape conditioning paradigm is discussed.

For such behaviorists as Watson (1925) and Skinner (1969), private events have no place in the science of psychology. Other writers, such as Pavlov (1927), Guthrie (1935), Tolman (1948) and Hull (1952) developed constructs to deal with the private events of human organisms. Within the behavior modification framework, investigators such as Wolpe (1958), Lazarus and Ambramovitz (1962) and Stampfl (1967) have employed the manipulation of imagery to modify covert and overt behaviors.

Two previous papers (Cautela, 1966, 1967) have described a procedure labeled "covert sensitization", designed to decrease the probability of maladaptive approach behavior. Covert sensitization follows the punishment paradigm in that an aversive stimulus accompanies or immediately succeeds the response to be decreased. The procedure is called "covert" because both the response to be decreased and the aversive stimulus are presented in imagination via instructions. Experimental evidence of the effectiveness of

---

*Reprinted with permission from the *Journal of Behavior Therapy and Experimental Psychiatry*, 1970, *1*, 273-278. ©Pergamon Press.

†This paper is based in part on a paper presented to the Conference on the Psychology of Private Events at West Virginia University, Morgantown, West Virginia, on 10 April 1970. The author expresses his appreciation to Miss Mary Grace Baron for her suggestions and careful reading of the manuscript.

covert sensitization has been provided by Ashem and Donner (1968); Barlow, Leitenberg and Agras (1969); Mullen (1968); Stuart (1967); Viernstein (1968) and Wagner and Bragg (1968).

More recently (Cautela, 1970), I have described a procedure to *increase* response probability by manipulation of imagery. This procedure is called "covert reinforcement". The patient is instructed to imagine he is performing the response to be increased; and when he indicates that the image is clear, the therapist pronounces the word, "reinforcement", which is the signal for the patient immediately to imagine a stimulus reinforceing to him (e.g. eating candy or making a grand slam in bridge). The patient is assigned the homework practice of scenes every day. A number of reports have supported the therapeutic efficacy of this technique (Cautela, Steffen and Wish, 1970; Cautela, Walsh and Wish, 1970; Flannery, 1970; Krop, 1970). Because it employs the positive reinforcement paradigm (i.e. the reinforcing stimulus is presented after the response to be increased), the technique is labeled "covert positive reinforcement" (CPR).

Although the CPR procedure can be applied to many behavioral problems, the author has encountered some difficulty with patients who claim they know of nothing reinforcing that they can imagine. When encouraged to imagine a possible reinforcing situation (e.g. winning a lot of money) they claim difficulty in obtaining a clear image. If these same patients are asked to imagine some disagreeable or anxiety-provoking experience, they may state that they are able to imagine such events because they have occurred so often in their lives. With this kind of patient I have developed a technique following the escape conditioning paradigm, labeled "covert negative reinforcement" (CNR). In the escape conditioning paradigm, a noxious stimulus is terminated when a response designated by the experimenter is performed by the subject. This procedure usually leads to an increase in the probability of the response designated (Dinsmoor, 1969).

It is the purpose of this paper to describe the CNR procedure and some examples of its clinical application; and to present some of the data from studies on escape conditioning which have been used to increase the effectiveness of the procedure. In addition, some recent experimental data will be reported showing that negatively reinforcing events presented in imagination can increase response probability.

DESCRIPTION OF THE PROCEDURE

After the usual behavior assessment (Cautela, 1968) and the determination that the CNR procedure will be used to modify the patient's behavior, he is given the following instructions:

"Experiments with animals and humans have shown that if a response is accompanied by the termination of a noxious or aversive stimulus, the probability of that response tends to increase in frequency. Now we are going to use the same procedure except that we are going to do the whole thing in imagination.'' The exact presentation of the rationale depends on sophistication and level of comprehension of the patient.

Elicitation of Aversive Stimuli

The Fear Survey Schedule (Wolpe and Lang, 1964) is followed by an interview to establish possible aversive stimuli. In the interview, the therapist asks such questions as the following:

''What is the most frightening scene or experience that you can imagine?''
''Tell me something you're afraid of that may not be on the questionnaire I just gave you.''

Some examples of responses to these questions are:

''I get very upset and up-tight when people yell at me.''
''I get very anxious when someone tells me to do something in a harsh tone.''

The therapist continues with further inquiry such as, ''Of the people that yell at you, who most upsets you when he or she yells at you?'' Having obtained an answer, the therapist instructs the patient in the following manner:

''Now close your eyes. I want you to imagine that your girlfriend's mother is yelling at you. Try to imagine you hear her voice and see her face in anger. All right, now try it. Raise you index finger when you feel that the scene is clear.'' When the patient signals, the therapist says, ''How clear did you get the scene? Did you get upset when your girlfriend's mother yelled at you?'' If the answer is in the affirmative, the therapist then says, ''All right, now I want you to imagine the scene again. This time, when you raise your finger, I will say the word, 'shift'. As soon as I do, quickly erase the scene from your mind.''

A suitable aversive stimulus has the following properties:

(1). The patient says the stimulus (e.g. rat) elicits fear.

(2). The patient reports he can clearly imagine the stimulus.

(3). The image of the stimulus produces responses similar to those to its external presentation (i.e. fear).

(4). The patient is able to terminate the image immediately at the request of the therapist with little or no residual discomfort. This is necessary to avoid contiguity between the aversive stimulus and the response to be increased. Otherwise, a *decrease* in the probability of the response may occur.

Instructions Given to the Patient

After the response to be increased has been determined the patient is given the following instructions:

''In a minute, I'm going to ask you to close your eyes. I will then ask you to imagine the scene in which you . . . (a description of the particular noxious scene chosen for use). When the scene is clear and you feel upset, raise your right index finger. I will then say the word, 'response'. Then immediately shift to the scene in which you . . . (a description of the response to be increased). As soon as that scene is clear, again signal with your right index finger.''

Great care is taken to insure that the patient can immediately withdraw the aversive stimulus upon request and replace it with the response to be increased. If, after a number of trials, there is still an overlap, a new aversive stimulus is chosen. Though the cessation of the noxious stimulus should occur as soon as the response to be increased occurs for optimal effectiveness, there is some evidence (Leitenberg, 1965) that in escape conditioning employing shock, delaying shock offset still leads to escape conditioning. Thus, in all probability, even if the patient does not report accurately the relationship between the aversive image and the response to be increased, the CNR procedure can be somewhat effective. Also if the patient reports that he has difficulty in terminating the noxious stimulus immediately upon the initiation of the response to be increased, it does not preclude the possibility of using CNR in an effective manner. In these cases, the patient's behavior should be carefully monitored to determine whether response probability is increasing or decreasing. There is no certain way to judge whether patients have practiced the procedure as instructed. However, it is presented in such a manner that they are usually not reluctant to report when they have not practiced.

With some patients there is a noticeable increase in the response (therefore, a decrease in the maladaptive behavior) after the first 2 or 3 sessions. In other cases, 5 or 6 sessions are needed. In general, no more than 15 sessions are needed to produce a great improvement in behavior. In the cases in which CNR has been used I estimate that it has been successful in 90 per cent.

Examples of CNR Scenes used to Treat Maladaptive Approach and Avoidance Behaviors

The following are examples in which CNR has been successfully applied. They are illustrations of the contexts of CNR procedure. Details of the treatment are not given.

Treatment of maladaptive avoidance behavior. A boy with a school phobia was asked to imagine that his arm was bleeding (aversive stimulus). He then shifted to the image of walking to school and saying to himself, ''It doesn't matter if the teacher criticizes me. I am going to school to learn what I can.''

A girl who would not leave her house because of fear of being sexually attacked was asked to imagine she was hearing sirens (which she reported as being highly aversive to her). She then shifted to walking outside her house on a bright sunny day. With repetition, she acquired feeling that it was great and safe to be out and enjoying the world. Removal of the anxiety response to walking outside the house combined with encouragement by the therapist actually to do so led to the performance of the behavior *in vivo* which she had previously practiced in imagination.

A man who was impotent was asked to imagine that his boss was yelling at him (aversive stimulus). Then immediately he switched to a scene in which he was lying in bed naked next to his wife and feeling relaxed.

A girl who was afraid to say anything at a party when a man walked up to her, imagined she was just about to fall off a high building (aversive stimulus) and then shifted to responding to a man's questions about her work, hobbies, etc.

Treatment of maladaptive approach behavior. A teenager, who wanted to stop smoking pot, was asked to imagine he was being ridiculed by his friends (aversive stimulus). He then switched to a scene in which he was refusing pot when it was offered to him.

An alcoholic who wished to be treated for that problem was told to imagine that his teeth were being drilled by a dentist (aversive stimulus) and then to shift to having an urge to drink, but saying, "It's stupid to drink", and finally deciding not to take a drink.

A homosexual imagined a rat approaching his throat (aversive stimulus); and then shifted to hugging a naked girl.

An obese girl imagined she was being called a "fat pig" by some handsome men (aversive stimulus). Then she switched to resisting an urge to eat between meals.

DISCUSSION

Experimental Bases for CNR Procedure

Empirical studies on escape conditioning have established some parameters relevant to the CNR procedure.

1. The rate of responding is a function of the intensity of the aversive stimulus. As the intensity of the aversive stimulus increases, there is a likelihood of increase in response probability (Reynolds, 1968, p. 105). An extremely aversive stimulus, however, can so disrupt the organism that the escape response is not apt to occur (Dinsmoor, 1968). The extremely aversive stimulus elicits responses incompatible with escape behavior.

2. The closer the response to be increased follows the termination of the noxious stimulus, the stronger will be the conditioning (Dinsmoor, 1968).

3. After training and maintainance of an escape response with an aversive stimulus of a high intensity, a stimulus of low intensity may be sufficient to maintain escape behavior, even though this low intensity was previously ineffective (Reynolds, 1968, p. 105).

4. A study performed by Cautela and Wisocki (1969) appears to be directly relevant to the CNR procedure. Forty-nine undergraduates received a checklist composed of 18 positive and 22 negative statements about elderly people. They were asked to rate how they felt about each item. One week later, about half of these students (the experimental group) were asked to imagine a scene

in which they were bleeding and in pain and were comforted by an elderly person. They were told to practice imagining this scene twice a day. Ten days later the experimental group showed a significant positive increase in attitude toward the aged (P <0.01), in contrast to the control group who did not imagine this scene. The control group scored a slightly negative nonsignificant change (P > 0.05). Ss who reported practicing the scene at home showed a significantly higher increase in scores (P < 0.01) than did the Ss who did not report home practice.

SOME PRACTICAL CONSIDERATIONS

1. When I first contemplated the use of the CNR procedure, I was concerned over the possibility of increasing the reaction to the aversive stimulus to such an extent that it would be detrimental to the patient. This concern, however, was not only not realized, but some patients actually reported a decrease in the aversive properties of the aversive stimulus. There are a number of possible reasons for this: (a) Satiation may have occurred as a result of repeated exposure. There is some experimental evidence that animals (Kellogg, 1941) and humans (MacDonald, 1946; Schneider and Baker, 1958; Seward and Seward, 1934) have decreased responding after repeated presentations of shock. In animals, sometimes higher levels of shock are needed to maintain responses such as leg flexion. In humans, decreases in physiological measures, general body movements, and verbal reports of painfulness have been noted. (b) The patient has control over the aversive stimulus and can terminate it when he so desires. This control over the aversive stimulus can result in a decrease in its aversive properties (Vernon, 1969). (c) The organism learns to make an adaptive response (even if it is unrelated to the aversive stimulus) when the aversive stimulus occurs. The aversive stimulus becomes associated with appropriate responding and therefore loses some of its aversive properties. For example, one patient who, with the CNR procedure, increased her distance of walking from her house, related that she walked five blocks (her previous level was four blocks) from her house one day when her stove blew up. She reported that previously she would have become upset and depressed "about something like this". This time she informed the appropriate people (landlord and husband), checked everything, and then decided that there was no point in brooding about it, and walked away from her house. A new adaptive response (calling the appropriate people) was substituted for "being upset and depressed".

2. It is probably not good procedure to use stimuli that produce nausea because it is unlikely that nausea will disapper immediately when the patient is requested to stop thinking of that stimulus. If the nausea is present when the response to be increased is presented, then by contiguous conditioning the response to be increased may acquire aversive properties, and thereby actually decrease response probability. There is some empirical evidence for this

assumption. In an experimental study on the effect of covert sensitization on alcoholism, Ashem and Donner (1968) found that in a backward conditioning group in which nausea was presented before the conditioned stimulus, the treatment was as effective as in a forward conditioning group in reducing alcohol intake. Some of the subjects in the backward conditioning group indicated that they felt nausea when the conditioned stimulus was presented in imagination.

3. While I agree with Skinner (1969), Rachman and Teasdale (1969) and others that whenever possible the use of positive reinforcement is to be preferred to negative reinforcement because it is more humane and is less apt to have maladaptive side-effects, yet, according to Dinsmoor (1968) negative reinforcement has some advantages over positive reinforcement. Responses are more firmly learned; there is less danger of satiation; and it is not necessary to deprive the organism. In the clinical use of reinforcement by imagery, negative reinforcement is necessary when the positive reinforcement procedure cannot be presented because of lack of cooperation by the patient who claims either a lack of available reinforcers or poor imagery of positive reinforcers. Also it is my impression that if a patient begins the therapy session in an anxious or hostile manner (because of events during the previous week or just prior to the therapy session), it is easier to begin almost immediately with CNR, whereas with conditioned positive reinforcement (CPR) the patient usually has to be calmed down a little before he can cooperate.

4. Sometimes the CPR can be combined with CNR and/or covert sensitization to modify behavior. Wisocki (1970) applied a combination of covert sensitization and CPR to eliminate severe compulsive behavior.

COMPARISON OF CNR AND THE CODITIONING OF "ANXIETY-RELIEF" RESPONSES

Wolpe has employed a procedure involving the conditioning of "anxiety-relief" responses which has some similarity to the CNR procedure (Wolpe, 1958, pp. 108-181). In the "anxiety-relief" procedure an aversive electrical shock is applied to the forearm and the patient is instructed to endure the shock until the desire to have it stop becomes very strong, and then to say the word, "calm", the current is turned off. After a number of conditioning trials, Wolpe reports that by saying the word, "calm", some patients can reduce the intensity of anxiety encountered in the course of day-to-day living. Meyer (1956) used the "anxiety-relief" method for desensitization of phobias by instructing the patient to say "calm" when in the presence of the specific anxiety-producing stimuli.

There are two major differences between the "anxiety-relief" conditioning and CNR:

1. In the CNR procedure the aversive stimulus is presented in imagination

through instructions. In the "anxiety-relief" procedure the aversive stimulus is externally applied.

2. The purpose of the CNR procedure is to increase response probability. The main object of the "anxiety-relief" procedure is to produce a reduction in anxiety (which may, of course, lead to the increase in probability of an approach response).

CONCLUSION

CNR appears to be an effective procedure for use in behavior modification. It can be used if the patient is capable of producing clear imagery in at least one or two sense modalities. Controlled studies are being planned for evaluation of the effectiveness of CNR. They include a study comparing the effectiveness of the CPR and CNR procedures, and a comparison with other procedures employing imagery, such as desensitization and implosive therapy.

REFERENCES

Ashem B. and Donner L. (1968) Covert sensitization with alcoholics: a controlled replication. *Behav. Res. & Therapy* **6**, 7–12.

Barlow D. H., Leitenberg H. and Agras W. S. (1969) Experimental control of sexual deviation through manipulation of the noxious scene in covert sensitization. *J. abnorm Psychol.* **5**, 596–601.

Cautela J. R. (1966) Treatment of compulsive behavior by covert sensitization. *Psychol. Rec.* **16**, 33–41.

Cautela J. R. (1967) Covert sensitization. *Psychol. Rec.* **20**, 459–468.

Cautela J. R. (1968) Behavior therapy and the need for behavioral assessment. *Psychother. Theory, Res., Pract.* 5, 175–179.

Cautela J. R. (1969) Behavior therapy and self-control: techniques and implications, in *Behavior Therapy: Appraisal and Status* (Edited by C. M. Franks). McGraw-Hill, New York.

Cautela J. R. (1970) Covert reinforcement. *Behav. Therapy* **1**, 33–50.

Cautela J. R., Steffen J. and Wish P. (1970) An experimental test of covert reinforcement. Paper presented at the American Psychological Association, Miami, Florida. (Mimeographed.)

Cautela J. R., Walsh K. and Wish P. (1970) The use of covert reinforcement to modify attitudes toward retardates. *J Soc. Psychol.* In press.

Cautela J. R. and Wisocki P. A. (1969) The use of imagery in the modification of attitudes toward the elderly: a preliminary report. *J. Psychol.* **73**, 193–199.

Dinsmoor J. A. (1968) Escape from shock as a conditioning technique. *Miami Symposium on the Prediction of Behavior, 1967: Aversive Stimulation.* (Edited by M. Jones), University of Miami Press, Miami.

Flannery R. (1970) An investigation of differential effectiveness of office vs. *in vivo* therapy of a simple phobia: an outcome study. Unpublished doctoral dissertation, University of Windsor.

Guthrie E. R. (1935) *The Psychology of Learning.* Harper, New York.

Hull C. L. (1952) *A Behavior System,* Yale University Press, New Haven.

Kellogg W. N. (1941) Electric shock as a motivating stimulus in conditioning experiments. *J. Gen. Psychol.* **25,** 85–96.

Krop H. (1970) The use of covert reinforcement to modify children's self-concept, Unpublished data, South Florida State Hospital.

Lazarus A. A. and Abramovitz A. (1962) The use of "emotive imagery" in the treatment of children's phobias. *J. ment. Sci.* **106,** 191–195.

Leitenberg H. (1965) Response initiation and response termination: analysis of effects of punishment and escape contingencies. *Psychol. Rep.* **16,** 569–575.

MacDonald A. (1946) The effect of adaptation to the unconditioned stimulus upon the formation of conditioned avoidance responses, *J. exp. Psychol.* **36,** 1–12.

Meyer V. (1956) Cited by J. Wolpe (1958) *Psychotherapy by Reciprocal Inhibition,* Stanford University Press, Stanford.

Mullen F. G. (1968) The effects of covert sensitization on smoking behavior. Unpublished study, Queens College, Charlottesville, North Carolina.

Pavlov I. P. (1927) *Conditioned Reflexes* (Translated by G. V. Anrep). Oxford University Press, London.

Rachman S. and Teasdale A. (1969) *Aversive Therapy,* University of Miami Press, Coral Gables, Florida.

Reynolds G. S. (1968) *A Primer of Operant Conditioning.* Scott, Foresman, Glenview, Illinois.

Schneider M. and Baker K. E. (1958) The drive-level of different intensities of electric shock. *Am. J. Psychol.* **71,** 587–590.

Seward J. P. and Seward G. H. (1934) The effect of repetition on reactions to electric shock: with special reference to the menstrual cycle. *Arch. Psychol.* **27,** 103 pages.

Skinner B. F. (1969). The machine that is man. *Psychology Today* **2,** 20–25.

Stampfl T. G. (1967) Implosive therapy, Part 1: The theory, in *Behavior Modification Techniques and the Treatment of Emotional Disorders* (Edited by S. G. Armitage), U.S. Publications, Battle Creek, Michigan.

Stuart R. (1967) Behavioral control of over-eating. *Behav. Res. & Therapy* **5,** 357–365.

Tolman E. C. (1948) Cognitive maps in rats and men. *Psychol. Rev.* **55,** 189–208.

Vernon W. M. (1969) Comparative aversiveness of self-delivered vs. other-delivered shock, *Proceedings 77th Annual Convention, American Psychological Association,* 813–814.

Viernstein L. (1968) Evaluation of therapeutic techniques of covert sensitization. Unpublished data, Queens College, Charlottesville, North Carolina.

Wagner M. K. and Bragg R. A. (1968) Comparing behavior modification methods for habit decrement-smoking. Unpublished data, V. A. Hospital, Salisbury, North Carolina.

Watson J. B. (1925) *Behaviorism.* Horton, New York.

Wisocki P. A. (1970) Treatment of obsessive-compulsive behavior by covert sensitization and covert reinforcement: A case report. *J. Behav. Ther. & Exp. Psychiat.* **1,** 233–239.

Wolpe, J. (1958) *Psychotherapy by Reciprocal Inhibition.* Stanford University Press, Stanford.

Wolpe J. and Lang P. J. (1964) A fear survey schedule for use in behavior therapy. *Behav. Res. & Therapy* **2,** 27–30.

Chapter 15
Covert Negative Reinforcement: An Experimental Test*

L. Michael Ascher and Joseph R. Cautela

Summary — Ss in the experimental group were asked to imagine an idiosyncratic noxious scene the cessation of which would be contingent upon imagining a neutral stimulus (a ringing bell). This was repeated 30 times. A second group was asked to imagine noxious and neutral scenes in an unpaired manner. A third group received no imagery training. In the experimental test phase, all Ss were asked to estimate the size of circles to establish a baseline. With Groups 1 and 2, E said the word "bell" when the Ss either overestimated (during the over-estimation condition) or underestimated (during the under-estimation condition) the size of the circles. Deviation of the estimates of circle size was influenced by use of the word "bell" in Group 1 only supporting the covert negative reinforcement hypothesis.

The experiment here described was designed to test covert negative reinforcement, a clinical procedure put forward by Cautela (1970a). Cautela (1970b) has previously described covert positive reinforcement in which the patient imagines reinforcing scenes following images of adaptive behavior. This technique of covert negative reinforcement follows the escape conditioning paradigm. The patient is asked to imagine an unpleasant situation, and then to imagine performing the adaptive response whose frequency the therapist wishes to increase. It is first necessary to identify several scenes which can serve as "noxious stimuli". Such scenes may be obtained from the Fear Survey Schedule (Wolpe and Lang, 1964) or from direct questioning (e.g.

*Reprinted with permission from the *Journal of Behavior Therapy and Experimental Psychiatry*, 1972, *3*, 1-5. ©Pergamon Press.

details about fears, disappointments, embarrassments). Terminating these unpleasant scenes after the image of the adaptive behavior, will then be a source of reinforcement.

An example of the application of covert negative reinforcement will clarify this description. A lawyer, preparing to take the Bar examination after having failed it several times, might complain of having so much anxiety that he has decided to wait and take it when he feels less anxious. Covert negative reinforcement would follow this outline: After identifying several noxious scenes, the therapist says "I want you to imagine (a particular) unpleasant scene. Signal by raising your right index finger when it is clear". The patient signals and the therapist says "Now I want you to imagine that you are doing all the things necessary before leaving your home for the exam. Signal when the image is vivid." The patient signals. After an interval, to prevent associating the offset of the adaptive image with the onset of the noxious image, the next pair of scenes is presented. "I want you again to imagine the unpleasant scene that you have previously described, and signal when it is clear." The patient signals. "Now imagine that you are in your car, driving to the place where the exam will be administered, and rehearsing some last minute information. Signal when this is clear." Each time, the noxious scene is presented first, followed by a step in the serial process which brings the patient from his home to the examination. The cessation of the noxious scene is always contingent upon the patient's imagining a scene in which he is performing the adaptive response. The present study is an attempt to provide some experimental validation for this clinical technique.

METHOD

Subjects

Thirty male and female college students ranging in age from 19 to 25 were randomly selected for this study.

Apparatus

The stimulus material consisted of eighteen 35 mm slides of circles whose diameter increased by 1 in. from 4 to 9 in. when projected on a screen 15 ft from the projector. Each circle size (4, 5, 6, 7, 8, 9 in. diameters) appeared three times. A standard beaded projection screen and Kodak Carousel projector were used to present the stimulus material.

Procedure

The thirty students were randomly assigned to three groups of ten Ss each.

(A) **Training phase.** The experimental Ss were individually given the following instructions:

> We have asked you here to participate in an experiment which deals with imagination and creativity. The first part of the study concerns your repeated imagination of two types of scenes one which you will create and one which I will instruct you to imagine. You will be asked to imagine the two scenes alternately in order that you do not become bored with either. Any questions which you may have will be answered at the conclusion of the experiment.
>
> I would like you to imagine the most noxious situation that you have ever experienced. There are many reasons why some event might be noxious; perhaps it was very frightening, disgusting, strange, disappointing etc. I want you to think for a few minutes and then describe, in as much detail as is possible, the scene which you feel is the most noxious that you have ever experienced.

When S reported an appropriate scene, E tried to make it as vivid as possible. This was done by questioning S regarding all details which seemed ambiguous, and by having S embellish the description with additional material. E then said:

> Now I want you to imagine the scene as we have described it. When it is clearly in your mind, please signal by raising the index finger of your right hand.

E waited 5 sec after Ss' signal before proceeding to the next step:

> Now I want you to imagine that a bell is ringing (E rang a medium sized bell, loudly for 5 sec). Imagine the bell is ringing, just as I have rung it for you. I want you to imagine that the bell is ringing, and as you imagine this, the noxious scene will disappear, and all that will remain is the sound of the ringing bell.

S was instructed to imagine the noxious scene, followed by the bell, on 30 occasions. Each time the instructions were the same. E first had S imagine the noxious scene as vividly as possible, for 5 sec. Then E said, ''bell.'' S was instructed to hold this image for 5 sec. A rest interval of 30 sec separated each pairing.

A similar training procedure was followed with Ss in control ''A'' except that the scenes of the noxious event and the ringing bell were not paired. S was first instructed to imagine a ringing bell; this was performed 30 times with a 15-sec intertrial interval. Following this, S was instructed to imagine the noxious scene 30 times, with a 15-sec intertrial interval.

Although Ss in control group ''B'' received no formal training instructions, they did take part in an informal interview situation during which the E spent approximately the same amount of time, prior to the testing phase of the experiment, as he did with the above two groups.

(B) **Testing phase.** Following the training session, each S was taken into a dark room in which the projector and the screen had previously been set up. The following instructions were then administered:

You are going to see a series of circles. I want you to estimate the size of their diameters in inches.

The stimuli were presented under three conditions using three different randomly determined orders. Each conditon involved the presentation of each of the six stimuli three times; thus each condition required 18 trials. Under the control condition, which occurred first, the stimuli were presented without comment by E. In the remaining two conditions, E said "bell", either after an over-estimation by S during the 'over-estimation' condition, or after an under-estimation during the 'under-estimation' condition. The latter two conditions were counter-balanced for each S within each S group (i.e. experimental, control "A", control "B"), and were separated by a buffer presentation of the stimuli during which E made no comments. Subjects who inquired about the E's sporadic reciting of the word "bell", were informed that questions would be answered at the end of the study. The Ss in control group "B" followed the same procedure during the experiment proper as was followed by the experimental group. Since they were matched controls, they were reinforced in a manner identical to their matched experimental group partners.

RESULTS

Table 1 shows the means and the standard deviations for performance under the three experimental conditions for each of the three groups. While the differences among these means are very small, the standard deviations are also extremely small. Inspection of the results indicates that the treatment means for the experimental group are in the direction predicted, i.e., the means increase from the under-estimation condition, through the control condition, to the over-estimation condition. The treatment means for the control groups are not in this predicted direction.

The results of the analysis of variance which was performed on the data of the three groups yielded significant differences for the overall group perfor-

Table 15.1 Means and Standard deviations of circle-size judgments for the three experimental conditions within the three subject groups

Group	X	SD	Under-estimation X	Under-estimation SD	Over-estimation X	Over-estimation SD
Exp	51·827	1·080	48·733	1·124	56·511	1·011
Con-A	52·200	1·374	52·357	0·527	51·621	0·887
Con-B	50·310	2·593	51·066	2·757	49·513	2·265

mances (F (2, 227) = 6 •08, P < 0 •01), for the overall treatment performances (F (2, 27) = 15 •64, P < 0 •001), and for the interaction (F (4, 54) = 40 •26, P < 0 •001). In order to determine which conditions were responsible for these significant differences, a Duncan Range test was performed which indicated that, in the case of the experimental group, the means for the under-estimation and over-estimation conditions were significantly different from the mean for the control condition (0 •05 and 0 •001 levels, respectively). The mean for the over-estimation condition was also significantly larger than that for the under-estimation condition (0 •001 level). No significant treatment differences were found within either of the two control groups. Overall, there were no significant differences (P70 •05) among any of the seven control conditions.

The Ss were given a short, post-experiment interview to determine if they knew the purpose of the experiment beforehand. The results of the interview indicated that the Ss did not guess the purpose of the experiment.

DISCUSSION

While the results of the present study support the hypotheses derived from the work of Cautela (1970a, b), the present experiment is actually an indirect test of Cautela's covert negative reinforcement procedure. This procedure, based on the escape conditioning paradigm, effects an increase in the probability of an adaptive response by pairing it directly with the cessation of some noxious stimulation. In the present case, a stimulus first associated with ending noxious stimulation was later used to increase the frequency of response with which it was associated. However, one could interpret Cautela's reported success with the covert negative response accruing reinforcement properties from being associated with ending the noxious stimulation. While this is not the typical method used to invest a neutral stimulus with secondary reinforcing properties, there is some literature which indicates that a neutral stimulus, when paired with the cessation of ongoing noxious stimulation, will come to acquire secondary reinforcing properties, there is some literature which indicates that a neutral stimulus, when paired with the cessation of ongoing noxious stimulation, will come to acquire secondary reinforcing properties (Barlow, 1956; Goodson and Brownstein, 1955; Mowrer, 1956; Mowrer and Aiken, 1954; Nefsger, 1957; Smith and Buchanan, 1954).

However, there is also a good deal of evidence which suggests that such a procedure is ineffective in generating secondary reinforcement (Beck, 1961; Siegel and Milby, 1969, Siegel and O'Bannon, 1969). These studies indicate that a neutral stimulus, applied when the shock ends, will not acquire secondary reinforcing properties. Since this paper proposes this negative reinforcement procedure as the basis of the present findings, it becomes necessary to consider possible alternative explanations for these findings.

The most obvious explanation, and one suggested by the work of Dulaney (1961), is that Ss had hypotheses about the purpose of the study which influenced their behavior. Several procedural components were incorporated to subvert such hypotheses: instructions were designed to suggest that the study had another purpose; questions were not answered until the experiment had been concluded; the relatively objective experimental task was difficult to fake. This explanation seems highly improbable, even though the information obtained from the Ss about their awareness of the purposes of the experiment at the post-experimental interview was probably not exhaustive.

Another hypothesis is suggested by the work of Asch (1954) and Luchins and Luchins (1968). These studies indicate that Ss' perceptual judgment of relatively objective stimuli are readily influenced by social reinforcement and social pressure. Applying such an hypothesis to the present data, it might be suggested that these results were not due to the proposed operation of covert negative reinforcement in investing "bell" with secondary reinforcing properties, but to the social reinforcement or pressure provided by E in simply making some verbal response differentially to Ss' behavior. However, the social reinforcement hypothesis becomes difficult to sustain when the control groups are considered. If we were simply dealing with a verbal reinforcement effect (e.g. Greenspoon, 1955), then the performance of control groups "A" and "B" would be closer to that of the experimental group.

REFERENCES

Asch S. E. (1958) Effects of group pressure upon the modification and distortion of judgements, *Readings in Social Psychology* (Edited by Maccoby E. E., Newcomb T. M., and Hartley E. L.) (3d. ed.), Holt, Rinehart and Winston, N.Y.

Barlow J. A. (1956) Secondary motivation through classical conditioning: A reconsideration of the nature of backward conditioning, *Psychol. Rev.* **63**, 406–408.

Beck R. C. (1961) On secondary reinforcement and shock termination, *Psych. Bull.* **58**, 28–45.

Cautela J. R. (1970a) Covert negative reinforcement, *J. Behav. Ther. & Exp. Psychiat.* **1**, 273–278.

Cautela J. R. (1970b) Covert reinforcement, *Behav. Ther.* **1**, 33–50.

Dulaney D. E., Jr. (1961) Hypotheses and habits in verbal "Operant conditoning", *J. Abnorm. Soc. Psychol.* **63**, 261–263.

Goodson F. E. and Brownstein A. (1955) Secondary reinforcing and motivating properties of stimuli contiguous with shock onset and termination, *J. Comp. physiol. Psychol.* **48**, 381–386.

Greenspoon J. (1955) The reinforcing effect of two spoken sounds on the frequency of two responses. *Am. J. Psychol.* **68**, 409–416.

Luchins A. S. and Luchins E. H. (1968) Motivation to tell the truth vs. social influences, *J soc. Psychol.* **76**, 97–105.

Mowrer O. H. (1956) Two-factor learning theory reconsidered, with special reference to secondary reinforcement and the concept of habit, *Psychol. Rev.* **63**, 114–128.

Mowrer O. H. and Aiken E. G. (1954) Contiguity vs. drive-reduction in conditioned fear: Temporal variations in conditioned and unconditioned stimulus *Am. J. Psychol.* **67**, 26–38.

Nefsger M. D. (1957) The properties of stimuli associated with shock reduction, *J. exp. Psychol.* **53**, 184–188.

Siegel P. S. and Milby J. B., Jr. (1969) Secondary reinforcement in relation to shock termination: Second chapter *Psych. Bull.* **72**, 146–156.

Siegel P. S. and O'Bannon R. (1969) Establishment of a conditioned reinforcer in relation to shock termination: An attempt to replicate, *Psychonomic Sci.* **17**, 158–159.

Smith M. P. and Buchanan G. (1954) Acquisition of secondary reward by cues associated with shock reduction, *J. exp. Psychol.* **48**, 123–126.

Wolpe J. and Lange P. J. (1964) A fear survey schedule for use in behavior therapy *Behav. Res. & Therapy* **2**, 27–30.

Chapter 16

The Use of Imagery in the Modification of Attitudes Toward the Elderly: A Preliminary Report*

Joseph R. Cautela and Patricia A. Wisocki

Summary — The purpose of the study was to attempt to change the attitudes of college students toward the elderly by the manipulation of imagery. It was hypothesized that pairing (in imagination) a reinforcing situation with an elderly individual would result in behavior change toward elderly people in general. Results indicated significant changes in the positive direction on an attitude questionnaire for the experimental group and no significant changes for the control group. Possible further studies in this are are discussed.

INTRODUCTION

There is ample evidence to indicate that elderly people as a class are the recipients of negative attitudes from the public in general (5, 17, 26, 27, 33) and from specific population groups, as college students (11, 23), juveniles (13), and professional personnel (14).

Little work has been done to develop a procedure to systematically change the attitudes of specific persons toward the elderly except through programs of education and training, such as the one reported by Farrar and Bloom (19).

Some studies utilizing a behavioral conditioning model have successfully

*Reprinted with permission from the *Journal of Psychology*, 1969, *73*, 193–199. ©The Journal Press 1969.

modified attitude behavior (6, 18). Buckhout and Rosenberg (6) manipulated two types of verbal reinforcement on attitudes expressed in a structured interview setting and found that a combination of positive and negative reinforcement produced a significant immediate modification of attitudes expressed in the interview. Whether this change generalized to the environment outside the interview setting is not known.

Early (18) employed a classical conditioning paradigm to significantly change the attitude behavior of elementary school children toward "social isolates" in the classroom. The measure of behavior used was change in free play activity toward each experimental isolate when contrasted with the same measure of behavior toward control isolates.

Both of the above conditioning studies have modified attitude behavior by manipulating external stimuli in relation to attitudes. Recent behavior therapy procedures indicate that behavior change can result from the manipulation of imagery.

Since 1958 when Wolpe (35) introduced the technique of systematic desensitization based on relaxation, the manipulation of imagery has become an important vehicle for behavior modification. Desensitization involves the presentation in imagination of anxiety-provoking items in hierarchical form ranging in degrees from least anxious to most anxious until the S can imagine the items without feeling nervous or upset. That this technique can successfully eliminate maladaptive avoidance behaviors has been demonstrated by Davison (15), Lang (24), Lang, Lazovik, and Reynolds (25), and Paul (31).

Covert Sensitization, a technique developed by Cautela (8, 9) for the modification of maladaptive approach behaviors, involves the pairing in imagination of aversive stimuli with the desirable stimulus (e.g., homosexual contact, food, alcoholic beverage, cigarette). The procedure has been found to effectively eliminate excessive alcoholic drinking (1, 2), obesity (32), smoking (30, 34), homosexuality (4, 12), and sadistic fantasy (16).

Lazarus and Abramovitz (26) developed the reciprocal inhibition technique of "emotive imagery" for the treatment of children's phobias. Instead of utilizing the usual Wolpe procedure of relaxation in desensitization, these authors induced certain emotion-arousing situations and presented them in imagination to children with various phobias. They reported that seven of nine children treated recovered in a mean of 3.3 sessions and that follow-up inquiries 12 months later revealed no relapse or symptom substitution.

While these techniques have been primarily applied to overt behavior problems, therapists working with patients have frequently noted that changes in thinking, personal feelings, and attitudes often result from changes in behavior (7). Several experiments and studies by various investigators concerned with the effects of self-evaluative statements on behavior (3, 20, 21, 22, 29) have indicated definite positive behavioral changes as a result of "self-reinforcing" statements. Marston (29) considers covert self-reinforcements to be as influential on behaviors as overt self-reinforcements. According to Cautela

(10), the behavior therapist can influence covert self-reinforcing responses in two ways: by reinforcing positive statements expressed by the patient or by modifying behavior in such a way that the patient is more likely to make self-reinforcing statements after he observes his own behavior.

The above studies demonstrate that behavior conditioning procedures can affect attitude change and that other kinds of behavior change have resulted from the manipulation of imagery.

The purpose of this study was to attempt to change the attitudes of college students toward the elderly by the manipulation of imagery. In this experiment we paired (in imagination) a reinforcing situation with an elderly person. It was hypothesized that the pairing of a reinforcing event with an elderly individual will be counter conditioning result in behavior change toward elderly people in general.

METHOD

1. Subjects

Ninety-three undergraduates at Boston College were used as *S*s. It was later necessary to exclude the data from 44 *S*s who were absent one or more times when the material was presented. As a result, data from 49 *S*s was considered acceptable. Eleven of this number were females. The experimental group was composed of 23 *S*s enrolled in a genral psychology class; the control *S*s (*N* = 26) were members of another general psychology class.

2. Procedure

An attitude questionnaire was constructed from a scale developed by Kogan (23) for the measurement of attitudes toward elderly persons. An additional six items were included by the experimenters, which resulted in a checklist of 18 positive statements and 22 negative statements concerning elderly persons. *S*s were asked to rate each item along a sclae of varying degrees of response intensity (i.e., Agree strongly; Agree; Disagree; Disagree strongly; No opinion).

Both the experimental and control groups were given the attitude questionnaire and told simply to complete it for a study. One week later the experimental group received the following instructions: I want you to imagine this scene as vividly as you can:

You have been in a car accident and are lying on the ground. An artery in your arm has been severed and is bleeding badly. You are in pain. A kind elderly man comes upon the scene and applies pressure to your wound with a clean handkerchief and holds your hand in a reassuring way, while he smiles at you. The police come and put you in an ambulance. The next day you hear two doctors talking and one says, "If it wasn't for that kindly old man, the patient would have died."

This scene was repeated for them by the experimenter and then the Ss were asked to imagine it once more, picturing themselves as the old man. Finally they were told to practice both scenes at home at least twice a day. No mention was made of the previously administered questionnaires, nor did any student ask questions concerning them. Five days after these scenes were presented in class, the experimenter reminded the group to practice them at home. He did not present the scenes again in class. Five days after this reminder, the attitude questionnaires were once more administered to both groups of Ss. At this time Ss in the experimental group were also asked to answer the following questions: (a) How many times did you practice the scenes at home? (b) Rate the clarity of the images on a scale from one to five, where five means "very clear." (c) What do you think was the purpose of the study?

Each questionnaire was scored after each presentation. Each S received a total positive and negative score, based on the way in which he answered each question and to what degree the response was made. Responses on the more extreme ends of the scale were weighted more heavily than the others. Responses of "no opinion" were not assigned a score. The total negative score was subtracted from the total positive score to achieve one composite score for each S.

RESULTS

There was a significant difference at the .01 level in a positive direction for the experimental group between the first and second administrations of the attitude questionnaires. There was no significant difference in the control group. In fact, there was a slight tendency for the scores in the control group to become more negative.

There also appears to be a relationship between the number of times the Ss reported practicing the scenes at home and the increase in positive scores. The Ss who practiced more often received a significantly ($p < .01$) higher score in the positive direction. A control group of Ss randomly selected not only did not increase their scores, but showed a decrease in scores in a decidedly negative direction. This relationship between the amount of practice and the degree of positive change can be expected from a conditioning paradigm.

CONCLUSIONS

It appears evident that in the sample population used for this study the attitudes about elderly persons which were expressed on self-report scales were changed significantly in a positive direction due to the imagery technique. If further experimentation reveals that the differences between the two groups are due to the experimental variable, the procedure promises to be a powerful tool in the alteration of attitudes. The procedure appears even more promising when one considers that most Ss practiced an extremely small amount of trials. This difference, of course, can be attributed to the higher motivation of patients to modify maladaptive behaviors rather than to merely cooperate with a professor.

It was not the purpose of this experiment to measure attitude changes by other methods which would provide more validation for the technique employed (e.g., observations of the Ss' behavior in social interactions with elderly persons), but such measures would certainly be important.

Further experimentation is currently underway to determine the effect of the manipulation of other variables on the use of a more refined imagery technique, called "Covert Reinforcement" in which Ss are reinforced with a pleasant scene each time they engage in anxiety-provoking behavior in imagination. Further studies are needed in which investigators attempt to measure: if the daily presentation of scenes by the experimenters will produce a greater or lesser degree of attitude change; how long the changes in attitude persist after discontinuance of the technique; and which types of reinforcing situations produce the highest degree of attitude change.

The implications of this study are far-reaching. If further experimentation demonstrates the continued efficacy of this technique in changing negative attitudes in a positive direction with the aged, an attempt can be made to change other negative attitudes in such areas as ethnic and minority groups, political systems, etc. It will also be necessary to consider the ethical implications of the availability of such a procedure and its application for attitude changes in a desired direction.

SUMMARY

Forty-nine undergraduate Ss received a checklist composed of 18 positive statements and 22 negative statements about elderly persons. Ss were asked to rate each item along a scale of varying response tendency according to how they felt about each item. One week later the experimental group of Ss was asked to imagine a scene in which their lives were saved by an elderly person. They were told to practice imagining this scene twice a day. Ten days later the experimental and control groups of Ss were given the same questionnaire. The experimental group showed a significant positive increase in attitudes toward the aged ($p > .01$). The control group scores showed a slightly negative nonsignificant change ($p > .05$). Ss who reported practicing the scene at home showed a significantly higher increase in socres ($p < .01$) than did the Ss who did not report additional trials.

REFERENCES

1. Anant, S. A note on the treatment of alcoholics by a verbal aversion technique. *Canad. J. Psychol.*, 1967, **8**, 19-22.

2. Ashem, B., & Donner. L. Covert Sensitization with alcoholics: A controlled replication. *Behav. Res. & Ther.*, 1968, **6**, 7-12.

3. Bandura, A., & Kupers, C. J. The transmission of patterns of self reinforcement through modeling. *J. Abn. & Soc. Psychol.*, 1964, **69**, 1-9.

4. Barlow, D., Leitenberg, H., & Agras, W. Preliminary report on the experimental control of sexual deviation by manipulation of the US in Covert Sensitization. Paper read at the Eastern Psychological Assoiacion Convention, Washington, D.C., April, 1968.

5. Barron, M. L. Minority group characteristics of the aged in American society. *J. Geront.*, 1953, **8**, 477-482.

6. Buckhout, R., & Rosenberg, M. Verbal reinforcement and attitude change. *Psychol. Rep.*, 1966, **18**, 691-694.

7. Cautela, J. R. Desensitization and insight. *Behav. Res. & Ther.*, 1965, **3**, 59-64.

8. _____. Treatment of compulsive behavior by Covert Sensitization. *Psychol. Rec.*, 1966, **16**, 33-41.

9. _____. Covert Sensitization. *Psychol. Rep.*, 1967, **20**, 459-468.

10. _____. Behavioral therapy and self-control: Techniques and implications. In C. M. Franks (Ed.), *Assessment and Status of the Behavior Therapies and Associated Developments*. New York: McGraw-Hill, 1968.

11. Cautela, J. R., & Kastenbaum, R. A reinforcement survey schedule for us in therapy, training, and research. *Phychol. Rep.*, 1967, **20**, 115-130.

12. Cautela, J. R., & Wisocki, P. A. The use of male and female therapists in the treatment of homosexual behavior. In R. D. Rubin & C. F. Franks (Eds.), *Advances in Behavior Therapy, 1968*. New York: Academic Press, 1969.

13. Cautela, J. R., Kastenbaum, R., & Wincze, J. The use of the RSS and FSS to survey possible reinforcing and aversive stimuli in a delinquent population. Paper presented at the Eastern Psychological Association Convention in Boston, Massachusetts, April, 1967.

14. Coe, R. M. Professional perspectives on the aged. *The Gerontologist*, 1967, **7**, 114-119.

15. Davison, G. The influence of systematic desensitization, relaxation, and graded exposure to imaginal aversive stimuli on the modification of phobic behavior. Unpublished Doctoral dissertation, Stanford University, Stanford, California, 1965.

16. _____. Elimination of a sadistic fantasy by a client-controlled counter-conditioning technique: A case study. *J. Abn. Psychol*, 1968, **73**, 84-89.

17. Drake, J. The Aged in American Society. New York: Ronald Press, 1958.

18. Early, J. Attitude learning in children. *J. Educ. Psychol*, 1968, **59**, 176-180.

19. Farrar, M., & Bloom, M. Social work education and the reduction of stereotypes about the aged. *Proc. Twentieth Ann. Meeting Geront. Soc.*, 1967, **47**.

20. Kanfer, F. The influence of age and incentive conditions on self-reward. *Psychol. Rep.*, 1966, **19**, 263-274.

21. Kanfer, F., & Marston, A. Conditioning of self-reinforcement responses: An analogue to self-confidence training. *Psychol. Rep.*, 1963, **13**, 63-70.

22. _____. Determinants of self-reinforcement in human learning. *J. Exper. Psychol,* 1963, **6**, 245-254.
23. Kogan, N. Attitudes toward old people: The development of a scale and an examaination of correlates. *J. Ban. & Soc. Psychol,* 1961, **62**, 44-54.
24. Lang, P. Experimental studies of desensitization therapy. In J. Wolpe, A. Salter, and L. J. Reyna (Eds.), *The Conditioning Therapies.* New York: Holt, Rinehart, & Winston, 1964, Pp. 38-53.
25. Lang, P., Lazovik, A., & Reynolds, D. Desensitization, suggestibility, and pseudotherapy. *J. Abn. Psychol,* 1965, **70**, 395-402.
26. Lazarus, A., & Abramovitz, A. The use of ''emotive imagery'' in the treatment of children's phobias. *J. Ment. Sci.,* 1962, **108**, 191-195.
27. Linden, M. E. Effects of social attitudes on the mental health of the aging. *Geriatrics,* 1957, **12**, 109-114.
28. _____. Relationships between social attitudes toward aging and the delinquencies of youth. *Amer. J. Psychiat.,* 1957, **114**, 444-448.
29. Marston, A. Self-reinforcement: The relevance of a concept in analogue research to psychotherapy. *Psychother.: Res. & Practice,* 1965, **2**, 1-5.
30. Mullen, F. The effect of Covert Sensitization on smoking behavior. Unpublished study, Queens College, Charlotte, North Carolina, 1968.
31. Paul, G. Insight *Versus* Desensitization Therapy. Stanford, Calif.: Stanford Univ. Press, 1964.
32. Stuart, R. Behavioral control of overeating. *Behav. Res. & Ther.,* 1967, **5**, 357-365.
33. Tuckman, J., & Lorge, L. Attitudes toward old people. *J. Soc. Psychol,* 1953, **37**, 249-260.
34. Viernstein, L. Evaluation of therapeutic techniques of Covert Sensitization on smoking behavior. Unpublished study, Queens College, Charlotte, North Carolina, 1968.
35. Wolpe, J. Psychotherapy by Reciprocal Inhibition. Stanford, Calif.: Stanford Univ. Press, 1958.

SECTION V
COVERT EXTINCTION

Chapter 17
Covert Extinction*
Joseph R. Cautela

Summary — A procedure labeled "covert extinction" (CE) is described. The label "covert extinction" is used because the procedure is based on the extinction paradigm and reinforcement is eliminated in imagination via instructions. A rationale for the procedure is presented together with examples of its application. A learning theory basis is presented for some of the parameters involved in the application of the procedure, together with some experimental evidence in support of the assumption that CE can bring about a decrement in response probability.

In previous papers the author has introduced behavior-modification procedures based on the assumption that stimuli presented in imagination via instructions have similar functional relationships to overt and covert behavior as do stimuli presented externally. These procedures have been labeled "covert sensitization" (Cautela, 1966; 1967), "covert positive reinforcement" (Cautela, 1970), and "covert negative reinforcement" (Cautela, 1971).

Covert sensitization is analogous to a punishment paradigm since the patient is asked to imagine that the is receiving noxious stimulation whenever he is about to perform an undesirable behavior. Experimental studies (Ashem & Donner, 1968; Barlow, Leitenberg, & Agras, 1969; Mullen, 1968; Stuart, 1969; Viernstein, 1968; Wagner & Bragg, 1969) indicate that covert sensitization can reduce the frequence of undesirable behavior.

In covert positive reinforcement, the patient is asked to imagine the behavior to be increased and then to imagine that he is receiving a reinforcing stimulus. Anecdotal reports and experimental evidence support the assumption that a reinforcing stimulus presented in imagination can result in an increase in the

*Reprinted with permission from *Behavior Therapy*, 1971, *2*, 192-200. ©Academic Press, Inc. 1971.

frequency of behavior (Cautela, Steffen, & Wish, in press; Cautela, Walsh, & Wish, in press; Flannery, 1970; Krop, in press).

Covert negative reinforcement is essentially an avoidance-conditioning procedure. The patient is instructed to imagine a strong aversive stimulus (e.g., being tied to a chair while a snake is about to strike and struggling to prevent it). Then, in his imagination, the patient has to shift immediately to the performance of the behavior to be increased (e.g., beginning to speak before a large audience). There is also some experimental evidence that this procedure results in an increase in the probability of response occurrence (Ascher & Cautela, 1970; Cautela & Wisocki, 1970).

COVERT EXTINCTION (CE)

Since punishing and reinforcing stimuli presented in imagination via instructions appear to function in a manner similar to externally applied punishing and reinforcing stimuli, it is reasonable to assume that, when a subject is instructed to imagine that reinforcing stimuli maintaining his covert or overt behavior do not occur, then that behavior will decrease in probability or be eliminated. Based on this assumption, the author has developed a behavior modification procedure labeled ''covert extinction.'' The procedure is labeled ''covert extinction'' since it involves the manipulation of imagery and is analogous to the experimental extinction paradigm. While the term ''extinction'' encompasses both classical and operant procedures, the technique presented here is essentially that of the operant paradigm.

Description of Procedure

A behavioral analysis (Cautela, 1968) first determines the behavior to be modified and the consequences maintaining the behavior. The patient is then given the following rationale:

> Your behavior (e.g., stuttering) occurs because it is maintained by the environment. Whenever you perform that behavior, it is reinforced (or rewarded) by other people or in some other way. There are many studies in the field of learning that show that if the reinforcing situation is prevented from occurring, the behavior that is influenced by reinforcement decreases in frequency (i.e., is weakened, is less apt to occur, or is even eliminated). We are going to have you imagine you are performing the behavior (stuttering) and then have you imagine that you are not being reinforced or rewarded. Do you understand? All right, now sit back and relax. Try to imagine the scene I am going to describe. Try to imagine that you are really there. Try not to imagine that you are simply seeing what I describe; try to use your other senses as well. If in the scene you are sitting in a chair, try to imagine that you can feel the chair against your body. If you are at a party, try to imagine that you can hear people talking and glasses tinkling. Now remember, the main point is you are actually there experiencing everything.

First, let us determine if you can imagine the scene clearly. Close your eyes and try to imagine everything I describe. Ready?

You are sitting in your school cafeteria. Choose a place in which you usually sit. (Pause) You can hear and see students walking around, eating and talking. (Pause) you are eating your favorite lunch. (Pause) There is an empty seat near you. (Pause) A pretty blonde girl comes over and asks you if she can sit down. (Pause) You stammer, 'Ya . . ya . . ya . . yes.' She absolutely reacts in no way to your stuttering.

The patient is asked if the scene was clear and how he felt about it. If the scene were clear and he could imagine the consequences as described (i.e., he had no difficulty imagining that the girl showed no reaction at all), he is then asked to imagine the scene by himself. (If there is any difficulty, the scene is repeated by the therapist with modified or elaborated instructions, depending on what was difficult for the patient to imagine.)

The patient is told that whenever he finishes imagining a scene by himself, he is to indicate this to the therapist by raising his right index finger. At that point, further inquiry is made about the clarity of the scene. The scene is then repeated 10 times by the therapist, alternating with 10 trials by the patient.

The patient is then asked to practice the scene at least 10 times a day at home. Sometimes he is asked to modify the scene slightly each day (e.g., each day a different girl is included in the scene). The behavioral analysis determines the situations which have to be practiced. In the case of a stutterer, for example, different scenes are presented, such as stuttering in response to a professor's question, stuttering whenever the patient is asked directions, and stuttering over the phone (in this case, he is assured that there is absolutely no reaction on the other end). Further sessions are devoted to these other situations in which the patient stutters until the most important (in terms of frequency) situations are covered. Fortunately, there is some generalization of extinction (Kimble, 1961, pp. 320–330) and some secondary extinction (Pavlov, 1927, p. 54), so that all situations do not have to be covered.

Further Examples of the Application of CE

As indicated in the following examples, CE is especially helpful when the reinforcing contingencies are difficult to control by environmental manipulation.

1. A hospitalized patient was considered functionally blind, i.e., he claimed he could not see, but observation by a number of individuals indicated that the patient had almost normal vision. Whenever the patient showed helpless, stumbling behavior while he was trying to walk, sit, or eat, someone would help him by guiding him or feeding him. This helping behavior occurred in spite of directions to all hospital personnel and patients not to help the patient. The patient was not malingering and really believed that he couldn't see. Evidently, many situations had become S^d (discriminative stimuli) for not

focusing on a particular object, since not focusing was reinforced by helping behavior. The staff was advised to tell the patient that even though he did not realize it, he was being made helpless by people paying attention to him when he was stumbling around, etc. A staff member presented scenes to the patient in which he was to imagine that he was stumbling over or couldn't find a chair, but that no one helped him or talked to him.

2. In a training school, a boy's disruptive behavior was reinforced by the laughter of his classmates and the attention of his teacher (Madsen, Becker, Thomas, Koser, & Plager, 1968, have indicated that disruptive behavior in the classroom can be maintained by teacher attention). In the case described here, the teacher and students would not cooperate with the therapist by ignoring the boy's disruptive behavior. Therefore CE was employed. The boy was asked to imagine performing the disruptive behavior, but no one noticed him. The disruptive behavior was eliminated in three weeks. His cooperation was ensured when he was informed that if his behavior did not change, he would be transferred from the public school to a home school on the grounds.

3. In many cases of multiple phobias, the husband, wife, or parents of the patient cannot follow the instructions not to reinforce certain behavior because they feel it would be cruel or that the patient would become angry. In these cases, the patients are asked to imagine that they are expressing the phobic behavior, but that no reinforcement is provided by others. The following is a typical example of treatment of fear of being left alone:

"You are home with your husband. He says he wants to go bowling. You tell him you don't want him to go because you are afraid of being left alone. But he says, 'I'm sorry. I'm going anyway.' and he leaves you alone." In these cases there is often great resentment by the individuals unwittingly administering the reinforcement because they feel trapped (they are!) by the patient's problem.

4. A homosexual who was reinforced for going into "gay" bars by admiring glances and approaches by other homosexuals was given the following scene:

"I want you to imagine you are walking into your favorite bar. You can hear the music and the noise of talking and glasses tinkling. You expect to be noticed, but no one notices you. They all act as if you weren't even there. It seems very strange . . . they pay no attention to you at all." The above procedure was combined with covert sensitization to sexual urges toward males.

5. A teenager in a training school who expressed many psychosomatic complaints to the cottage staff was asked to imagine he was telling the staff he had a headache or that his feet hurt, etc., but they paid no attention to him.

6. The following is a case of administering CE to nonsocial reinforcement. A woman who was being treated for obesity was asked to imagine that she was tense and lonely at night, but that she couldn't find any food in the house (or, in some scenes, that all restaurants were closed).

7. A patient who was being treated for severe self-injurious behavior (eye-poking and tongue-biting) was asked to imagine that he poked at his eyes and ran out into the hospital corridor, but that the staff paid no attention to him.

In this case, CE was combined with a number of other behavior modification procedures to decrease self-injury.

LEARNING THEORY BASIS FOR CE PROCEDURE

In a previous article, the author attempted to relate learning theory and empirical data to the covert reinforcement procedure (Cautela, 1970). Similar considerations yield the following provisional conclusions with respect to covert extinction.

1. Number of Extinction Trials

Response strength weakens as a function of the number of extinction trials (Skinner, 1938; pp. 74–76; Pavlov, 1927, p. 49). If the patient does his homework and has weekly therapeutic sessions, then 90 extinction trials per week are performed (20 trials in the office, and 70 at home). The importance of practice is stressed and inquires are made concerning the amount of practice each week.

2. Prevention of Spontaneous Recovery

When more extinction trials are given, there is less chance of spontaneous recovery (Pavlov, 1927, p. 58; Lawson, 1960, p. 250). In some cases, spontaneous recovery may be eliminated by continuing extinction trials beyond zero; i.e., after the response has been eliminated (Pavlov, 1927, p. 57).

3. Massed and Distributed Practice

In general, massed practice hastens extinction (Pavlov, 1927, p. 53; Rohrer, 1947; 1948). According to Hull (1952), this is due to the accumulation of Ir. Spontaneous recovery is less apt to occur with distributed extinction trials, and more new reinforcement trials are needed to reach preextinction habit strength (Pavlov, 1927, p. 52). It is desirable, therefore, to mass extinction trials in the office sessions, while distributing practice by assigning daily homework sessions.

4. Amount of Effort as Related to CE

Tasks requiring more effort extinguish faster than tasks requiring less effort (Capehart, Viney, & Hulicka, 1958; Solomon, 1948). Whenever possible, this finding is utilized by requiring the patient to expend more effort (covertly) performing the task, e.g., stuttering a great deal; running around a lot in the classroom trying hard to get attention from his classmates.

5. Similarity of Training Conditions

Increasing the irregularity of the training conditions increases resistance to extinction (McNamara & Wike, 1958). It is important, therefore, both to vary the scenes for generalization purposes yet to keep them relatively constant in order to increase extinction effects.

6. Variation of Reinforcement

Variation of reinforcement for the same task does not influence resistance to extinction (Logan, Beier, & Kincaid, 1956). Therefore, the fact that maladaptive behavior is usually maintained by a variety of reinforcers does not necessarily mean that resistance to extinction will be greater. But it does necessitate a greater variety of extinction scenes in order to cover all possible reinforcing situations. It is also fortunate that responses reinforced by a variety of reinforcing stimuli of diverse intensities do not necessarily extinguish faster than responses reinforced by one magnitude (Logan, Beier, & Kincaid, 1956), since, in everyday life, the amount of reinforcement for any given reponse tends to fluctuate.

7. Latent Extinction.

The reduction of response strength due to non-occurrence of the response in a situation where it is usually reinforced is referred to as latent extinction (Kimble, 1961, p. 320; Moltz, 1955). This principle is utilized when instructing the patient to imagine himself in a particular situation without making the response, e.g., being in a classroom without showing disruptive behavior; talking to someone without stuttering.

8. Generalization of Extinction.

The generalization of extinction is similar to the generalization of reinforcement (Hovland, 1937; Kimble, 1961, p. 333). It is not necessary to extinguish every behavior along a continuum to eliminate the behavior.

PROBLEMS ENCOUNTERED IN THE APPLICATION OF CE

A few patients claim they cannot achieve clear imagery. In such circumstances, it is helpful to describe the pertinent scenes in greater detail and instruct the patient to observe all aspects of the stimulus situation when encountered externally. In some subjects, clear auditory imagery can be obtained but not visual imagery. For these patients, descriptions of the scenes should emphasize more auditory details. Sometimes clarity is increased simply with practice and concentration.

Occasionally, it is difficult to convince the patient that particular contingencies control his behavior. In these cases, it helps to cite experimental data or even anecdotal incidents. Once in a while, a patient reports that he was too busy or forgot to practice. For these individuals, it is helpful to set up a particular schedule for practicing, emphasizing all the while the necessity for practice.

It is important to point out to the patient that withdrawal of reinforcement is sometimes followed by a temporary increase in responding (Lawson, 1960, p. 256). Another possible side effect of reinforcement withdrawal is instigation of aggression (Skinner, 1953, p. 69). Some patients report great resentment at being asked to imagine that reinforcement is being withheld. For example, a female became angry at her husband when she was asked to imagine that he did not respond to her psychosomatic complaints. As the patient continues the treatment sessions, the resentment usually decreases. It sometimes helps to explain that resentment is a natural consequence of reinforcement withdrawal. Also, if necessary, covert reinforcement can be used to decrease resentment.

Extinction in the laboratory shows a gradual decline in the strength of the conditioned response (or operant). This constant gradual decline usually does not occur in the CE procedure since there may be days where the response is reinforced by the physical or social environment. As a result, the patient may report that he has had a 'bad day' because there was an increase in maladaptive behavior. Therefore, he has to be reassured that his therapeutic progress will have its ups and downs, that he will have his good and bad days. Gradually, there will be fewer bad days and more good days until eventually the response will hardly occur at all or will be entirely eliminated.

It is possible that, after treatment is terminated, additional reinforcement trials by other individuals may reinstate the maladaptive behavior. If this occurs, another series of CE trials will weaken the maladaptive behavior. These further extinction trials usually decrease the maladaptive behavior at a faster rate than the previous extinction trials (see Pavlov, 1927, pp. 53–54; Lawson, 1960, p. 250).

CE COMBINED WITH OTHER PROCEDURES

The use of CE need not preclude instructions to others to withhold reinforcement. It is important that extinction (inhibitory effects) become more powerful than reinforcement effects. One must be careful to avoid positive reinforcement effects.

Though there are data which show that punishment is more effective if antagonistic responses are reinforced (Bandura, 1969, p. 348), no such data are available to indicate that extinction is facilitated by reinforcing antagonistic responses. A study by Leitenberg, Rouson, and Bath (1970) suggests that, at first, extinction is facilitated by reinforcement of antagonistic responses, but when reinforcement for completing behavior is withdrawn, the original behavior is resumed with no over-all saving in total responses to extinction. The author has found that covert extinction effects occur faster and are more enduring if the CE procedure is combined with covert reinforcement. It is also important to provide the subject with other reinforcers to take the place of those which are being extinguished, i.e., to increase his own reinforcement repertoire.

DISCUSSION

Research data are needed to confirm the clinical impression that covert extinction affects behavior in a manner similar to overt extinction. Studies of vicarious extinction (Kanfer, 1965) and modeling (Bandura, 1969, pp. 143–167) suggest that the individual does not have to experience extinction directly for a particular behavior to be weakened.

While Pavlov (1955, p. 285) and Skinner (1969, p. 242) both seem to agree that covert and overt stimuli obey the same laws, controlled research concerning this issue is needed. A recent controlled study by Ascher (1970) utilized overt reinforcement to produce an increase in response strength and then employed covert extinction to bring about a response decrease. In this study, college students were covertly reinforced for choosing particular pronouns for sentence construction. In one group, pronoun usage was extinguished by having them imagine the pronouns without covert reinforcement. Another group was not presented with the pronouns, but spent the same amount of time conversing with the experimenter. Results show that a reduction in pronoun usage occurred in the extinction group, but not in the conversation group.

There is some reason to have confidence in the assumption that covert extinction is an effective technique for use in the practice of behavior therapy and that it functions in a manner similar to overt extinction. More further controlled research and clinical exploration are, of course, essential before these new covert techniques can be unequivocally accepted into the armamentarium of the behavioral scientist.

REFERENCES

Ascher, L. M. Covert extinction: An experimental test. Unpublished data, State

University of New York, Fredonia, 1970.

Ascher, M., & Cautela, J. R. Covert negative reinforcement: An experimental test. Unpublished data, New York State University at Fredonia, 1970.

Ashem, B., & Donner, L. Covert sensitization with alcoholics: A controlled replication. *Behaviour Research and Therapy,* 1968, **6,** 7–12.

Bandura, A. *Principles of behavior modification.* New York: Holt, Rinehart and Winston, 1969.

Barlow, D., Leitenberg, H., & Agras, W. S. The effect of instructions in the use of covert sensitization. Unpublished study, University of Vermont, 1969.

Capehart, J., Viney, W., & Hulicka, I. N. The effect of effort upon extinction. *Journal of Comparative and Physiological Psychology,* 1958, **51,** 505–507.

Cautela, J. R. Treatment of compulsive behavior by covert sensitization. *Psychological Record,* 1966, **16,** 33–41.

Cautela, J. R. Covert sensitization. *Psychological Record,* 1967, **20,** 459–468.

Cautela, J. R. Behavior therapy and the need for behavioral assessment. *Psychotherapy: Theory, Research and Practice,* 1968, **5,** 175–179.

Cautela, J. R. Covert reinforcement. *Behavior Therapy,* 1970, **1,** 33–50.

Cautela, J. R. Covert negative reinforcement. *Behavior Therapy and Experimental Psychiatry,* 1971, in press.

Cautela, J. R., Walsh, K., & Wish, P. The use of covert reinforcement to modify attitudes toward retardates. *Journal of Psychology,* in press.

Cautela, J. R., Steffen, J., & Wish, P. An experimental test of covert reinforcement. *Journal of Clinical and Consulting Psychology,* in press.

Cautela, J. R., & Wisocki, P. A. The use of imagery in the modification of attitudes toward the elderly: A preliminary report. *Journal of Psychology,* 1969, **73,** 193–199.

Flannery, R. An investigation of differential effectiveness of office vs. *in vivo* therapy of a simple phobia: An outcome study. Unpublished doctoral dissertation. University of Windsor, 1970.

Hovland, C. I. The generalization of conditioned responses with varying frequencies of tone. *Journal of Genetic Psychology,* 1937, **17,** 125–148.

Hull, C. L. *A behavior system.* New Haven: Yale University Press, 1952.

Kanfer, F. H. Vicarious human reinforcement: A glimpse into the black box. In L. Krasner and L. P. Ullmann (Eds.), *Research in behavior modification.* New York: Holt, Rinehart, and Winston, 1965. Pp. 244–267.

Kimble, G. A. *Hilgard and Marquis' Conditioning and learning.* New York: Appleton-Century-Crofts, 1961.

Krop, H. The use of covert reinforcement to modify children's self-concept. *Behavior Therapy,* in press.

Lawson, R. *Learning and behavior.* New York: Macmillan, 1960.

Leitenberg, H., Rouson, R. A., & Bath, K. Reinforcement of competing behavior during extinction. *Sience,* 1970, **169,** 301–302.

Logan, F. A., Beier, E. M., & Kincaid, W. D. Extinction following partial and varied reinforcement. *Journal of Experimental Psychology,* 1956, **52,** 65–70.

McNamara, H. J., & Wike, E. L. The effects of irregular learning conditions upon the rate and permanence of learning. *Journal of Comparative and Physiological Psychology,* 1958, **51,** 363–366.

Madsen, C. H., Jr., Becker, W. C., Thomas, D. R., Koser, L., & Plager, E. An analysis of the reinforcing function of ''sit down'' commands. In R. K. Parker

(Ed.), *Readings in educational psychology.* Boston: Allyn and Bacon, 1968. Pp. 265–278.

Moltz, H. Latent extinction and reduction of secondary reward value. *Journal of Experimental Psychology,* 1955, **49,** 395–400.

Mullen, F. G. The effect of covert sensitization on smoking behavior. Unpublished study, Queens College, Charlottesville, North Carolina, 1968.

Pavlov, 'I. P. *Conditioned reflexes.* Translated by G. V. Anrep. London: Oxford University Press, 1927.

Rohrer, J. H. A motivational state resulting from nonreward. *Journal of Comparative and Physiological Psychology,* 1949, **42,** 476–485.

Rohrer, J. H. Experimental extinction as a function of the distribution of extinction trials and response strength. *Journal of Experimental Psychology,* 1947, **37,** 473–493.

Skinner, B. F. *The behavior of organisms: An experimental analysis.* New York: Appleton-Century-Crofts, 1938.

Skinner, B. F. *Science and human behavior.* New York: Macmillan, 1953.

Skinner, B. F. *Contingencies of reinforcement.* New York: Appleton-Century-Crofts, 1969.

Solomon, R. L. Efforts and extinction rate: A confirmation. *Journal of Comparative and Physiological Psychology,* 1948, **41,** 93–101.

Stuart, R. Behavioral control of over-eating. *Behaviour Research and Therapy,* 1967, **5,** 357-365.

Viernstein, L. Evaluation of therapeutic techniques of covert sensitization. Unpublished data, Queens College, Charlottesville, North Carolina. 1968.

Wagner, M. K., & Bragg, R. A. Comparing behavior modification methods for habit decrement-smoking. Mimeo, V. A. Hospital, Salsbury, North Carolina, 1969.

Chapter 18

An Experimental Study of Covert Extinction*†

L. Michael Ascher and Joseph R. Cautela

Summary — A 2×3 study, using performance on a pseudo concept formation task as the dependent variable, tested the efficacy of covert extinction (CE). Groups received either CE instructions, overt extinction (OE) instructions, or no instructions, and either reinforcement or no reinforcement. The data revealed no significant difference between the unreinforced CE and OE groups, but did indicate significant differences between these groups and the reinforced group receiving no instructions. Parallel results were obtained for the three similar reinforced groups. The conclusion, based on these data, was that CE was effective in facilitating the course of extinction whether or not the environment continued to provide reinforcement for the specific response.

Basing his work on the assumption that a stimulus presented in imagination can affect overt and covert behavior in a manner similar to a stimulus presented externally, Cautela (1967, 1970a, 1970b, 1971) has developed a number of behavior modification procedures which require the manipulation of imaginal stimuli and responses in ways analogous to the manipulation of overt stimuli and responses. For example, in the case of patients who avoid performing a specific adaptive response due to contingent anxiety, Cautela (1970a) uses a technique called covert positive reinforcement. This involves instructing the patient to pair in his imagination, images of performing the anxiety provoking

---

*Reprinted with permission from the *Journal of Behavior Therapy and Experimental Psychiatry*, 1974, 5, 233–238. © Pergamon Press.

†This study was partially supported by a Grant awarded to the senior author from The State University College at Fredonia and the Research Foundation of the State University of New York, Fredonia.

response with images of idiosyncratic reinforcing scenes. The typical result is that the patient performs the adaptive response at a higher rate (e.g. Ascher, 1973). The imaginal covert positive reinforcement technique is similar to the secondary reinforcement procedure in which a neutral external stimulus is paired with a reinforcing external stimulus resulting in the neutral stimulus taking on reinforcing properties (Kimble, 1961).

If the assumptions of covert positive reinforcement are correct, then it follows that when the subject imagines a response which is being maintained by external reinforcement, but imagines the response without the favorable environmental contingency, then the probability of occurrence of the response without the favorable environmental contingency, then the probability of occurrence of the response should decrease. The procedure has been labeled covert extinction (CE) because it is analogous to the operant extinction paradigm, i.e. withholding the reinforcing stimulus after the emission of the instrumental response, but it occurs in the subject's imagination. For example, the CE technique was used by the senior author to reduce the probability of occurrence of a maladaptive response with an obese patient (i.e. eating some fattening food which was difficult for the patient to give up). The subject of this treatment was asked to imagine that he was seated in a delicatessen and that the waitress had brought two bagels stuffed with cream cheese and Nova Scotia lox (the troublesome food). His mouth was watering; he could not wait to devour them. He took the first bite but was somewhat disappointed because the food did not seem to have the usual amount of flavor. He opened the bagel, looked at the lox, smelled it, but everything seemed to be normal; he put some salt on it and took a second bite. He experienced even less flavor than before. With each successive mouthful there was less and less flavor, until, when the first bagel was finished, he did not bother to eat the second one. The subject was instructed to imagine this several times each day, and especially before engaging in the maladaptive behavior. After two sessions during which CE was extensively employed, the patient reported that he no longer desired bagels and lox; for 3 months following, he avoided this food.

The purpose of the present study is to provide a context for an investigation of the efficacy of the CE procedure which may be more controlled than, and relatively free of the complexities of, a clinical setting. The present paper reports an experiment designed to study the effectiveness of CE in reducing the probability of occurrence of an externally reinforced response.

METHOD

Subjects

Ninety college students were tested in the present experiment.

Apparatus

A "BCI SR-400 Programmer" (#A10068) was used to present verbal material to all Ss; this device permits a choice of one of four responses on each trial. A "BCI Scoring Indicator" (#A10026) monitored the number of responses which each S made, and a "BCI Token Dispenser" (#A10077), operated by E, administered the reinforcement.

Procedure

Six groups were used in the study, with fifteen Ss randomly assigned to each.

Phase one. All Ss were informed that E was interested in studying the relationship between concept formation and imagination. The Ss were instructed to look at the Programmer which presented a row of four words. They were told that each set of four words related to a different concept and that they were to demonstrate their understanding of the task by selecting the word which best illustrated each concept. An example was presented to S and corrected by E if necessary; reinforcement was also presented at this time. Subjects were instructed to indicate their choices by pressing the button which represented the appropriate word for the trial. After every response, the Programmer advanced and a new set of four words appeared. A "correct" response was indicated by the Token Dispenser which lit up and noisily dispensed a token. Although the tokens could not be redeemed for additional reinforcement, Ss were informed that a coded list of the performance of all Ss would be posted enabling them to judge their skill at concept formation in comparison to their fellow students. In fact, no concepts existed, thus permitting E to reinforce S randomly. Each S was presented with the same set of 200 different four word groups. Following five of the first 20 responses (the 7th, 10th, 11th, 15th, and 20th) a reinforcement was administered irrespective of the specific choice of S. After the 25th response E told S to stop performing. He asked how many reinforcements S had received and when informed of the number E suggested that this indicated good performance. He spent approximately 2 min. "fixing" the Programmer and the Token Dispenser. Each of the six groups then received the following differentiating instructions.

Phase two.   Group I (CE instructions without additional reinforcements) Ss were given CE training as follows:

I want you to imagine that you are responding to the words presented on the Programmer but are receiving no tokens. Each time you press a button, a new group of words appears, but no token is dispensed.

These CE instructions were presented 30 times. After each block of five presentations, S was instructed to imagine that he was responding to some type of machinery which typically dispensed some type of reinforcement (e.g. candy machine, public telephone, sandwich vendor), but consistently failed to receive the appropriate reinforcement. The purpose of these interspersed images were to prevent the S from becoming bored with the 30 repetitions of the CE instructions. After the CE imagery (requiring about 15 min), Ss were told that they could continue to work as long as they wanted, at which point E left the room. No additional reinforcement could be obtained by these Ss.

Group 2 (CE instructions with continued reinforcement) received CE training identical to that administered to Group 1 (30 presentations). They were then told that they should continue to work for as long as they wished. The E then left the room and entered an adjacent experimental chamber in order to be able to dispense reinforcement randomly on a VR 10 schedule.

Group 3 (no instructions and no additional reinforcement) Ss were engaged in approximately 15 min of random conversation by E. At the conclusion of this period, they were told that the purpose of the conversation was to give them some rest and that they could now continue for as long as they desired to work. The E then left the room and permitted S to work by himself. No additional reinforcement was administered to these Ss.

Group 4 (overt extinction [OE] instructions without additional reinforcement) Ss were also encouraged to converse with E for 15 min. Following this period they were told that there was something wrong with the reinforcing mechanism and that no more tokens would be dispensed. However, they were informed that they could continue to work for as long as they liked. The E then left the lab and allowed S to work undisturbed. No additional reinforcement was presented to these Ss.

Group 5 (no instructions and continued reinforcement) was similar to Group 3 in that E conversed with these Ss for 15 min after which they were told that they could continue to work for as long as they wished. The E then left the lab and entered the adjacent experimental chamber in order to be able to dispense reinforcement on a VR 10 schedule for Ss' responses.

Group 6 (overt extinction [OE] instructions with continued reinforcement) Ss received the same extinction instructions as did Group 4 Ss. However, following the departure of E, Ss continued to receive reinforcement on a VR 10 schedule.

Thus the study employed a 3×2 design. Three sets of instructions (CE, OE, no instructions) were each utilized with pairs of groups; one of each pair was continued on reinforcement after the first 20 trials — the second group of each pair received no further reinforcement after the first 20 trials.

The criterion of extinction was reached when S took his possessions and left the lab. At this point E, who was waiting outside, escorted S to his office where he conducted a post-experimental interview to determine whether S understood the purpose of the study. Subsequent to the completion of the experiment, all Ss were informed as to the nature and the results of the study.

RESULTS

Table 1 illustrates the mean number of responses and the standard deviation to the criterion of extinction for the six groups.

The results of an analysis of variance on these data are reported in Table 2. A Duncan Range test was then performed indicating the following relationships among the six groups. The first comparison was conducted with Groups 1 (CE instructions without additional reinforcement), 3 (no instructions and no additional reinforcement), and 4 (OE instructions without additional reinforcement), and indicated that Groups 1 and 4 were not significantly different from each other ($P > 0 \cdot 05$), but that Group 3 differed significantly from these latter two ($P < 0 \cdot 001$). A second comparison revealed that Group 5 (no instructions and continued reinforcement) differed significantly from the remaining five groups ($P < 0 \cdot 001$). The final comparison was undertaken between Group 2 (CE instructions with continued reinforcement), on the one hand, and Groups 1, 3, 4, and 6 (OE instructions with continued reinforcement), on the other. This comparison indicated that Group 2 differed significantly from Groups 1 and 4 ($P < 0 \cdot 001$), but did not differ from Groups 3 and 6 ($P > 0 \cdot 05$).

The results of the post-experimental interview revealed that in no instance was the S able to explain the purpose of the study.

Table 18.1. Means and standard deviations to criterion
for six experimental groups

		Type of instructions		
		Covert extinction	Overt extinction	No instructions
Reinforcement	$\overline{X}$	82·078	84·478	166·133
continued in phase 2	S.D	14·069	12·042	42·249
Reinforcement not	$\overline{X}$	33·133	29·333	77·133
continued in phase 2	S.D	11·389	15·727	18·784

Table 18.2. Analysis of variance of trials to extinction

Source	SS	df	MS	F
A (Reinforcement)	92933·889	1	92933·889	183·57*
B (Instructions)	82780·111	2	41390·056	81·67*
A × B	7065·522	2	3532·761	69·78*
Error	42525·598	84	506·257	

* $P < 0 \cdot 001$.

DISCUSSION

The results of the present study suggest that the procedure described by Cautela (1971), and labeled covert extinction (CE), is effective in facilitating the extinction of a previously reinforced overt response, whether or not external conditions are favorable to the extinction of this response. When Ss were exposed to CE training which preceded the cessation of reinforcement (Group 1) their responses extinguished as quickly as did those of Ss who were directly informed that no additional reinforcement could be obtained (Group 4); and, their responses extinguished significantly faster than did those of Ss who received no information prior to extinction (Group 3). This might suggest that when environmental factors are appropriate for the extinction of a specific response, i.e. when an S no longer receives the typical reinforcing consequences for the behavior, the CE technique will facilitate the course of extinction by reducing the reinforcing imagery and thus reducing the number of responses to the extinction criterion. This is supported, in the present study, by the finding that the responses of the group which received CE training and no additional reinforcement (Group 1) extinguished significantly faster than did those of the group which also received no additional reinforcement but did not obtain information in advance of this change.

It is possible that in spite of the fact that Ss claimed ignorance of the purpose of the study, a more detailed post-experimental interview might have revealed that the CE instructions did provide an instructional set similar to that resulting from E's indication to Ss in Group 4 that no additional reinforcement could be obtained. Of course, one could argue that when Ss do not receive reinforcement for a number of trials an instructional set results anyway. One way to investigate the possible additional set component provided by CE is to conduct a parametric study designed to determine the relationship between the number of CE trials and the resultant resistance to extinction (assuming that sufficient CE trials are presented to provide the opportunity for the possible instructional set to occur). It would be hypothesized that if this relationship proved to be positive, then the results of the CE procedure could be considered to be more analogous to the results of overt extinction than to the verbal signal that no additional reinforcement is forthcoming. On the other hand, if different numbers of CE trials resulted in similar resistance to extinction then the hypothesis that the verbal signal accounted for the effects of the CE technique would receive strong support.

In practice, the environment does not always support the efforts of the therapist in reducing maladaptive approach responses. In fact, Cautela (1971) has used CE in cases where dieting women are continuously tempted by their husbands who persist in offering these obese women fattening foods. Thus, while patients may be receiving CE training during their therapy sessions, and may be practicing the technique each day, they may still experience reinforcement from the environment for performing the maladaptive overt response. In the present study, Group 2 represented the analogue of this common circumstance (CE with continued reinforcement). Although Ss in this group received training identical to those in Group 1 (CE without additional reinforcement), Group 2 Ss also continued to receive reinforcement while Group 1 Ss did not. As would be expected, the responses of Group 1 extinguished far sooner than did those of Group 2. More important, the results indicated that when an S received CE training, in spite of the fact that he was still able to obtain the typical reinforcement from his environment, his responses to the criterion of extinction were markedly reduced in number from those of Ss who continued to receive reinforcement at the same rate but did not experience CE training (Group 5).

No significant difference was found in the number of responses to criteria between Ss in Group 2 which received CE training and intermittent reinforcement, and Ss in Group 3 which received no information regarding the succeeding reinforcement schedule and then experienced extinction. This comparison suggests that with respect to the extinction of responses maintained on a partial schedule of reinforcement, the removal of reinforcement without specific related information regarding the future of contingent maintaining stimuli, may not produce extinction any more rapidly than administering CE training and permitting the S to continue to receive diminishing partial reinforcement outside therapy. This would seem to have implications for the use of CE in the alleviation of narcotics and alcohol addictions (Wisocki, 1973; Gotestam and Melin, 1974).

When Ss continue to receive reinforcement, the CE procedure appears to be as effective in producing extinction as is telling the individual that he will no longer be able to obtain reinforcement. This was indicated by the failure to find a significant difference between Group 2 and Group 6 (in which Ss received reinforcement in spite of being informed that they would not). In practice, it would be incorrect to tell the patient that although he may experience the maladaptive approach stimulus (e.g. food), he will not experience reinforcement because in fact he will receive the typical reinforcement contingent upon the appropriate approach response. The CE procedure, on the other hand, suggests that there will be a diminution of reinforcement and the decrement will increase with each trial. If nothing else, this is at least the more credible alternative.

The question may arise whether the CE technique is analogous to the conventional extinction procedure, i.e. whether CE has similar effects upon covert stimuli and responses that conventional extinction has on overt stimuli and responses. In operant terms, extinction may be defined as the withholding of the reinforcing stimulus which previously followed a response. This typically results in the reduction of the probability of the occurrence of the response on future occasions. Cautela (1971) described the CE technique as requiring S to imagine that reinforcing stimuli maintaining some maladaptive overt response does not occur. Thus S imagines making the overt response, but does not imagine being contingently reinforced. On the basis of this article (Cautela, 1971), and the results of the present study, it would appear as though CE is a procedure which has effects similar to those of conventional extinction (the OE instructions of the present study). That is, CE, when appropriately utilized with covert representations of overt behavior, appears to facilitate the extinction of this overt behavior. It is hypothesized that CE facilitates the extinction of an overt response by requiring S to imagine making this overt response without imagining the occurrence of the reinforcer. While the present paper supports the hypothesis that CE facilitates the extinction of overt behavior, this study does not bear on explanations regarding the mechanisms whereby CE effects this facilitation. In fact, it is not clear how CE operates with respect to the extinction of overt behavior. Although the present authors hypothesize that the mechanisms of CE are analogous to those of overt extinction, other explanations are also possible and will be referred to later in this section.

Further evidence regarding the similarity of covert and overt extinction procedures might be obtained from studies which would focus on parameters whose effects are known in relation to the conventional extinction of overt responses (as was suggested above in another context). Such studies might vary relevant parameters in studies which investigated CE to determine whether the results which have been obtained with overt extinction are similar to those obtained with covert extinction. For example, the number and schedule of reinforcements during the acquisition of a covert response could be varied. It would then be assumed that CE, if it were similar to conventional extinction, would produce extinction most rapidly with responses acquired on a continuous reinforcement schedule as opposed to a partial reinforcement schedule.

Although both Cautela (1971) and the present authors have considered CE within an operant framework, there is no reason that the CE technique cannot be adapted to a classical conditioning mode. Extinction as a classical phenomenon involves the repeated presentation of the CE without the UCS, resulting in a reduction of the probability of eliciting the CR. The CE technique described by Cautela (1971) could be modified by having S imagine a stimulus (CS) which is typically followed by continuously associated internal stimuli (CR). The S would thus be instructed to imagine that the CS is presented, but that the CR does not occur. For example, a snake phobic would be asked to imagine that he is in the presence of a snake (CS) but does not become afraid (CR), i.e. he does not experience the autonomic arousal which usually occurs in the presence of snakes. Or, in another case, a pedophiliac might imagine that he is in the presence of very attractive female child (CS) but does not become appropriately aroused (CR). This is in contrast to the application of CE to instrumental behavior where the response is imagined repeatedly without the maintaining stimuli.

Thus the data support the hypothesis that the CE technique facilitates the extinction of overt responses whose covert representations are incorporated in the CE imagery when images of the contingent overt reinforcement are excluded.

REFERENCES

Ascher L. M. (1973) An analogue study of covert positive reinforcement, *Advances in Behavior Therapy* (Edited by Rubin R.), Academic Press, New York.

Cautela J.R. (1967) Covert sensitization, *Psychol. Rep.* **20**, 459–468.

Cautela J. R. (1970a) Covert reinforcement, *Behav. Ther.* **1**, 33–50.

Cautela J. R. (1970b) Covert negative reinforcement, *J. Behav. Ther. & Exp. Psychiat.* **1**, 273–278.

Cautela J. R. (1971) Covert extinction, *Behav. Ther.* **2**, 192–200.

Gotestam K. G. and Melin L. (1974) Covert extinction of amphetamine addiction, *Behav. Ther.* **5**, 90–93.

Kimble G. A. (1961) *Hilgard and Marquis' Conditioning and Learning,* Appleton-Century-Crofts, New York.

Wisocki P. A. (1973) The successful treatment of a heroin addict by covert conditioning techniques, *J. Behav. Ther. & Exp. Psychiat.* **4**, 55–61.

Chapter 19
Covert Extinction of Amphetamine Addiction*†
K. Gunnar Gotestam and Lennart Melin

Summary — A covert extinction paradigm is developed and applied to four addicts, with long-term and heavy intravenous abuse of central stimulants. The technique included the imaginative presentation of the patient's injection ritual, repeated 15 times a day. Three of the addicts have not taken amphetamines during a 9-month follow-up period.

Aversive conditioning procedures have been employed to eliminate drug-taking behavior of persons addicted to morphine, heroin, and demerol, and recently covert conditioning techniques have been used with heroin addicts (O'Brien, Raynes, & Patch, 1972). Cautela's (1970, 1971a) covert techniques offer several advantages over alternative behavior-modification procedures. First, they enable one to use more vivid situations (the complete addiction situation) compared to the simple items one could otherwise use in the ward (syringes, capsules, etc.); second, there are modest or no equipment requirements; and third, Cautela (1971b) has reported better patient participation and lower drop-out rates.

FOUR CASE PRESENTATIONS

Four female amphetamine addicts (mainlining 100–200 mg three to five

*Reprinted with permission from *Behavior Therapy*, 1974, 5, 90–92. © Academic Press, Inc. 1974.

†This research was supported in part by Anton and Dorotea Bexelius' Foundation.

times/day) were interviewed to obtain details of the circumstances under which they injected themselves with the drug. Two or more frequent injection situations were recorded. During a treatment trial one of these situations was presented to the patient, making sure that she could follow and vividly imagine the situation (see Cautela, 1970). Finally, the patient was told to imagine that she got no "flash," and that she felt no effect whatsoever.

The patient began training guided by a member of the staff. Later she did more and more by herself for a total of 8–15 trials a day, in two or three sessions. Each trial took 3–4 min.

Case Reports

Case 1. A 30-year-old woman, who had worked periodically, had taken amphetamine for 8 years, the last 6 years intravenously. Upon admission she was disturbed, showing an amphetamine psychosis with symptoms of delusions of persecution for a period of 1 month. At the start of the treatment she was taking chlorpromazine (75 mg daily).

The training trials comprised the imagination of a situation where she bought the drug at a market place, and then went alone to a public toilet where she prepared the syringe and injected the solution. After about 100 trials she absented herself without leave (AWOL) and took one injection of amphetamine. She reported afterwards that this produced no feeling at all. She was readmitted to the ward and completed a treatment with about 100 more trials. Thereafter she went home, and has taken no drug during a follow-up period of 9 months. (Our follow-up system includes contact with the patient after 2, 4, and 6 weeks, and 3, 6, 9, 12, and 24 months after discharge. At the same time we make contact with some person in the patient's environment, i.e., family, social worker.) She has started high school courses in an education program. She has continued the procedure when she feels a craving and reports that the craving disappears more quickly with this technique.

Case 2. A 47-year-old housewife with two children in the twenties had used amphetamine, together with her children, for about 18 months. She has worked periodically.

Her imagination training consisted of a situation where she went to a park with some friends, and there prepared a solution and injected it. The extinction treatment was performed 10 days, before she went AWOL. She took one injection in a park but did not experience the flash. She therefore took another injection, something she had never done before. She then felt the flash and continued to inject herself about 15 times during 1 week but under different circumstances. She came back to the ward but was discharged before therapy was completed. During the follow-up period of 9 months, she has not injected amphetamine but has been using alcohol during weekends. This was not a new behavior but represented an increase in frequency of an old one.

Case 3. A 16-year-old schoolgirl with a poor social adjustment had smoked cannabis for 4 years and injected amphetamines for 6 months.

During stimuli presentations she simply imagined injecting herself. After 12 trials she went AWOL and took three consecutive injections during 1 day. During these injections she did not experience a flash but only palpitations and nausea. This feeling had also been present during most of the training trials, though we tried to avoid both aversive and reinforcing stimuli. After she tried the drugs again, it was difficult to go on with the extinction trials because of tension symptoms. After another 3 weeks of relaxation training the extinction treatment continued and she was discharged to a new foster home. The 9-month follow-up shows that she has not taken amphetamine since the discharge.

Case 4. A 25-year-old woman started taking amphetamine 7 years ago. During periods of work which lasted up to 8 months she could be drug-free. However, she says she would return to amphetamine to reduce her increased weight and after about 1 or 2 weeks would be unable to continue work.

The stimuli presentations used were situations similar to those reported in Case 3. After 1 week's training she went AWOL. She took another dose of amphetamine together with a friend, with whom she shared the drug. The friend experienced the usual flash and euphoria but she herself did not. She continued to take drugs for 1 week, injecting herself about 20 times. She relapsed later in amphetamine-taking after 2½ months.

DISCUSSION

In our first four cases we have found that after about 1 week of treatment with the extinction procedure of about 100 trials, the patient does not react to addiction situations with autonomic symptoms. Even when they have taken amphetamine later, they have not experienced the flash.

The present study is not controlled and there are no self-administration animal studies on long-term effects of extinction in the literature. There are, however, some animal studies showing that the traditional therapeutic alternative, withdrawal of the drug, does not greatly affect later drug-taking behavior. Wikler and Pescor (1967, 1970) have shown that animals withdrawn from morphine for periods up to 1 year again self-administer morphine when given the opportunity. Wikler (1971) has also proposed the use of an extinction paradigm in the treatment of drug addiction.

REFERENCES

Cautela, J. R. Covert reinforcement. *Behavior Therapy*, 1970, **1**, 33–50.

Cautela, J. R. Covert extinction. *Behavior Therapy,* 1971a, **2**, 192–200.

Cautela, J. R. Covert conditioning. In A. Jacobs & L. B. Sachs (Eds.) *The psychology of private events.* New York: Academic Press, 1971b. Pp. 112–130.

O'Brien, J. S., Raynes, A. E., & Patch, V. D. Treatment of heroin addiction with aversion therapy, relaxation training and systematic desensitization. *Behaviour Research and Therapy,* 1972, **10**, 77–80.

Wikler, A. Some implications of conditioning theory for problems of drug abuse. *Behavioral Science,* 1971, **16**, 92–97.

Wikler, A. & Pescor, F. T. Classical conditioning of a morphine-abstinence phenomenon, reinforcement of opioid-drinking behavior and "relapse" in morphine-addicted rats. *Psychopharmacologia,* 1967, **10**, 255–284.

Wikler, A., & Pescor, F. T. Persistence of "relapse-tendencies" of rats previously made physically dependent on morphine. *Psychopharmacologia,* 1970, **16**, 375–384.

SECTION VI
COVERT MODELING

Chapter 20

The Present Status of Covert Modeling*

Joseph R. Cautela

Summary — In the covert modeling (CM) procedure, a client is asked to imagine he is observing a model behaving in various situations. CM is a covert conditioning procedure analogous to overt modeling. In this paper, the description of the procedure is presented together with relevant experimental data which support the assumption that CM can be as effective as overt modeling. Evidence is also cited which tends to indicate that the same parameters are involved in both CM and overt modeling. Advantages and cautions in the use of CM are discussed.

In recent papers (Cautela, 1967, 1970a, b, 1971a, 1973), I have reiterated the assumption that covert events obey the same laws as overt events. This view is consistent with the views of learning theorists such as Pavlov (1927); Guthrie (1935); Skinner (1938); Hull (1943) and Spence (1956). Experiments (Miller, 1935; Cohen, 1969; Schwartz and Higgins, 1971) comparing physiological responses during overt and covert activity lend support to the assumption. Indirect evidence is also presented by the many anecdotal and empirical studies demonstrating the effectiveness of procedures which I have subsumed under the rubric of ''covert conditioning'' (Cautela, 1973).

Studies on observational learning or modeling (Bandura, 1969, 1970, 1971; Bandura and Barab, 1973) indicate that modeling effects can be obtained without the presentation of live or film models. Bandura theorizes that mediational processes such as symbolic coding and covert rehearsal are crucial elements in observational learning. He also presents data to support this assumption (Bandura and Barab, 1973).

In view of the above considerations, it appeared that it would be fruitful,

---

*Reprinted with permission from the *Journal of Behavior Therapy and Experimental Psychiatry*, 1976, 7, 323-326. © Pergamon Press.

clinically and otherwise, to devise a procedure in which all the elements are manipulated covertly (Cautela, 1971b). The procedure is designated "covert modeling" since the subject (in an experiment) or the client (in a clinical setting) is given instructions to imagine observing a model performing various behaviors with particular consequences.

The procedure was initially developed for clients who claimed they could not imagine themselves performing behaviors in other covert conditioning techniques. They claimed that while it was difficult for them to imagine themselves performing behaviors, they could clearly imagine someone else doing the behavior.

DESCRIPTION OF THE PROCEDURE

First, the client is given the following rationale:

> The procedure we are going to use is based on a number of experiments in which people learn new habits by observing other people in various situations. The way this is usually done is that people actually observe others doing things. What I am going to do is vary this procedure somewhat by having you observe certain scenes in imagination rather than having you directly observe a movie or actual interaction among people. I am going to use scenes that I think will help you change the behavior we agreed needs changing. In a minute, I'll ask you to close your eyes, and try to imagine, as clearly as possible, that you are observing a certain situation. Try to use all the senses needed for the particular situation, e.g. try to actually hear a voice or see a person very clearly. After I describe the scene, I will ask you some questions concerning your feelings about the scene and how clearly you imagined it.

The client is then given a specific scene to imagine, and after that he is asked how clearly he imagined it and to describe his feelings during particular parts of it — whether they were pleasant, unpleasant, or neutral? He is also asked if the therapist described the scene too rapidly. On the basis of his replies, the scene may be modified before being presented again. When the client is able to report that the scene was clearly imagined, and the rate of presentation was satisfactory, he is asked to repeat the whole scene by himself. The scene is then repeated four times more by the therapist and four times by the client. The client is asked to practice each scene at home at least ten times per day. He is cautioned not to go through the scenes in a perfunctory or mechanical manner, but to imagine them as clearly as possible, in great detail.

Construction of Scenes

Factors relating to the clients' specific problems and parameters known to affect overt modeling are taken into account in the construction of modeling scenes. Some of these parameters are: behaviors that follow the behavior of the model, attentional processes, retention capacity of the observer, the number of trials of overt rehearsal of modeled responses, the covert practicing of modeled responses, the prestige of the model (Bandura, 1969, pp. 118–216), drive state (Schachter; 1964), age of the model (Bandura and Kupers; 1964) and consequences of behavior (Bandura, 1969, p. 128.

Examples of scenes used clinically are as follows:

(1) A client used to blush every time that words relating to homosexuality were spoken. He was afraid that his blushing would cause others to think that he was a homosexual. He reported that he could not obtain clear imagery of himself in situations concerning his blushing. However, he could clearly imagine someone else in those same situations. The imaginary model was meant to be used to extinguish his fear of the consequences of blushing.

I want you to imagine that there are two couples (about the same age as you) seated at a table in a restaurant. The restaurant is quite busy. All the tables are occupied and waiters are walking by the table. The people at the table seem to be enjoying their dinner. One of the men at the table says loudly, 'There's a gay bar next door'. The other fellow blushes, but nobody seems to notice and they start talking about how delicious the food is.

Thereafter, in a nearly identical situation the model did not blush at hearing the homosexual-related words. Similar modeling scenes were employed for other social situations.

(2) A client who liked to brag in front of women (for their approval) but who was extremely hurt by their criticism was given the following scene. The model, similar to the client in age, sex and occupation, displays coping behaviors.

I want you to imagine that you see a man about your age and a woman working together behind a counter in a restaurant. (The restaurant is described in some detail.) The man says to the woman, 'Next week I'm going to New York and have an audition for a play. Then maybe I'll get a job and make lots of money.' The woman looks disgusted and says, 'Boy, do you have pipe dreams; and besides, why are you always thinking about money? After she says this, the man starts to look upset and then sort of laughs to himself and continues his work, whistling. It is clear that criticism didn't bother him at all.

Other modeling scenes used in this case involved the model attenuating the bragging behavior and then being very socially reinforced.

EXPERIMENTAL DATA

The assumption of functional similarity between overt and covert events leads to a number of important empirical questions concerning CM. How does CM compare with overt modeling in terms of efficacy of behavior modification? Are the same parameters involved in both overt modeling and CM? Can the efficacy of CM be demonstrated experimentally with a clinical population?

Cautela, Flannery and Hanley (1974) have attempted to provide some data bearing on the first question. Kazdin (1973, 1974a, 1974b) in a series of studies has addressed himself to the investigation of the parameters of covert modeling and its efficacy on a clinical population under controlled conditions.

The first obvious step in a research strategy was to determine if CM would exhibit an effect under laboratory conditions while at the same time comparing its efficacy with overt modeling. Cautela, Flannery and Hanley (1974) found overt modeling and CM equally effective in the reduction of fear of rats in a laboratory situation.

Kazdin (1973, 1974a, b) has set out to systematically explore the effectiveness and parameters of CM. Kazdin (1973) investigated the efficacy of CM in reducing snake avoidance. He also tried to determine if the same parameters of overt modeling applied to CM. Kazdin found that treatment effects were better with CM using a coping model as compared with a mastery model. This finding is similar to that observed in overt modeling (Meichenbaum, 1971).

In another study, Kazdin (1974a) replicated the finding of the superiority of coping models in CM and also demonstrated that perceived similarity to the model in CM enhances imitation. This result replicates the finding in observational learning that the greater the perceived similarity of a model to the observer, the greater the imitation (Bandura, Ross and Ross, 1963; Burnstein, Stotland and Zander, 1971; Stotland, Zander and Natsoulas, 1961).

Kazdin (1974b) also examined CM with persons referred from a clinic for their poor assertive behavior. He found that CM which resulted in favorable consequences to the model's behavior was more effective than modeled behavior with no consequences.

The above results indicate that:

(1) CM can be as effective as overt modeling in modifying behavior (Cautela, Flannery and Hanley, 1974).

(2) The same parameters that effect overt modeling should have similar effects on CM (Kazdin, 1973, 1974a).

(3) CM can be tested and shown effective with clinical populations (Kazdin, 1974b).

(4) CM can be made more effective if the consequences of the model's behavior are also manipulated (Kazdin, 1974b).

AREAS CALLING FOR RESEARCH

Besides further verification of the general efficacy of the procedure, a number of empirical questions need investigation:

(1) What are the determinants of particular persons' inability to to imagine themselves in situations while able to imagine others?

(2) Does it affect clinical effectiveness if the client observes himself rather than someone else as the model?

(3) How does the efficacy of CM compare with that of desensitization?

(4) How does CM compare with overt modeling on such parameters as prestige of model?

(5) What is the relevance of particular model characteristics, such as an idealized model, abstract model without particular features, a specific individual known and admired by the client?

REFERENCES

Bandura, A. (1969) *Principles of Behavior Modification*, Holt, Rinehart & Winston, New York.

Bandura A. (1970) Modeling theory, *Psychology of Learning Systems, Models, and Theories* (Edited by Sahakian W. S.), Markham, Chicago.

Bandura A. (1971) Psychotherapy based upon modeling principles, *Handbook of Psychotherapy and Behavior Change* (Edited by Bergen A. E. and Garfield S. L.), Wiley, New York.

Bandura A. and Barab P. G. (1973) Processes governing disinhibitory effects through symbolic modeling, *J. abnorm. Psychol.* **82**, 1–9.

Bandura A. and Kupers C. J. (1964) Transmission of patterns of self-reinforcement through modeling, *J. abnorm. soc. Psychol.* **69**, 1–9.

Bandura A., Ross D. and Ross S. A. (1963) Imitation of film-mediated aggressive models, *J. abnorm. soc. Psychol.* **66**, 3–11.

Burnstein E., Stotland E. and Zander A. (1961) Similarity to a model and self-evaluation, *J. abnorm. soc. Psychol.* **62**, 257–264.

Cautela J. R. (1967) Covert sensitization, *Psychol. Rep.* **20**, 459–468.

Cautela J. R. (1970a) Covert negative reinforcement, *J. Behav. Ther. & Exp. Psychiat.* **1**, 273–278.

Cautela J. R. (1970b) Covert reinforcement, *Behav. Therapy* **1**, 33–50.

Cautela J. R. (1971a) Covert extinction, *Behav. Therapy* **2**, 192–200.

Cautela J. R. (1971b) Covert modeling, Paper presented to the Association for the Advancement of Behavior Therapy, Washington, D.C.

Cautela J. R. (1973) Covert processes and behavior modification, *J. nerv. ment. Dis.* **157**, 27–36.

Cautela J. R., Flannery R. and Hanley S. (1974) Covert modeling: An experimental test, *Behav. Therapy,* in press.

Cohen J. (1969) Very slow brain waves relating to expectancy: The contingent negative variation (CNV), *Average Evoked Potentials: Results and Evaluations* (Edited by Duchin E. and Lindsley D. B.), U.S. Government Printing Office, Washington, D.C.

Guthrie E. R. (1935) *The Psychology of Learning*, Harper, New York.

Hull C. L. (1943) *Principles of Behavior*, Appleton-Century-Crofts, New York.

Kazdin A. E. (1973) Covert modeling and the reduction of avoidance behavior, *J. abnorm. Psychol.* **81**, 78–95.

Kazdin A. E. (1974a) Covert modeling, model similarity, and the reduction of avoidance behavior, *Behav. Therapy* **5**, 325–340.

Kazdin A. E. (1974b) Effects of covert modeling and the reinforcement of assertive behavior, *J. abnorm. Psychol.* (in press).

Meichenbaum D. H. (1971) Examination of model characteristics in reducing avoidance behavior, *J. Pers. Soc. Psychol.* **17**, 298–307.

Miller N. E. (1935) The influence of past experience upon the transfer of subsequent training. Ph.D. Dissertation, Yale University.

Pavlov I. P. (1927) *Conditioned Reflexes* (Translated by Anrep G. V.), Oxford University Press, London.

Schachter S. (1964) The interaction of cognitive and physiological determinants of emotional state, *Advances in Experimental Social Psychology* (Edited by Berkowitz L.), Vol. 1, Academic Press, New York, pp. 49–60.

Schwartz G. E. and Higgins J. D. (1971) Cardiac activity preparatory to overt and covert behavior, *Science* **173**, 1144–1146.

Skinner B. F. (1938) *The Behavior of Organisms: An Experimental Analysis,* Appleton-Century-Crofts, New York.

Spence K. W. (1956) *Behavior Theory and Conditioning,* Yale University Press, New Haven.

Stotland E. Zander A. and Natsoulas T. (1961) The generalization of interpersonal similarity, *J. abnorm. soc. Psychol.* **62**, 250–256.

Chapter 21
Covert Modeling: An Experimental Test*
Joseph R. Cautela
Raymond B. Flannery, Jr.
and Stephen Hanley

Summary — The effects of covert modeling, overt modeling, and attention placebo were compared in the reduction of fear of rats in a laboratory situation. There was no difference between the overt and covert groups on three behavioral or two subjective measures. The overt group was superior on one subjective measure. This supports other experimental and anecdotal evidence that covert and overt modeling are equally effective.

Covert conditioning procedures (cf. Cautela, 1971a) have been labeled Covert Sensitization (Cautela, 1966; 1967), Covert Reinforcement (Cautela, 1970a), Covert Negative Reinforcement (Cautela, 1970b), and Covert Extinction (Cautela, 1971b). The main assumption underlying these procedures is that a stimulus presented in imagination via instructions can affect covert and overt behavior in a manner similar to a stimulus presented externally. Recently, Cautela (1971c) has developed a clinically effective procedure designated Covert Modeling (CM) in which the modeling situation is presented completely in the imagination via instructions.

The purpose of this paper is to compare the effectiveness of the CM procedure with overt modeling (OM) and attention placebo groups in a controlled laboratory situation. (Cf. a comparable but less controlled study by Bandura, Blanchard, and Ritter, 1969, who investigated the differential effects of OM, Systematic Desensitization and Contact Desensitization.)

---

*Reprinted with permission from *Behavior Therapy*, 1974, *5*, 494–502. © Academic Press, Inc. 1974.

METHOD

Subjects

Thirty female undergraduates were selected in a two-step procedure. Individuals who reported strong aversions to laboratory rats on the Fear of Laboratory Rats Survey were asked to come to the laboratory to approach, stroke, and hold the phobic stimulus. Two attitudinal questionnaires were then completed in an adjoining office. Thirty subjects were chosen on the basis of the data (criteria discussed below) and allocated at random to one of three equated groups.

Measures

Behavioral measures.   A laboratory rat roaming about freely on a 1-ft sq. platform on top of a 4-ft-high wooden stand was used as the fear-evoking stimulus. The experimenter and the subjects wore heavy duty leather gloves with 4-inch nylon cuffs in the handling of the animal. The Approach measure consisted of 10 1-ft increments which were crossed when a subject moved toward the animal platform. The point at which the subject chose to stop was recorded. The Stroke measure consisted of touching the rat and stroking its back twice. Credit was given for the last behavioral measure, Hold, if the subject was able to pick up and hold the actual fear stimulus for 1 min. The last two measures were scored in a dichotomous fashion (''yes'' or ''no''). Because of the factorial complexity of fear (Lang, 1969), these three measures were considered to be uncorrelated.

Subjective measures. The Fear Intensity Scale (cf. Lang & Lazovik, 1963; Flannery, 1972) ranged from ''no fear'' (1) to ''very intense fear'' (7).
The Fear of Laboratory Rats Survey, an initial classroom screening device describing five levels of avoidance or fear of laboratory rats, was employed.
Two additional attitudinal subjective measures were a semantic differential measurement of the actual fear and a specially constructed questionnaire to assess the subjects' fear of the laboratory rats in six different settings. These two measures were similar to those employed by Bandura *et al.* (1969), except that the name of the fear object was changed. Again, the subjective measures were not assumed to be necessarily correlated.

PROCEDURE

Pretreatment Stage

Each subject who had reported strong aversions on the Fear of Laboratory Rats

Survey was asked to complete the two attitudinal measures and given a brief test for adequate visual imagery in which she was requested to describe the food colors at her last meal (Cautela, 1970a). No subject was rejected for lack of visual imagery. Then she went to the laboratory where she was asked to approach the animal, stroke it twice, and hold it for 1 min. Still in the presence of the actual fear stimulus, she completed the Fear Intensity Scale. All laboratory pretesting was done by the second author to hold constant the effects of model prestige (Bandura, 1969) and minimize experimenter bias, (Rosenthal & Rosnow, 1969). In addition the second author stood 4 ft away from the fear stimulus to avoid vicarious learning or counterconditioning (Davison, 1968).

The 30 selected individuals were put into two treatment groups (overt modeling versus covert modeling) or the control group for attention effects. Subjects ranged in their approach behavior from 2 ft to 8 ft with a mean of 6 ft (see Table 1).

When asked to stroke the animal, two of the 30 subjects forced themselves forward in an attempt to stroke the rat, then ran quickly from the laboratory and reported intense, subjective fear. None of the remaining 28 subjects would hold and stroke the rat.

On the Fear Intensity Scale, subjects, scores ranged from mild (2) to very intense (7), with a mean of 3.6 for each group. On the semantic differential and attitudinal measures, the mean level of avoidance for each group was substantial.

No group was statistically different from any other on any of the above measures.

Apart from their use in previous research (Barlow *et al.*, 1969; Flannery, 1972), these criteria meet the ethical consideration of choosing a problem not central to daily living of the subjects concerned (DeMoor, 1970).

Treatment Stages

Each subject was seen for three 50-min sessions within a 7-day period. For the treatment group observing the model and actual fear stimulus covert modeling) (T_1), the subject was immediately taken to the laboratory and placed in a chair 8 ft away from the experimental animal. The model explained to each subject that experiments had proved that just by watching other people say or do things, the behavior of a person is influenced. An example was given and the subject instructed to observe the second author until he said the word "stop," at which time she was asked to sit in a second chair 10 ft away from the laboratory and the model. She was instructed to return to the chair at the laboratory door when the model indicated that the next observational period was to begin. The observational periods consisted of six 2-min scenes, at intervals of 1 min, modeled by the second author from a previously written and rehearsed script. The scenes included the model familiarizing himself with the laboratory, talking to the animal in his cage, taking the animal out of his cage, watching the animal roam freely on the platform, stroking the actual fear stimulus twice, and holding it for 1 min. The script, written to describe the actual laboratory, fear-evoking stimulus, and model attempted to include the correct behavioral responses, the discriminative stimuli, the reinforcement contingencies, and the prestige of a model who was always referred to as "doctor" (Bandura, 1969, pp. 118–216).

During covert modeling the subject imagines someone else engaged in the behavioral repertoire. It was decided to incorporate a second experimenter for four reasons: First, an experimenter reading the CM scene is consistent with the clinical procedure being evaluated. Second, if the first experimenter read the CM scenes, overt modeling would occur. The experimenter would be present, relaxed, asking the subject to image himself, while the subject actually heard his relaxed voice. All of these comprised OM and could have enhanced fear reduction. Third, if the first experimenter read the scenes, CM would be given an experimental advantage due to the enhanced learning situation. Finally, if the present investigation led to meaningful data, another experiment could be conducted with the same experimenter serving for all three groups.

For the treatment group observing the model and fear-evoking stimulus covertly (covert modeling) (T_2), each subject remained in an office with the third author, the second experimenter. He read the following instructions, the same as those used clinically (Cautela, 1971c), to each subject after the brief explanation of vicarious learning given to the subjects in T_1:

"What I am going to do is vary this modeling procedure somewhat by having you observe certain scenes in imagination rather than have you directly observe a movie or actual interaction among people. I am going to use scenes that I think will help you change the behavior we agreed needs changing. In a minute I'll ask you to close your eyes, and try to vividly imagine, as clearly as possible, that you are observing a certain situation. Try to use all the senses needed for the particular situation, e.g., try to actually hear a voice or see a person very quickly. After I describe the scene, I will ask you some questions concerning your feeling about the scene and how clearly you imagined it."

The third author then proceeded to read the six scenes from the same script being modeled in the laboratory. Again, each scene was interspersed with an intertrial rest period of 1-min duration. However, each subject remained in the office.

The attention control group (C_1) subjects likewise spent their three individual sessions in the office with the third author. They were told that a discussion of fear of laboratory rats would result in insight that would help change his fear. To equalize demand characteristics these sessions were spent exploring the origin and nature of the subjects' fears.

Posttreatment Stage

At the end of the third and last experimental session, each subject was submitted once more to the three behavioral measures — approach, stroke, hold — and asked to complete the Fear Intensity Scale in the laboratory and the two attitudinal measures in the office. All posttesting in the laboratory was conducted by the second author.

RESULTS

Behavioral Indices

Subjects approached the rat more closely after treatment, and more subjects in these two treatment groups stroked the rat and held it after treatment than before (Table 1). No appreciable change in these measures was observed for the attention control group which continued to show the same amount of fear as all subjects had during the initial exposure to the rat. One exception to this was a slight increase in the number of attention control group subjects who would stroke the animal after treatment. Furthermore, the treatment group presented with the actual fear stimulus during treatment sessions (T_1) appeared to decrease its fear somewhat more than the treatment group presented with the fear stimulus in imagination only (T_2). Significant main and interaction effects were found for the repeated factor (pre- and posttreatment) ($F(1,27) = 26.2$) beyond the .01 level, and for the interaction effect ($F(2,27) = 4.92$) at the .05 level. As in the rest of this study, individual comparisons were carried out by the more conservative post hoc Newman-Keuls procedure (Winer, 1962). Each of the two treatment groups significantly increased the number of feet approached to the fear stimulus ($p < .01$). The control group did not significantly change its approach measure. It should be noted that all groups had been equated for the initial approach measure so that differences in rate of fear reduction, i.e., rate of increase in approach, would also reflect differences in final fear of the rat. No significant difference as found in fear reduction among the three groups, and no significant difference in rate of fear reduction was found between the two treatment groups.

For the other two behavioral measures, stroke and hold, nonparametric tests measuring the number of subjects reducing their fear were carried out. To measure within group changes, McNemar's test was used (Siegel, 1956). Initially, one subject in T_2 and C_1 would stroke the animal; however, all groups at first displayed the same inability to hold the rat. In T_1, nine subjects changed from not being able to stroke the animal to stroking it. One subject who initially refused to stroke the animal continued to do so. This change was significant ($X^2(1) = 6.1; p < .02$). Similarly, eight of these subjects, who

Table 21.1 Mean Number of Feet Approached to Fear Stimulus, and Mean Scores on the Self-report Fear and Attitude Measures for Pre- and Posttreatment (SD in parenthesis)

	Groups					
	T_1		T_2		C	
	Pre	Post	Pre	Post	Pre	Post
Measures	treatment		treatment		treatment	
Approach	6.4	9.6	6.4	9.3	6.4	6.7
	(± 1.70)	($\pm .97$)	(1.90)	(1.89)	(1.90)	(2.54)
Fear Intensity Scale	3.6	1.5	3.7	1.9	3.6	3.8
	(1.26)	(.85)	(1.39)	(1.20)	(1.51)	(2.09)
Semantic Differential	44.4	24.9	44.8	21.1	42.5	36.7
	(.93)	(.96)	(.98)	(1.14)	(1.07)	(1.24)
Attitude Scale	39.7	16.9	39.5	22.5	38.7	38.0
	(.90)	(.79)	(1.20)	(1.66)	(1.18)	(1.88)

Number of Subjects Who Stroked and Held Fear Stimulus
on Pretreatment and Posttreatment Conditions

	Groups					
	T_1		T_2		C	
	Pre	Post	Pre	Post	Pre	Post
Measures	treatment		treatment		treatment	
Stroke	0	9	1	9	1	3
Hold	0	8	0	5	0	0

refused to do so previously, held the rat. The other subjects continued to refuse to hold the animal. This increase in the number of subjects reducing their fear was also significant ($X^2(1) = 6.1$; $p < .02$). In the T_2 group, one subject stroked the animal both before and after treatment, one refused to do so at either time, and eight subjects who initially refused to stroke the animal did so after treatment. The number of subjects changing in stroking the rat was significant at the .02 level ($X^2(1) = 6.1$). Five subjects decided to hold the rat after treatment, whereas the remaining five subjects continued to refuse to hold the animal. This difference was almost significant the .05 level (observed $X^2(1) = 3.2$; expected $X^2 = 3.84$). In the control group (C_1), two subjects who initially refused to stroke the animal now stroked it after treatment, one subject continued to stroke it both before and after treatment, and six subjects refused to stroke it. This difference in the number of subjects willing to stroke the animal after treatment was not significant ($X^2(1) = .5$). No significant change was found in the number of subjects unable to hold the rat. In fact, not one subject changed after treatment.

Fisher exact probabilities tests (Siegel, 1956) were carried out in comparing differences between groups for the number of subjects who reduced their fear as measured by the stroke and hold measures. Significantly more T_1 subjects decreased their unwillingness to stroke ($p < .01$) and hold ($p < .005$) the rat than the control group. Similarly, T_2 subjects also significantly decreased their unwillingness to stroke ($p < .01$) and hold ($p < .05$) the animal more than the control group. No significant difference was found between the number of T_1 and T_2 subjects who changed their initial unwillingness to hold the actual fear stimulus.

T_1 did not differ significantly from T_2 on any measure. Presenting the actual fear stimulus during treatment did not result in significantly greater behavioral gains than presenting the fear stimulus in imagination.

Subjective Measures

There appeared to be appreciable decreases in fear measure and the two attitudinal measures for both treatment groups. Only on the semantic differential attitude measure did the control group appear to show any decrease (Table 1).

A repeated measures analysis of variance for the fear intensity scale and the two attitudinal measures was carried out to determine the significance of the observed outcome differences. Significant main and interaction effects for the fear intensity scale were found for groups at the .05 level ($F(2,27) = 4.2$), the repeated factor (pre- and posttreatment scores) at the .01 level ($F(1,27) = 5.6$), and the double interaction effect at the .001 level ($F(2,27) = 20.1$). Each treatment group significantly decreased their subjective fear to the actual fear stimulus ($p < .01$). The control group did not change its level of fear intensity significantly. All groups had been equated for the initial fear intensity measure so that differences in rate of fear reduction, i.e., rate of decrease in intensity of self-reported fear to the actual fear stimulus, would also reflect differences in final fear of the rat. Each treatment group significantly decreased its subjective fear intensity to the animal more than the control group at the .01 level. In addition, the T_1 group differed significantly from the T_2 group in its reduction in intensity of fear ($p < .01$).

The first attitude measure was the adapted semantic differential. A significant main and interaction effect was found at the .01 level for the repeated factor (pre- and posttreatment) ($F(1,27 = 51.9$) and the interaction effect ($F(2,27) = 5.7$). Individual comparisons were again carried out by the post hoc Newman-Keuls procedure. Each of the two experimental groups significantly increased their positive evaluations of the animal at the .01 level of significance. There was no significant change in the positive feelings of the control group. No significant difference was found among the three groups; nor did group T_2 differ significantly from the T_2 group on this measure.

The second attitudinal measure assessed the subjects' distress of the rat in a variety of situations. Again, significant main and interaction effects at the .01 level were found for the repeated factor (pre- and post-treatment scores) ($F(1,27) = 24.5$) and the interaction effect ($F(1,27) = 5.96$). Individual comparisons by the Newman-Keuls procedure indicated that both treatment groups significantly decreased their attitudes of being afraid of the actual fear stimulus in a wide variety of situations at the .01 level, while the attitudes of the control group did not change significantly. The subjects in T_2 did not differ significantly from the subjects in T_2 on this measure.

Presenting the actual fear stimulus during treatment had a greater effect in the reduction of self-reported fear than the other types of treatment. Further, both forms of modeling treatment led to significantly more positive attitudes on both questionnaires than did discussion alone.

DISCUSSION

CM can be as effective as OM in reducing college students' fears of laboratory rats. Only on one measure, the fear index, was OM superior to CM, perhaps because the fear index was obtained in the presence of a rat after the behavioral measures were completed. Subjects in the CM group reported that at the postexperimental inquiry they were somewhat taken aback by the squirming of the rat and did not know how to handle the squirming animal. Thus, this group reported fear at that time greater than the OM group who had had a chance to observe the experimenter holding the rat during the OM procedure.

The decision to employ a second experimenter (third author) was justified since the CM group treatment effects were not enhanced unduly and were consistent with the OM group. Also, the difference in results between the Attention Control and CM groups using the same experimenter did not appear to lead to behavioral changes by demand characteristics in the Attention Control group (cf. Kazdin, 1963).

Recent studies by Kazdin (1973; 1974) add further support to the assumption that OM and CM are influenced by similar parameters. Kazdin (1973) reasoned that as CM had similar properties to OM, then the results of Meichenbaum (1971) using film models should be duplicated. Meichenbaum found that, when a model is initially anxious (similar to the anxious observer) and overcomes his anxiety (i.e., a coping model), greater anxiety reduction in the observer results than with a model who appears completely unafraid (i.e., a mastery model). Using CM, Kazdin (1973) found that both a coping group and a mastery group had significant fear reduction in snake avoidance, but that the coping group had greater change on posttests. No difference was reported in the nonmodeled scene control group. In another study, Kazdin (1974), found that using a covert model of the same age and sex as the subject had a greater effect in reducing fear in snake avoidance than using a covert model who was older and of the opposite sex (cf. Bandura, Ross, & Ross, 1963; Hicks, 1965).

REFERENCES

Bandura, A., Blanchard, E., & Ritter, B. G. Relative efficacy of desensitization; and modeling approaches for inducing behavioral, affective, and attitudinal changes. *Journal of Personality and Social Psychology,* 1969, **13**, 173–199.

Bandura, A., Ross, D., & Ross, S. Imitation of film-mediated aggressive models. *Journal of Abnormal and Social Psychology,* 1963, **66**, 3–11.

Barlow, D., Leitenberg, H., Agras, W., & Wincze, J. The transfer gap in systematic desensitization: An analogue study. *Behaviour Research and Therapy,* 1969, **7**, 191–196.

Cautela, J. R. Treatment of compulsive behavior by covert sensitization. *Psychological Record,* 1966, **16**, 33–41.

Cautela, J. R. Covert sensitization. *Psychological Record,* 1967, **20**, 459–468.

Cautela, J. R. Covert reinforcement. *Behavior Therapy,* 1970 (a), **1**, 33–50.

Cautela, J. R. Covert negative reinforcement. *Journal of Behavior Therapy and Experimental Psychiatry,* 1970 (b), **1**, 273–278.

Cautela, J. R. Covert conditioning. In A. Jacobs & L. B. Sachs (Eds.), *Psychology of private events.* New York: Academic Press, 1971 (a), pp. 112–130.

Cautela, J. R. Covert extinction. *Behavior Therapy,* 1971 (b), **2**, 192–200.

Cautela, J. R. Covert modeling. Paper presented at the Fifth Annual Meeting of the Association for Advancement of Behavior Therapy, Washington, D. C., September, 1971 (c).

Davison, G. Systematic desensitization as a counterconditioning process. *Journal of Abnormal Psychology,* 1968, **73**, 91–99.

DeMoor, W. Systematic desensitization versus prolonged high intensity stimulation (flooding). *Journal of Behavior Therapy and Experimental Psychiatry,* 1970, **1**, 45–52.

Flannery, R. B., Jr. A laboratory analogue of two covert reinforcement procedures. *Journal of Behavior Therapy and Experimental Psychiatry,* 1972, **3**, 1–7.

Hicks, D. J. Imitation and retention of film-mediated aggressive peer and adult models. *Journal of Personality and Social Psychology,* 1965, **2**, 97–100.

Kazdin, A. Covert modeling and the reduction of avoidance behavior. *Journal of Abnormal Psychology,* 1973, **81**, 87–95.

Kazdin, A. Covert modeling, model similarity, and reduction of avoidance behavior. *Behavior Therapy,* 1974, **5**, 325–340.

Lang, P. The mechanics of desensitization and the laboratory study of human fear. In C. M. Franks (Ed.), *Behavior therapy: Appraisal and status.* New York: McGraw-Hill, 1969, pp. 160–191.

Lang, P. J., & Lazovik, A. D. Experimental desensitization of a phobia. *Journal of Abnormal and Social Psychology,* 1963, **66**, 519–525.

Meichenbaum, D. Examination of model characteristics in reducing avoidance behavior. *Journal of Personality and Social Psychology,* 1971, **17**, 298–307.

Rosenthal, R., & Rosnow, R. *Artifacts in behavioral research.* New York: Academic Press, 1969.

Siegel, M. *Nonparametric statistics for the behavioral sciences.* New York: McGraw-Hill, 1956.

Winer, B. *Statistical principles in experimental design.* New York: McGraw-Hill, 1962.

Chapter 22
Covert Modeling and the Reduction of Avoidance Behavior*†
Alan E. Kazdin

Summary — The present study investigated the effect of covert modeling in reducing snake avoidance. Covert modeling entails the modeling paradigm without live or film models. A model who executed behaviors which would be anxiety provoking for the subject was imagined by the subject. Different model descriptions were used: a coping model who was depicted as initially anxious but eventually fearless in fear-relevant scenes and a mastery model who was depicted as performing fearlessly throughout the scenes. A scene control group received similar scenes as modeling groups without the presence of the model. A delayed-treatment control group was used to assess the effects of repeated testing at pretreatment and posttreatment assessments and received no intervening treatment. Subsequently, this group received convert modeling without specification of affective cues of the model. In two sessions, all covert modeling groups showed significant increases in approach behavior and reductions in emotional arousal and anxiety ratings. Changes in attitudes were less consistent across treatments. No-treatment and scene control groups did not improve on any of the measures. As predicted from previous work on attributes of the model, a coping model led to greater change at postest than the mastery model. The effect of both treatment conditions was maintained at a 3-week follow-up assessment.

Recently, several investigators have demonstrated the efficacy of modeling techniques in altering persistent avoidance behaviors (Bandura, Blanchard, & Ritter, 1969; Bandura, Grusec, & Menlove, 1967; Bandura & Menlove, 1968; Blanchard, 1970; Geer & Turteltaub, 1967; Hill, Liebert, & Mott, 1968; Meichenbaum, 1971). In the usual modeling procedure, live or symbolic (film) models are employed. An essential feature of observational learning via

*Reprinted with permission from the *Journal of Abnormal Psychology*, 1973, *81*, 7-95. ©The Americal Psychological Association 1973.

†This research was supported by a grant from the Pennsylvania State University, Liberal Arts College Central Fund for Research.

modeling is that no apparent overt responses are performed. Hence, covert processes or imaginal representations of the observed performance are assumed to guide behavior in the observer. Thus, external stimuli cues (live or filmed performance of a model) are coded and represented symbolically by the observer (Bandura, 1970). This explanation of modeling suggests that direct observation of a model is not essential for altering performance as long as the covert processes which guide behavior are modified. One way to achieve modeling effects is with verbal instructions (Bandura, 1970). To the extent that instructions convey response information which can guide behavior, they serve a modeling function.

Cautela (1971) has proffered another modeling technique which can be conducted without live or film models. The procedure is referred to as covert modeling because the subjects imagines a model (or models) engages in various behaviors. The behaviors performed in imagination by the model are those behaviors which are to be altered in the subject. Interestingly, with this paradigm the representational images which are assumed to be altered as a function of live modeling (Bandura, 1970) can be focused upon directly to alter behavior. One purpose of the present investigation was to determine if modeling stimuli can be presented covertly via instructions to achieve a reduction in avoidance behavior.

Similarity of the model and observer is important in modeling. Generally, the greater the perceived similarity, the greater the imitation (Burnstein, Stotland, & Zander, 1961; Flanders, 1968; Rosekrans, 1967), although there are some exceptions (Hicks, 1965). Using film models, Meichenbaum (1971) found that a model who is initially anxious (similar to the anxious observer) but overcomes his anxiety (i.e., a coping model) results in greater anxiety reduction in the observer than a model who is completely fearless (i.e., a mastery model). It was predicted in the present study that similarity of the covert model would influence imitation as it has with film models. The coping model was predicted to result in greater behavior change than a mastery model and a model in which no affective cues were present.

The present experiment examined the effectiveness of covert modeling and the influence of a model characteristic in reducing avoidance behavior. One model was depicted as initially anxious but eventually fearless; another model was depicted as fearless throughout the covert modeling procedure. Two control groups were included in the design to control for the effects of imagining fear-relevant scenes and the influence of repeated assessment on avoidance behavior.

METHOD

Subjects

The Ss were 20 male and 44 female undergraduate students enrolled in introductory psychology at Pennsylvania State University. These Ss were included from a pool of 80 students who reported extreme fears of nonpoisonous harmless snakes on the Fear Survey Schedule (Geer, 1965) and failed to touch a small snake on a behavioral test. The subjects were screened from 647 volunteers.

Assessment of Avoidance Attitudes and Behavior

After selecting extremely fearful subjects on the Fear Survey Schedule, subjects were met individually by a female experimenter who administered attitude and behavioral measures of avoidance. The assessment battery was administered at pretreatment, posttreatment, and 3 weeks following treatment.

Attitude measures. Two measures of attitudes toward snakes were administered prior to the behavioral test. First, a semantic differential rating (Osgood, Suci, & Tannenbaum, 1967) of "snakes" was used. This included 11 bipolar adjectives reflecting the evaluative dimension. A second measure was a snake attitude survey consisting of six items describing encounters with snakes (Bandura et al., 1969). Ratings from 1 (strong dislike) to 7 (strong enjoyment) were made for each item.

Behavioral test and Fear Thermometer. The behavioral test of avoidance, similar to the procedure used by other investigators (Davison, 1968; Lang & Lazovik, 1963), consisted of 14 tasks requiring increasingly intimate contact with a caged snake (1½ feet in length). The tasks included approaching the snake cage with progressively greater proximity, handling the snake first with and then without gloves, holding the snake on one's arm, and holding the snake about 10 inches from one's face for 30 seconds.

Prior to the avoidance test, factual information was given describing characteristics of snakes. Subjects were informed that snakes were not slimy, felt cool because they take on the temperature of their environment, and may use their tongue as an exploratory rather than an agressive device. This procedure was used to exclude subjects whose performance gains in retesting might reflect the effect of incidental information acquired from the test (Bandura et al., 1969). Subjects were told to enter the room where the snake was caged. If subjects could not do this a score of zero was given. If subjects entered the room, the series of graded tasks was presented. The subject's score consisted of the number of tasks completed. Subjects who could touch the snake at all were excluded from the study.

While subjects performed the behavioral test, measures of fear arousal were obtained. After each task was completed, the subject was asked to rate his anxiety on a zero (no anxiety) to 10-point (most anxiety ever felt) scale. The assistant stood behind and out of direct view of the subject as she described the task to avoid providing cues and expectancies for performance. The assistant was "blind" as to the hypotheses and experimental conditions.

Anxiety after behavioral test. The final measure administered was an adjective checklist for anxiety (Zuckerman. 1960). After completing the behavioral test, subjects completed this checklist to describe their feelings at that moment. The maximum score on the checklist was 21, indicating high anxiety.

Treatment Conditions

Subjects were individually matched on the basis of their pretreatment avoidance on the behavioral test and assigned randomly to one of four conditions. Each group contained 16 subjects. Subjects were randomly assigned to one of four experimenters, with the restriction that each experimenter have the same number of subjects in each experimental condition. The experimenters (three males, one female) were senior psychology undergraduates. Two experimenters had participated in pilot work the previous term and had extensive experience with similar treatments. The experimenters were ''blind'' to the specific hypotheses of the study. For each treatment group, subjects were told that they were to imagine various scenes but were not informed that the procedures might effect behavior change. The procedures were presented as a basis from which information could be obtained about measuring fears.

Treatment was administered in two sessions. In the first session, subjects practiced visualizing two scenes, one involving a college student (the model) ''similar in age and sex'' to the subject and the other involving the snake. The subject was asked to describe the practice scenes as imagined and queried for details. Subjects were encouraged to imagine scenes as vividly as possible and were given examples of dimensions to notice. After the practice scenes, the 14 treatment scenes were presented. The scenes, taken directly from the 14 tasks in the behavior approach test, involved increasingly intimate interaction with the snake. When presented with a scene description, subjects were instructed to signal by raising a finger to note when the image was pictured clearly. Descriptions of treatment scenes were not solicited from the subject. Each scene was held for 15 seconds from the time the subject signaled that the image was clearly picuted. During each treatment session, the same 14 scenes were presented once. Each treatment session lasted approximately 15 minutes. The following treatments were used.

Covert coping model. Subjects in this condition imagined 14 treatment scenes in which the covert model (same-sexed college student) was depicted as anxious, hesitant, and worried in his (her) approach to the task. In each scene, the model eventually coped with the task by taking deep breaths to relax and become confident. A typical scene was:

Imagine that the person (model) puts on the gloves and tries to pick up the snake out of the cage. As the person is doing this he sort of hesitates and avoids grasping the snake at first. He stops and relaxes himself, feels calm, and picks up the snake.

Within each scene, the model eventually coped with his anxiety and performed the task calmly. Across all 14 scenes, the model became less anxious and more confident so that by the last two scenes there were only confident approach responses. These last *two* scenes were worded identically for coping and mastery conditions. For example, the last scene was:

Imagine the person holding the snake in his (her) hands about 10 inches away from the face. Imagine the person very calm and relaxed. Picture him (her) smiling because he (she) is not bothered. He (she) can look at the snake without fear.

Covert Mastery model. Subjects in this condition imagined treatment scenes in which the model was depicted as confident, unbothered, and completely at ease while performing the tasks. A typical scene was: "Imagine that the person puts on the gloves and picks up the snake out of the cage. Picture him (her) doing this confidently and holding the snake close to his (her) body." Descriptive phrases in the scenes included performing the tasks without hesitation, while smiling, remaining calm, looking confident, and appearing relaxed.

No-model scene control. Subjects in this group practiced visualizing a model and snake. During each treatment session, 14 scenes were presented of the snake and snake cage in order of increasingly more arousing scenes which paralleled those of the behavioral test. However, no model interacting with the snake was included in the scenes (e.g., "Imagine the snake sticking its head outside of the cage.") This group controlled for the effect of imagining scenes involving increasingly greater proximity to snakes.

Delayed-treatment control. This group received no treatment between the first two assessments (i.e., pretreatment and posttreatment). After the initial assessment was completed, these subjects returned for reassessment. Reassessment was timed so that a control subject came in when the other subjects in the block of four subjects (one from each group) were scheduled for reassessment. Thus, the interval between assessment and reassessment was similar for all treated and control subjects. These control subjects were treated with covert modeling in two sessions following the posttreatment assessment. The treatment used the 14 scenes employed with coping and mastery groups. The only difference was that behaviors of the model were not included in the scenes which conveyed either model anxiety or calmness. A typical scene was "Imagine the person holding the snake in his hands about 10 inches away from his face."

The purpose of the delayed-control group, then, was twofold: (*a*) to provide a base rate of change from preassessment to postassessment with no intervening treatment with which treated groups could be compared, and subsequently (*b*) to determine the effects of a "pure" covert model procedure in which characteristics of the model related to fear were left unspecified.

For the mastery, coping, and scene control groups, follow-up assessment was made approximately 3 weeks after the posttest. For the delayed-treatment control group, the third assessment was actually a posttest rather than follow-up, because this group was not given treatment in the original pre-post interval. A follow-up (fourth assessment) on this delayed-treatment control group was not possible due to the completion of the academic term.

RESULTS

Analysis of the pretreatment performance of all groups indicated no significant differences on any dependent variable. At posttreatment and follow-up, no differences obtained between experimenters on the dependent measures.

To evaluate the effect of treatment, the data were analyzed separately at posttreatment and follow-up, no differences obtained between experimenters on the dependent measures.

To evaluate the effect of treatment, the data were analyzed separately at posttreatment and follow-up. Separate one-way analyses of covariance were computed for each dependent variable with pretreatment measurement as the covariate. Table 1 and Table 2 present the effects of treatment, differences between pairs of treatment conditions, and changes within each group on each of the dependent measures at posttreatment and follow-up, respectively.

Posttreatment Results

Approach behavior. The mean approach responses performed by the subjects in each of the four groups at pretreatment and postreatment are included in Figure 1. Within-group changes (correlated t tests) indicated that neither the scene nor delayed-treatment control groups changed at posttreatment (see Table 1). On the other hand, two treatment groups significantly increased in approach behavior and were significantly different from controls in paired-comparison tests. As predicted, coping covert modeling produced greater behavioral change than mastery covert modeling. This is shown by a greater within-group change for the coping covert modeling group and by a significant difference between the two treatments ($p < .02$).

A rigorous test of reduction avoidance is the percentage of subjects who performed the terminal behavioral task at posttest (i.e., held the snake close to their face for 30 seconds). The rates were 31% for the coping group, 12.5% for the master group, and 0% for each of the control groups ($x^2 = 10.73, p < .01$).

Fear arousal during approach behaviors. The extent of fear arousal depends upon the threat value of the responses being performed. One measure of fear was made by comparing mean fear arousal for approach responses subjects performed prior to treatment with the mean fear arousal for those *same*

Table 22.1. Significance of Treatment Effects, Intergroup Differences, and Within-Group Changes for Each Dependent Measure at Posttest

Response measure	Treatment effect (F test)	Comparison of pairs of treatment conditions (F test)						Pre-Post within-group changes (t tests)			
		Coping vs. mastery	Coping vs. scene control	Coping vs. no treatment	Mastery vs. scene	Mastery vs. no treatment	Scene vs. no treatment	Coping	Mastery	Scene control	No treatment
Approach behavior	20.47***	6.20*	44.75***	40.58***	17.64***	15.05***	.10	7.25***	5.12***	1.58	1.85
Fear arousal											
Initial tasks	4.21**	.02	9.30**	3.13	8.53**	2.69	1.64	−3.03**	−4.17***	−.56	−2.08
Total tasks	1.33							−1.35	−2.00	.43	−1.30
Anxiety checklist	3.79*	.37	7.95**	5.95*	4.93*	3.35	.15	−2.56*	−2.03	1.71	−.49
Semantic differential	4.26**	.23	8.29**	.71	11.36**	1.74	4.16*	1.63	3.02**	−1.44	1.00
Snake attitude survey	3.58*	3.57	1.61	3.24	6.05*	8.94**	.28	1.24	3.04**	1.52	−1.11

*p < .05.
**p < .01.
***p < .001.

Table 22.2 Significance of Treatment Effects, Intergroup Differences, and Within-Group Changes for Each Dependent Measure at Follow-up

Response measure	Treatment effect (F test)	Comparison of pairs of treatment conditions (F test)						Pre-Post within-group changes (t tests)			
		Coping vs. mastery	Coping vs. scene control	Coping vs. no-cue CM	Mastery vs. scene	Mastery vs. no-cue CM	Scene vs. no-cue CM	Coping	Mastery	Scene control	No-cue CM
Approach behavior	9.43***	1.72	25.81***	7.29**	14.29***	1.93	5.71*	6.46***	5.23***	1.85	3.95**
Fear arousal											
Initial tasks	5.49**	.22	13.45***	.61	10.30**	.10	8.41**	-3.62**	-4.63***	-1.24	-4.74***
Total tasks	3.19*	.12	8.07**	1.18	6.25*	.56	3.06	-3.33**	-3.22**	-.55	-2.53*
Anxiety checklist	5.15**	.42	13.32***	.53	9.00**	.01	8.53**	-3.74**	-3.87**	.82	-4.54***
Semantic differential	5.55**	.15	11.22**	.23	13.99***	.76	8.29***	1.71	3.02**	-2.19*	1.52
Snake attitude survey	2.60	1.32	2.46	.52	7.40**	3.49	.72	1.25	2.67*	.12	.53

*p < .05.
**p < .01.
***p < .001.

212

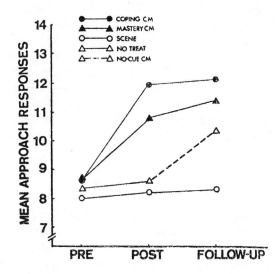

Fig. 22.1 Mean number of approach responses performed before, immediately after, and 3 weeks subsequent to treatment.

responses at posttreatment (i.e., initial approach responses). Another measure of fear was made on the mean arousal for all behavioral tasks passed on the pretest with all those completed in the posttest (i.e., total approach responses).

Considering only those initial approach responses, subjects in both treatment groups reported significantly less anxiety at posttest, whereas control subjects did not (Table 1). At posttreatment, both covert modeling groups were significantly less aroused than the scene control group, although not different from each other. The delayed-treatment group tended to decrease in arousal at retesting ($p < .06$). However, the two control groups were not significantly different in arousal.

The results for the mean arousal for pretreatment approach responses relative to mean arousal for total approach responses at posttreatment indicated no overall treatment effect.

Anxiety checklist responses. An analysis of covariance of checklist data at posttreatment showed a significant treatment effect (Table 1). A significant within-group reduction of anxiety was noted for the coping covert modeling group ($p < .05$) but less so for the mastery covert modeling group ($p < .07$). Each treatment group differed from each control group. Yet neither the treatment groups nor the control groups differed from each other.

Attitude measures. Analysis of semantic differential ratings of the concept "snakes" showed a significant treatment effect. Within-group comparisons revealed a significant change for the mastery covert modeling group only. Both treatment groups were highly significantly different from the scene control group but not different from the delayed-treatment control group. The treatment groups were not different from each other. Interestingly, the delayed-treatment control group was different from the scene control, even though the former did not make a significant within-group change.

The snake attitude survey results show a significant within-group change for the mastery covert modeling group only. The mastery covert modeling group was significantly different from both control groups. No other significant differences obtained.

Treated Controls

Following the second assessment, subjects in the delayed-treatment control group received a covert modeling procedure in which cues were omitted that described the model as anxious or confident. In evaluating the efficacy of this no-cue covert modeling procedure, t tests for correlated means were computed for changes in performance of delayed-treatment control subjects after they have received treatment relative to their second assessment scores. During the post-follow-up interval in which the delayed controls received treatment, the no-cue covert modeling treatment dramatically increased approach behavior ($t = 4.07, p < .001$), reduced fear arousal on initial behavioral tasks ($t = 5.04, p < .001$) and over total tasks ($t = 2.51, p < .05$), and reduced anxiety on the checklist measure ($t = 3.48, p < .01$). However, no attitude changes were found on the semantic differential ratings ($t = .92$) or snake attitude survey ($t = 1.34$).

Follow-up Results and Maintenance of Changes

Approximately 3 weeks after the posttreatment session, mastery and coping covert modeling groups and the scene control groups were called back for follow-up assessment. It was during the posttreatment and follow-up assessment that the delayed-treatment control received treatment. The thrid assessment was follow-up for three groups and a posttreatment assessment for the delayed-treatment control group which received the no-cue covert modeling treatment.

Analyses of covariance were made on each of the dependent measures using the pretreatment assessment as the covariate. Separate one-way analyses of variance made for the third assessment (follow-up) for the treatment groups, paired-comparison tests, and within-group changes are presented in Table 2.

On the approach test, the three covert modeling procedures changed significantly form pretreatment to follow-up, whereas the scene control group did not. Each group was significantly different from the scene control group (Table 2). The coping covert modeling group was significantly different from the no-cue covert modeling procedure. The superiority of the coping covert modeling group over the mastery group which obtained at posttreatment was no longer evident at follow-up. Nevertheless, the slight superiority of the coping covert modeling group is shown in a difference over the no-cue covert modeling group (Figure 1). The mastery and no-cue covert modeling groups were not significantly different on the approach test at follow-up. Within-group change during the posttreatment and follow-up interval was significant for the mastery covert modeling group ($t = 3.10$, $p < .01$) but not for the coping covert modeling group. Not only were the gains made with treatment maintained at follow-up, but subjects in the mastery covert modeling group made additional gains in approach responses.

On the measures of fear arousal, all three covert modeling groups significantly changed from pretreatment to follow-up over the initial approach items (Table 2). At follow-up, all treatments were significantly different from the scene control group, although not different from each other. Within-group changes on arousal for initial approach tasks from posttreatment session to follow-up showed no significant differences for coping, mastery, and scene control groups. Thus, the effects of treatment were maintained at follow-up.

A significant treatment effect obtained for the total arousal across all items completed on the behavioral test (Table 2). The three treatment groups showed significant within-group changes, whereas the scene control did not. The coping and mastery covert modeling groups were significantly different in total arousal scores from the scene control group, although the no-cue covert modeling group was not ($p < .10$). The treatments were not significantly different from each other on total arousal at follow-up. Within-group change between posttreatment and follow-up was nonsignificant for the mastery covert modeling group. The coping covert modeling group, however, did show a significant reduction in total arousal in this interval ($t = 3.03, p < .01$).

For the anxiety checklist, the three covert modeling procedures significantly changed at follow-up whereas the scene control did not. Highly significant differences obtained between each treatment group and the scene control group but not between covert modeling treatments (Table 2). Within-group post-follow-up t tests showed significant decreases in anxiety for the coping ($t = 2.81, p < .01$) and mastery ($t = 2.42, p < .03$) groups. Thus, the improvements made during treatment increased further in the follow-up interval. Again, the scene control group did not change during the follow-up interval.

Semantic differential ratings of snakes at follow-up showed that only the mastery covert modeling group made a significant within-group improvement. The scene control group became significantly less favorable in their ratings of snakes at follow-up relative to pretreatment scores. Each of the three treatments was significantly different from the scene control group, although not different from each other. No significant changes were made from posttreatment to follow-up assessments for mastery and coping covert modeling groups, indicating maintenance of improvements in attitude after treatment.

On the snake attitude survey only the mastery covert modeling group changed significantly in the pretreatment-follow-up interval (Table 2). At follow-up, only the mastery covert modeling group was significantly different from the scene control. No group changed in the post-follow-up interval.

Relationship between Attitude and Behavior Changes

To ascertain the relationship between attitude and behavior changes as a result of treatment, product-moment correlations were computed for change between pretreatment and follow-up for the three covert modeling groups on attitude and behavior measures. Correlations were computed separately within each treatment group. No significant differences obtained between groups, so they were averaged across groups by Fisher's z transformation. For the treatment groups, behavior change, as indicated by the approach test, was positively correlated with attitude change, as measured by the semantic differential ratings ($r = .29$, $p < .05$) and snake attitude survey ($r = .25$, $p < .09$). Severity of initial avoidance behavior was not a significant predictor of attitude change, and initial attitude was not a predictor of behavior change.

DISCUSSION

Covert modeling was highly effective in producing enduring changes in avoidance behavior. The three covert modeling treatments significantly increased approach behavior and reduced emotional arousal and anxiety. Additionally, some increases in favorable attitudes were shown. The improvements do not appear to result merely from imagining fear-relevant scenes which might be considered sufficient for extinction of avoidance responses. Subjects in the scene control group, who imagined fear relevant scenes with no model, failed to show improvements on any dependent measure.

Of the coping and mastery modeling treatments, the coping model was predicted to show greater avoidance reduction. This was supported on the behavior approach test at posttreatment and follow-up. Whereas the coping covert modeling group tended to show greater change in approach behavior, the mastery group tended to show greater changes in attitude measures. Other studies have reported higher correlations between changes in attitudes and behavior when treatment is more intensive and administered for a greater number of sessions (Bandura et al., 1969; Blanchard, 1970).

The results of the coping and mastery model manipulation are partially consistent with those of Meichenbaum (1971), who found that filmed coping models led to greater approach responses than mastery models. However, Meichenbaum used multiple film models, whereas a single covert model was used in the present study. Further, the greatest changes in Meichenbaum's study were made following exposure to coping models who verbalized self-instruction and self-reinforcing statements as they performed the tasks. The role of these instructions although not examined in the present study certainly needs to be investigated further.

The results of the present study fit nicely with reports of live and film modeling procedures which have been used to reduce avoidance behavior (Bandura et al., 1967; Bandura et al., 1969; Bandura & Menlove, 1968; Blanchard, 1970; Geer & Turteltaub, 1967; Hill et al., 1968; Meichenbaum, 1971). Modeling is concerned primarily with the processes by which representation of patterned activities serves a response guidance function, rather than the mode by which the information is transmitted to the subject (Bandura, 1970). Using a covert model can be viewed as another way to present the stimulus material. Yet not all modeling procedures convey equivalent levels of information. For example, modeling with guided participation (contact desensitization; see Ritter, 1969) provides modeling cues plus direct proprioceptive feedback for performance. It is no surprise that this is superior to other forms of modeling (Bandura et al., 1969). Perhaps, in vivo performance is an important ingredient in treatment. However, it may be possible to increase the strength of the covert procedure by experimentally manipulating attributes of the model or consequences which follow the model's performance. The covert procedure may be restricted to those individuals whose imagery is sufficiently vivid to provide the requisite information and representational coding. This area remains to be explored. Interestingly, vividness of imagery seems to be unrelated to decreases in avoidance behavior in desensitization (McLemore, 1972).

A potential implication of the research on covert modeling is that the interpretation of other therapies which rely on covert processes might be clarified. For example, covertly observing oneself perform anxiety-provoking tasks, which occurs in desensitization, may be tantamount to observing another individual perform these tasks (covert modeling) and lead to similar cognitions (Bem, 1967). A modeling interpretation of procedures as desensitization (i.e., self-modeling) suggests several well-investigated variables which may be evaluated (see Bandura, 1969, 1971; Campbell, 1961). The similarities between and relative efficacy of desensitization and covert modeling remain to be explored.

REFERENCES

Bandura, A. *Principles of behavior modification.* New York: Holt, Rinehart & Winston, 1969.

Bandura, A. Modeling theory. In W. S. Sahakian (Ed.), *Psychology of learning: Systems, models, and theories.* Chicago: Markham, 1970.

Bandura, A. Psychotherapy based upon modeling principles. In A. E. Bergin & S. L.

Garfield (Eds.), *Handbook of psychotherapy and behavior change.* New York: Wiley, 1971.

Bandura, A., Blanchard, E. G., & Ritter, B. Relative efficacy of desensitization and modeling approaches for inducing behavioral, affective, and attitudinal changes. *Journal of Personality and Social Psychology,* 1969, **13,** 173–199.

Bandura, A., Grusec, J. E., & Menlove, F. L. Vicarious extinction of avoidance behavior. *Journal of Personality and Social Psychology,* 1967, **5,** 16–23.

Bandura, A., & Menlove, F. L. Factors determining vicarious extinction of avoidance behavior through symbolic modeling. *Journal of Personality and Social Psychology,* 1968, **8,** 99–108.

Bem, D. Self perception: An alternative interpretation of cognitive dissonance phenomena. *Psychological Review,* 1967, **74,** 183–200.

Blanchard, E. Relative contributions of modeling, informational influences, and physical contact in extinction of phobic behavior. *Journal of Abnormal Psychology,* 1970, **76,** 55–61.

Burnstein, E., Stotland, E., & Zander, A. Similarity to a model and self-evaluation. *Journal of Abnormal Psychology,* 1961, **62,** 257–264.

Campbell, D. T. Conformity in psychology's theories of acquired behavioral dispositions. In I. A. Gerg & B. M. Bass (Eds.), *Conformity and deviation.* New York: Harper & Row, 1961.

Cautela, J. R. Covert modeling. Paper presented at Fifth Annual Meeting of the Association for the Advancement of Behavior therapy, Washington, D. C., September 1971.

Davison, G. C. Systematic desensitization as a counterconditioning process. *Journal of Abnormal Psychology,* 1968, **73,** 91–99.

Flanders, J. A. review of research on imitative behavior. *Psychological Bulletin, 1968,* **69,** 316–337.

Geer, J. H. The development of a scale to measure fear. *Behaviour Research and Therapy,* 1965, **3,** 45–53.

Geer, J., & Turteltaub, A. Fear reduction following observation of a model. *Journal of Personality and Social Psychology,* 1967, **6,** 327–331.

Hicks, D. J. Imitation and retention of film-mediated aggressive peer and adult models. *Journal of Personality and Social Psychology,* 1965, **2,** 97–100.

Hill, J., Liebert, R., & Mott, D. Vicarious extinction of avoidance behavior through films: An initial test. *Psychological Reports,* 1968, **12,** 192.

Lang, P., & Lazovik, A. Experimental desensitization of a phobia. *Journal of Abnormal and Social Psychology,* 1963, **66,** 519–525.

McLemore, C. W. Imagery in desensitization. *Behaviour Research and Therapy,* 1972, **10,** 51–57.

Miechenbaum, D. H. Examination of model characteristics in reducing avoidance behavior. *Journal of Personality and Social Psychology,* 1971, **17,** 298–307.

Osgood, C. E., Suci, G. J., & Tannenbaum, P. H. *Measurement of meaning.* Urbana: University of Illinois Press, 1957.

Ritter, B. The use of contact desensitization, demonstration plus participation and demonstration alone in the treatment of acrophobia. *Behaviour Research and Therapy,* 1969, **7,** 157–164.

Rosekrans, M. Imitation in children as a function of perceived similarity to a social model and vicarious reinforcement. *Journal of Personality and Social Psychology,* 1967, **7,** 307–315.

Zuckerman, M. The development of an affective adjective checklist for the measurement of anxiety. *Journal of Consulting Psychology,* 1960, **24,** 457–462.

Chapter 23

The Effects of Covert and Overt Modeling on Assertive Behavior*†

Ted L. Rosenthal and Susan L. Reese

Summary Three modeling therapy formats (overt modeling with a standard hierarchy of situations, covert modeling with the standard hierarchy, and covert modeling with a self-tailored hierarchy) were compared to assess their relative efficacy in developing assertive skills. Half the subjects in each treatment condition received or did not receive generalization training. Significant within-group improvement was indicated on four self-report measures. Overall, the results suggest that covert modeling was as effective as overt modeling or covert modeling plus self-tailoring instating assertion among nonassertive college women.

Research on modeling therapies has explored the efficacy of covert modeling in treating behavioral dysfunctions (Cautela, Flannery and Hanley, 1974; Kazdin, 1973, 1974). Covert modeling is a technique in which the subject imagines modeling situations (including the appropriate behavior to be developed or altered) without the use of live or filmed models. Thus far, covert modeling has effectively reduced avoidance responses to rats (Cautela *et al.*, 1974), to snakes (Kazdin, 1973), and has successfully produced assertive behavior in nonassertive clients (Kazdin, 1974). This latter finding is particularly significant since the acquisition of assertive responses entails developing

*Reprinted with permission from *Behaviour Research and Therapy*, 1976, *14*, 463-469. © Pergamon Press.

†This experiment was submitted to the Department of Psychology in partial fulfillment of the requirements for the degree of Master of Arts at the University of Arizona.

skill rather than just restoring simple motor approach behavior previously inhibited by fear.

Although the effectiveness of covert modeling has been demonstrated, little research has addressed the relative efficacy of covert and overt modeling. The single study reported (Cautela *et al.*, 1974) explored analogue fears in college students and suggested that overt and covert modeling were equally effective in reducing avoidance responses to rats.

Thus, the present research compared the utility of covert and overt modeling for developing assertive skills. Unlike the simple, discrete actions required to approach small animals, acquisition of assertive skills requires a broader repertoire of social responses and greater sensitivity to a variety of discriminative cues signaling appropriate assertive behavior. It was therefore anticipated that, in the more complex case of assertion training, overt modeling would be superior to covert modeling as a behavior change technique. Three modeling therapy variations were studied. One group received overt modeling and another covert modeling using the same standard stimulus hierarchy. The third group received covert modeling with self-tailoring of the situational hierarchy to each subject's personal experience. It was predicted that the self-tailoring procedure would enhance efficacy of the covert modeling technique because the specific instances imagined would have greater subjective vividness and relevance for the client.

In addition, half the subjects in each modeling group were encouraged to think of new situations for which the modeled behavior would be appropriate. Research on diverse behavioral treatments suggests that clients may fail spontaneously to transfer their specific treatment experiences to related situations (Rosenthal, in press). Thus directions to generalize have been studied, but these efforts have been confined to quite limited prompts, which failed to assure that clients could bridge the training-transfer gap. For example, in a study of Hersen, Eisler, and Miller (1974, p. 300), the instructions, very narrow in scope, were as follows:

Remember what you have learned in the training sessions and apply this to the new situations you will be exposed to. We would like you to continue standing up for your rights and expressing yourself better.

Prior to the post-test, subjects received another brief set of similar instructions. In contrast, the present generalization prompts aided clients to entertain concrete behavioral and situational alternatives that were related to the training paradigm. This assured that clients devoted some thought to assertive behaviour in relevant situations not specifically included in training. The remaining subjects in each group did not receive this guidance. It was predicted that such cognitive generalization practice would facilitate transfer of the modeled behaviors to subjective and behavioral post-test measures.

METHOD

Subjects

Thirty-six female volunteers, distressed by their lack of appropriate assertive behavior were recruited from undergraduate psychology courses at the University of Arizona. Using a reduced set of the Wolpe and Lazarus (1966) Assertive Questionnaire items, subjects were screened by telephone, matched in sextets, and randomly assigned to one of six treatment groups.

Treatment Procedures

Nine assertive modeling situations were presented to all subjects individually over three treatment sessions. Sessions consisted of three scenes presented twice in succession, requiring about three minutes in duration, and depicting a social situation followed by an appropriate assertive response.

Alternative treatment variations involved: (a) overt modeling with standard hierarchy, (b) covert modeling with the same standard hierarchy, or (c) covert modeling with self-tailoring of the standard hierarchy. The standard hierarchies were determined by administering a modified version of the Interpersonal Behavior Test (Lawrence, 1969) including 57 assertive situations and responses. Thirty-seven undergraduate volunteers, not participating in the present study, rated each situation and the given response on a scale from 1 (very easy) to 8 (very difficult). The nine situations rated most difficult comprised the standard hierarchy of modeling scenes which were presented in ascending order of difficulty. In brief, the content of the hierarchy was as follows: (1) A customer, having noticed that others coming after her are being helped first, demands immediate service. (2) Confronted with evaluating her friend's artwork, a person tactfully expresses her criticism. (3) A person politely requests that a classmate refrain from loud gum chewing. (4) A young woman, unfamiliar with the guests at a social gathering, approaches an attractive man and initiates conversation. (6) A woman openly explains her feelings of platonic friendship for a man who considers their relationship to be more serious. (7) A young woman, engaged in private discussion with her friend, suggests that an unexpected visitor return at a later time. (8) A young woman expresses her disappointment at her fiance's decision to terminate their relationship. (9) A woman explains to her friend that she would like to postpone a prior commitment to accept an invitation from a special man.

For the covert modeling condition with standard hierarchy, the same stimulus material was recast in words item by item, to encourage subjects' imaginal participation. To create the self-tailored format, each item of the standard covert hierarchy was presented to the subject who then provided a personal experience most similar to the given situation. This personally relevant content thus formed a set of self-tailored items parallel to the standard hierarchy.

For the overt modeling procedure, college volunteers assisted the experimenter in presenting the assertion-relevant scenes. Clients were instructed to pay close attention as the models enacted each episode. For the covert modeling with standard hierarchy condition, clients were encouraged to attend diligently as the experimenter verbally described the situations. Upon completion of the description, subjects were instructed to close their eyes and imagine the sequence for a duration approximately equal to the time required to enact the situation in the overt condition. The self-tailored covertly modeled treatment was similarly structured.

Treatment groups were further differentiated through generalization practice variations which included: (a) providing information to help the client tie her specific therapy experiences to related situations, or (b) omission of such guidance. For those clients receiving generalization training, each treatment scene was followed by examples describing three other situations in which assertive responses similar to those specifically modeled were appropriate. For example, one item depicted a woman waiting patiently in a department store queue when she noticed that others were pushing ahead of her. During generalization training, three other situations in which a person was required to wait an unreasonably long time were illustrated: in a college walk-through queue for registration; in a queue to enter a movie theatre; and while trying to obtain information by telephone. In addition, subjects were encouraged to think of other personally relevant situations in which responses similar to the modeled example would be appropriate.

Self-Report Measures

Four self-report measures were used to assess assertive performance. A modified version of the Interpersonal Behavior Test (Lawrence, 1969) consisted of 37 items involving social competence which the client rated in terms of how much difficulty she would have executing such a task. The rating scale ranged from 1 (very easy) to 8 (very difficult). The modified Wolpe–Lazarus (1966) Assertion Scale consisted of 18 Yes/No questions relating to the subjects' handling of assertion issues. The Percentage Estimate measure was a modified version of item 1 of the Conflict Inventory Scale (McFall and Lillesand, 1971); clients were required to estimate the percentage of other people who were more assertive than themselves. The five semantic differential items assessed on Good–Bad, Strong–Weak, and Active–Passive dimensions the client's perceptions (and later changes) regarding neutral and assertion relevant content. The items so judged were as follows: (1) self perception of assertive ability; (2) clients' perceptions of other peoples' assertive skills; (3) clients' subjective feelings about the doorknob of their room (control item);

(4) self-ratings of own physical appearance; (5) clients' perception of how others would rate their assertive skills.

In addition to the foregoing pre-post measures, a set of 'mini' measures were administered after the first and second treatment sessions. These were intended to compare the rate of short term change among the treatment variations and consisted of seven Likert-type rating items. Clients' overall feelings toward the therapy session were assessed, as were their perceptions regarding the relevance of the treatment procedures in addressing their specific assertion problems. For example, "How confident or optimistic are you that you can apply today's training in your own daily life?" Scale points ranged from Extremely to Not-At-All. For all covert treatment conditions, clients rated how clearly they visualized each scene, from 1 (very clear) to 4 (not clear at all). After the third treatment session, information was collected as to whom the subject had imagined (self or other) performing the assertion relevant tasks.

Behavioral Measures

Non-laboratory indices of assertiveness were administered following the treatment sessions. A survey-taking behavioral test required the subject to approach two strangers and request their completion of an attitude survey. The time it took to approach each person and the time elapsed until the subject completed the task recorded. Clients also rated their own comfort or discomfort in accomplishing the task. Part of the follow-up procedures included a surreptitious phone call. An assistant, posing as a representative of a local advertising agency, requested the subjects' participation in a consumer study. The number of refusals prior to compliance was recorded.

Design

The main analysis of variance involved a 3 (overt, covert with standard hierarchy or covert with self-tailored hierarchy) × 2 (cognitive generalization practice or not) pictorial design. *Post-hoc* testing was accomplished via the Neuman Keuls Studentized Range Statistic (or, in one instance, by a trend test).

RESULTS

Pre-Post Self-Report Changes

Statistical analysis of the Wolpe–Lazarus measure yielded a significant trials effect showing increased assertiveness from before to after treatment (see Table 1). However, type of treatment ($F = 0.10$, $df = 2/30$, NS) and generalization training ($F = 0.42$, $df = 1/30$, NS) had no discernible effects.

A similar pattern was found on both the Percentage Estimate item and the modified Interpersonal Behavior Test, where significant pre-post treatment changes were found (see Table 1) but no main effects for type of modeling format or generalization training (largest $F = 0.69$, $df = 2/30$ and $1/30$ respectively, NS). No significant interactions were found.

'Mini' (Process) Measures

No significant differences among groups across treatment sessions were found on item 1 (attitude toward treatment), item 2 (ability to grasp situations in a life-like way), item 3 (amount of experienced anxiety during treatment) or item 7 (enthusiasm regarding the upcoming treatment session). On item 4 (perceived helpfulness of therapy) there was a significant treatment effect ($F = 5.59$, $df = 2/30$, $p < 0.01$). A trend analysis ($F = 4.99$, $df = 1/30$, $p < 0.05$) suggested that covert modeling with self-tailored hierarchies ($\bar{x}=2.63$) produced the most favorable ratings of perceived helpfulness Covert modeling with standard hierarchies ($\bar{x} = 3.56$) and overt modeling ($\bar{x} = 3.79$) produced less favorable ratings in that order. There was also a significant generalization practice by trials interaction ($F = 5.64$, $df = 1/30$, $p < 0.025$). Neuman Keuls tests indicated that subjects who received generalization training perceived trial 2 ($\bar{x} = 2.83$) as more helpful ($p < 0.05$) than trial 1 ($\bar{x} = 3.39$), whereas, for subjects not given generalization training, there was no difference between trial 1 ($\bar{x} = 3.39$) and trial 2 ($\bar{x} = 3.69$). Furthermore, within trial 2, subjects given generalization training ($\bar{x} = 2.83$) perceived treatment as more helpful ($p < 0.05$) than their no-generalization counterparts ($\bar{x} = 3.69$). Over-all, the interaction effects on perceived helpfulness suggested some subjective advantages for providing generalization training.

On item 5 (clients' self-confidence in applying training to their own lives) there was a significant improvement ($F = 4.89$, $df = 1/30$, $p < 0.05$) between the first ($\bar{x} = 3.72$) and the second ($\bar{x} = 3.25$) trial, but no difference based on training format. The same pattern was found on item 6 (expected difficulty in utilizing training) where scores improved significantly ($F = 5.79$, $df = 1/30$, p

Table 23.1 Summary of pre-post means and analysis of variance for self-report measures

Response Measure	Means		df	F-Value for Trials Change
	Before	After		
Wolpe–Lazarus	9.89	7.61	1/30	31.33*
Percentage estimate	62.08	48.06	1/30	29.53*
Interpersonal behavior test	4.96	3.81	1/30	139.00*

*$p < 0.001$

< 0.05) from the first (x = 4.31) to the second (x = 3.69) trial but with no other treatment effects.

Semantic Differential Items

Table 2 presents the group means by item and rating dimension and F values for all scales which changed significantly from before to after treatment. On item 1 (self perceptions of assertive ability) there were significant pre-post improvements on each rating dimension (Table 2) but no other significant effects. There were parallel pre-post improvements on item 5 (perception of fellow students' evaluation of subject's assertive ability) on all three scale dimensions and a trials × generalization interaction on the Good–Bad dimension ($F = 6.71, df = 1/30, \rho < 0.025$) suggesting that generalization training produced more favorable change in perceptions across trials than was created without such training. The over-all pattern of more favorable self-reactions apparently generalized to item 4 (ratings of subjects' physical appearance) where there were significant pre-post improvements on both the valuation and the potency dimensions (Table 2) but not on activity. No significant changes involving type of treatment were obtained on any item.

Table 23.2 Summary of pre-post means and analysis of variance for semantic differential items

Semantic differential item	Means*		
	Pre	Post	Trials F
1. Own Assertiveness			
Good–Bad	4.28	3.06	40.74‡
Strong–Weak	4.64	3.22	31.14‡
Active–Passive	5.00	3.39	32.44‡
2. Physical Appearance			
Good–Bad	3.44	2.92	11.65†
Strong–Weak	3.81	3.17	12.05†
3. Other's Evaluation Of Assertiveness			
Good–Bad	4.47	3.25	40.13‡
Strong–Weak	4.67	3.28	37.74‡
Active–Passive	4.86	3.36	41.33‡

*Note: All dfs = 1/30. Smaller mean values are always in the direction of better, stronger, and more active ratings.
†$\rho < 0.01$
‡$\rho < 0.001$

In contrast, very negligible semantic differential results were found on item 2 (client perceptions of other peoples' assertive skills) and item 3 (clients' subjective feelings about the doorknob of their room). These control items produced no main effects on any response dimension as a function of type of treatment, nor any significant overall pre-post changes. Several significant interaction terms were found on the control items but subsequent *post hoc* testing failed to disclose significant cell differences. In summary, the analyses indicated that treatment substantially improved clients' rated attitudes toward themselves but had minor effects on their perceptions of both social and nonsocial content which was distinct from the goals of treatment. Although clients did not perceive any change in other people's capacity to engage in appropriate assertion, their perception of their own assertive ability improved after therapy.

Behavioral Test Data

No significant effects were obtained on either behavioral measure (latency of approach or total time to complete the task) of the survey taking test (largest $F = 1.83$, $df = 2/30$, NS). There was some self-report evidence that throughout the survey taking procedure clients became progressively more comfortable. Thus, they rated their comfort as greater while administering the survey ($\bar{x} = 2.47$) than at the point of approaching ($\bar{x} = 2.89$) respondents ($F = 6.02$, $df = 1/30$, $\rho < 0.025$).

The telephone solicitation data produced no discernible differences among groups. In fact, only one client initially refused the request, while another asked just one relevant question prior to compliance.

Covert Process Reports

The type of covert modeling procedures which clients were exposed to produced sharp differences in whether clients imaged themselves or another person enacting the assertion tasks. Thus, clients who received covert modeling with self-tailored hierarchy typically visualized themselves participating in the assertion relevant situations, while clients receiving covert modeling with the standard hierarchy imagined other people displaying the appropriate assertive skills corrected for continuity, ($X^2 = 8.17$, $df = 1$, $\rho < 0.01$). In relation to how vividly clients reported imagining the scenes, generalization training interacted with type of covert modeling procedure ($F = 12.05$, $df = 1/20$, $\rho < 0.005$). Generalization training enhanced the clarity of the situations visualized for clients receiving covert modeling with the standard hierarchy ($\bar{x} = 1.35$), but reduced scene vividness for covert modeling with the self-tailored hierarchy ($\bar{x} = 2.09$). The covert groups not given generalization practice were more comparable between standard ($\bar{x} = 1.98$) and self-tailored ($\bar{x} = 1.50$) hierarchy conditions. The analysis of covert process reports failed to produce any other significant effects.

DISCUSSION

Overall, the results confirmed the worth of standard covert modeling which required less time, and no staff assistance, but produced assertion progress comparable to the more costly overt modeling tactics. One must recall that clients were college students, a population superior in symbolic ability. Hence the advantages of covertly modeled assertion still need to be demonstrated with clients average or below in cognitive skills.

Self-tailored hierarchies, which demanded more time, proved no more effective than covert modeling with a standard hierarchy. Although self-tailoring clients perceived their treatment as more helpful, they failed to differ from their standard hierarchy counterparts on any behavioral or self-report measures of assertion. The functional equivalence of the two covert modeling variations is intriguing because there were sharp group differences in the models they imagined: the standard hierarchy group visualized other people, and the self-tailoring group themselves, in the assertion scenes. Such data suggest that our grasp of the relationships between the content of cognition and its impact on action and self-perception is still rather primitive (Mahoney, 1974; Rosenthal, in press). For example, research suggests that overt modeling creates stronger gains than systematic desensitization (e.g., Bandura, Blanchard and Ritter, 1969). Yet, (the component of relaxation training aside), the present self-tailoring group adopted phenomenology akin to systematic desensitization, but with outcome results comparable to overt modeling. There is further evidence that similarity between client and covert model is helpful (Kazdin, 1973), but the standard and self-tailored covert modeling groups differed precisely in this aspect of what they imagined, without any outcome differences. One explanation for these results may lie in closer scrutiny of the self-tailoring procedure, which required more time and interchange between client and therapist than did both other treatment methods. This individual attention may have led clients to perceive self-tailoring as more helpful. Lack of outcome differences between the standard and self-tailored groups may have stemmed from the impromptu nature of the self-tailored hierarchies which were generated on-the-spot and lacked the refinement possible in administering the standard hierarchy. Thus, caution is needed before dismissing the potential value of self-tailored covert modeling in clinical settings.

Generalization practice received some support as a useful tool to produce therapeutic gain, since it had favorable effects on several self-report items. Generalization practice enhanced clients' ratings of the clarity with which they visualized assertion scenes, but this only held significantly for the standard hierarchy covert modeling group, and was reversed in the self-tailored condition where eliciting related examples was a necessary and integral component in the construction of self-tailored hierarchies. Thus, generalization practice may have added substantially less information for self-tailored clients than for those given standard covert modeling.

A surreptitious phone call making 'unreasonable' demands failed to create any significant group differences. This was consistent with investigations of assertive training using related telephone follow-up tests (e.g., Kazdin, 1974; McFall and Lillesand, 1971). Although behavioral tests failed to disclose reliable treatment differences, anecdotal data suggested that clients did transfer their laboratory experiences to real life situations. One client reported that 'I was able to tell two guys this weekend that I'm not interested (in dating them). Usually, I'd just avoid them, but I just sat them down and told them how I felt.' Another client, who was having disputes with her father, related this example: 'I found my father looking through my drawers. I stood up for myself without crying or yelling. There have been other situations, too.' A third woman described her feelings this way: 'Treatment has really helped me. I'm sticking up for myself all over the place and just don't back down anymore. I guess psychology does work.' Given such encouraging free reports, it appeared that the present treatments had favorable impact on clients' spontaneous assertion in real life situations. However, there remains a need to devise sensitive and valid nonlaboratory measures to reflect unobtrusively clients' relative progress after diverse behavioral treatments for enhancing assertives.

REFERENCES

Bandura A., Blanchard E. and Ritter B. (1969) The relative efficacy of desensitization and modeling approaches for inducing behavioral, affective and attitudinal changes. *J. Person. soc. Psychol. 13*, 173-199.

Cautela J. R., Flannery R. and Hanley S. (1974) Covert modeling: An experimental test. *Behav. Therapy 5*, 494-502.

Eisler R., Hersen M. and Miller P. (1973) Effects of modeling on components of assertive behavior. *J. Behav. Therapy exp. Psychiat. 4*, 1-6.

Hersen M., Eisler R. and Miller P. (1974) An experimental analysis of generalization in assertive training. *Behav. Res. and Therapy 12*, 295-310.

Kazdin, A. (1973) Covert modeling and the reduction of avoidance behavior. *J. abnorm. Psychol. 81*, 87-95.

Kazdin A. (1974) Effects of covert modeling and model reinforcement on assertive behavior. *J. abnorm. Psychol. 83*, 240-252.

Lawrence P. (1969) The assessment and modification of assertive behavior. Unpublished manuscript, Arizona State University.

Mahoney M. (1974) *Cognition and Behavior Modification*. Ballinger Publishing Co., Cambridge, Mass.

McFall R. and Lillesand D. (1971) Behavior rehearsal with modeling and coaching in assertion training. *J. abnorm. Psychol. 77*, 313-323.

Rosenthal T. L. Modeling therapies. In *Progress in Behavior Modification* (Eds. M. Hersen, R. Eisler and P. M. Miller), vol. 2., Academic Press, New York.

Wolpe J. and Lazarus A. (1966) *Behavior Therapy Techniques*. Pergamon Press, London.

Chapter 24

Covert Modeling, Imagery Assessment, and Assertive Behavior*†

Alan E. Kazdin

Summary The purpose of the present investigation was (a) to examine the effect of two variables in developing assertive behavior using covert modeling and (b) to develop a technique to assess ongoing imagery during treatment. In a 2 × 2 design, the number of models imagined (imagining several models versus imagining a single model perform assertively) and model reinforcement (imagining favorable consequences following model behavior versus imagining no consequences) were combined. A nonassertive-model control group that imagined assertion-relevant scenes was included in the design. The results indicated that imagining multiple models or model reinforcement enhanced behavior change across self-report inventories and a behavioral role-playing test. Treatment effects transferred to novel role-playing situations and were maintained at a 4-month follow-up assessment. Assessment of imagery during the session corroborated the adherence of subjects to the imagery conditions to which they were assigned. However, subjects systematically introduced elaborations into the scenes. The data suggest the importance of assessing imagery in covert conditioning therapy studies.

Covert modeling is a therapy technique in which individuals imagine a model engage in the behaviors they wish to develop (Cautela, 1971). Recently, analogue studies have suggested that covert modeling is an effective technique (Kazdin, 1973, 1974a, 1974b, 1974c) that may be as effective as live modeling (Cautela, Flannery, & Hanley, 1974) in reducing subphobic levels of avoidance. Unfortunately, covert modeling has not been extensively

---

*Reprinted with permission from the *Journal of Consulting and Clinical Psychology*, 1975, *43*, 716-724. © The American Psychological Association 1975.

†This research was supported by Grant MH23399 from the National Institute of Mental Health.

evaluated with behaviors that more closely resemble clinical problems than do mold fears of college students. In one report (Kazdin, 1974d), covert modeling was effective in developing assertive behavior of clients carefully screened for inadequate social skills. Interestingly, the gains were maintained up to 3 months after treatment.

The present investigation extends previous work in developing assertive behavior with covert modeling and by evaluating parameters that may influence modeling effects. Specifically, two variables important in live modeling were evaluated including the number of models and the consequences that follow model behavior (Bandura, 1971; Rachman, 1972). In overt modeling, observing several models is superior to observing a single model (Bandura & Menlove, 1968). In addition, favorable consequences that follow model behavior enhance performance of the observer (Bandura, 1965; Bandura, Ross, & Ross, 1963). Previous analogue research has shown that imagining either multiple covert models or favorable consequences following model behavior tends to influence client performance (Kazdin, 1973, 1974a). The present investigation evaluated the separate and combined effects of multiple models and favorable model consequences in developing assertive behavior.

Aside from evaluating parameters of covert modeling, this study also developed a methodology to enhance evaluation of covert techniques in general. Assessing imagery is a problem for covert conditioning techniques. By their very nature, private events such as images are not readily accessible to the experimenter. Although the experimenter instructs the client to imagine specific material, there is not way to ensure that the client actually is imaging the events as presented. However, claims are frequently made about the crucial events that must be imagined to achieve behavior change via covert techniques. Depending on the specific technique, various events are assumed to be essential for behavior change such as imagining a model (covert modeling) or reinforcing or punishing events after behavior (covert reinforcement and punishment, respectively). In fact, subjects may not consistently imagine the supposedly crucial ingredients of therapy. Informal reports sometimes reveal that imagined scenes depart from those presented verbally by the experimenter (Davison & Wilson, 1973; Weitzman, 1967). Assessment of imagery during treatment might help to determine whether subjects adhere to the scenes presented. The present investigation assessed ongoing imagery during treatment and evaluated compliance with specific imagery conditions and imaginal correlates of therapy outcome.

In summary, the purpose of the present investigation was twofold. First, the two parameters important in live modeling were examined in the context of covert modeling to develop assertive behavior. In a 2 × 2 design, the number of models (imagining a single covert model perform assertively across treatment sessions versus imagining several models) was combined with model reinforcement (imagining favorable consequences following covert model behavior versus no consequences). A nonassertive-model group was included in the design to control for imagining assertion-relevant scenes in the absence of an assertive model. The second purpose was to assess ongoing imagery during the therapy sessions. Tape-recorded narrations of imagery were analyzed across a number of dimensions.

METHOD

Subjects

Subjects were solicited from newspaper and television advertisements as well as by local posters offering free assertion training. Of the 74 individuals who responded, 54 participated in the project (24 females, 30 males). The participants ranged in age from 18 to 61 years (*Mdn* = 21). The subjects who participated met the screening requirements detailed below and submitted a refundable deposit ($10) to ensure their completion of the program.

Overview of Procedure

Individuals who responded to advertisements received an initial interview and were administered the assessment battery. Subjects were then assigned randomly to one of five treatment conditions administered individually in four therapy sessions. The stimulus material (covert modeling scenes) used in treatment was standardized across groups, varying only in the parameters under investigation, and presented on tape. During treatment the subjects described their ongoing imagery that was tape-recorded. Immediately after treatment and at a 4-month follow-up, the subjects were reassessed.

Assessment of Assertive Skills

Self-report. Four self-report pencil-and-paper measures assessed the extent to which subjects could assert themselves, refuse others, and cope with anxiety-provoking social situations. The measures included (a) the Conflict Resolution Inventory, (b) the Wolpe-Lazarus Assertive Training Scale, (c) the Rathus Assertiveness Schedule, and (d) the Willoughby Scale.

Behavioral role-playing test. After completing the self-report measures, a behavioral role-playing test was administered. The test required the subjects to respond spontaneously to prerecorded situations in which an assertive response would be appropriate (cf. McFall & Marston, 1970; Rehm & Marston, 1968). A subject was told to respond as if actually in the situation and to play the role of the person to whom the events were happening. At the end of the prerecorded situation, a bell signaled the subject to respond. All subjects' responses were recorded. Two sets of 10 role-playing situations were used. One of the sets was administered at pretest. At posttreatment, the pretest set was re-presented and followed by the new set of situations (that served as the generalization measure). The two sets were counterbalanced across subjects.

The primary dependent measure from the behavioral test was an assertiveness rating of the subject's role-playing responses (1 = not at all and 5 = very assertive). Additional measures included latency of response after the signal and the duration of the assertive response. These measures were derived from tape recordings after the experiment was terminated. Judges, unaware of the purpose of the study, rated the tapes in random order. The preassessment and postassessment data for a given subject were not on the same tape and were not rated in sequence. A final measure taken during the behavioral test was the subject's pulse rate measured by a Pulsemeter (2D16—Medical Systems Corporation) connected to the subject's left index finger.

Subject screening. To participate in the assertive training clinic, subjects had to meet at least two of the following requirements: (a) rate their lack of assertiveness as a "significant problem" (defined as 65 or greater on a scale in which 1 = no problem, 100 = very significant problem), (b) rate their assertiveness at the 25th percentile or lower relative to others in our culture, and (c) respond with a greater number of nonassertive than assertive responses on the 35 refusal items of the Conflict Resolution Inventory. Finally, each subject was not to reply assertively to more than one of the behavioral role-playing test situations at pretest. Global ratings of role-playing responses made at the time of assessment by a research assistant (1 = no response, 2 = inassertive, 3 = assertive) were used for *screening* only. Interrater agreement on the scoring of pretest behavioral responses was checked on four occasions across a total of 115 responses with perfect agreement for 90.4% of the responses. Of the initial clients, 20 failed to meet the screening requirements.

Follow-up. Approximately 4 months after treatment, the Conflict Resolution Inventory and the Wolpe-Lazarus scale were sent to each subject.

Covert Modeling Treatment Stimuli

Thirty-five treatment scenes were used during treatment. The scenes were prerecorded, and presentation was controlled by the therapist (with a remote on-off switch). Each scene consisted of three parts: (a) a description of the *context* and situation in which an assertive response was appropriate, (b) a *model* who made an assertive response, and (c) *favorable consequences* that resulted from the model's assertive response. The partitioning of scenes in this fashion permitted careful delineation of the experimental conditions. A typical scene is illustrated below:

1. The person (model) is eating in a restaurant with friends. He (she) orders a steak and tells the waiter he (she) would like it rare. When the food arrives the person begins to eat and apparently finds something wrong with the steak.
2. He (she) immediately signals the waiter. When the waiter arrives, the person says ''I ordered the steak rare, and this one is medium. Please take it back and bring me one that is rare.''
3. In a few minutes the waiter brings another steak and says he is very sorry this has happened.

Assessment of Imagined Scenes

A major purpose of the study was to assess aspects of the subjects' imagery as they imagined scenes in the treatment sessions. Subjects were instructed to verbalize or narrate the scene they were imagining aloud after the scene had been presented and clearly pictured. The verbalizations by the subjects while imagining the scenes were tape-recorded. The tapes subsequently were evaluated to assess the extent to which subjects adhered to the presented scenes and elaborated specific components of the scenes. Each scene was scored to assess the presence or absence of particular characteristics* (a) *Scene components*. Three categories assessed whether the specific components of the scene were reported by the subject and whether the narrative was consistent with the scene as presented. The three components included the context, the model's assertive response, and whether favorable consequences followed model behavior. (b) *Elaboration of scene*. This measure assessed whether subjects elaborated or introduced additional descriptive material about the scene, model, or consequences, and (c) *Completed scene*. The final measure assessed whether or not the subject was able to complete his description of the scene in the time alloted for imagery.

Treatment Conditions

Subjects were assigned randomly to one of five groups and to one of five therapists with the restriction that each therapist saw subjects in each condition. Graduate or senior undergraduate students (two females, three males) served as therapists. Treatment was administered individually in four sessions over a 2-week period. In the initial session, the therapist discussed the treatment rationale and required the subjects to practice imagining scenes in which a model similar in age and of the same sex was present. Practice material was unrelated to assertiveness but provided subjects with an opportunity to imagine scenes carefully, describe their imagery, and receive instructions and direction from the therapist.

In the first session, all subjects were told that the person imagined in the practice scenes was to be imagined in the treatment scenes. In subsequent

---

*All Newman-Keuls comparisons reported as significant met the .05 level of confidence.

sessions, all subjects imagined a practice scene that differed across experimental conditions, if the model was to be altered. Assertion training scenes followed the practice scenes in each session. Each scene was held for 35 sec, beginning when the subject signaled that the image was clear. The scenes employed in each session were imagined twice. At the end of each session, subjects completed a questionnaire in which they rated their clarity of imagery, anxiety experienced during the session, the amount of the material presented that they could successfully imagine, and various features of the model (e.g., age and sex).

The five groups included a 2 × 2 factorial combination of the number of models (imagining one model versus imagining four different models over the course of treatment) and model reinforcement (favorable consequences following model performances versus no consequences). A nonassertive-model control group was included in the design. Because previous research employing the assessment battery and screening requirements indicated no changes over time without treatment and a relatively limited number of subjects was available, a no-treatment group was not included in the design (Kazdin, 1974c, 1975). The following groups were employed.

Single model/reinforcement. Subjects ($n = 11$) imagined a person similar to themselves in age and of the same sex as the model in all treatment sessions. Prior to each session, subjects practiced imagining the same person at the beginning of the session. The scenes used in reatment consisted of the context in which an assertive response was appropriate, the model's assertive response, and favorable consequences following model performance.

Single model/no reinforcement. Subjects ($n = 11$) imagined the same model throughout treatment sessions as did the previous group. The treatment scenes employed for this group did *not* include the favorable consequences following model performance. Subjects received only the context and the model's assertive response in each scene.

Multiple models/reinforcement. Subjects ($n = 11$) imagined a *different* model in each treatment session. Across the four treatment sessions the models were similar in age and of the same sex, older and of the opposite sex, older and of the same sex, and similar in age and of the opposite sex, respectively. The scenes used in treatment consisted of the context, the model's assertive response, and favorable consequences.

Multiple models/no reinforcement. Subjects ($n = 11$) imagined a different model in each treatment session. The treatment scenes employed for this group did *not* include the favorable consequences. Only the context and the model's assertive response were presented.

Nonassertive-model/control. Subjects ($n = 10$) received only one portion of the treatment scenes, namely, the *context* in which an assertive response was appropriate. A person or model *was* imagined in the scene as the previous groups. However, *no assertive response* was made by the model *nor* did *consequences* follow model performance. The person in the scene was imagined as part of the context (i.e., to whom an event occurred that provided impetus for an assertive response).

RESULTS

Treatment

Preliminary one-way analyses of variance indicated no differences among groups on any dependent measure at pretreatment nor significant differences at posttreatment resulting from therapists. Also, groups did not differ on the postsession questionnaires on rated clarity of imagery, anxiety experienced during the sessions, and in the amount of material presented that could be successfully imagined. With the exception of one dependent variable, mentioned below, sex of subject was not related to performance. Two-way analyses of covariance (using pretreatment performance as the covariate), Newman-Keuls comparisons including nonassertive-model controls, and within-group t tests from pretreatment to posttreatment were employed to evaluate the data.

Self-report inventories. The results for the two-way analyses of covariance for the major dependent variables appear in Table 1. The Conflict Resolution Inventory showed the effect of the number of models, and the Wolpe-Lazarus scale showed the effect of model reinforcement. Subjects who imagined several models rather than a single model or favorable consequences rather than no consequences were more assertive on both measures. The means for the Conflict Resolution Inventory data are presented in Figure 1. Multiple comparisons revealed that each covert modeling group differed from nonassertive-model controls.* Also, multiple model/reinforcement subjects were more assertive than all other groups. On the Wolpe-Lazarus scale, all groups except the single model/no-reinforcement group were more assertive than nonassertive-model controls.

---

*Several additional variables other than those included here were assessed such as whether the subjects (a) imagined themselves being assertive; (b) described feelings of the characters in the scenes; (c) described the setting; (d) described physical characteristics of people in the scenes; and (e) repeated, continued, or altered the scene when it was imagined the second time. These variables did not yield significant results and are not detailed in this article.

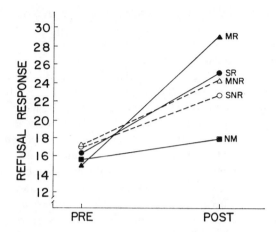

Fig. 24.1. Mean refusal responses on the Conflict Resolution Inventory for single model/reinforcement (SR), single model/no-reinforcement (SNR), multiple model/ reinforcement (MR), multiple model/no-reinforcement (MNR), and nonassertive-model control (NM) groups.

Analysis of Willoughby Scale responses also showed an effect of model reinforcement (see Table 1) indicating that imagining favorable consequences led to greater assertive behavior than imagining no consequences. Multiple comparisons indicated that all modeling groups were superior to nonassertive-model controls, but they did not differ from each other. The final self-report inventory, the Rathus Assertiveness Schedule, revealed no differences among treatment conditions.

Within-group increases in assertive behavior from pretreatment to posttreatment for the self-report inventories appear in Table 2. The t tests indicated that covert modeling groups tended to show consistent increases in assertive behavior across measures, whereas the nonassertive-model control group did not.

Behavior role-playing test. Responses to the behavior role-playing test were recorded and subsequently scored in random order across pretreatment and posttreatment. Two judges completed the ratings for assertiveness, latency, and duration of responses. Interjudge agreement was computed separately for each dependent variable. Ratings of assertiveness were made for each response (5 point scale: 1 = not at all, 5 = very assertive). The correlation between judges across 125 responses of 12 randomly selected subjects was .94. For latency and response duration, each situation was scored as an agreement if the estimate of both judges agreed within .5 or 1.0 sec, respectively. D disagreement was scored if the estimate exceeded the criterion. Reliability was calculated as agreements divided by agreements plus disagreements and multiplied by 100 to form a percentage. Across 110 responses of 10 subjects, reliability was 87.3% for latency and 89.1% for duration.

For rated assertiveness, on the role-playing test both the number of models and model reinforcement were significant (see Table 1). The means for assertiveness ratings for each group appear in Figure 2. Each treatment group was more assertive at posttreatment than controls. Multiple model/reinforcement subjects were rated as more assertive than all other groups. Analysis of response latency revealed a significant effect of model reinforcement with subjects imagining favorable model consequences showing a shorter response latency than nonreinforcement subjects (see Table 1). Only multiple model/reinforcement subjects were different from control subjects.

Analysis of response duration indicated no difference among treatment conditions. During the behavioral test, the pulse rate of the subjects was recorded immediately after a role-playing situation was presented. At post-treatment, groups did not differ in pulse rate.

Within-group changes on the behavior role-playing test (see Table 2) were evident for each of the treatment groups. Although the nonassertive-model control group improved in rated assertiveness, the change was markedly less than for the covert modeling groups. In any case, the within-group improvements were relatively consistent for the covert modeling groups.

Behavior role-playing test: Generalization. Subjects also responded to novel role-playing situations at posttreatment to determine whether treatment effects generalized. Performance on the novel situations was similar to performance on the previous retest situations. For ratings of assertiveness in the novel situation, significant effects were obtained for number of models,

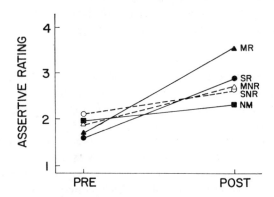

Fig. 24.2 Mean assertive rating on the behavior role-playing test for single model/reinforcement (SR), single model/no-reinforcement (SNR), multiple model/reinforcement (MR), multiple model/no-reinforcement (MNR), and nonassertive-model control (NM) groups.

Table 24.1 Two-Way Analyses of Covariance at Posttreatment

Source	cf	Self-report inventories				Behavior role-playing test		
		CRI refusal	Wolpe-Lazarus scale	Willoughby scale	Rathus schedule	Asser-tiveness	Latency	Duration
No. models (A)	1	4.77*	3.82	<1	<1	5.36*	<1	<1
Model reinforce-ment (B)	1	6.40*	4.58*	4.54*	2.00	7.39**	5.02*	1.95
A × B	1	<1	<1	<1	<1	3.32	2.83	<1
Error	39							

Note. CRI = Conflict Resolution Inventory.
*$p < .05$.
**$p < .01$.

Table 24.2 Within-Group Changes From Pretest to Posttest Assessments (*t* Tests)

Response measure	Group				
	Single model/ reinforcement	Single model/ no reinforcement	Multiple model/ reinforcement	Multiple model/no reinforcement	Nonassertive model
Self-report					
Conflict resolution inventory	7.57***	4.40**	9.00***	4.42**	1.73
Wolpe-Lazarus scale	4.25***	4.00**	6.83***	5.30***	.97
Rathus schedule	1.62	2.49*	1.03	2.38	−1.77
Willoughby Scale	4.18**	3.31**	6.19***	3.19**	1.68
Assertive ability (self-rate)	4.47***	1.94	4.10**	4.20**	3.55**
Saying ''no'' (self-rate)	1.99	3.38**	2.44*	3.47**	1.63
Extent of problem (self-rate)	1.98	4.12**	2.79*	2.34*	2.37*
Behavior role-playing test					
Assertiveness	7.66***	5.61***	11.25***	7.72***	2.29*
Response latency	2.82*	1.84	4.03**	3.07*	1.78
Response duration	2.61*	.95	3.61**	2.72*	.78
Pulse rate	2.67*	.61	2.25*	−.12	.34

*$p < .05$.
**$p < .01$.
***$p < .00i$.

240

$F(1, 39) = 10.22, p < .01$, model reinforcement, $F(1, 39) = 8.68, p < .01$, and the interaction, $F(1,39) = 4.90, p < .05$. The interaction resulted from the marked effect of favorable consequences for multiple-model subjects. Indeed, multiple model/reinforcement subjects were significantly greater in assertiveness than all other groups. Latency of responses to the novel role-playing situations yielded a significant effect of model reinforcement, $F(1, 39) = 4.34, p < .05$, but no other effects. Reinforcement subjects showed a shorter latency than did nonreinforcement subjects. There were no differences among groups in response duration on the novel role-playing situations.

Global self-ratings. Subjects rated how assertive they were, the extent to which they could say "no" to others, and the degree to which saying "no" was a problem (each on a $1-100$-point scale). Groups did not differ in global self-ratings. Each group improved on at least one of three global self-ratings (see Table 2). The only sex difference obtained in the investigation resulted from males rating themselves as having less of a problem in saying no at posttreatment than did females, $F(1, 52) = 6.27, p < .05$.

Follow-Up

Four months after treatment, the Conflict Resolution Inventory and the Wolpe-Lazarus Assertive Training Scale were mailed to each subject. Thirty-eight (or 70.4%) of the subjects returned the questionnaires. Two-way analysis of variance of follow-up data (unweighted-means solution) yielded a significant effect of model reinforcement on the Conflict Resolution Inventory, $F(1, 28) = 4.99, p < .05$. Reinforcement subjects were more assertive than nonreinforcement subjects. Both single model/reinforcement and multiple model/reinforcement subjects were significantly different from nonassertive-model controls, but they did not differ from each other. On the Conflict Resolution Inventory, within-group increases in refusal responses from pretreatment to follow-up were significant for single model/reinforcement, $t(8) = 2.32, p < .05$, multiple model/no-reinforcement, $t(7) = 5.18, p < .01$, multiple model/reinforcement, $t(8) = 8.36, p < .001$, and nonassertive-model control subjects, $t(5) = 3.16, p < .05$.

Although there were no differences among groups of the Wolpe-Lazarus scale, within-group improvements from pretreatment to follow-up were evident for single model/no-reinforcement, $t(5) = 5.72, p < .01$, multiple model/no-reinforcement, $t(8) = 3.68, p < .01$, and nonassertive-model control subjects, $t(5) = 3.93, p < .05$.

Within-Session Report of Imagery

Verbalizations of subjects during the treatment sessions while subjects were imagining the scenes were tape-recorded and evaluated by two judges (different from the judges who rated the role-playing test). Interobserver agreement was assessed by comparing agreements and disagreements for each scene across 200 scenes of 10 randomly selected subjects. An agreement was counted if observers' responses were identical for a specific category during a given scene. A disagreement was noted for nonidentical scoring. Reliability was calculated by dividing agreements by agreements plus disagreements and multiplying by 100 to form a percentage. Reliability was 83.0% for whether subjects finished the scenes they were verbalizing, 93.2% for whether the model was described as asserting himself in the scenes, 88.6% for scoring whether the subject described consequences following model behavior, and 83.6% for whether the subject elaborated portions of the scenes.

Model assertiveness and consequences. One-way analyses of variance were completed across each variable. Significant differences among the groups were attained for the number of scenes in which an assertive model was included in the verbal description, $F(4, 49) = 28.93, p < .001$. All treatment groups reported substantially more scenes with an assertive model than did nonassertive-model controls. Modeling groups did not differ from each other. This finding was expected because only the treatment groups were instructed to imagine an assertive model in the scenes. Groups also differed in their verbalizations of consequences following model behavior relative to all other groups. This, too, was expected from implementation of the experimental manipulations. Overall, the within-session imagery data indicated that treatment conditions differed along experimentally manipulated dimensions as intended (i.e., whether an assertive model or favorable consequences were imagined).*

Scene deviation and scene elaboration. Although subjects reported imagining material that closely adhered to the material presented, in a few instances subjects introduced material not associated with their condition. That is, subjects sometimes deviated from the condition to which they were assigned. For example, although nonassertive-model control subjects never were instructed to imagine an assertive model in the scenes, a mean of 8.9% of

---

*Postsession questionnaire responses corroborated the within-session verbalizations. Questionnaire responses at the first and last sessions indicated that 90.9% and 95.5% of the model subjects, respectively, reported imagining an assertive model. In these sessions, 100% and 97.7% of the subjects, respectively, reported imagining a model appropriate in age and sex to their experimental condition. Also, 86.4% of the subjects (for the first and last sessions) indicated imagining consequences as appropriate to their experimental condition (i.e., favorable consequences or no consequences). For the nonassertive-model control subjects, 80% and 90% reported the model did not assert himself/herself during the first and last session, respectively. These results indicate that subjects reported adhering closely to the conditions to which they were assigned.

the scenes described included an assertive model. Similarly, although both groups included in the model/no-reinforcement condition never were instructed to imagine favorable consequences, a mean of 6.2% of the scenes reported included favorable consequences. Overall, subjects followed the presented scenes but on some occasions added modeling material and consequences.

Aside from introducing ingredients associated with specific treatment conditions (e.g., assertive model behavior or model consequences), the verbalizations were evaluated for the extent to which subjects elaborated upon the scenes presented. Elaboration of the scenes referred to including "extra" descriptive material beyond the material presented. A two-way analysis of variance indicated that model/reinforcement subjects elaborated significantly more on the scenes presented than did nonreinforcement subjects, $F(1, 40) =$ 6.70, $p < .05$. Elaboration of the treatment scenes by the reinforcement subjects may explain why these subjects were scored as having completed their descriptions of fewer scenes during treatment than did nonreinforcement subjects, $F(1,40) = 6.30$, $p < .05$.

Imagery and Treatment Outcome

To evaluate the relationship between within-session verbalizations of imagery and behavior change, within-cell correlations (averaged by Fisher's z) were computed between verbalization measures and pre-post changes in assertiveness. In general, various features of imagery (e.g., describing feelings of the model or features of the setting) did not consistently relate to changes in assertive behavior. Similarly, postsession questionnaire self-ratings of clarity of imagery, anxiety while imagining treatment scenes, and amount of material that was successfully imagined did not reliably relate to increases in assertive behavior.

DISCUSSION

The results indicated that (a) imagining several models engage in assertive performance led to greater changes in assertive behavior than did imagining a single model, (b) imagining favorable consequences following model performance enhanced modeling effects, (c) imagining assertion-relevant scenes without an assertive model was not as consistently associated with changes in assertive behavior as were covert modeling conditions, (d) the gains effected with covert modeling transferred to novel role-playing situations and tended to be maintained for up to 4 months of follow-up on a self-report measure, and (d) the within-session reports of imagery were useful in determining the extent to which subjects adhered to the imagery conditions to which they were assigned and in revealing divergence from the scenes presented.

As expected, covert modeling groups showed consistently more assertive behavior than did nonassertive-model control subjects. Imagining multiple models and model reinforcement enhanced the effects of covert modeling. These findings are consistent with results from overt modeling (Bandura, 1971; Rachman, 1972). Favorable model consequences appeared to effect behavior change to a greater extent than did multiple models, as shown in the number of dependent variables affected and in within-group improvements from pretreatment to posttreatment assessment. These findings replicate earlier work on the effect of model consequences (Kazdin, 1975).

The present results suggest that variations of parameters of imagery influence behavior change. Future work can continue to explore features of imagery that can be manipulated to enhance treatment. However, an important priority for research is the use of direct comparative studies assessing the relative efficacy of procedures based on imagery alone with those based upon overt behavior (e.g., behavioral rehearsal). In various areas of treatment, both techniques based on imagery and overt rehearsal claim effectiveness. Some direct comparisons need to be made because there is suggestive evidence that symbolic rehearsal and imagery-based procedures are not as effective as overt behavioral rehearsal in altering behavior (e.g., Bandura, Blanchard, & Ritter, 1969). Comparative studies might reveal the priority with which imagery-based treatments should be accorded.

A major purpose of this study was to assess aspects of imagery during treatment. Within-session verbalizations were useful in determining whether subjects imagined specific features of the material presented. Generally, subjects adhered closely to the imagery conditions to which they were assigned. However, verbalizations also revealed some changes from the scenes presented. Although the deviations were relatively infrequent, they are worth examining.

An interesting finding from the assessment of imagery was that model/reinforcement subjects added descriptive material to the treatment scenes to a greater extent than did nonreinforcement subjects. This finding leads to the interesting speculation that elaboration of scenes rather than model reinforcement mediated the superior performance on measures of assertiveness achieved by the reinforcement groups. The present investigation only raises this issue. Future research might profitably focus on manipulated and nonmanipulated aspects of imagery to determine more specific correlates of behavior change.

The extent to which scene deviation occurs in covert therapy investigations should always be determined. A failure of ''different'' treatment conditions to have different effects on behavior may result from relatively large subject deviations from the scenes presented. The actual imagery on the part of the subjects may make diverse experimental conditions less distinct than originally intended by the experimenter. In effect, subjects may imagine features that ''alter'' the treatment conditions to which they were assigned. Although this occurred infrequently in the present study, deviation from presented scenes has both methodological and substantive implications that need to be addressed.

REFERENCE NOTE

1. Cautela, J. R. *Covert modeling*. Paper presented at the fifth annual meeting of the Association for the Advancement of Behavior Therapy, Washington, D.C., September 1971.

REFERENCES

Bandura, A. Influence of models' reinforcement contingencies on the acquisition of imitative responses. *Journal of Personality and Social Psychology*, 1965, 1, 589-595.

Bandura, A. Psychotherapy based upon modeling principles. In A. E. Bergin & S. L. Garfield (Eds.), *Handbook of psychotherapy and behavior change*. New York: Wiley, 1971.

Bandura, A., Blanchard, E. B., & Ritter, B. Relative efficacy of desensitization and modeling approaches for inducing behavioral, affective, and attitudinal changes. *Journal of Personality and Social Psychology*, 1969, *13*, 173-199.

Bandura, A., & Menlove, F. L. Factors determing vicarious extinction of avoidance behavior through symbolic modeling. *Journal of Personality and Social Psychology*, 1968, *8*, 99-108.

Bandura, A., Ross, D., & Ross, S. Vicarious reinforcement and imitative learning. *Journal of Abnormal and Social Psychology*, 1963, *67*, 601-607.

Cautela, J., Flannery, R., & Hanley, E. Covert modeling: An experimental test. *Behavior Therapy*, 1974, *5*, 494-502.

Davison, G. C., & Wilson, G. T. Processes of fear-reduction in systematic desensitization: Cognitive and social reinforcement factors in humans. *Behavior Therapy*, 1973, *4*, 1-21.

Kazdin, A. E. Covert modeling and the reduction of avoidance behavior. *Journal of Abnormal Psychology*, 1973, *81*, 87-95.

Kazdin, A. E. Comparative effects of some variations of covert modeling. *Journal of Behavior Therapy and Experimental Psychiatry*, 1974, *5*, 225-231. (a)

Kazdin, A. E. Covert modeling, model similarity, and reduction of avoidance behavior. *Behavior Therapy*, 1974, *5*, 325-340. (b)

Kazdin, A. E. The effect of model identity and fear-relevant similarity on covert modeling. *Behavior Therapy*, 1974, *5*, 624-635. (c)

Kazdin, A. E. Effects of covert modeling and reinforcement on assertive behavior. *Journal of Abnormal Psychology*, 1974, *83*, 240-252. (d)

Kazdin, A. E. Effects of covert modeling, multiple models and model reinforcement on assertive behavior. *Behavior Therapy*, 1975, in press.

McFall, R. M., & Marston, A. R. An experimental investigation of behavior rehearsal in assertive training. *Journal of Abnormal Psychology*, 1970, *76*, 295-303.

Rachman, S. Clinical applications of observational learning, imitation, and modeling. *Behavior Therapy*, 1972, *3*, 379-397.

Rehm, L. P., & Marston, A. R. Reduction of social anxiety through modification of self-reinforcement: An instigation therapy technique. *Journal of Consulting and Clinical Psychology*, 1968, *32*, 565-574.

Weitzman, B. Behavior therapy and psychotherapy. *Psychological Review*, 1967, *74*, 300-317.

Chapter 25

The Adaptation of Covert Modeling Procedures to the Treatment of Chronic Alcoholism and Obsessive-Compulsive Behavior: Two Case Reports*†

William M. Hay, Linda R. Hay, and Rosemery O. Nelson

Summary — Covert modeling procedures were employed in the treatment of a 48-year-old male with a 30-year history of excessive alcohol consumption, and a 27-year-old female with a 6-year history of obsessive-compulsive behaviors. The covert modeling procedure in the first case consisted of practicing in imagination appropriate responses to excessive drinking stimuli. Throughout the 11-month posthospitalization follow-up period, the subject remained almost totally abstinent and maintained full-time employment. In the second case, a multiple baseline design was used to evaluate the effectiveness of the covert modeling procedure on each of the subject's obsessive-compulsive behaviors. The covert modeling procedure consisted of practicing in imagination appropriate behavior in situations where obsessive-compulsive behaviors had previously been exhibited. At 6-month follow-up, the subject was no longer engaging in the obsessive-compulsive behaviors. The therapeutic value of teaching the covert modeling procedure as a self-control technique was discussed.

*Reprinted with permission for *Behavior Therapy*, 1977, *8*, 70-76. © The Association for Advancement of Behavior Therapy 1977.

†Portions of this paper were presented at the Annual Meeting of the Association for Advancement of Behavior Therapy, San Francisco, December 1975.

Cautela (Note 1) suggested that the use of covert modeling procedures, where the modeled sequence is viewed in imagination, may be as effective as overt modeling procedures. Cautela, Flannery, and Hanley (1974) found that overt and covert modeling were equally efficacious in reducing college subjects' avoidance of laboratory rats. Further support for the use of covert modeling techniques has been provided by a series of studies where covert modeling was experimentally demonstrated to be an effective technique for reducing snake avoidance behavior and developing assertive behaviors in nonclinical college subject populations (Kazdin, 1973, 1974a, 1974b, 1974c, 1974d, 1975).

Case studies have been reported in which covert modeling procedures were employed with nonanalogue populations (Cautela, Note 1). Similarly, Flannery (1972) used the covert modeling procedure to teach a drug-dependent college student appropriate decision-making skills concerning the continuation of a relationship with her boyfriend. The present cases extended the demonstration of the utility of covert modeling procedures to two additional clinically relevant target behaviors: excessive drinking and obsessive-compulsive behaviors.

CASE 1

Subject

A 48-year-old male with a 30-year history of excessive alcohol abuse, a tenth grade education and from a rural southeast community, had been committed by the courts to a state institution for detoxification and rehabilitation. Numerous previous hospitalizations had not been successful in altering his drinking behavior. The longest period of abstinence reported by the subject was during a year in prison.

Treatment

A behavioral alcohol interview questionnaire[1] was utilized to analyze functionally the antecedents, response parameters, and consequences of his drinking pattern. The therapist, in close conjunction with the client, used this information to formulate five treatment scenes. These scenes sampled "trigger" situations in which the subject most frequently drank to excess. The subject's participation in the formulation of the treatment scenes allowed the specification of many of the situational parameters that precipitated and accompanied excessive drinking by the subject in his home environment. In

---

[1] A copy of this questionnaire is available upon request to the first author.

addition, his input was used to develop the alternative coping strategy that was incorporated into each treatment scene. Over the course of treatment, the content of the treatment scenes was modified to include any relevant stimulus conditions that would function to make the scenes closer approximation of actual ''trigger'' situations.

The treatment rationale outlined for the subject stressed the use of covert modeling as a generalized self-control skill. Specifically, he was told to use the procedure at any time that he either anticipated or found himself in a high probability drinking situation.

During each treatment session, the therapist described the scene and coping response for each of the five excessive drinking ''trigger'' stimuli situations. The subject was instructed to imagine each scene and to signal by raising his right index finger when the details of the scene were vivid. At that point, the therapist continued to embellish the scene for an additional 30 sec. A scene was presented twice during each therapy session. An example of a treatment scene is:

Imagine yourself walking in town and running into a group of your old drinking buddies. They have already been drinking heavily and ask you to join them. They are drinking white lightening. They look happy and you are alone. In the past you would have taken a drink and probably have become drunk. Now cope with the situation. Imagine yourself feeling the ''urge'' to drink but refusing and slowly turning and walking down the street.

The subject met with the therapist for two 30-min sessions each week during his 3-week period of hospitalization. In addition, he rehearsed the treatment scenes each day between therapy sessions with the aid of a tape recording prepared by the therapist. The tape consisted of the same five scenes and responses that were presented during the therapy sessions. In addition, he was involved in ward group treatment activities and given training in muscle relaxation to help relieve tremors and other alcohol related withdrawal symptoms.

Results and Discussion

Upon discharge, the subject was given a supply of stamped and addressed self-report postcards and told to mail a postcard each day on which the quantity and type of any alcoholic beverage consumed was recorded. In addition, the therapist phoned him once per month. After 2 months, the daily report was faded to weekly postcards and finally to monthly phone calls alone. During the first 6 months posthospitalization, he was seen as an outpatient for three 1-hr sessions and the covert modeling scenes previously practiced during treatment were rehearsed.

Throughout the first 8 months of follow-up, the subject reported total abstinence. This self-report was corroborated through bimonthly telephone contact with the subject's sister. Following this 8-month period of abstinence, the subject did report one 3-day excessive drinking incident. However, the subject has remained abstinent for an additional 3 months since that time. Thus, the subject reported drinking on only 3 days during the 11-month posthospitalization period. Throughout the posthospitalization period, the subject has maintained full-time employment without requiring rehospitalization.

The situation associated with the subject's 3-day relapse was not one of the specific scenes used in treatment. During treatment it probably is not possible to provide exhaustive coverage of all the situations that "trigger" excess drinking for any particular subject. One difficulty is that the majority of clients have not developed the self-observation skills necessary to delineate all the stimulus parameters eliciting their excessive drinking. In the present case study, although the use of covert modeling as a self-control skill was stressed, no specific training in applying these procedures to extratherapeutic situations was provided. Perhaps the generalization of the covert modeling skills would have been facilitated by the occasional presentation of additional trigger scenes for which the subject would have been asked to generate appropriate coping responses. These additional scenes would have provided a measure of how well the subject could adapt the covert modeling procedures to trigger situations not presented during treatment.

CASE 2

Subject

A 27-year-old female inpatient, diagnosed as having an obsessive-compulsive personality, anxiety neurosis, and depressive neurosis, had been married for 9 years, with two children, but had been separated from her husband for the past 1½ years. Prior to admittance, she and her children were living with her mother and grandmother.

The subject stated that her obsessive-compulsive behaviors began about 6 years ago following the birth of her second child. At that time, she became preoccupied with cleanliness, changing her children's clothing at the slightest sign of dirt and continually cleaning her house. She reported that she wanted to keep her house so spotless that "the family could eat off the floor if necessary." In addition, she became obsessed with the manner in which she performed perfunctory activities, such as turning on and off light switches and opening and closing doors. She complained of compelling desires to check that she had done things correctly, and frequently returned several times to check that the lights were off and that various doors were closed. For 4 years prior to her admission to the hospital, she received outpatient psychiatric care, including psychotherapy, medication, and EST. Since these procedures were unsuccessful, her psychiatrist suggested that she voluntarily admit herself to the state hospital.

While in the hospital, the subject was no longer exceptionally concerned with cleanliness but still engaged in ritualistic behaviors when turning off lights and closing her hospital room door. In addition, urges to check the lights and door increased in frequency and intensity. The subject also reported a new obsession: a preoccupation with being third and anxiety concerning the number "3." This obsession interfered with a variety of activities. For example, the subject would not get on a bus or ride in a care with only two other people, she would throw away the third item in a box, and she refused to carry three things. The subject believed that, if she failed to perform any of these behaviors correctly, then something "terrible" would happen to her.

Treatment

Since the subject's obsessional thoughts occurred almost continuously, it was decided that it would be more feasilbe for her to record occurrences of the overt behaviors that resulted from the obsessional thoughts rather than the obsessional thoughts themselves. The three obsessive-compulsive behaviors that the subject exhibited in the hospital were chosen for modification: checking that the room lights were off; checking that she had closed her room door; and behaviors concerning the number "3." Throughout baseline and all phases of treatment she self-recorded the daily frequency of each of these behaviors. Following a week of baseline recording, she was introduced to the covert modeling procedure. Although the subject concurrently recorded all three behaviors, the covert modeling procedure was applied to only one behavior at a time. This multiple baseline design allowed for the experimental evaluation of the utility of the covert modeling procedure in treating this subject's obsessive-compulsive behaviors.

During treatment weeks 1 and 2, the therapist presented the scenes and responses while the subject practiced in imagination that she was coping with urges to check that she had switched off the lights. Specifically, a series of eight scenes was imagined during each treatment session so that the subject could rehearse overcoming urges to check the lights in various settings. No mention of either closing the door or urges to check that the door was closed was made during these sessions. The subject was instructed to signal when the scene was vivid and to maintain the image until she had successfully coped with the situation. Each scene was presented twice during a therapy session. Forty-five minute therapy sessions were held twice a week. In addition, she practiced the scenes daily with the aid of a tape prepared by the therapist.

During the third and fourth weeks, the same covert modeling procedure was utilized to teach the subject to cope with urges to check her room door.

Treatment during the fifth and sixth weeks focused on practicing in imagination appropriate behaviors in situations where the subject's concern with the number "3" had previously interfered with her behavior.

Results and Discussion

There was a substantial decrease in the frequency of all three behaviors during the 6 weeks of treatment (Fig. 1). The subject reported that the urges to perform these behaviors had also decreased during this time. Furthermore, even when an ''urge'' was experienced she now felt that she had the skills to cope with it.

Examination of Fig. 1 suggests close correspondence between checking the lights and checking the door. The attenuated effect of the covert modeling procedure in reducing light checking behavior during treatment weeks 1 and 2 may have resulted from this relationship. The subject herself reported difficulty in separating these behaviors: Once she had returned to her room, regardless of whether she had experienced an urge to check the lights or the door, she would check both the light and door. The subsequent significant decrease in both light and door checking behaviors during the weeks that the covert modeling procedure was applied to door checking behavior corroborates the lack of independence of these target behaviors. By viewing these two checking behaviors as a single target behavior, it seems reasonable to assume from the multiple baseline design that the covert modeling procedures were responsible for the sequential attenuation of checking behaviors and behaviors related to the number ''3.''

The subject was discharged from the hospital 1 week following the termination of the treatment sessions. At 3- and 6-month follow-ups, the subject's self-report indicated that she was no longer engaging in obsessive-compulsive behaviors. Telephone contacts with her mother substantiated the subject's

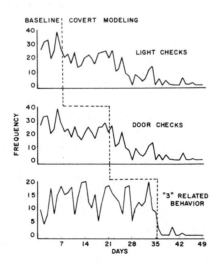

Fig 25.1 A multiple baseline analysis of the effects of covert modeling on the frequency of the three obsessive-compulsive behaviors in Case 2.

report. The subject stated that she had been able to adapt the treatment procedures to the obsessive-compulsive cleanliness that she had previously exhibited exclusively at home. Although no longer performing these obsessive-compulsive behaviors, she still felt depressed at times. She attributed these episodes of depression to her inability to secure employment.

DISCUSSION

One advantage of covert procedures, as utilized in the present studies, is that they do not require elaborate therapeutic aids. Thus, covert modeling procedures may be tuilized when the nature of the presenting problem prohibits the use of live or filmed models. Additionally, the results suggest the potential therapeutic value of teaching covert modeling procedures as a self-control skill. Anecdotal reports from the subjects indicate that they were both able to generalize the covert modeling procedure to other problems that were not directly dealt with during the therapy sessions. The subject of Case 1 reported adapting the covert modeling procedures to rehearse appropriate responses to trigger situations not practiced in therapy. The fact that he did drink excessively over one 3-day period, however, indictes that he was not entirely successful in generalizing the covert modeling procedures. The subject of Case 2, however, not only used the covert modeling procedure to deal with obsessive-compulsive behaviors that she exhibited in her home environment, but also adapted the procedures to practice appropriate job-interviewing behaviors.

In the present cases, subjects were instructed to imagine themselves as coping models. Kazdin has systematically examined the effects of varying several parameters of the covert modeling technique in analogue studies employing nonclinical college subject populations. The efficacy of covert modeling was enhanced by imaging a coping rather than a mastery model (Kazdin, 1973), a similar rather than a dissimilar model (Kazdin, 1974b), a reinforced rather than a nonreinforced model (Kazdin, 1975), and multiple as opposed to a single model (Kazdin, 1974a). Whether subjects imagined themselves or another person as the covert model did not differentially affect treatment results (Kazdin, 1974c). No attempt was made in the present cases to manipulate these parameters. Delineation of the influence of each of these parameters on therapeutic outcome with clinical nonanalogue populations awaits further experiment.

REFERENCE NOTE

1. Cautela, J. R. *Covert modeling*. Paper presented at Fifth Annual Meeting of the Association for Advancement of Behavior Therapy, Washington, DC, September 1971.

REFERENCES

Cautela, J. R. Flannery, R. B., Jr., & Hanley, S. Covert modeling: An experimental test. *Behavior Therapy,* 1974, **5,** 494–502.

Flannery, R. B., Jr. Use of covert conditioning in the behavioral treatment of a drug-dependent college dropout. *Journal of Counseling Psychology,* 1972, **6,** 547–550.

Kazdin, A. E. Covert modeling and the reduction of avoidance behavior. *Journal of Abnormal Psychology,* 1973, **811,** 87–95.

Kazdin, A. E. Comparative effects of some variations of covert modeling. *Journal of Behavior Therapy and Experimental Psychiatry,* 1974, **5,** 225–231. (a)

Kazdin, A. E. Covert modeling, model similarity and reduction of avoidance behavior. *Behavior Therapy,* 1974, **5,** 325–340. (b)

Kazdin, A. E. The effect of model identity and fear-relevant similarity on covert modeling. *Behavior Therapy,* 1974, **5,** 624–635. (c)

Kazdin, A. E. Effects of covert modeling and model reinforcement on assertive behavior. *Journal of Abnormal Psychology,* 1974, **83,** 240–252.

Kazdin, A. E. Covert modeling, imagery assessment, and assertive behavior. *Journal of Counsulting and Clinical Psychology,* 1975, **43,** 716–724.

SECTION VII
COVERT RESPONSE COST

Chapter 26
Covert Response Cost*
Joseph R. Cautela

Summary — The paper introduces the technique of covert response cost, which involves having the client imagine a behavioral response which he wishes to reduce in frequency paired with the imagined loss of a reinforcer. Methodological considerations, research and clinical evidence of the effectiveness of this procedure, and suggestions for further research are discussed.

In the view point of many professionals, and the lay public, behavior modification has often been identified with aversive control. Investigators such as Braff (1973) postulate that misuse and unclear use of such terms as aversive stimulation and negative reinforcement may lead to unnecessary restrictions of the techniques available to the clinician. One problem with this identification has been the inclusion of procedures such as psycho-surgery and drugs under the rubric of aversive control. Also, aversive control usually is identified with electric aversion therapy. As a matter of fact, there are many more procedures included under the construct of aversive control. By aversive control is meant the modification of response rate through the use of a stimulus which an individual is likely to avoid. A classification of aversive control procedures is presented in Table 1.

There are three general classes of procedures. The first class, AD, involves the use of aversive stimuli and results in the decrement of response. In the second class, a positive reinforcer is involved in some manner and results in response decrement. In the third class, aversive stimuli are involved, but the result is an increase in response rate. By an aversive stimulus is meant a stimulus which the organism tends to avoid and not to approach, or a stimulus which can be used to suppress behavior. By reinforcement is meant a consequence which increases the response probability when presented (positive

*Reprinted with permission from *Psychotherapy: Theory, Research and Practice*, 1976, *13*, 397-404.

Table 26.1 Aversive Controls

General Class	Specific Class	Procedure
AD		
A– Aversive stimulus is involved; a stimulus which the organism attempts to avoid	AD-P	Punishment
	AD-S	Conditioned suppression
D– Procedure results in probability of response decrement	AD-R	Physical restraint
RD		
R– Reinforcer is involved; a stimulus which the organism attempts to approach	RD-E	Extinction- Reinforcement is not presented
D– Procedure results in probability of response decriment	RD-T	Time-out- Reinforcement is not available for a period of time
	RD-S	Satiation- Repeated presentations of reinforcement which results in response decriment
	RD-O	Omission training- Reinforcement is not presented when undesirable response is made or reinforcement for omitting a response
	RD-C	Response cost- Reinforcement is taken away from the organism
AI		
A– Aversive stimulus is involved; a stimulus which the organism attempts to avoid	AI-E	Escape conditioning
	AI-A	Avoidance conditioning
I– Procedure results in probability of response increase		

reinforcement), or when an event is withdrawn after a behavior (negative reinforcement).

If aversive controls have to be used, then procedures that involve less coercion, "pain," and subjective distress are more desirable from the client's point of view. In a discussion of ethics, Bandura (Note 1) has advocated the use of "symbolic" or covert methods of aversive stimulation as a more human alternative to overt stimulation. Also, if aversive procedures can be used as self-control or self-management, then the client or therapist is more apt to use them when indicated, either alone or with other procedures. Indeed, some investigators hold that it can be considered unethical to withhold a procedure that can suppress a personally damaging or anti-social behavior simply because it is labeled an "aversive control procedure". It is desirable, as Skinner (1974, p. 181) points out, to use positive reinforcement whenever possible, but at the present state of our knowledge, we have not reached the point at which an aversive control is never necessary.

The author has developed a number of covert conditioning procedures, some of which involve aversive stimulation. The procedures are categorized as covert conditioning since the client or subject is instructed to imagine both the response to be modified and the consequences. The procedures are based on the assumption that overt and covert behaviors obey the same laws. This is consistent with the view of theorists such as Pavlov (1927) and Skinner (1969, p. 242), and is also supported by some recent evidence (Baron, Note 2; Cautela, Flannery, & Hanley, 1974; Epstein, 1973; Kazdin, 1973a, 1974a, 1974b; Schwartz and Higgins, 1971). There is both anecdotal and experimental evidence that the covert conditioning procedures of covert reinforcement (COR) (Cautela, 1970b), covert negative reinforcement (CNR) (Cautela, 1970a), covert extinction (CE) (Cautela, 1971), covert sensitization (CS) (Cautela, 1967), and covert modeling (CM) (Cautela, in press) are effective (Cautela, 1973).

In general, the purpose of this paper is to present another covert conditioning method that involves aversive control, that can be used as a self-control procedure requiring the cooperation of the client and thereby, decreasing the likelihood of forced control by others. Specifically, the purpose of the paper is to describe the procedure of covert response cost (CRC). Some clinical experience and preliminary experimental results will be presented. Before discussion of CRC, a brief description of overt cost and some of its characteristics will be presented.

OVERT RESPONSE COST

Response cost has been defined as the removal or conditioned reinforcers contingent upon a response (Kazdin, 1972), or as physical cost or effort (Azrin, 1958). In this paper, response cost is referred to as the removal of a positive reinforcer contingent upon a response.

Compared to other aversive control procedures, response cost has only recently been investigated in the laboratory and researched and utilized in applied settings. Laboratory investigations were originally systematically carried out by Weiner (1962, 1963, 1964, 1965a, 1965b, 1969). More recently, investigators such as Kazdin (1972) and Rimm and Masters (1974, pp. 394-397) advocate the use of response cost as an effective means to suppress maladaptive behaviors. In an excellent review article, Kazdin (1972) points to the effectiveness of response cost in a wide variety of applied settings and with problematic behaviors. Response cost has demonstrated superiority in group therapy (Harmatz & Lapuc, 1968). In another study, response cost plus token reinforcers found greater efficacy than token reinforcers alone (Phillips, et al., 1971). Also, it appears that by response cost, behaviors suppressed often do not recover when response cost is withdrawn (Kazdin, 1972; Phillips, et. al., 1971; Siegel, et. al., 1969). Kazdin (1973b) has reported generalized effects in suppression of speech disfluencies.

Another relevant characteristic of response cost is that it does not appear to have some of the side effects associated with punishment such as escape (Phillips, et. al., 1971) or disruptive behaviors (Schmauk, 1970). In view of the above observations concerning response cost, it is surprising that tests concerned with aversive conditioning make little reference to the response cost procedure.

WHY CRC?

If the literature indicates that covert sensitization is an effective technique to decrease undesirable behavior, what is the purpose of adding another covert technique that involves aversive control. There are a number of reasons that covert response cost (CRC) should be included in the behavior therapy repertoire of procedures. For most clients, it is necessary to develop more than one behavior and occasionally clients report becoming bored with repeating the same technique. I have found that the client is more apt to do homework and appear more alert if we alternate CS and CRC scenes.

Occasionally, a client reports a dearth of stimuli that register an aversive or report disgust when CS is employed. Since it is important in CS, as with COR, to avoid the adaptation or satiation effect, it is necessary to employ many aversive stimuli. In these cases, CRC can be either added to CS or employed instead of CS. With some clients, when CS is employed, the particular undesirable behavior does not appear to be reducing rapidly enough so that CRC is added or substituted. Some clients report a greater emotional response with CRC than with CS. In these cases, I have employed CRC rather than CS, assuming the stronger emotional response could make CRC more effective.

DESCRIPTION OF CRC

In employing covert response cost (CRC), the client is instructed to imagine both the response to be reduced and the loss of a reinforcer; e.g. a watch, money, jewelry. After a behavior analysis has determined the target response and that CRC is going to be one of the treatment procedures, the client is given the following rationale.

He is told that experimental and clinical findings indicate that if a particular behavior is followed by a deprivation of something of value, often that behavior tends to decrease. "We have found that in many instances if we ask people to imagine they are being deprived of, or lose something, after they imagine doing something undesirable, such as smoking or even feeling anxious, they are less apt to perform the undesirable behavior."

After the rationale is given and the client indicates willingness to co-operate with the procedure, he is asked to fill out the covert response cost survey schedule (CRCSS). See Table 2.

Table 26.2 Covert Response Cost Survey Schedule (CRCSS)

Directions: Check how much the following situations would disturb, bother or upset you at the moment you discover that they have occurred.					
	Not at all	a little	a fair amount	much	very much
1. You lose your pocketbook					
2. You lose your wallet					
3. You lose your favorite coat					
4. You lose your rubbers					
5. You lose your umbrella					
6. You lose your watch					
7. Your automobile is stolen					
8. You lose your favorite piece of jewelry					
9. You lose $10					
10. You lose your favorite shoes					
11. You lose your paycheck					
12. Your house or apartment burns down					
13. You break your favorite record					
14. Your television is stolen					
15. Your favorite piece of furniture breaks or is stolen					
16. You lose your bankbook					
17. You arrive a half hour late for work or school					
18. You lose your ticket to an important event, e.g. concert, sporting event, play					
19. You lose your house and/or car keys					
20. Arriving home you find you were short changed $5 by a store clerk					
Add any other items you feel are valuable and that you would not want to lose.					

The CRCSS consists of twenty items in which there is an indication of a loss of something valuable to the client. He is asked to report the amount of disturbance he feels over the loss of each item, ranging from not at all to very much. The client is also asked if he can think of any other losses that would upset him. Then he is asked to imagine a setting in which he has indicated a loss would be either disturbing or very much disturbing. This is done to determine the clarity of imagery and the degree of subjective distress incurred. The following is a typical example of the investigation of an item for its possible inclusion in a CRC scene.

"I am going to ask you to imagine losing your car. Would that bother you a lot? In this scene try to imagine that you are really there; that it is really happening. Then I am going to ask you how clearly you imagined the scene on a one to five scale, where one is 'not clear at all' and five is 'very clear' and where you can see it really happening. Also, I will ask on a one to five scale, where one is 'not at all' and five is 'very much', how much the scene bothers you. Remember that it is important to believe that the situation I am going to describe is really happening.

"You are coming out of a neighbor's party. You know that you parked your car right in front of the house, but it is not there. You can not believe your eyes. The car is gone. You look up and down the street and it is nowhere to be seen. Suddenly, you realize that it has been stolen.

"Now I am going to ask you to imagine, the response to be decreased (the one we agreed upon). You are parked next to a high school. You open the car door and expose yourself to a group of young girls walking by. Remember how we practiced this scene before?" The client is then told when the image of this scene is clear, he is to signal by raising his right index finger. The therapist then says, "shift" and the client imagines he is incurring a response cost (e.g. he finds when he gets home that his car is stolen.) The therapist questions the client concerning the clarity of imagery and how much distress he could feel when imagining the response cost situation. If the client reports the imagery as clear and he feels some discomfort at the response cost, he is then asked to practice the whole procedure by himself, signalling when he has completed imagining the response cost situation.

In any one treatment session, ten scenes are described to the client in which he is to imagine the response cost. Each scene is first described by the therapist. This is alternated with scenes in which the client is told to practice both scenes by himself; that is, he imagines that he is about to do the undesirable behavior and then shifts to the response cost, e.g. "you are about to take a drink of alcohol; you have lost your wallet."

Due to the possibility of the adaptation effect, it is probably a good idea to use three or four different response cost scenes at any one session. The client is then instructed to practice the scenes at home ten times each day. He is also told to vary the response cost scenes. If he finds that the scenes are losing their distressing qualities, he is told to stop using those particular scenes and choose others.

TYPICAL EXAMPLES OF CRC

CRC can be applied to both maladaptive approach behaviors and maladaptive avoidance behaviors. In general, it is used in maladaptive approach behaviors such as alcoholism, smoking, overeating, and sexual problems. Sometimes, CRC is also used for excessive avoidance behaviors, e.g. fear of tunnels and bridges. As in all the covert conditioning procedures, a hierarchy does not have to be constructed as a logical order is usually followed. For example, an alcoholic, who used to begin his weekend drinking immediately after coming home from work on Friday night, was given the following scene sequence:

"As you walk into the house after work, you say to yourself, 'I think I'll start out with a belt'." When he signals that the scene is clear, the therapist says "Shift". He then imagines that his new is smashed against a tree. When he signals that the image is clear, he is told to imagine that he is walking toward the liquor cabinet to pour himself a straight shot before his wife knows that he is home. "Shift". (Smashed car scene). The next scene he is told to imagine is that he opens the bottle and raises it to his lips. "Shift."

Of course, before the sequence was initiated, the scenes were checked for clarity and aversiveness. Also, the sequence was gradually built up by doing the first scene, then the first and second scenes, and finally the first, second, and third scenes. After each description by the therapist and the imagining by the client, the client then repeated the procedure without the description by the therapist. In each session a sequence of scenes is usually used. The following are individual scenes which are part of a sequence.

A pedophiliac was given this scene as a part of a sequence employed to build up avoidance behavior (sexual) to children. "You are walking into the locker room after a basketball game to watch the youngsters undress and to look at their penises. You are now opening the door. Shift. Now imagine you are at a restaurant reaching for your wallet to pay the waiter and you find that the wallet is missing. (This scene was highly aversive since it involved the loss of many credit cards and license.)

A woman treated for overeating was asked to imagine that she was about to open the refrigerator to get something to eat before going to bed. "Shift. You are meeting your husband at the theatre. He askes for the tickets and you suddenly remember that you left them at home on the table."

The following is an example of the use of CRC with excessive avoidance behavior, e.g. a fear of driving through tunnels. "You decide that this time you are not going to get upset and anxious and you are going to drive through the Sumner Tunnel. Immediately, you get anxious and think, 'Oh my God, what if I panic!' Shift. You are in the ladies room in a restaurant. As you wash your hands, you notice that your diamond ring is missing." After the scene is described once, the therapist has only to say "shift" and the client imagines the CRC scene without it being described. On an a prior basis, it might appear that if an anxiety response is followed by an aversive stimulus that the anxiety could worsen. However, anecdotal evidence and empirical test (Scott, et al., Note 3) indicates this does not appear to be a danger in employing CRC to reduce avoidance behavior.

INDICATIONS OF EFFECTIVENESS OF CRC

While CRC is a relatively new covert conditioning procedure, anecdotal results are encouraging. As in other procedures of behavior therapy, systematic research is needed as the ultimate test of the efficacy of the procedure and the determination of the process involved. There are some preliminary results that are encouraging, but more extensive and well controlled studies are needed.

In 1965, Weiner found that both the real costs of losing points on a counter by pressing a key and imagined cost (instruction to imagine losing the points each time the key was pressed) had suppressive effect upon inter-reinforcement responses relative to no cost on a FI-10 second schedule. As a result of his experiment, Weiner concluded that "This supports those behavior therapists (e.g. Wolpe, 1958) who claimed that the effects produced by the actual occurrence of aversive events can be reintegrated to some extent by verbal instruction to imagine the aversive event." (1965, p. 662)

In a more recent experiment, Tondo, Lane & Gill (1975) employed CRC in target responses of eating specific food by subjects in a weight reduction program. They utilized a single case design with two subjects. The data indicated that CRC was effective in producing reliable decreases in the amount of target food consumed. Inter- and intra-subject replications were obtained.

Scott & Jackson (Note 3) compared the effect of CRC, covert reinforcement, and a control group on test anxiety. There were no differences, $p < .05$, between the covert reinforcement and CRC groups in reducing test scores. Both groups differed from the control group. This study indicated that an anxiety response can be viewed as an operant and can be suppressed by aversive consequences.

The anecdotal evidence from the clinical situation and the three experiments just cited, indicate that CRC should receive serious consideration by the clinical and researcher concerned with covert processes.

FUTURE RESEARCH

The development of a new treatment procedure usually results in research questions involving degree of efficacy, process, and theoretical implications. Accordingly, the CRC procedure usually results in research questions involving degree of efficacy, process, and theoretical implications. Accordingly, the CRC procedure results in research questions such as the following:

1. How effective is CRC; how many trials are needed before a change in the behavior is noticed? (Anecdotally, we have noticed that around sixty trials are required.) Does the procedure have differential effectiveness on different behaviors? How long does the behavior remain suppressed when treatment is complete? (Of course, the answer to the last question depends on variables such as the number of trials to suppression and the number of overlearning trials performed.)
2. Does it make a difference whether the imagined loss involves something actually in the subject's possession or a loss not involving such an object, e.g. imagining having an expensive sports car stolen when the subject does not have one.
3. How does CRC compare with covert negative reinforcement and covert sensitization?
4. How does CRC compare with overt response cost? Are they both equally effective? Do the same parameters apply to overt and covert response cost?

The answers to such research questions are important in determining whether or not CRC should be employed as a clinical method and how to optimize its use. Also, research questions, such as question number four, bear directly on the assumptions of covert conditioning.

CRC COMBINED WITH OTHER PROCEDURES

As with other covert conditioning procedures, and indeed with other behavior therapy procedures, in clinical practice a combination of procedures is used to increase or decrease behavior. Only in attempting to experimentally verify the procedure are they isolated for treatment effect. As mentioned previously, one reason for developing CRC was to provide more variety in the use of procedures designed to reduce maladaptive approach behaviors, thereby avoiding a type of satiation effect by concentrating only on CS. Therefore, CRC is often combined with CS.

There is some evidence that aversive control is more effective if behavior antagonistic to the target behavior pinpointed for deceleration is reinforced (Azrin & Holz, 1966). This general finding appears also true of combining response cost with reinforcement of antagonistic behavior (Kazdin, 1971). In a previous example given in which CRC was employed with a fear of tunnels, COR was also employed to increase approach behavior to tunnels. In maladaptive approach behavior, COR is combined with CRC as a self-control response, e.g. COR for deciding not to take a drink. For the pedophiliac described previously, COR was employed for sexual approach behavior to adult females. Of course, other procedures such as thought stopping, relaxation, contingency contracting, etc., are also taught. The procedures are taught as self-control techniques to be used by the client after formal therapy is terminated.

ADVANTAGES OF CRC AS COMPARED TO ORC

1. The development of another covert procedure has heuristic value in terms of investigating the relationship of covert conditioning to overt conditioning; i.e., the assumption that covert processes follow the same principles and parameters as overt process.
2. In CRC, there is more flexibility in terms of the number of reinforcements which can be removed. The client does not have to have the reinforcement in his immediate possession in order to have an aversive effect of imagining that he is losing it; i.e., losing a sweepstake ticket which is a winner even though the client never bought a ticket or won.
3. CRC is more readily used as a self-control and self-management procedure.
4. The agent who removes the reinforcement does not have to be a member of the staff or the therapist. The scene can be so constructed as to leave them out of the situation. This could result in decreasing the tendency of the client to build up a resentment toward the individual removing the reinforcement as may happen in overt response cost.
5. Many more trials of CRC can take place in a specific period of time than with overt response cost. Of course, the implicit assumption here is that the more trials, the greater the suppression of behavior.

GENERAL CONSIDERATIONS

It is important to exercise care in selecting a reinforcer. If a very powerful reinforcer is used such as the loss of a loved one, the resulting affect may be too disturbing to the client. It is important, as in CS and COR, to vary the specific consequences removed to avoid the satiation effect. Satiation can occur no matter how strong the individual emotional response. There are some side advantages of this since this effect tends to decrease the probability of phobic responses the individual may develop concerning the loss of objects.

If the client indicates that he has difficulty in imagining the scenes, imagery may be made clearer by describing the situation in more detail, practicing in vivo, looking at objects in a particular place and then looking at the place with the object removed. Often, imagery gets clearer with sheer practice. In imagining scenes, even though a client may report poor imagery in one or two sense modalities, the imagery is often adequate to excellent in other sense modalities. The Imagery Survey Schedule (ISS) has been developed to determine which sense modalities have greater clarity and ease (latency) of response (Tondo & Cautela, 1974). Therefore, in describing scenes, it is important to use as many sense modalities as possible.

When applying CRC, the therapist should be careful to inquire whether the client is able to immediately shift from the undesirable behavior scene to the CRC scene. The immediate aversiveness is more effective than if a delay occurs. When employing CRC to eliminate anxiety, e.g., eliminate a plane phobia, the therapist should monitor the anxiety level to insure that it does not increase the anxiety level. It is especially important to avoid contiguity of anxiety with the loss by making sure the scene shift is immediate.

In summary, anecdotal and experimental evidence indicate that CRC is effective in suppressing behavior. It is another procedure that can be used by the clinician to suppress behavior without the side effects usually associated with punishment. Covert response cost is another method which can be employed by the researcher to investigate the characteristics of covert behavior.

REFERENCE NOTES

1. Bandura, A. *Legal and ethical issues in behavior therapy*. Paper presented at the Eighth Annual Meeting of the Association for Advancement of Behavior Therapy, Chicago, November 1974.
2. Baron, M. G. *The experimental analysis of imagery: The parameters of covert reinforcement*. Unpublished doctoral dissertation, Boston College, 1974.
3. Scott, D., & Jackson, W. *Covert response cost: An experimental test*. Unpublished manuscript, Boston College, 1974.

REFERENCES

Azrin, N. H. Some effects of noise on human operant behavior. *Journal of the Experimental Analysis of Behavior*, 1958, *1*, 183-200.

Azrin, N. H. & Holz, W. C. Punishment. In W. K. Honig (ed.), *Operant behavior: Areas of research and application*. New York: Appleton-Century-Crofts, 1966, pp. 380-447.

Braff, D. L. Clinical and theoretical consequences of the misuse of basic behavior therapy concepts. *American Journal of Psychiatry*, 1973, *130* (7), 818-819.

Cautela, J. R. Covert sensitization. *Psychological Reports*, 1967, *20*, 459-468.

Cautela, J. R. Covert negative reinforcement. *Journal of Behavior Therapy and Experimental Psychiatry*, 1970, *1*, 273-278. (a)

Cautela, J. R. Covert reinforcement. *Behavior Therapy*, *1*, 33-50. (b)

Cautela, J. R. Covert extinction. *Behavior Therapy*, 1971, *2*, 192-200.

Cautela, J. R. Covert processes and behavior modification. *The Journal of Nervous and Mental Disease, 1973, 157* (1), 27-36.

Cautela, J. R. Covert modeling: Currant status. *Journal of Behavior Therapy and Experimental Psychiatry*, in press.

Cautela, J. R., Flannery, R. B., & Hanley, S. Covert modeling: An experimental test. *Behavior Therapy*, 1974, *5*, 494-502.

Epstein, L. H. & Peterson, G. L. Differential conditioning using covert stimuli. *Behavior Therapy*, 1973, *4*, 96-99.

Harmatz, M. G. & Lapuc, P. Behavior modification of overeating in a psychiatric population. *Journal of Consulting and Clinical Psychology*, 1968, *32*, 583-587.

Honig, W. K. (ed.). *Operant Behavior: Areas of research and application*. New York: Appleton-Century-Crofts, 1966.

Kazdin, A. E. The effect of response cost in suppressing behavior in a prepsychotic retardate. *Journal of Behavior Therapy and Experimental Psychiatry*, 1971, *2*, 137-140.

Kazdin, A. E. Response cost: The removal of conditioned reinforcers for therapeutic change. *Behavior Therapy*, 1972, *3*, 533-546.

Kazdin, A. E. Covert modeling and the reduction of avoidance behavior. *Journal of Abnormal Psychiatry*, 1973, *81*, 87-95. (a)

Kazdin, A. E. The effect of response cost and aversive stimulation in suppressing punished and nonpunished speech disfluencies. *Behavior Therapy*, 1973, *4*, 73-82. (b)

Kazdin, A. E. Covert modeling, model similarity and reduction of avoidance behavior. *Behavior Therapy*, 1974, *5*, 325-240. (a)

Kazdin, A. E. Effects of covert modeling and reinforcement on assertive behavior. *Journal of Abnormal Psychology*, 1974, *3*, 240-252. (b)

Moore, W. H. & Ritterman, S. I. The effects of response contingent punishment upon the frequency of stuttered verbal behavior. *Behavior Research and Therapy*, 1973, *11*, 43-48.

Pavlov, I. P. *Conditioned Reflexes*. London: Oxford University Press, 1927.

Phillips, E. L., Phillips, E. A., Fixsen, D. L., & Wolf, M. M. Achievement place: Modification of the behaviors of pre-delinquent boys within a token economy. *Journal of Applied Behavior Analysis, 1971, 4*, 45–59.

Rimm, D. C. & Masters, J. C. *Behavior Therapy: Techniques and Empirical Findings*. New York: Academic Press, 1974.

Schmauk, F. J. Punishment, arousal, and avoidance learning in sociopaths. *Journal of Abnormal Psychology*, 1970, *76*, 325-335.

Schwartz, G. E. & Higgins, J. D. Cardiac activity preparatory to overt and covert behavior. *Science*, 1971, *173*, 1144-1146.

Siegel, G. M., Lenske, J., & Broen, P. Suppression of normal speech disfluencies through response cost. *Journal of Applied Behavior Analysis*, 1969, *2*, 265-276.

Skinner, B. F. *Contingencies of reinforcement*. New York: Appleton-Century-Crofts, 1969, p. 242.

Skinner, B. F. *About behaviorism*. New York: Alfred A. Knopf, 1974, p. 181.

Suinn, R. M. The STABS, a measure of test anxiety for behavior therapy: Normative data. *Behavior Research and Therapy*, 1969, *7*, 335-339.

Tonda, T. R., & Cautela, J. R. Assessment of imagery in covert reinforcement. *Psychological Reports*, 1974, *34*, 1271–1280.

Tonda, T. R., Lane, J. R., & Gill, K. Jr., Suppression of specific eating behaviors by covert response cost: An experimental analysis. *Psychological Record*. 1975, *25*, 187–196.

Weiner, H. Some effects of response cost upon human operant behavior. *Journal of the Experimental Analysis of Behavior*, 1962, *5*, 201-208.

Weiner, H. Response cost and the aversive control of human operant behavior. *Journal of Experimental Analysis of Behavior*, 1963, *6*, 415-421.

Weiner, H. Response cost effects during extinction following fixed-interval reinforcement in humans. *Journal of the Experimental Analysis of Behavior*, 1964, *7*, 333-335.

Weiner, H. Real and imagined cost effects upon human fixed-interval responding. *Psychological Reports*, 1965, *17*, 659-662. (a)

Weiner, H. Conditioning history and maladaptive human operant behavior. *Psychological Reports*, 1965, *17*, 935-942. (b)

Weiner, H. Controlling human fixed-interval performance. *Journal of the Experimental Analysis of Behavior*, 1969, *12*, 349-373.

Winkler, R. C. Management of chronic psychiatric patients by a token reinforcement system. *Journal of Applied Behavior Analysis*, 1970, *3*, 47-55.

Wolf, M. M., Hanley, E. L., King, L. A., Lachowicz, J., & Giles, D. K. The timer-game: A variable internal contingency for the management of out-of-seat behavior. *Exceptional Children*, 1970, *37*, 113-117.

Chapter 27

Suppression of Specific Eating Behaviors by Covert Response Cost: An Experimental Analysis*†

Thomas R. Tondo, James R. Lane, and Kinloch Gill, Jr.

Summary — A combination of multiple baseline and reversal designs were used to investigate effects of covert response cost (CRC) on maladaptive eating in 2 overweight females. The S's consumption of both target and non-target foods and beverages was monitored. During control phases E met with S and instructed her to imagine "lunchtime" scenes in which she is about to make the maladaptive target response. During treatment phases E instructed S to imagine response cost scenes contingent upon both imaginary and real-life lunch situations in which S is about to make the target response. Data indicate that the systematic presentation, withdrawal, and representation of CRC produced corresponding decreases, increases, and decreases in consumption of target foods only.

Cautela (1972) has reported utilizing successfully two covert conditioning procedures (covert sensitization and covert reinforcement) in the treatment of

---

*Reprinted with permission from *The Psychological Record*, 1975, 25, 187-196. © The Psychological Record.

†The authors would like to thank Ramona Trujillo (Director of the Personal Adjustment Center, Oxford, MS) and Barbara Smith (Research Assistant) for their valuable assistance and cooperation.

overeating, and a number of research studies have supported the effectiveness of such techniques in the treatment of obesity (Ashem, Poser, & Trudall, 1970; Janda & Rimm, 1972; Lick & Bootzin, 1971; Manno, 1972; Manno & Marston, 1972; Meynen, 1970; Sachs & Ingram, 1972; Stuart, 1967).

Recently, Cautela (1974) developed another covert conditioning technique, covert response cost (CRC), in order to supplement his treatment program for overeating and other maladaptive habits. The CRC procedure follows a punishment paradigm, the goal being to decrease the frequency of occurrence of a maladaptive behavior by making covert (imaginal) aversive responses (response cost scenes) contingent on the behavior. In the treatment of obesity the CRC procedure entails presenting to the patient a number of covert conditioning trials in which he is instructed to imagine scenes in which he is incurring a response cost (RC) (i.e., loss of a positive reinforcer) contingent upon the imagination of scenes in which he is about to make a maladaptive eating response. The patient is also instructed to administer additional covert conditioning trials at home and to imagine the RC scenes (i.e., self-punishment) in real-life situations whenever he is tempted to make an actual maladaptive eating response (see Cautela, 1974).

Kazdin (1972) has reviewed the experimental and applied studies on RC, and because of its apparent relative effectiveness and its advantages over other punishment procedures, he has recommended that RC be utilized more frequently as a behavior therapy technique, both as an overt procedure and as a "covert procedure, 'practice' in imagination." To date, only one study (Weiner, 1965) has been reported in which the possible effectiveness of a covert RC technique was investigated. In that study it was demonstrated that verbal instructions to imagine occurrences of cost (point loss) contingent upon interreinforcement responding under an FI 10-sec. schedule of point reinforcements) did suppress such responding, but the effect was not as marked and consistent as that produced by a real point loss.

In view of the possible clinical utility of a covert RC technique in the treatment of obesity, the purpose of the present study was to investigate (by means of a combination of multiple baseline and reversal designs) the effectiveness of Cautela's (1974) CRC procedure in the suppression of specific maladaptive eating behaviors.

METHOD

Subjects

The Ss were two adult overweight females who were day-care patients at a local personal adjustment center. Both Ss were selected from a group who indicated an interest in participating in a research project on weight reduction and who reported being able to experience images elicited by various items on the Imagery Survey Schedule II.*

Experimental Situation

The Ss were observed 3 to 4 days per week during lunch in a private dining area reserved for Ss in the present study and for two other Ss who were participating in another study. In order to minimize modeling effects, a four-way divider was used to shield each S from view of other Ss. Two main observers (one who observed Ss in the present study and one who observed Ss in the other study) and a third independent O (who checked the reliability of the two main Os) were also present during each lunch session. The two main Os sat at opposite ends of the dinner table, while the third sat beside the particular O whose impressions were being checked during the session. A two-way divider, placed between the third O and the main O, insured independence of recordings. Taped dinner music was played throughout the sessions in order to mask any extraneous sounds, as well as the auditory cues which S generated while eating.

Observation and Measurement

Throughout the lunch sessions the main O (who was unaware of when the control and treatment phases were in effect) watched both Ss and recorded the amount of food and beverage consumed. For solid foods, O counted the number of "bites" taken. A "bite" was defined as a 1-2-3 movement, consisting of bringing the food up to the mouth, putting a "regular" amount of the food into the mouth, and then taking the remainder of the food (or the utensil upon which the food was placed) away from the mouth. In the case of liquids, O counted the number of "sips" taken. A "sip" was defined as a 1-2-3 movement, consisting of bringing the beverage up to the mouth, pouring a "regular" amount of it into the mouth, and then taking the remainder of the beverage away from the mouth. In addition, the number of grams of peanut butter cups and corn chips consumed by each S per session was measured.

Reliability Measures

The third O (who was completely unaware of the purpose of the experiment) checked the reliability of the main O's recordings during certain sessions. Monitoring only one S per session, he checked approximately one quarter of the observations on each S.

---

*J. R. Cautela and T. R. Tondo. The Imagery Survey Schedule II. Unpublished questionnaire, Boston College, 1971.

Stability Criterion

In the present study "stability" was defined as less than 20% variability in the amount of target food consumed across three consecutive sessions. Thus stability during any phase was reached only when the amount (number of "bites") of target food consumed during any one of three consecutive sessions was within ± 10% of the mean for those three sessions.

Design and Procedure

Prior to the experiment, both Ss were given the following "expectancy" instructions:

During this research project, I will be using a number of different techniques which may or may not help you to cut down on your eating of certain fattening foods. The purpose of this research is to find out which of these techniques, if any, will in fact help you to control your eating of specific fattening foods. Thus at certain times you may find that what I do, or tell you to do, will help you to control your eating of fattening food; at other times you may notice no change in your eating patterns; and, finally, at other times you may find that you are actually eating more of the fattening foods than you were before.

A combination of multiple baseline and reversal designs was used with both Ss. However, because of minor differences in methodology the design and procedure for each S will be described separately.

Subject 1. Throughout the experiment S_1 brought a sandwich and a bottle of Coca-Cola to lunch. In addition, during each lunch session E (the senior author) provided her with a measured amount (100g) of the target food (Fritos Corn Chips), whose consumption was considered maladaptive *only if it occurred excessively at the end of the meal* (i.e., after S_1 had finished eating her sandwich).

The experimental phases for S_1 consisted of baseline, control, covert response cost, control, and covert response cost. Each new phase was begun only after the amount of target food consumed per session during the previous phase had reached stability. During baseline S_1 simply was observed eating, and the number of "bites" and "sips" taken of each food or beverage was recorded. The grams of target food consumed was also noted.

Throughout the control phases E met with S_1 for approximately 15 min. per day prior to each lunch session. During these phases S_1 was instructed to imagine the following "lunch time" scene five times:

Imagine it is lunch time at the Personal Adjustment Center and you are sitting at the dinner table [pause 5 sec.]. Try to feel as though you are actually there. Use as many of your senses as possible and concentrate on all of the details [pause 5 sec.]. Next, imagine that you are eating your sandwich and that you are just now taking the last bite of it. Concentrate on all of the sensations you would experience, especially those of taste and smell [pause 5 sec.]. Then, imagine that you see the crisp, salty, Fritos corn chips in front of you, and you begin to reach for another handful [pause until S_1 indicates the scene is completed].

The present phase was included as a control for a number of variables, such as interaction between E and S_1, instructions to imagine various events, including the response to be decreased (i.e., reaching for the target food).

During the treatment (CRC) phases, E once again met with S_1 prior to each lunch session for approximately 15 min., with the exception of the first treatment session of the first treatment phase, which lasted approximately 30 min. The first treatment session was used for identification and assessment of a number of possible RC scenes. The Covert Response Cost Survey Schedule* was administered to S_1, and a number of RC scenes based on items rated as "very unpleasant" were then constructed jointly by S_1 and E. These scenes were assessed further by instructing S_1 to imagine each one five times and to rate the scene's ease, clarity, and unpleasantness after each trial. In addition, E timed the latency of completion of each scene on each trial. Throughout the assessment procedure S_1 was told to concentrate on experiencing an unpleasant reaction while imagining each RC scene, and she was instructed to signal when the scene was completed and an unpleasant reaction experienced.

On the basis of the above assessment procedure, two RC scenes were selected. One scene was based on Item #3 ("You lose your favorite coat") of the Covert Response Cost Survey Schedule. S_1 was instructed to imagine that she accidentally burns a hole in her cashmere coat while smoking a cigarette in her car. In the other scene (the "Car Key Scene"), based on Item #19, S_1 was asked to imagine that while getting into her car, she discovers that her car keys have been stolen.

In each of the remaining treatment sessions, S_1 was given five trials in which she was instructed to imagine one of the RC scenes contingent upon completion of imagination of the "Lunch Time Scene" (i.e., reaching for more Fritos at the end of the meal). Although the same RC scene was used within a session, the two RC scenes were alternated between sessions.

At the end of each treatment session (with the exception of the first one) S_1 was instructed to imagine the same RC scene practiced within that session whenever she was tempted to reach for more Fritos at the end of the next in vivo lunch session. It should be noted that although S_1 was not given the above in vivo CRC instructions during the second control phase, neither was she told to discontinue use of the procedure.

Subject 2. Throughout the experiment, S_2 brought a sandwich and a bottle of Tab to lunch. In addition, during each lunch session E provided her with a

---

*J. R. Cautela. The Covert Response Cost Survey Schedule. Unpublished questionnaire, Boston College, 1973.

set amount (three 22-g cups) of the target food (Reese's Peanut Butter Cups), whose consumption was considered maladaptive *only if it occurred excessively* (i.e., if S_2 ate more than one cup per meal).

The experimental phases for S_2 consisted of control, covert response cost, control, and covert response cost. Each new phase was begun only after the amount (number of "bites") of target food consumed per session during the previous phase had reached stability.

The procedure during the first control phase was the same as that for S_1, with the exception that the following "Lunch Time" scene was used:

Imagine it is lunch time at the Personal Adjustment Center and you are sitting at the dinner table [pause 5 sec.]. Try to feel as though you are actually there. Use as many of your senses as possible and concentrate on all of the details [pause 5 sec.]. Next, imagine that you have just finished eating your sandwich and that you are now smoking a cigarette [pause 5 sec.]. Then, imagine that you see some of those sweet, chocolate, peanut butter cups and, after some deliberation, you decide to have just one. So you take the first one and begin to eat it. Concentrate on all of the sensations you would experience, especially those of taste and smell [pause 5 sec.]. Now, imagine that you have just finished eating the first peanut butter cup and you are about to reach for a second one [pause until S_2 indicates the scene is completed].

During the treatment phases the procedure was also basically the same as that used with S_1, with the exception that for S_2 the first treatment session of the first treatment phase was used for both assessment and treatment. Consequently, the session lasted approximately 45 min.

The assessment procedure for S_2 was essentially the same as that used with S_1, except that because of time limitations, S_2 was instructed to imagine each RC scene three times instead of five. Four RC scenes, based on the following items of the Covert Response Cost Survey Schedule were selected: Item #7 ("Your automobile is stolen"), Item #9 ("You lose $10), Item #12 ("Your house or apartment burns down"), and Item #16 ("You lose your bankbook"). As with S_1, the scenes were constructed and modified jointly by S_1 and E. For example, in the scene based on Item #9, S_2 was instructed to imagine that she discovers that $100 has been stolen from her, and in another scene based on Item #16 she was instructed to imagine that while attempting to purchase an item at a local department store, she discovers that her checkbook is missing.

Unlike the procedure for S_1, at the end of the first treatment session S_2 was given five trials in which she was instructed to imagine one of the RC scenes contingent upon imagination of the "Lunch Time Scene" (i.e., reaching for the second peanut butter cup). In addition, S_2 was instructed to imagine the RC scene during the next in vivo lunch session whenever she was tempted to take more than one peanut butter cup. However, whereas S_1 was never told to discontinue the in vivo RC procedure during the second control phase, S_2 was specifically told *not* to use the procedure during that phase.

RESULTS

Reliability Measures

Interobserver reliabilities were measured in terms of percentage of agreement on frequency of occurrence of those responses (i.e., "bites" or "sips" of each type of food or beverage) checked during a particular session. Percentage of agreement on the frequency of occurrence of a particular response was computed simply by dividing the smaller frequency by the larger one and then multiplying by 100. For S_1, the percentage of agreement ranged from 85% to 100%, whereas for S_2, it ranged from 88% to 100%.

Subject 1

As can be seen in Figure 1, during the baseline phase S_1 took an average of 28.67 "bites" of Fritos per session. During the first control phase the average dropped only slightly to 24.00 "bites" per session. However, although the number of "bites" of Fritos increased slightly during the first session (Session 7) of the first CRC phase, it dropped to an average of 18.00 by the last session

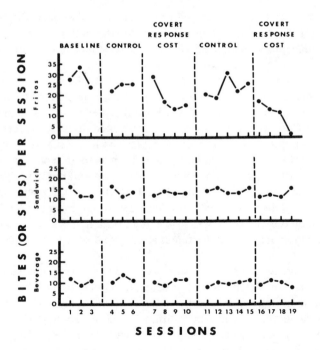

Fig. 27.1. Bites of target food (Fritos) and bites and sips of a nontarget food and beverage, respectively, for S_1 during each lunch session.

of that phase. Upon returning to the control phase, the number of "bites" of Fritos increased slightly during Sessions 11 and 12 but then increased sharply to a mean of 22.00 by the end of the second control phase. Reinstatment of the CRC procedure led to an immediate decrease in number of "bites" of Fritos, and during the last session of that phase, the number of "bites" dropped sharply to almost zero, yielding an average of 10.75 "bites" per session during the second CRC phase.

The grams of Fritos consumed per session paralleled the data on "bites" per session, and the number of "bites" and "sips" of other foods and beverages, respectively, per session remained relatively stable throughout the experiment.

Subject 2

Figure 2 shows that during the first control phase S_2 took an average of 20.00 "bites" of peanut butter cups (the target food) per session. During the first CRC phase the number of "bites" of target food increased slightly and then dropped sharply to an average of 12.50 for that phase. Upon return to the control phase, the number of "bites" of target food increased immediately to approximately its original control level (19.00). Reinstatement of the CRC

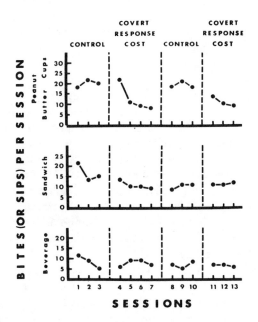

Fig. 27.2. Bites of target food (peanut butter cups) and bites and sips of a nontarget food and beverage, respectively, for S_2 during each lunch session.

procedure led to a reliable drop in the number of ''bites'' of target food, yielding a mean of 11.00 during that phase.

The grams of target food consumed per session paralleled the data on ''bites'' per session, and the number of ''bites'' and ''sips'' of other foods and beverages, respectively, per session remained relatively stable throughout the experiment.

DISCUSSION

The data of the present experiment demonstrate the effectiveness of the CRC procedure in controlling the amount of target food consumed by each S. Furthermore, the data from the control phases indicate that the suppressive effects of the CRC procedure cannot be attributed to such variables as interaction with the therapist or instructions to imagine scenes related to the target food.

One variable which may account for the present findings, however, is the ''expectancy'' of each S concerning the relative therapeutic effectiveness of the CRC procedure. Although Barlow, Agras, Leitenberg, Callahan, and Moore (1972) were able to rule out S expectancies as the critical variable in covert sensitization by experimentally manipulating therapeutic instructions designed to create positive and negative expectancies, because of time limitations it was not feasible to include similar manipulations in the present experimental design. As an alternative, an attempt was made to hold S expectancies constant throughout the experiment by presenting, prior to the experiment proper, instructions indicating that a number of different techniques would be tried and that each ''may or may not'' be helpful in the control of eating. It is realized, of course, that the present instructions may not in fact have created constant expectancies about the effectiveness of each procedure. One might have asked each S at the end of the experiment what her expectancies were, but such *post hoc* questioning was considered of little value since research has shown that Ss tend to change their ''cognitions'' in order to make them consistent with their past behavior (Festinger, 1957). Borrowing from a suggestion made by Hampton (1973), perhaps the subjective effects of the expectancy instructions should have been checked prior to the first lunch session of each new phase. Future research should be oriented toward assessing the relative contribution of S expectancy to the CRC procedure as well as to other covert conditioning techniques.

A somewhat surprising finding was that the introduction, removal, and reinstatement of the CRC procedure led generally to quick, respective decreases, increases, and decreases in the occurrences of target responses of both Ss. According to conditioning principles, one would have expected more gradual changes. One possible explanation of the results is that the in vivo application of the RC scenes was the more important variable in the immediate suppression of the target behavior. If the Ss had not been instructed to use the RC scenes in vivo during the CRC phases, suppression of the target behavior may not have been as rapid. This hypothesis is supported by the fact that during the second control phase S_2, who had been instructed to discontinue use of the in vivo CRC technique, showed an immediate increase in consumption of target food, whereas S_1, who had not been instructed to discontinue use of the in vivo technique, failed to show a similar effect at the beginning of that phase. The relative importance of the in vivo application of RC scenes, as well as other covert scenes, during covert conditioning therapy, needs to be assessed.

A third finding pertains to the apparent *specificity* of the CRC treatment effect, whose evaluation was made possible by the multiple baseline component of the design. The data indicate that while the CRC treatment procedure led to a reduction in consumption of target foods during treatment phases, it had no effect on the concurrent consumption of nontarget foods and beverages. In the treatment of alcoholism and obesity by covert sensitization, Cautela (1967) notes that, ''An important characteristic of the covert sensitization procedure is that its effects are very specific. If one treats for aversion to beer, there will be very little generalization to wine and whiskey [p. 462].'' The present findings imply that Cautela's (1967) statement concerning the specific effects of covert sensitization can be extended to the effects of CRC.

In conclusion, the present data represent the first demonstration of the effectiveness of Cautela's (1974) CRC procedure in the suppression of maladaptive approach behavior (i.e., excessive eating of specific target foods). Future research should be oriented toward substantiating the present findings, as well as assessing the relative efficacy of CRC vs. covert sensitization and other self-control techniques (e.g., those described by Ferster, Nurnberger, & Levitt, 1962; Goldiamond, 1965; Harris & Bruner, 1971; Hall, 1972; Stuart, 1967) in the suppression of maladaptive eating.

REFERENCES

Ashem, B., Poser, E., & Trudall, P. 1970. The use of covert sensitization in the treatment of over-eating. Paper presented at the meeting of the Association for the Advancement of Behavior Therapy, Miami.

Barlow, D. H., Agras, W. S., Leitenberg, L., Callahan, E. J., & Moore, R. C. 1972. The contribution of therapeutic instruction to covert sensitization. *Behaviour Research and Therapy*, **10**, 411-415.

Cautela, J. R. 1967. Covert sensitization. *Psychological Reports*, **20**, 459-468.

Cautela, J. R. 1972. The treatment of over-eating by covert conditioning. *Psychotherapy: Theory, Research and Practice*, **9**, 211-216.

Cautela, J. R. 1974. Covert response cost. Unpublished manuscript, Boston College.

Ferster, C. B., Nurnberger, J. I., & Levitt, E. B. 1962. The control of eating. *Journal of Mathetics*, **1**, 87-109.

Festinger, L. A. 1957. *A theory of cognitive dissonance*. Evanston: Row, Peterson.

Goldiamond, I. 1965. Self-control procedures in personal behavior problems. *Psychological Reports,* **17,** 851-868.

Hall, S. M. 1972. Selfcontrol and therapist control in the behavioral treatment of overweight women. *Behaviour Research and Therapy,* **10,** 59-68.

Hampton, P. T. 1973. Placebo control treatments in behavior ttherapy research. *Behavior Therapy,* **4,** 481-482.

Harris, M. B. & Bruner, C. G. 1971. A comparison of a self-control and a contract procedure for weight control. *Behaviour Research and Therapy,* **9,** 347-354.

Janda, L. H., & Rimm, D. C. 1972. Covert sensitization in the treatment of obesity. *Journal of Abnormal Psychology,* **80,** 37-42.

Kazdin, A. E. 1972. Response cost: The removal of conditioned reinforcers for therapeutic change. *Behavior Therapy,* **3,** 533-546.

Lick, J., & Bootzin, R. 1971. Covert sensitization for the treatment of obesity. Paper presented at the meeting of the Midwestern Psychological Association, Detroit.

Manno, B. 1972. Weight reduction as a function of the timing of reinforcement in a covert aversive conditioning paradigm. *Dissertation Abstracts International,* **32(7-B),** 4221.

Manno, B., & Marston, A. R. 1972. Weight reduction as a function of negative covert reinforcement (sensitization) versus covert positive reinforcement. *Behaviour Research and Therapy,* **10,** 201-207.

Meynen, G. E. 1970. A comparative study of three treatment approaches with the obese: Relaxation, covert sensitization, and modified systematic desensitization. *Dissertation Abstracts International,* **31(5-B),** 2998.

Sachs, L. B., & Ingram, G. L. 1972. Covert sensitization as a treatment for weight control. *Psychological Reports,* **30,** 971-974.

Stuart, R. 1967. Behavioral control of over-eating. *Behaviour Research and Therapy,* **5,** 357-365.

Weiner, H. 1965. Real and imagined cost effects upon human fixed interval responding. *Psychological Reports,* **17,** 659-662.

SECTION VIII
CLINICAL APPLICATIONS
OF COMBINED COVERT
CONDITIONING
TECHNIQUES

Chapter 28
Multifaceted Behavior Therapy of Self-Injurious Behavior*
Joseph R. Cautela and
Mary Grace Baron

Summary — Learning principles were used to overcome the severe self-injurious behavior (eye-poking and lip- and tongue-biting) of a 20-yr-old male, diagnosed as schizophrenic. In individual treatment sessions, relaxation, thought-stopping and desensitization were used to render stimuli antecedent to self-injurious behavior ineffective. Withdrawal of reinforcement and covert sensitization were used directly to diminish self-injurious behavior. Reinforcement (overt and covert) and instruction were employed to teach appropriate behaviors. Three shifts of ward staff were instructed and monitored in the application of reinforcement principles. Self-injury ceased after 3 months. Nine months later the patient was discharged. A 2-yr follow-up indicates no recurrence of the maladaptive behavior and a normal adjustment.

The development of self-injurious behavior has been examined in operant laboratories. Conditions are established so that a stimulus which is ordinarily aversive (e.g. shock, white noise) is made to be reinforcing (Ayllon and Azrin, 1966; Brown, 1965; Hendry, 1969, p. 358; Honig, 1966, p. 418; Sandler and Quagliano, 1964). In such cases, the aversive stimulus is presented only when a reinforcer is also presented, so that the aversive stimulus becomes a discriminative stimulus associated with reinforcement. The presentation of the aversive stimulus then does not result in avoidance behavior but may lead to increase of response frequency. Anyone observing these subjects administering aversive stimuli to themselves would call the behavior "masochistic"

*Reprinted with permission from the *Journal of Behavior Therapy and Experimental Psychiatry*, 1973, *4*, 125–131. © Pergamon Press.

were he not aware of the conditioning history. These studies support the behavioral analysis of cases of self-injurious behavior.

Behavior therapy efforts to deal with self-injurious behavior have usually centered upon a punishment paradigm in which strong aversive shock is made contingent upon the occurrence of self-injurious behavior (Marks, Rachman and Gelder, 1965; Tate and Baroff, 1966). Other studies (Bucher and Lovaas, 1968; Lovaas *et al.*, 1965; Risley, 1968) have demonstrated that the withdrawal of social reinforcement (when self-injurious behavior occurs) combined with the administration of electric shock (when the behavior occurs) more effectively decreases it.

This paper describes the application of behavior therapy techniques to the treatment of a severe case of self-injurious behavior (eye-poking and lip- and tongue-biting). This case was unique because of the combination of the following features:

(1) The patient was hospitalized and diagnosed as "schizophrenic" by previous therapists. "Schizophrenic" was also the diagnostic label used by the staff in the hospital in which the treatment occurred.

(2) The senior author was informed that if the self-injury continued, the patient would be dead in 3 months.

(3) A number of other therapeutic attempts (including insight therapy and a methodologically inappropriate reinforcement therapy) had failed to modify the patient's behavior.

(4) Usually with severe cases of self-injurious behavior aversive electric current is used. Rather a wide gamut of procedures (e.g. covert sensitization, thought-stopping, desensitization, reinforcement sampling) were employed not only to control the self-injury, but also to reinstate appropriate social behaviors.

(5) Treatment techniques were taught to and applied by a number of personnel in the therapeutic environment of the patient.

(6) The notoriety of the case invited close public examination and following of the progress of therapy.

(7) It has been well over 2½ yr since the patient has engaged in inappropriate behavior and he seems well-adjusted.

CASE HISTORY

When our treatment began, this single, 20-yr-old, white, male college student had been engaging in eye-poking for 16 months and lip- and tongue-biting for 6 months. A description of early history and family relations is not included here for reasons of privacy and because this information in no way determined our treatment procedures. Two years before treatment, the patient had withdrawn from school because he was failing his courses and found life at the university meaningless. He had worn contact lenses for a number of years, but claimed he had never become fully adjusted to them and had to remove them 3 or 4 times a day. His eyes had begun to irritate him, so that he began to rub them continuously. The irritation persisted, and after a team of opthalmologists had found no cause for the irritation, the patient announced to the doctors and to his mother that he nevertheless had urges to rub his eyes very hard. During the next few weeks, he would often retire to his room and reappear before his mother with his eyes red and swollen. Eventually, he began jabbing his eyes with his thumb. At this time, the mother sought psychiatric treatment for him.

For the first 3 months during which he exhibited eye-poking, the patient was seen in private therapy and diagnosed as obsessive-compulsive. His self-injurious behavior increased, however, and he was then hospitalized for 1 month for a series of electro-shock treatments. The frequency and severity of poking further increased, and he was transferred to another private hospital where he was placed under constant observation and was seen by a psychiatrist 2 or 3 times a week.

During an 11-month stay at this hospital, the self-injurious behavior increased and his admission diagnosis of "borderline state with psychotic decomposition" became "schizoaffective". Attempts to suppress poking by putting the patient in arm restraints resulted in the new self-injurious behavior of biting the lips and tongue. A wide variety of drugs (Chloralhydrate, Thorazine, Artane, Elavil, Mellaril, Librium, Paraldehyde and Stelzaine) were administered, often in large doses, but self-injurious behavior continued at a high rate.

Financial pressures necessitated transfer of the patient to a state hospital. Even though he was again on constant observation and in weekly private therapy, his first 2 months there were marked by increased biting and poking. In the third month, the patient was transferred to a surgical ward for sleep therapy. After 2 weeks of this, he exhibited some "grogginess" but continued poking, causing further damage to his eyes. The patient's eyes were then stitched shut to prevent further damage. He was kept almost constantly in arm restraints, with a tongue-blade depressor in his mouth securely tied to his head.

At the time of our intervention, the patient had been diagnosed as "schizophrenic" by the psychiatrist in charge of the case. He was poking and/or biting almost daily. He had completely lost the sight of one eye and inflammation of the other eye prevented a definite assessment of its status. He had completely bitten off some lower lip tissue and a considerable portion of the upper lip. Resultant scar-tissue formation had reduced the size of his mouth opening to one-half. He displayed swelling and bleeding of the eyes and face, dripping saliva from the mouth, and nearly continuous shaking or jerking of his body. The hospital staff reported that all dealings with him were highly unpleasant. His increasing self-injury and lack of responsiveness to treatment created a common opinion among the staff that any further therapeutic attempts would be futile.

PLANNING THE TREATMENT PROGRAM

By the time we started treatment, the patient was completely blind. The damage was later shown to be so extensive that even corneal transplants could not restore vision. The main aim of our treatment program was to eliminate the self-injurious behaviors of poking and removing particles of his eyes and biting off lip and tongue tissue. Another goal was to have the patient discharged and able to lead a ''happy'', fruitful life.

In designing treatment we assumed that: 1. Particular stimuli elicited the self-injury; and 2. The consequences of self-injury maintained the behavior. Effective treatment would have to render the controlling stimuli ineffective and decrease the frequency of self-injury by removing all observable maintaining consequences (e.g. social reinforcement).

The senior therapist would meet the patient weekly in his private office away from the hospital grounds. Here he would introduce the self-control techniques (Cautela, 1969), assess treatment progress and adjust the program as needed. The co-therapist would meet the patient in his hospital room twice a day, 3 days per week, to practice the self-control procedures. She would also be available on the ward to direct staff behavior in a manner consistent with reinforcement principles.

The hospital administration and staff agreed to waive their usual treatment procedures and support the implementation of the behavior therapy program. Medical personnel (opthalmologist, ward doctor, nurses) examined the patient periodically to assess his general health and to note any changes due to self-injury. The nursing staff on all three shifts recorded previously identified classes of the patient's behavior, e.g. social interactions, disruptive episodes.

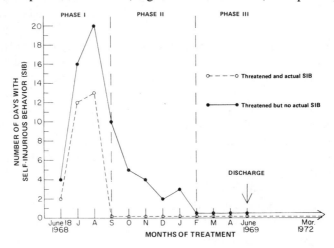

Fig. 28.1. Frequency of threatened and actual self-injurious behavior during treatment and follow-up (2½ yr after termination of treatment).

TREATMENT

The incidence of self-injurious behavior (i.e. the number of days on which such behavior was reported by the staff) shows three relatively distinct phases. During the first 2½ months (Phase I) both threatened and actual self-injurious behavior occurred at a high rate. During the 5 months of Phase II, there was no self-injurious behavior, and threats of self-injury decreased. No self-injury either occurred or was threatened in the final phase (5 months).

PHASE I

During this phase, treatment focused on diminishing self-injurious behavior. The stimulus conditions of self-injury were so varied and pervasive that episodes were reported in the day, at night, in social situation, during inactive periods, and at times when the patient reported feeling tense and restless. The behavior itself, however, was always preceded by an "urge", i.e. a thought or feeling that he must poke (or bite) immediately. The behavior varied little in form or duration, but invariably resulted in bleeding, loud protests of pain from the patient, which would move the staff or other patients to intervene.

Individual Treatment Sessions

Rationale. The patient was told that the authors did not regard him as "schizophrenic" or "psychotic", but rather as someone who was engaging in certain inappropriate behaviors which led to and maintained his removal from society. Also, it was explained to him that he engaged in self-injurious behavior not because he was a "masochist" or enjoyed the pain, but that his self-injurious responses were strong, learned habits that he needed to unlearn. The patient thought the rationale was logical and agreed to try to practice the techniques. He warned, however, that we should not be too optimistic, for "nothing seems to work on me".

    Relaxation and thought-stopping. In order to weaken the association between the antecedents of poking (e.g. having an "urge", being restless), and actual self-injurious behavior, the patient was taught relaxation and instructed to use it whenever he had an "urge" or felt tense. Thought-stopping (Wolpe, 1969) was demonstrated by stopping the thought, "I've got to poke", and the accompanying behavior of lifting his right arm toward his eye. The patient was urged to practice these techniques as often as he could, and particularly whenever he felt tense or nervous.

    Covert sensitization. Covert sensitization (Cautela, 1969) was used to decrease the actual self-injurious behavior. For example, the patient was instructed to imagine a sequence of events leading up to biting his lips. As soon as he reported he could clearly imagine having an ''urge'' to bite, he imagined that he felt sick to his stomach. The covert sensitization trials were alternated with trials in which he imagined a sequence of events leading up to the injurious behavior, but in which he resisted the ''urge'' and felt good.

Strengthening behaviors incompatible with self-injurious behavior. Since feeling calm and relaxed was a desirable behavior, *covert reinforcement* (Cautela, 1970) was used to increase its probability. Reinforcers listed by the patient on the Reinforcement Survey Schedule (Cautela and Kastenbaum, 1967) included items inaccessible to him because he was confined to a hospital (e.g. dating) or because of his physical condition (e.g. eating fried chicken). *Reinforcement sampling,* a technique recommended by Ayllon and Azrin (1969, pp. 75–122) to increase familiarity with potential reinforcers, was also done in imagination. *Covert reinforcement sampling* was continued throughout all treatment phases.

Contracting (Homme, 1970). [*This*] was used to insure that the patient practiced his assigned homework, e.g. if he reported practicing each technique 10 times, a session with the cotherapist could be spent discussing only pleasant scenes or in conversation. Also a contract was drawn up stating that when a 2-month period with no self-injurious behavior had occurred, plans for plastic surgery of the lips would be initiated.

While discussing the fear-producing situations in his life, the patient reported that because of his appearance and his inability to see, he was very much afraid to meet new people. *Systematic desensitization* was employed to combat this fear. After 2 weeks, when he reported he could imagine the top item in the hierarchy and not feel anxious and he said he was comfortable in social situations, desensitization was discontinued.

Participation by the Ward Staff

Since it was important to decrease the probability of social reinforcement for the self-injurious behavior, the co-therapist instructed the ward staff in: (1) the experimental analysis of the patient's behavior, which soon led them to view the self-injurious behavior as an operant, (2) the self-control techniques being taught to the patient in the individual sessions which demonstrated that the same rationale was the basis for individual treatment and ward programs, and (3) appropriate ways of responding to self-injurious and disruptive behavior.

For example, a particulary disruptive behavior was the patient's yelling in loud, excited tones for ''help to keep from biting''. Usually in this situation, all staff and even some patients would drop anything they were doing and go to his assistance. They were now instructed to quietly approach the patient and escort him back to his room, reminding him to use his self-control techniques and contracting to come and spend time with him when he was in control. Figure 2 shows the number of loud requests for staff aid before and during the proposed treatment. With the removal of some of the social reinforcement, the number of demands temporarily increased (the "extinction effect" (Reynolds, 1968, p. 28)). On the fourth day of extinction, the behavior did not occur. However, reinforcement by one staff member on the fifth day temporarily increased the behavior. After 7 more days of extinction the behavior decreased to zero and never reappeared.

Treatment Effects

At the end of Phase I, threatened self-injurious behavior continued at a high rate (see Fig. 2) and the patient continued to report constant "urges" to poke or bite. However, the actual behavior ceased, and the amount of shaking, jerking, fidgeting behavior was greatly reduced. The staff reported that the patient seemed calm in social interactions, but he was still very demanding, disruptive and "spoiled".

In order to combat the general sluggish behavior of the patient and to increase the probability of mobility and alertness, and, in general, to facilitate learning, the patient's Thorazine was reduced from 300 to 50 mg twice daily.

PHASE II

This 5-month phase emphasized more practice in self-control techniques. On September 1 the physician reported no new lacerations of the patient's tongue since the last weekly exam. However, many convulsive-like behaviors that

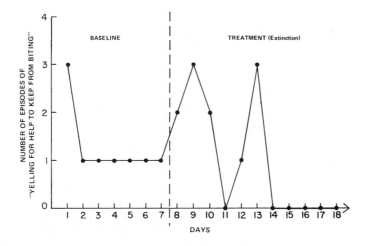

Fig. 28.2 Baseline and extinction frequencies of loud requests for staff aid.

characteristically preceded and accompanied self-injurious behavior endured. Such behaviors were sufficiently similar to self-injurious behavior to be labelled by the staff as self-injury and are charted in Fig. 1 as "threatened but not actual self-injurious behavior". The continuance of these behaviors, though not self-injurious, increased the ward staff's aversion to the patient, and thus increased the danger of reconditioning of the self-injurious behavior. Therefore, we planned the elimination of these disruptive behaviors by thought-stopping and covert sensitization. Incompatible behaviors (e.g. sitting calmly, playing the guitar) would be reinforced by therapists and staff.

Individual Treatment Sessions

Thought-stopping and covert sensitization were applied to the antecedent behaviors of "feeling miserable" and having an "urge" to bite or poke. Whenever the patient said he had done his homework and the staff reported a decreased number of "urges", the rest of a session was spent in pleasurable practice — relaxation and covert reinforcement.

These sessions also focused on analysis of ward problems arising from the patient's demanding behavior or from the behavior of some of the staff. *Behavioral rehearsals* were done to teach the patient how to handle these social problems, e.g. asking for something diplomatically. *Reinforcement sampling* was continued to strengthen behaviors incompatible with self-injury. For example, recorded books and a record player were loaned from the local library for the blind; an instructor of the techniques of daily-living for the newly blinded was recruited; and the patient's own clothes and a guitar were brought from his home.

Participation of the Ward Staff

The staff were quite consistent in removing all reinforcement for his convulsive-like behaviors, and in engaging him in conversation or somehow paying attention to him whenever his behavior was appropriate. He was assigned a daily ward job and was highly reinforced by the staff for carrying it out.

Treatment Effects

Throughout Phase II, the physicians reported no new injury to eyes or mouth. The number of convulsive-like episodes decreased, and the patient reported only occasional "urges" to "just touch my eye or tongue , but not to poke or bite". The staff reported that the patient was much easier to deal with, more friendly, and more interesting.

PHASE III

No destructive or disruptive behaviors were reported by the patient, the ward staff, or the physicians from the ninth month of treatment until discharge. Treatment concentrated on: (a) eliminating any maladaptive thoughts reported by the patient, (b) sampling of reinforcers outside the hospital, and (c) arranging corrective plastic surgery.

Individual Treatment Sessions

The patient often wondered whether he might sometime poke again even though he no longer had urges to do so. A *thought-stopping* session dealing with these thoughts was tape-recorded and the patient played the tape whenever he had the thoughts. *Reinforcement sampling* included renewing old acquaintances, exploring career choices and eating in restaurants. All medications were eliminated and never again reintroduced. In keeping with the original *contract* (i.e. plastic surgery of the lips after 2 months without self-injurious behavior), plans were drawn up for surgery during the eleventh month (even though the psychiatric staff prognosticated that as soon as plastic repair was completed the patient would probably again mutilate his lips). The operation was performed under local anesthesia. The patient recuperated on the surgical ward and was enthused at the prospect of increased eating, talking, and singing abilities, and at his improved appearance.

Participation by Ward Staff

The staff gave minimal reinforcement to any verbalizations about "disturbing" thoughts and continued to reinforce with attention and approval any appropriate behaviors of the patient, e.g. good grooming, friendly conversation.

Treatment Effects

During this phase no self-injurious behavior was exhibited or even threatened. Disturbing thoughts were eliminated and the patient's appearance and social manner improved markedly. He remarked more frequently that he would like to be out of the hospital for good.

Throughout treatment, he was given the hope that a corneal transplant might restore vision to his one eye. However, the consulting ophthalmologists pronounced his eye damage as irreversible.

After working (without pay) as a receptionist in the medical building for 1 month, he was discharged in June, 1969 (1 yr after treatment began), with instructions to contact us if any problem behaviors developed. Three months after discharge, he began a 16-week rehabilitation program for adjustment to blindness. During his stay at the rehabilitation center, the staff reported that he was well-adjusted. Upon completion of the program, he was interviewed and accepted by a major university to continue his undergraduate studies. Recently he married. The authors attended the wedding, and the patient, his wife, and his mother all reported that he was enthusiastic about the future and very happy.

DISCUSSION

This case illustrates how, in clinical practice, a wide variety of procedures can, and often must, be employed. Of course, this makes it impossible to assess the overall effects of any one procedure.

A clear lesson that emerges from this case is the extent to which the treatment of a hospitalized patient depends upon the co-operation of ward personnel. Another lesson is that labelling such cases as "hopeless" and "schizophrenic" should not deter therapists from applying behavior modification procedures.

An unusual feature of this treatment was that electrical aversion therapy was not used. When the therapist can arrange it, covert sensitization is probably preferable since it entails features of self-control. A drawback, however, is that covert sensitization may require more time and greater numbers of trials. In some cases, it may be necessary immediately to use electrical aversion to prevent permanent injury or death.

Though we received a great deal of co-operation throughout the entire hospital, the effects of the program would have been maximized if it had been conducted in a behavior modification ward. However, the favourable outcome demonstrates the practicality of behavior modification even within a non-behaviorally oriented institution.

REFERENCES

Ayllon T. and Azrin N. H. (1966) Punishment as a discriminative conditioned reinforcer with humans, *J. exp. Analysis Behav.* **9**, 411–49.

Ayllon T. and Azrin N. (1969) *The Token Economy*, Appleton-Century-Crofts, New York.

Brown J. S. (1965) Theoretical note: A behavioral analysis of masochism, *J. exper. Res. Person.* **1**, 65–70.

Bucher B. and Lovaas O. I. (1968) Use of aversive stimulation in behavior modification, *Miami Synposium on the Prediction of Behavior, 1967: Aversive Stimulation* (Edited by Jones M. R.), pp. 77–145, University of Miami Press, Coral Gables, Florida.

Cautela J. R. (1969) Behavior therapy and self-control: Techniques and implications, *Behavior Therapy, Appraisal and Status* (Edited by Franks C.), pp. 323–340, McGraw-Hill, New York.

Cautela J. R. (1970) Covert reinforcement, *Behav. Therapy,* **1,** 33–50.

Cautela J. R. (1971) Covert conditioning, *The Psychology of Private Events* (Edited by Jacobs A. and Sachs L. B.), Academic Press, New York.

Cautela J. R. and Kastenbaum R. (1967) A Reinforcement Survey Schedule for use in therapy, training and research, *Psychol. Rep.* **20,** 1115–1130.

Hendry D. (1969) *Conditioned Reinforcement,* Dorsey Press, Homewood, Illinois.

Homme L. (1970) *How to Use Contingency Contracting in the Classroom,* Research Press, Champaign, Illinois.

Honig W. (1966) *Operant Behavior, Appleton-Century-Crofts, New York.*

Lovaas O. L., Freitag G., Gold V. J. and Kassorla I. C. (1965) Experimental studies in childhood schizophrenia: Analysis of self-destructive behavior, *J. exp. Child Psychol.* **2,** 67–84.

Marks I. M., Rachman S. and Gelder M. G. (1965) Methods for assessment of aversion treatment in fetishism with masochism, *Behav. Res. & Therapy* **3,** 253–258.

Reynolds G. (1968) *A Primer of Operant Conditioning,* Scott-Foresman, Atlanta.

Risley T. R. (1968) The effect and side-effect of punishing the autistic behaviors of a deviant child, *J. appl. Behav. Anal.* **1,** 21–34.

Sandler J. And Quagliano J. (1964) *Punishment in a signal avoidance situation.* Paper read at the Southeastern Psychological Association Meeting, Gatlinburg, Tennessee.

Tate B. G. and Baroff G. S. (1966) Aversive control of self-injurious behaviour in a psychotic boy, *Behav. Res. & Therapy,* **4** 281–287.

Wolpe J. (1969) *The Practice of Behavior Therapy,* Pergamon Press, New York.

Chapter 29

Treatment of Obsessive-Compulsive Behavior by Covert Sensitization and Covert Reinforcement: A Case Report*†

Patricia A. Wisocki

Summary — In a 27-year-old female, a multiplicity of obsessive-compulsive behaviors were eliminated in eight 2-hr sessions by covert sensitization and covert reinforcement. Covert sensitization was used to condition an aversive response to the performance of the obsessive-compulsive behaviors; covert reinforcement to reinforce other responses in place of these behaviors.

INTRODUCTION

Behavior therapy treatment of obsessive-compulsive behavior has employed two strategies:

1. Eliminating the anxiety antecedents of the behavior (the conditioned autonomic drive) primarily through the use of systematic desensitization (Bevan, 1960; Wolpe, 1964, 1969: Walton, 1960; Walton and Mather, 1964 and Haslam, 1965).

*Reprinted with permission from the *Journal of Behavior Therapy and Experimental Psychiatry*, 1970, *1*, 233–239. © Pergamon Press.

†The author gratefully acknowledges the critical assistance and encouragement of Dr. Joseph R. Cautela in the preparation of this manuscript.

2. Eliminating the habit that constitutes the obsessive-compulsive behavior by using techniques of thought-stopping (Taylor, 1963; Cautela, 1969), inhibition by electrical stimulation (Wolpe, 1954; McGuire and Vallance, 1964) and covert sensitization (Cautela, 1966, 1967; Stuart, 1967; Mullen, 1968; Anant, 1967; Ashem and Donner, 1968; Kolvin, 1967; Barlow, Leitenberg and Agras, 1968; Viernstein, 1968; Cautela and Wisocki, 1969). These techniques have been effective in reducing various forms of obsessive thoughts and compulsive behaviors.

This paper presents a case example of a treatment that carries out both aims but uses covert sensitization to condition an aversive (avoidance) response to the performance of the obsessive-compulsive behavior, and covert reinforcement (Cautela, 1970) to reinforce responses antagonistic to obsessive-compulsive behavior. Covert sensitization is the simultaneous presentation in imagination of both the response to be extinguished and the stimulus to an aversive response.

A strong avoidance response is likely to inhibit the undesirable response and result in a measure of conditioned inhibition of that response (Wolpe, 1969, p. 201). Covert reinforcement is an operant technique in which both the response to be reinforced and the reinforcer of that response are presented in imagination. The theoretical and empirical bases of this technique have been provided by Cautela (1970).

This case was one of three of obsessive-compulsive behavior successfully treated in this way during the past year. Although it required twice as many sessions as the other two, it is presented because it was particularly challenging. The patient had been hospitalized twice and was considered 'schizophrenic' by the hospital psychiatrist; earlier attempts to treat the obsessive-compulsive behavior by relaxation and desensitization had been unsuccessful and she did not altogether desire the treatment to succeed, because success would increase responsibility and effort and decrease the time she could spend with her husband.

Four other behavior therapy procedures — progressive relaxation, systematic desensitization, assertive training, and thought stopping — were employed in treating other problems of this patient. No further mention will be made of them, since they were not applied to the obsessive-compulsive behavior directly.

CASE REPORT

The patient was an attractive 27-year-old female. She lived with her husband and two small children in a large home in a Southern state. In November 1967 she visited a psychiatrist because of feelings of anxiety, depression, confused thinking, and concern over her meticulous and slow performance of household duties. She was distressed at the fact that her husband had proposed the sixth move of their household in the 7 years of their marriage. She felt unable to face the problems of packing, moving, and cleaning once again. The psychiatrist diagnosed her as a "severe obsessive-compulsive individual with marked rituals who might very well border on a schizophrenic reaction".

In December she was hospitalized for 13 days and put on 5 mg of Navane and 2 mg of Cogentin once or twice daily. Fourteen months later, she was admitted to another hospital because her behavior had progressively worsened. She had been neglecting her housework and personal appearance altogether. Her husband reported a worsening in their sexual relations as well. She was making suicidal threats and frequently her body would 'shake all over'; she would wring her hands, pace the floor, bite her nails. She spent hours on such tasks as folding clothes, making beds, and putting groceries away. If anyone upset her routine or 'messed up' the house by using the dishes to eat, unfolding clothes to wear, etc., she became extremely angry and upset. Two days before her second hospital admission, she began smoking, pulling her hair and hitting her head. In the hospital she was again diagnosed as "obsessive-compulsive personality", although the psychiatrist thought she was "definitely schizophrenic".

A social worker trained in behavior modification principles and procedures taught the patient relaxation and began a program of desensitization to dirt and disorder in the house and to certain household tasks. This produced no noticeable change in the compulsive behavior, but the patient did notice a decrease in anxiety regarding how she felt about dust, order and her home. On 9 April 1969, after approximately eight sessions, therapy was discontinued because the patient's husband had decided to move to Massachusetts and she was referred to the author.

TREATMENT

Before therapy was begun a behavioral analysis was done (after Cautela, 1968). Then the relaxation procedure was revised and she was taught the thought-stopping technique. She was instructed to shout, "Stop", covertly to herself whenever disturbing thoughts entered her mind during the week. She was also told to practice relaxation twice a day.

It was agreed that therapy would be conducted for two consecutive hours each week since the patient would be coming from a distance of 150 miles and because of her husband's insistence that she quickly assume her "responsibilities as a wife and mother".

The patient's obsessive-compulsive behavior was exhibited exclusively in her housework activity. The primary problem area, the habit of folding clothes several times until they were completely wrinkle-free, consumed most of the patient's time and caused the greatest amount of anxiety. The therapist therefore focused on it first.

Ordinarily the patient spent from 5 to 10 min folding each item of clothing she had washed, depending on how flat and simple it was. If her anxiety reached a level where she could not face the chore, she left the clothes in the drier until she felt calmer. (She had managed to reduce time spent in folding by hanging in the closets as many clothes as possible, e.g. slips and undershirts.) After folding an item, the patient would spend another 5 or 10 min putting it away in a drawer. Her response sequence was as follows: (a) ends of clothes brought together: (b) wrinkles smoothed out: (c) item folded carefully once; (d) item unfolded and smoothed over again; (e) folded neatly a second time (this process might be carried out several more times until she was satisfied as to the lack of wrinkles); (f) carried to a dresser drawer across the room (each item carried individually); (g) drawer opened and item carefully placed on appropriate pile of clothing. If it became wrinkled at this point, it was refolded. (It was also sometimes necessary to refold the entire pile of clothes.) (h) drawer closed; (i) drawer opened to check neatness; (j) drawer closed; (k) patient turns attention to next item.

COVERT SENSITIZATION

In applying the covert sensitization procedure the therapist instructed the patient to relax and imagine herself in various scenes in which she was (a) thinking of performing the compulsive action, (b) about to engage in the compulsive action; (c) engaging in the compulsive action. At each stage, either in intention or in actual performance, the patient was told to imagine herself vomiting profusely over every aspect of the situation described by the therapist.

A typical sequence was:

You're in the laundry room. There is a pile of clothing in front of you. You take one thing . . . it's a towel . . . and you fold it once and put it aside. You look over at it and think that it's not quite wrinkle-free and you decide to refold it. As soon as you have that thought, you get a queasy feeling in the pit of your stomach. Vomit comes up into your mouth. It tastes bitter and you swallow it back down. Your throat burns. But you take the towel and start to refold it anyway. Just as you do that, your stomach churns and vomit comes out of your mouth — all over the clean clothes, your hands, the table, over everything. You keep vomiting and vomiting. Your eyes are watering; your nose has mucus coming out of it. You see vomit all over everything. You think that you should never have tried to fold that towel a second time — a few slight wrinkles make no difference — and you run from the room. Immediately you feel better. You go and clean yourself up and smell fresh and feel wonderful.

The patient was told to imagine this scene while the therapist described it to her and then to imagine it by herself, trying to achieve as much clarity and vividness of imagery as possible. The therapist and patient alternated descriptions of the scene for 20 more trials. The scene was then assigned for 'homework' practice by the patient ten times twice a day.

Such a covert sensitization scene may be divided into each of its three parts (intention, precipitation and action) composing shorter scenes to which the aversive stimulus may be applied — making a greater number of trials. This modification is only employed after the patient is readily able to imagine the complete covert sensitization scene vividly. For example, after a few weeks of practice, the patient was instructed to imagine herself in the laundry room *thinking about* folding a piece of clothing for the second time. When this image was clear, she signalled by raising her finger and the therapist responded with the word "vomit" (or "worms", "maggots", "crawling insects" — items for which she had previously indicated extreme displeasure) and the patient immediately imagined herself vomiting on (or seeing worms, etc., crawling over) her clothes. Similar scenes in which she quickly imagined herself *just about to perform* the obsessive-compulsive behavior and or was *performing them* were described and the stimulus word then presented.

Together with scenes of folding clothes, other scenes were constructed in which the patient imagined vomiting on herself as she returned to rearrange the clothes placed in the dresser drawers. These were also presented and practiced for 20 alternating trials.

Half of each therapy session (1 hr) was spent in applying the covert sensitization technique to the obsessive-compulsive behavior; the other half was spent in the application of the covert reinforcement procedure.

COVERT REINFORCEMENT

A crucial assumption in the covert reinforcement procedure is that a stimulus presented in imagination can have reinforcing properties similar to a stimulus presented externally (e.g. food, money, praise). That is, a stimulus presented in imagination can have the same functional relation to covert or overt behavior as a stimulus presented externally. Cautela (1970) reports that he has successfully treated phobias, obsessions, homosexuality, obesity problems and problems involving maladaptive thoughts with the covert reinforcement technique.

Before applying covert reinforcement it is first necessary to select appropriate stimuli that could function as reinforcers. Ordinarily this is done from the patient's responses to the Reinforcement Survey Schedule (Cautela and Kastenbaum, 1967). Any item to which the patient has indicated intense pleasure is tested for visual clarity, which Cautela (1970) suggests is indicative of its reinforcing quality. Another criterion for inclusion of items in the reinforcement repertoire is the ability of the patient to obtain the image within five seconds of its presentation.

In this case the patient indicated only five items (of a possible 139) on the Reinforcement Survey Schedule with a high reinforcing value. From direct questioning four more items were added to the list of reinforcers. The final list in rank order was: practicing ballet, sipping sweet tea, eating Italian food, golfing, walking in a forest, completing a difficult job, being praised, having people seek her out for company, happy people. A variety of reinforcers was especially important for this patient in order to avoid the problem of satiation (Ayllon and Azrin, 1968).

In applying the covert reinforcement procedure the therapist instructed the patient to imagine herself in various scenes involving two types of behavior: (1) refraining from repeating the obsessive-compulsive behavior; (2) making both overt and covert responses antagonistic to the obsessive-compulsive behavior. When an appropriate response was imagined, the patient signalled and the therapist immediately used the word ''reinforcement'' which was the cue for the patient to imagine one of the (pre-determined) reinforcing items. Thus, imagining the appropriate behavior was paired with a reinforcing stimulus. The imagined behaviors were reinforced in the following sequence:

1. Folding clothes only once.
2. Folding clothes quickly, leaving them slightly wrinkled.
3. Stacking clothes up quickly and putting them all in a drawer together, rather than one item at a time.
4. Closing the dresser drawer without going back to check the neatness of the clothes.

Examples of both types of this application are these:

A. ''Relax and imagine that you are in the living room, feeling content.'' (The word ''Reinforcement'' is spoken by the therapist at this point and the patient imagines, for instance, that she is sipping sweet tea.)
''You think to yourself 'I have a few minutes; I guess I'll go downstairs and fold some clothes' ('Reinforcement').
You walk casually toward the laundry room and stop to look at the kids playing outdoors ('Reinforcement').
You saunter into the laundry room and look at the clothes piled up, thinking to yourself 'This will only take a few minutes' ('Reinforcement').''

B. ''Relax and imagine that you you are in the laundry room, standing in front of the day's laundry. You think to yourself that you'll really have to hurry folding these clothes so that you can go shopping with a friend ('Reinforcement'). You impatiently shove the clothes to one side ('Reinforcement'). You fold your daughter's pajamas and quickly put them aside ('Reinforcement'). You take the next item, fold it quickly and it's a little wrinkled, but you put it on top of the other things ('Reinforcement').''

Each scene is practiced 20 times in alternating sequence. The therapist describes it once and then the patient imagines it by herself once, etc. Each scene practised is also assigned for 'homework'.

The second type of covert reinforcement application (i.e. making antagonistic obsessive-compulsive behavior responses) may be divided into increasing overt and covert responses. An example of an overt response for this case was throwing her son's unmatched sock into the drawer and shutting it quickly. This scene was imagined several times and reinforced with an image of the patient eating an Italian sandwich or practising ballet.

Examples of covert responses which were reinforced with scenes of walking in a forest or practising golf are these:

"Imagine this thought: 'I don't care if it's wrinkled; it doesn't matter' ('Reinforcement'). Imagine this thought: 'Getting disturbed over folding clothes is a ridiculous thing' ('Reinforcement')."

Both types of scenes were practised several times and assigned for homework as well. In order to provide the therapist with an efficient means of assigning scenes for practice outside the office and as a helpful reminder to the patient, a homework assignment form has been developed (Wisocki, 1969).

DISCUSSION

The outcome of this case appears impressive in view of the fact that the patient had been hospitalized twice for her obsessive-compulsive behaviors, had been labeled a "schizophrenic", was incapable of functioning adequately as a wife and mother before therapy, exhibited a large complexity of behavioral problems — and "as relieved of her obsessive-compulsive behaviors in eight 2-hr sessions.

Since a variety of procedures were employed for the modification of the various maladaptive behaviors exhibited by this patient, and since expectancy on the part of the patient may possibly have had a role in the outcome, it cannot be proved that the decline of the obsessive-compulsive behaviors was entirely due to covert reinforcement and covert sensitization. There is presumptive evidence, however, in favor of this. We used relaxation, assertive training, thought-stopping and desensitization only minimally and for other purposes. Previous use of relaxation and desensitization at another center to diminish anxiety connected with the obsessive-compulsive behavior had not reduced the obsessive-compulsive behavior. Covert sensitization and covert reinforcement were alone directly applied to the obsessive-compulsive behaviors and in correlation with the procedures there was reduction in the obsessive-compulsive behavior. It decreased rapidly and steadily (except for 1 week in which her folding behavior worsened as a result of familial problems) until the termination of therapy. The obsessive-compulsive behaviors of other patients treated by the same methods followed a similar steady pattern of decrease.

It is quite possible that either one of the two procedures used alone could have modified the obsessive-compulsive behaviors exhibited by this patient, but it appeared that each of them exerted controlling effects. According to Cautela (personal communication) covert sensitization or covert reinforcement used singly in the treatment of obsessive-compulsive behaviors requires a greater number of treatment sessions than when the two techniques are jointly used. The issue can only be resolved by experimentation.

RESULTS

This patient was seen in therapy for a total of eight 2 hr sessions. One session was devoted to a behavioral analysis, relaxation training and instruction in the application of covert sensitization and covert reinforcement to her obsessive-compulsive behaviors.

Within those 6 weeks after the first application of these two procedures to her folding behavior, the patient reported a general decrease in all of her obsessive-compulsive behaviors. Bed-making decreased from 30 min to 10 min; rinsing dishes from 60 min to 20 min. After the second week she reported an increase in her folding behavior which she attributed to excessive worry about moving into a new house which her husband had purchased, the possibility of interference from her father, her ability to accept responsibility, and what people were thinking about her as a former mental patient. She had also had arguments with her mother-in-law about proper care of her children. None of these problems had been treated up to this point. However, during this generally bad week, she experienced enjoyable sexual relations with her husband for the first time in more than 2 years. (The previous week covert reinforcement had been applied to this behavior.)

After that single decline in behavioral progress, the patient's obsessive-compulsive behaviors steadily decreased. She began cleaning the new house for their move into it and eventually became cheerful about it. By the sixth treatment session her folding was done quickly, some clothes were left slightly wrinkled, clothes were piled up and put into drawers in one trip, bed-making was down to 5 min, and rinsing dishes required only a brief time. She enjoyed having people in for dinner and making snacks for her husband and children without worrying about getting the dishes dirty or leaving them unwashed for a few hours. In an interview with the therapist, her husband reported satisfaction with her performance as a housewife and mother.

Two weeks later the patient was seen again and covert reinforcement was employed for the first time with her behavior of vacuuming cans and washing items to be refrigerated. Since thoughts about moving began to bother her again, trials of thought stopping were reinstated. Identical treatment was given in the next session, together with a discussion of her relationship with her husband. Unfortunately at this time, in spite of the therapist's insistence on the need for overlearning (Pavlov, 1928, p. 57; Cautela, 1968) and the necessity of placing the new behavior patterns under the control of adequate reinforcers, the patient's husband decided against continuing therapy, since the obsessive-compulsive behaviors had been eliminated. A self-control program was then outlined by the therapist for use by the patient if ever the need arose.

Three months after the termination of theray the patient indicated that she was experiencing no problems with the previous maladaptive behaviors. Although she reported that she was still a "neat" housekeeper, her housework was performed rapidly and without anxiety.

A 12-month follow-up indicated that the obsessive-compulsive behavior had not returned. Both the patient and her husband expressed a great deal of satisfaction with her current performance. She feels that she can finally exert control over her environment and this results in a feeling of happiness.

REFERENCES

Anant S. S. (1967) A note on the treatment of alcoholics by a verbal aversion technique, *Canad. Psychol.* **1**, 19–22.

Ashem B. and Donner L. (1968) Covert sensitization with alcoholics: A controlled replication, *Behav. Res. & Therapy* **6**, 7–12.

Ayllon T. and Azrin N. (1968) *The Token Economy*. Appleton-Century-Crofts, New York.

Barlow D., Leitenberg H. and Agras W. S. (1968) Preliminary report of the experimental control of sexual deviation by manipulation of the US in covert sensitization. Paper presented at the Eastern Psychological Association Convention, Washington, D.C.

Bevan J. R. (1960) Learning theory applied to the treatment of a patient with obsessional ruminations, in *Behavior Therapy and the Neuroses* (Edited by H. J. Eysenck), pp. 165–167. Pergamon Press, New York.

Cautela J. R. (1966) Treatment of compulsive behavior by covert sensitization, *Psychol. Rec.* **16**, 33–41.

Cautela J. R. (1967) Covert sensitization, *Psychol. Rec.* **20**, 459–468.

Cautela J. R. (1968) Behavior therapy and the need for behavioral assessment, *Psychotherapy: Theory. Res. & Prac.* **5**, 175–179.

Cautela J. R. (1969) Behavior therapy and self-control: Techniques and implications, in *Behavior Therapy: Appraisal and Status* (Edited by C. Franks), McGraw-Hill, New York.

Cautela J. R. (1970) Covert reinforcement. *Behav. Therapy,* **1**, 33–50.

Cautela J. R. and Kastenbaum R. (1967) A reinforcement Survey Schedule for use in therapy, training and research. *Psychol. Rep* **20**, 1115–1130.

Cautela J. R., Steffen J. and Wish P. A. (1969) Covert reinforcement: An experimental test. Unpublished study, Boston College.

Cautela J. R. and Wisocki P. A. (1969) The use of male and female therapists in the treatment of homosexual behavior, in *Advances in Behavior Therapy, 1968.* (Edited by C. Franks and R. Rubin) Academic Press, New York.

Cooper J., Gelder M. and Marks I. (1965) Results of behavior therapy in 77 psychiatric patients, *Brit. med. J.* **1**, 1222–1225.

Cowden R. C. and Ford L. I. (1962) Systematic desensitization with phobic schizophrenics, *Am. J. Psychiat.* **119**, 241–245.

Haslam M. T. (1965) The treatment of an obsessional patient by reciprocal inhibition, *Behav. Res. & Therapy* **2**,, 213–216.

Jacobson E. (1938) *Progressive Relaxation*. University of Chicago Press, Chicago.

Kolvin I. (1967) Aversive imagery treatment in adolescents, *Behav. Res. & Therapy* **5**, 245–249.

McGuire R. and Vallance M. (1964) Aversion therapy by electric shock: A simple technique, *Brit. Med. J.* **1**, 151–153.

Meyer V. and Crisp A. (1966) Some problems in behavior therapy, *Brit. J. Psychiat.* **112**, 367–381.

Mullen F. G. (1968) The effect of covert sensitization on smoking behavior. Unpublished study, Queens College, Charlotte, North Carolina.

Pavlov I. P. (1928) *Lectures on Conditioned Reflexes*. International Publications, New York.

Rubin R. D. (1967) Treatment of obsessions by conditioned inhibition, *Conditional Reflex* **2**, 167–168.

Salter A. (1949) *Conditioned Reflex*. Farrar, Strauss, New York.

Stuart R. (1967) Behavioral control of overeating, *Behav. Res. & Therapy* **5**, 357–365.

Taylor J. G. (1963) A behavioral interpretation of obsessive-compulsive neurosis, *Behav. Res. & Therapy* **1**, 237–244.

Viernstein L. (1968) Evaluation of the therapeutic technique of covert sensitization. Unpublished study, Queens College, Charlotte, North Carolina.

Walton D. (1960) The relevance of learning theory to the treatment of an obsessive-copulsive state, in *Behavior Therapy and the Neuroses* (Edited by H. J. Eysenck) ergamon Press, New York.

Walton D. and Mather M. (1964) The application of learning principles to the treatment of obsessive-compulsive states in the acute and chronic phases of illness, in *Experiments in Behavior Therapy* (Edited by H. J. Eysenck) Macmillan, New York.

Wisocki P. A. (1969) Homework Assignment Form, unpublished data, Boston College, Chestnut Hill, Mass.

Wolpe J. (1954) Reciprocal inhibition as a main basis of psychotherapeutic effects. *Am. med. assoc. arch. Neurol. & Psychiat.* **72**, 205–226.

Wolpe J. (1958) *Psychotherapy by Reciprocal Inhibition*, Stanford University Press, Stanford.

Wolpe J. (1964) Behavior therapy in complex neurotic states, *Brit. J. Psychiat.* **110**, 28–34.

Wolpe J. (1969) *The Practice of Behavior Therapy*. Pergamon Press, New York.

Chapter 30

Case Conference: A Transvestite Fantasy Treated by Thought-Stopping, Covert Sensitization and Aversive Shock*†

Louis Gershman

Summary — The subject of this case conference is a 22-year-old college senior with a transvestite fantasy whose origin dated back to preschool days. It was successfslly treated in six sessions using the behavioral techniques of thought-stopping, covert sensitization and aversive shock. Questions concerning goals, procedures, timing of approaches, and practical issues are discussed.

Mr. M., 22, is a college senior who complained of a transvestite fantasy that dominated his sex life. This had been treated unsuccessfully at a Psychological Services Center before he was referred to me for behavior therapy. Since the case involves only six sessions, I shall describe what took place at each of these.

*Reprinted with permission from the *Journal of Behavior Therapy and Experimental Psychiatry*, 1970, *1*, 153–161. © Pergamon Press.

†This case was presented to a seminar conducted by Dr. Joseph Wolpe at the Eastern Pennsylvania Psychiatric Institute. Participants in the discussion were: Gregory Woodham, M.D., Joseph Wolpe, M.D., Alan J. Goldstein, Ph.D., and John Bambeck, Ph.D.

FIRST SESSION

Early recollections date back to a preschool memory of fighting with his sister, while taking a bath with her, about who should wear a plastic raincoat in the tub. In kindergarten he remembers being especially attracted to a little girl friend who wore a plastic raincoat. In elementary school he loved to wear a raincoat, especially the plastic kind, but because he was afraid his friends might call him a sissy, he often desisted. By the time he entered junior high school, M.'s affinity for raincoats had extended to girls' boots. In the eighth grade, he bought a pair of girls' boots and walked outdoors in the deep snow, which hid the boots. To the question, ''How did you feel when you put on these boots?'' he answered: ''Nothing special, I just liked the idea of wearing the raincoat and the boots''.

One day, at age 14, while rummaging in the basement, he discovered a woman's dress. He slipped it on and inspected himself in a large mirror. After disrobing, he masturbated. The sexual arousal during the early years of his problem was elicted by wearing women's garments. For example, he would put on boots or a raincoat and then proceed to masturbate. For the last 5 years, however, imagining himself in any kind of women's apparel has been a sufficiently exciting stimulus to be followed by masturbation. He enjoyed the act for itself, without associating with it any other thought, feeling, or imagery.

M. made several trips to the basement in his early high school years for the purpose of dressing in women's clothes. One day, after draping himself in an old dress, raincoat and boots, he heard his sister's footsteps on the cellar stairs. He quickly hid, terribly frightened. After she left, he masturbated and removed the clothes. During the next year he had several experiences involving wearing a maid's uniform and his mother's underwear, boots, raincoat and scarf. He would venture outdoors only in the dark, not willing to risk recognition.

Starting with his sophomore year in high school, he dated girls from one to three times weekly. There was no petting, but after each date, he masturbated. As a junior in high school, he stopped dressing in girls' clothing. The fantasy of imagining himself in girls' attire was sufficient to elicit masturbation. A few years later in college, he participated heavily in sports, and masturbation decreased to approximately twice weekly.

The previous summer he had met a girl, Jessica, at a seashore resort whom he liked very much and with whom he had his first sexual intercourse. This had evoked in him depressed feelings about his sexual potentiality. The intercourse was disappointing: he described it as ''Scary — it was just like masturbating''. Before and during the sex act, he could not get rid of the image of himself in girl's clothing. ''It's as if my girl isn't there. The fantasy takes over and sticks with me''. This generated the thought that he was perverted. Subsequent sex experiences with Jessica always had the same sequel.

Second Session

I probed the family relationships. M.'s father was a strict military career man, who routinely punished his children for violations of protocol. M. had learned to fear him, becoming more or less alienated from him since early childhood days. These feelings had persisted until about a year earlier when he had received a warm reply to a letter he had sent his father from aboard ship while carrying out compulsory duties as part of his naval training. For the first time in his life, he sensed that his father really did care for him. Ever since, M. has been able to communicate more freely and satisfactorily with him. His mother, on the other hand, was M.'s refuge. In the early days, to escape the ire of his father, he would run to mother. This pattern of behavior continued throughout his growing-up years. As M. says, ''Everything about her was golden and great''. Both parents argued incessantly, often in the presence of the children. M.'s mother had confided to him about a year previously that the only reason that she hadn't left her husband was her concern for the children.

Going steady with Jessica has helped M. to gain a different perspective about his relationship with his parents. (Jessica herself is being counselled at the University Psychological Services Center.) In serious discussions about life, the future, etc., she has convinced M. that the real problem in his life is his mother. According to Jessica, M.'s dependence on his mother and his inability to relate in proper masculine manner to his father are the causes for his sexual difficulties. I should point out that M. had confided to Jessica his masturbation problems but not his transvestite proclivities. It was due to Jessica's persuasiveness that M. sought psychological treatment.

I explored more specifically the fantasy, trying to pinpoint where, when and in what circumstances it appeared. Stimuli such as the following were effective in its arousal: seeing girls in class, at lunch, in the hallways, etc.; and pictures of girls in magazines. Generalization had become so rampant that any female apparel was a sufficient stimulus to evoke the fantasy no matter where he was.

Woodham: Will you say once again what the fantasy is?

Gershman: He imagines himself clothed in women's apparel. This is tipped off by any of the above stimuli I just mentioned.

Wolpe: Does the fantasy also lead to sexual desire or not?

Gershman: Yes and no. For many years, the masturbation which followed the fantasy seemed to be sufficient in itself. At the present time, it would be difficult, especially since M. has already had heterosexual experience, to say that this is true.

Wolpe: I'm puzzled about one thing. You speak about masturbation being sufficient. Where do you make the separation between the impulse that leads to masturbation and what you call sexual desire?

Gershman: According to M., when he looks at a girl at the present time, his desire can go in two directions: to heterosexual desire or to fantasy. He seems to make this distinction in his own mind. It is not apparent what specific circumstances are necessary to swerve his response in one direction or the other.

Wolpe: Is it something like this? He looks at a woman. His impulses could branch off in either of the two directions. He is sexually aroused and will usually move toward gratification in fantasy and consequent masturbation; but may be impelled toward normal sexual relations in favourable circumstances.

Gershman: He was unable to have an erection unless he conjured up the fantasy. From the very first experience with Jessica last summer, he could not maintain an erection unless he had the fantasy. Unless he had the image, he could not even get an erection.

Goldstein: Did he say specifically why he wanted treatment? Does he want to get rid of the fantasy or does he want to enjoy sexual intercourse?

Gershman: Both. He wants to marry this girl. He realizes that he cannot have intercourse without calling forth the fantasy. With serious prospects of marriage facing him, he is very much concerned. He is bothered about this "perversion". He wants to get rid of it.

I would like to mention a few other stimuli that help to evoke the fantasy. Rain is an effective stimulus. Rain, you will remember, is associated with raincoat, a female object which was so important in his early years. Also, when he sees girls' clothes hanging, for example, in a closet, department store, etc., the image is inevitably elicited.

At this session, I initiated treatment. I started with the "stop" technique (Wolpe, 1969), using it in this manner: I asked him to evoke the fantasy, to stop it, and then to shift to something which was reinforcing. Since I had already found out that he likes to read and to tinker with mechanical things, I asked him to focus on interesting scenes of this sort after stopping the image. We practiced this sequence in the office several times. After about the fourth or fifth repetition, it was obvious that he would be able to do it on his own. As a homework assignment, he was required to carry out this sequence three times daily, approximately six times at each session, adding up to a minimum of 18 times per day.

I emphasized the deliberate evocation of the fantasy. The purpose was mainly to institute the factor of control. Naturally, he would also get this fantasy during the day without purposely arousing it. He was directed to make use of the "stop" technique on these occasions also.

At this session I also started a covert sensitization* scene (Cautela, 1967).

Goldstein: Excuse me. Is this because you anticipated lack of success in the "stop" technique?

Gershman: No. Not exactly for that reason . . .

Goldstein: Just an additional measure?

Gershman: Right. According to my treatment program, covert sensitization

---

*This consists essentially of pairing the image one wishes to attack with an aversive image, that, for example, produces nausea.

was the next step. I had no way of telling how successful the ''stop'' technique itself would be, but I never really expected it to be sufficient by itself. It was a necessary beginning because in addition to the positive effects which could evolve from making use of a tool that is always available, I wanted to institute greater self-control efforts in my patient.

Wolpe: Did you have any concern about doing away with sexual arousal?

Gershman: No. I realize the significance of your question. However, the kind of sexual arousal that M. wanted was disturbed by these images. For instance, in making love to his girl, the intrusion of the image impeded real sexual arousal for his girl.

Goldstein: You said before that he wasn't able to get an erection without the image?

Gershman: That is correct. If he maintained the image, then he was able to engage in sexual follow-up.

Goldstein: Pleasurably?

Gershman: Yes, but primarily in a physical sense. The knowledge that what he was doing was not right was beginning to disturb him.

Wolpe: Then was he able to sustain the erection?

Gershman: Off and on. Though he got the erection, it was not to his satisfaction. At times, he would have an orgasm and other times, none. It was an on-and-off proposition, creating anxiety. What plagued him most was the fact that he could not regard the girl as his girl because he was not responding to her as he ought. It bothered him that when he had difficulty in erecting and coming to a climax, he would have to call forth the image to help.

Wolpe: Is this fantasy that he has a stereotyped fantasy?

Gershman: It varies. He's not always wearing the same undergarments, or clothes, or raincoat.

Goldstein: What is he doing in the fantasy?

Gershman: He is not doing anything. He sees himself dressed in these clothes.

Goldstein: Just standing there?

Gershman: Yes. In the past, when he put on the clothes, he would observe himself in the mirror. Sometimes this was reinforcing. Other times, however, the view was disappointing. The reinforcement, as you can see, was intermittent.

THIRD SESSION

M. was very enthusiastic about his success with the ''stop'' technique. He was able to conjure up an image purposely and to eliminate it. This was very encouraging. With further probing, he estimated his success to be about 60 percent. The greatest difficulty in stopping the image occurred at bedtime. During the week he had made love to Jessica three times: having an erection three times, and an orgasm each time; but he had had to conjure up the fantasies on each occasion.

I discussed with him my intention of associating the fantasy with aversiveness by making use of the covert sensitization technique and perhaps other aversive methods. I explained my reasons for doing so. Because of his success with the "stop" technique, he was highly motivated to go along with my suggestions.

For homework, I gave him the following: (1) Continue with the "stop" technique, (2) repeat the covert sensitization scenes at least twice during the day, and (3) associate his feces with the image. Direction for the latter called for his deliberately placing his head close to his feces and conjuring up the image. In leaving the toilet area, he was to feel relieved, breathe fresh air — following the covert sensitization routine. M. Pointed out that it was his house job to clean the cat's litter two or three times during the week. He despised doing this. I required him as the fourth item in his homework schedule to associate the fantasy with the cat's litter in the same way as with the feces.

FOURTH SESSION

It was obvious even before we started that M. was feeling very chipper. He eagerly pointed out that the only time he had had any fantasies during the past few days was when he let them appear. He could stop them any time he wanted. He was enjoying the newly-found control which the "stop" technique had given to him. Also, he had had intercourse with Jessica the previous night, had an erection without a fantasy and penetrated her without a fantasy. This was the first time he had done this. "I felt like I was on Cloud 9 last night," he said. However, he was unable to have an orgasm because Jessica was very tired and he had to stop. He felt he could have had it without conjuring up the image if intercourse had continued.

Several other significant things had happened this past week. As a result of stomach trouble, he had vomited five times over a period of a few days. Remembering the important association that had been stressed between the image and aversiveness, every time he vomited in the toilet bowl, he brought up the image — boots, raincoat, often the total image — in fantasy. He had also cleaned the cat's litter twice, making use of the same type of aversive association. A few days earlier Jessica had come into his apartment wearing a raincoat and he had succeeded immediately in stopping the image which was evoked. Also, whenever he had looked at nude female pictures in *Playboy* magazine which one of the boys in his house brought in, he was sexually aroused toward Jessica. There were no exceptions.

During the session I made use of several covert sensitization scenes and revived his vomiting experiences in imagery. In both instances, I followed this with the image of Jessica in the nude and M. and Jessica in sexual intercourse.

At this time I speculated whether merely to continue the ongoing procedures, or to try by other means to accelerate change. I decided to add aversive shock. My reason was that since aversiveness was working well, why not introduce another weapon to the arsenal to make it even more effective. I used shock in this manner. I had M. deliberately call forth the image, and say "Stop", upon which I shocked him and then immediately gave him the pleasurable image of himself and Jessica in sexual intercourse. I gave him a portable shocker and assigned him to use this technique the following week in addition to continuing the assignments of the week before.

Goldstein: Then the 'stop' is conditioned to the shock?

Gershman: Yes.

Goldstein: The stopping is made aversive?

Wolpe: I am puzzled that you brought in this shock technique when you were doing so well without it.

Gershman: Well, I was thinking of Guthrie who points out that a learning process is improved when the desirable response is made in different situations with different stimuli present.

Wolpe: Will you spell this out?

Gershman: Guthrie contends that for successful learning of a skill that can be widely used we have to practice the behavior in different situations. He gives as an example, I believe, a person who is learning to play a piece of music on the piano, or learning a poem, etc. When he practices the piano, he is always in the same room, in the same position, in the same chair, facing in the same direction, the walls are always the same color — everything's pretty much the same. In other words, the stimuli are more or less the same. But when he plays the piano in some other room where many stimuli would naturally be different, he will tend to falter. Basically this is Guthrie's idea. Therefore, if we can build up a wide range of experiences, there is a greater probability of comprehensive learning taking place. In S-R learning terms, what we are doing is to connect numerous stimuli with a particular response. This strengthens the whole S-R situation.

Wolpe: I don't see the relevance here when you were trying to *eliminate* a response.

Gershman: I was trying to eliminate the fantasy response. My aim was to strengthen the elimination process. Remember, the "stop" technique is something M. will always have available. If I could strengthen it, why not?

Wolpe: Well, I think there is also another question here. What are you inhibiting? You are using the word "Stop" to inhibit a response and then you are following that with a shock. Is there not a danger of producing an inhibition of inhibition?

Gershman: I felt that the association of the stop and shock being used in a practically simultaneous manner would make out of both stimuli a simple totality.

Goldstein: Do you have any reason to think that it was more effective this way?

Gershman: It was very effective.

Wolpe: Was it necessary?

Gershman: This is debatable. My interpretation was that it would add strength to the whole situation.

Goldstein: Does he used "Stop" while engaged in intercourse?

Gershman: Yes.

Goldstein: Wouldn't that be perhaps a contra-indication to the use of shock therapy, because the shock would also evoke anxiety?

Gershman: No. Remember, I had been seeing this boy only a few times, and I felt that the success which I was having could very well wear off with time. I didn't want to chance that. I felt that shock could be used very effectively at this particular time as a strengthening process.

Wolpe: I can't argue against a measure that you say has succeeded. What I'm concerned about is the possibility of negative effects on responses to normal sexual stimuli, since these are being paired with aversive consequences.

Gershman: Remember, that following shock, I make use of the image of pleasant sexual intercourse with his girl. This was very reinforcing for him. If I had perhaps made use of some other image, a neutral image, for instance, what you are suggesting might very well occur. But I deliberately made use of sexual intercourse *per se* as a pleasant experience that *followed* the image-cum-shock.

Bambeck: Guthrie's postulate is really weak and not of much value, don't you think?

Gershman: My impression is that Guthrie is on firm ground with this postulate. As you know, it is difficult to test much of Guthrie's theory because of the multiple S-R movements that are involved. However, empirically Guthrie's ideas are quite practical. As a matter of fact, we can translate this particular postulate into Skinnerian or Hullian terminology without any trouble.

FIFTH SESSION

M.'s feelings about the fantasy-image were undergoing radical change. It had become repugnant, sickening. This was the significant theme of the whole session. He had had two intercourse experiences with Jessica during the week. The first time he had for quite a time maintained an erection without the fantasy. He again had to stop without reaching orgasm because Jessica was tired. Again he felt that he could have reached it if he had been able to continue. The second intercourse was retrogressive. Because he desperately wanted to have the orgasm that he had missed the last two times, after a few minutes he deliberately called forth the image which eventually led to an orgasm. I explained to him in learning terms that this sequence was to be avoided at all costs.

Goldstein: If you are going to operate from a conditioning model and you have a CS, the image, and you want him to develop orgasmic potential without the image that is attached to other stimuli, then why not make use of the CS you have at your disposal. It may be the only one you'll ever have.

Gershman: What are you referring to?

Goldstein: I'm saying that he has only had orgasms under a very specific stereotyped condition. This can be to your advantage rather than disadvantage in developing normal sexual arousal.

Gershman: No, the orgasm is unpredictable; sometimes it comes, sometimes it doesn't. According to M., he feels confident that the orgasm could come without the image. The previous night he was tight and frustrated and since he had experienced two frustrating sexual experiences, he called forth the image deliberately. The image was no longer the problem. He controlled it. Previously, the image was the problem. Now, he can stop it anytime he wants. What are you suggesting?

Goldstein: I'm suggesting that when he has intercourse, he should call up the image if that is what is required to have an orgasm. We can predict in terms of straightforward conditioning that all the other stimuli in the situation will become conditioned to the response of orgasm.

Gershman: However, this image is very repugnant to him now.

Goldstein: I understand this, but the point is you've got to have another response which is an alternative one before you knock out the one which is unadaptive.

Gershman: I agree with the logic of your statement, but my interpretation of the conditions is different. I am trying to overcome the necessity of achieving success by evoking the image, which has been the uncontrollable variable for so many years.

Goldstein: It's the same principle as treating a homosexual through aversive training without being concerned about first giving him an alternative response to females.

Gershman: What you are saying is that when he has sexual intercourse he should purposely bring up the image and then have his orgasm.

Goldstein: Yes.

Gershman: What would we be doing? Strengthening the association between the orgasm and the image which already existed before and which we are trying to get rid of.

Goldstein: It's the unconditioned stimulus in this particular situation.

Gershman: Sure, but there are other important unconditioned stimuli also present. You are really suggesting that he continue what was for him normal before the treatment, and for which he came for treatment — that in the sexual situation, he should evoke the image, get raised excitation and then have the intercourse. It seems to me quite reasonable that if we can eliminate the image, there will be some measure of direct conditioning of the erotic response plus erection to the sexual situation — by-passing the image. In this way we can hope to build up the sexual response without the image — which essentially seems to have happened here. At the present time, there's no question about the increase in sexual desire without the image. As a CS the image is quite weak, now, sickening. By merely seeing Jessica in the nude now, he is always sexually stimulated. It was different before. What you are saying makes a great deal of sense, in homosexual cases, but I would not do it in this case unless it was the only alternative left.

Wolpe: Isn't there evidence that one can get conditioning of sexual responses without orgasm?

Gershman: I believe so.

Bambeck: Before he started treatment and when he had to use the image to elicit orgasm, or even an erection, how did he feel immediately after intercourse?

Gershman: Disappointed. Because to him this intercourse was just like the masturbation process.

Bambeck: Wouldn't this make the idea invalid about trying to link the image, the fantasy, with satisfaction, since the consequence was really disappointing?

Gershman: I think so. All techniques used — stop, covert sensitization, and shock — were for the purpose of eliminating the fantasy. If were were to do what has been suggested, we might very well bring back the bogey man once again — the fantasy — and associate it with a high reinforcement. I think we would be back where we started.

Goldstein: I would suggest to you that the fantasy played a large part in conditioning him to respond sexually to Jessica. Had he not had a girlfriend and you have used the same treatment approach, you would have closed off a possibility of normal sexuality. Apparently, what has happened is that enough has developed to make sexual responsiveness transferable.

Gershman: I think that makes good sense. The existence of a girlfriend to whom he was highly motivated was definitely important.

Wolpe: I had a case about 3 years ago which was not dissimilar to this one. A young man of about 22 couldn't enjoy sexual intercourse unless he had an image of a large female who would be punishing him in some way. He was finally able to enjoy normal sexual intercourse after the image was eliminated by aversive conditioning.

Goldstein: May I ask you a question about a side issue. Did this person that you treated begin masturbation at a very young age — like 6? The reason I ask is because every time I've seen a case where there is a very stereotyped sexual response in terms of the stimuli that are elicited, there always has been a history of very early masturbation. Apparently, the younger one starts, the more stereotyped the response becomes. I don't know.

Gershman: M. also started masturbating at an early age.

Goldstein: There was a girl I saw who could only masturbate by crossing her legs in a particular way and imagining that she had to urinate. It started when she was very young, 6 or 7. When she was in a car, she would cross her legs and the motion of the car would masturbate her. The reason she got away with it was that she told her parents she had to go to the bathroom. So it developed into a very stereotyped kind of a response just as we have here. I wonder if the age at which one starts . . .

Wolpe: You're raising a question with wide ramifications. Very little work has been done on the specific factors that play a part in neurotic conditioning. It's about time somebody began working on the kind of questions you're raising in relation to this case, and similar questions in relation to other kinds of cases. What are the factors that determine neurotic conditioning of different kinds? What are the factors that favor homosexual conditioning? What are the factors making for a predisposition to agoraphobia?

Goldstein: I think one has to be careful about getting into the same bind that analysts do, by depending upon subjective reports of occurrences in the past, which are not terribly reliable. When delving into what happened when someone was 6 years old, one could get "information" to confirm an analytic model or "information" to confirm any other model.

Wolpe: There are obviously methodological problems, but the researcher has to insure that his information is reliable. When you are pressing for details of a past that is hazy, there is a factor at work that inclines people to give you the information that you want. But if you were to interview 100 fetishistic cases and a large percentage were spontaneously to tell you that they masturbated at the age of 6 or so, this would be, I think, impressively unusual.

SIXTH SESSION

This session took place several weeks later. It was short. M. was having no trouble with erection or orgasm. During the past 2 weeks, he had engaged in inercourse several times without difficulty. He was looking forward to his marriage with Jessica the next month. Most of the session dealt with a review of the techniques which had been used to counter-condition the fantasy-masturbation sequence. M. was most cheerful, was looking forward to the marriage and feeling extremely confident that he would be able to function normally. On leaving, he agreed that if any difficulty were to arise in the future, he would contact me immediately. Six months have passed without any telephone call.

REFERENCES

Cautela J. R. (1967) Covert sensitization. *Psycholog. Reports* **20**, 459–468.
Wolpe J. (1969) *The Practice of Behavior Therapy*. Pergamon Press, New York.

Chapter 31

The Use of Covert Conditioning in the Treatment of Drug Abuse*

Joseph R. Cautela and Anne K. Rosenstiel

Summary — It appears that behavioral techniques show some promise in treating drug abuse. Recently the covert conditioning procedures have been employed to modify drug-taking behavior. Covert conditioning procedures involve the manipulation of imagery in a manner similar to the overt operant procedures. The covert conditioning procedures of covert sensitization, covert positive reinforcement, and covert extinction are described, and studies presented where these procedures have been applied to the treatment of drug abuse. The studies cited involve various drug-taking behavior such as heroin, amphetamine (intravenously injected), and LSD. A behavioral model is presented concerning the application of a number of behavioral techniques to modify the antecedents and consequences of drug-taking behavior. It is indicated that a comprehensive drug treatment approach should also use the behavioral procedures to insure educational, vocational, social and sexual and marital adjustment.

The treatment of drug abuse has shown little promise in developing a standardized treatment with low relapse rates. Hunt et al. (1971) reviewed data that indicate that almost 80% of heroin addicts relapse 12 months after treatment terminated. The application of behavioral techniques to drug abuse shows some promise in the treatment of drug abuse. Droppa (1973) has recently reviewed a general behavioral approach to drug addiction. The purpose of this paper is to focus on the specific behavioral techniques of covert conditioning (Cautela, 1973) which have been used with some success with drug addiction and to outline a comprehensive treatment approach.

*Reprinted with permission from the *International Journal of the Addictions*, 1975, *10*, 277-303. © Marcel Dekker, Inc. 1975.

REVIEW OF BEHAVIORAL
APPROACHES TO DRUG ABUSE

Behaviorists have applied the learning theory approach to the treatment of drug abuse with moderate success. Treatment has been aimed at eliminating antecedent conditions or focusing on the target behavior.

A number of investigators (Boudin and Valentine, 1973; Cahoon and Crosby, 1972; Wikler, 1965) have found that environmental events act as cues for drug-taking behavior. This led investigators such as Kraft (1969a, 1969b, 1970a, 1970b) to treat drug abuse by using systematic desensitization to neutralize the influence of cues (antecedent conditions).

Cahoon and Crosby (1972) stated that reinforcement, both in the form of social reinforcement and reinforcement in the drug itself, is one of the variables responsible for maintaining the use of drugs. Therefore, it would follow that pairing an aversive stimulus with the drug, thereby creating an aversion to the drug, would eliminate one of the variables maintaining the behavior. Both electrical and chemical aversion have been used to overcome the reinforcing properties of the drug itself (Lesser, 1967; Liberman, 1968; Raymond, 1964; Wolpe, 1965). Lesser (1967) combined electrical aversion with relaxation and assertive training. Wolpe (1965) used an electrical shock contingent on the use of drugs as part of a treatment which also included assertive training. Although the study by Lesser was successful, Wolpe's subject relapsed after 12 weeks. Raymond (1964) and Liberman (1968) used a form of chemical aversion. Liberman reports that one out of two subjects became readdicted. Raymond's procedure proved successful with the one case reported.

Boudin (1972) and Boudin and Valentine (1973) report the successful use of contingency contracting, but they conclude that the approach they used was extremely time consuming. Boudin and Boudin and Valentine also report successfully using aversion therapy in some cases. The aversive stimulus consisted of shock or *in vivo* negative reinforcers administered right before the subject injected himself. O'Brien et al. (1971) and Gotestam et al. (1972) used a form of token economy with hospitalized narcotic addicts. They were successful in increasing certain behaviors, but these behaviors were not directly related to drug usage itself.

In summary then, investigators either tried to eliminate antecedent cues using reciprocal inhibition techniques such as systematic desensitization, assertive training, or relaxation, or focused on the target behavior by aversion therapy or contingency contracting.

It would appear that a comprehensive treatment of drug abuse would involve the elimination of undesirable antecedent cues and the manipulation of consequences. This approach is exposed by a number of investigators such as Wikler (1965) and Cahoon and Crosby (1972). While the elimination of antecedents and consequences should probably involve a number of behavioral techniques, the following section will focus specifically on a description of the covert conditioning techniques and the use of covert conditioning to eliminate antecedents and consequences.

THE USE OF COVERT CONDITIONING TO MODIFY ANTECEDENT CONDITIONS AND CONSEQUENCES

The covert conditioning techniques are a systematic way of changing covert and overt behavior. The assumption underlying covert conditioning is that a stimulus presented in imagination via instructions can effect overt and covert behavior in a manner similar to a stimulus presented externally. It is also assumed that the parameters effecting overt operant conditioning are similar to those operating in covert conditioning.

Cautela has developed six covert conditioning techniques which are conceptualized within the operant framework (see Cautela, 1973, for a detailed description of techniques). The following three techniques have been specifically applied to drug abuse.

The Modification of Antecedent Conditions

The rationale for covert positive reinforcement (Cautela, 1970a) is that a behavior followed by a reinforcer will increase in response probability. It is analogous to overt reinforcement and is used when an increase in response probability is desired. The client imagines the thought or behavior to be increased and then follows it with a reinforcer. Covert reinforcement can be used to modify both maladaptive approach and avoidance behavior. Many experiments (Blanchard and Draper, 1973; Cautela et al., in press; Cautela et al., 1971; Flannery, 1972; Krop et al., 1971; Krop et al., in press; Steffen, 1971; Wisocki, 1973a) have shown that it is an effective technique. The technique is used in the following manner:

Covert reinforcement can be used to eliminate cues that are likely to lead to drug-taking behavior. The first step is to find possible reinforcers. The Reinforcement Survey Schedule (Cautela and Kastenbaum, 1967) can be used for this purpose. To supplement the RSS, the therapist can ask the client and people with whom he interacts if there are additional reinforcers. The client is then asked to close his eyes and try to imagine a possible reinforcing scene, such as laying on a beach, relaxing in the sun, or listening to his favorite music. The therapist describes the scene in some detail. If the client can imagine the reinforcing scene within 5 seconds and he reports that the image is clear and pleasurable, the scene is used as a reinforcer.

The client is then asked to imagine the response to be increased. He is asked to imagine that he is really there rather than viewing the scene. When he has that image clear, he is asked to raise his right index finger. The therapist says reinforcement and the client then switches to the previously practiced reinforcing scene. When the reinforcing scene is clear, the client signals again. Since there is some evidence that continued and massed reinforcement can lead to satiation (Allyon and Arzin, 1968, pp. 119–120), reinforcing scenes should be alternated.

In the office the client practices the scene 20 times. The scene is presented 10 times by the therapist alternating 10 trials fo the same scene by the client. The client is asked to practice the scene at least 10 times a day at home.

If, for example, criticism is apt to be followed by drug-taking behavior, the individual can be desensitized to criticism by using covert reinforcement. A typical scene might be:

Imagine that you are at work and you're talking to some of your colleagues. Your boss comes over to you and criticizes you for some work you did previously. You think to yourself, I can't always perform perfectly. I'm not going to let that criticism upset me. Reinforcement. Imagine yourself sailing on a boat. You can smell the water and feel the breeze against your body. You are enjoying yourself and the scenery around you. You feel calm and relaxed.

If the client reports being anxious in social situations, and this is a cue for taking drugs, a scene which could be used to desensitize the client might be:

Imagine that you're at a party talking to a girl you just met. You can hear the other people talking around you. You can hear the music playing and the people dancing. As you're talking to her you feel good; you feel totally relaxed. Reinforcement. Imagine yourself at a football game. You can feel the bleacher you're sitting on and hear the noise and commotion around you. Your favorite player has just run 40 yards to make a touchdown. Everybody stands up and cheers.

The Manipulation of Consequences

Covert sensitization, covert extinction, and covert reinforcement of incompatible responses can be used to modify consequences.

The Use of Covert Sensitization.

The rationale behind covert sensitization (Cautela, 1966, 1967) is that a response followed by an aversive or noxious stimulus will decrease in frequency. It is analogous to overt punishment. The client imagines the behavior to be decreased followed by an aversive stimulus. In this way, aversion is conditioned to the undesirable behavior. Experimental evidence shows that covert sensitization is effective in treating maladaptive approach behavior such as sexual disorders (Barlow, Leitenberg and Agras, 1969; Barlow et al., 1972; Callahan and Leitenberg, 1973; Curtis and Presley, 1972; Segal and Sims, 1972), alcoholism (Asherᵱ and Donner, 1968; Cautela, 1970b; Fleiger and Zingle, 1971; Miller and Hersen, 1972), obesity (Cautela, 1972; Janda and Rimm, 1972; Manno and Marston, 1972; Sachs and Ingram, 1972; Stuart, 1967), and smoking (Cautela, 1970c; Irey, 1972; Primo, 1972).

The procedure consists of the client imagining the response to be decreased followed by an aversive stimulus. Although vomiting is the most commonly aversive stimulus used, other stimuli can be employed. For example, Wisocki (1973b) found that a client equated vomiting with a good grade of heroin, and aversive stimuli such as bees swarming around him were used.

As in covert reinforcement, the scene is practiced 20 times in the office, alternating between the therapist presenting scenes and the client practicing it by himself. The client is then asked to practice it at home at least 10 times a day.

In the treatment of drug abuse, scenes are constructed in which a chain of responses leading to injection are punished. This would include thinking about shooting up, going to see the pusher, and injecting the drug. Examples to typical scenes which might be used are as follows.

Thinking about shooting up:

Imagine that you are at your friend's house and the thought passes through your mind how great it would be to get high. As soon as you start to think that, bitter spit comes into your mouth. You swallow the sour spit and think how much better you'll feel once you have a fix. You think about going into the bathroom and shooting up. Suddenly you vomit. There is vomit all over your body; all over your clothes. It smells foul, it feels slimy. You start retching: you have dry heaves. You decide it's not worth it. You decide not to shoot up. As soon as you think that you feel better. You take a shower and feel glad that you stopped thinking about shooting up.

Going to see the pusher:

Imagine that you're in your car going to meet your pusher. You can feel the steering wheel in your hands and can see vividly the street you're driving on and the other cars. As you approach his house, rats start crawling about you on the seat. As you slow down the car, the rats start climbing up your arms. They smell of sewage. As you park and turn off the engine, they jump all over your face. They cling to your body as if they won't let go. They start defecating all over you. You decide its not worth it. You turn on the engine and as you start to leave, the rats start to disappear. You feel good that you resisted the temptation.

Injecting the drug (this scene is similar to the one used by Wisocki, 1973b):

Imagine that you're in your room and you decide that you want a fix. You get up from the chair you're sitting in to get the syringe. Just as you get up a wasp flies into the room. It starts buzzing. You get a little fearful as the brown, ugly wasp flies in front of you. As you get the syringe and get the fix ready, you see more wasps flying around the room: they are now getting louder. You think how nice it will be once you shoot up and try to forget about the wasps flying around you. Just as you put the syringe to your arm a whole mess of wasps attack your body: they're clinging to your face and your arms. You can feel them stinging your whole body. Their high buzzing pierces your ears. They get into your clothes. You decide it's not worth it and throw down the syringe and start to leave the room. As you're leaving the room the wasps start flying away. The farther you go the less wasps there are. You feel much better. Everything is quiet and you feel good that you resisted the fix.

The client is instructed that everytime he has the urge to inject the drug, no matter where he is, to imagine getting sick and vomiting, or some other aversive stimulus.

The Use of Covert Extinction. The assumption in covert extinction (Cautela, 1971) is that imagining a response without a reinforcer would decrease response probability. It is analogous to overt extinction and is used to extinguish a conditioned response. In this technique the client imagines the behavior to be decreased and then imagines that he is not receiving the reinforcement that is maintaining that behavior. An experiment done by Ascher (1970) has tested its effectiveness.

In a behavior such as drug abuse, covert extinction may involve not having the drug be reinforcing or getting no social reinforcement from peers following drug-taking behaivor. As stated previously by Cahoon and Crosby (1972), both types of reinforcement (the drug itself and social reinforcement) serve to maintain drug abuse.

Scenes are constructed in the office where the client imagines the response to be decreased followed by no reinforcement. As in other techniques, scenes are practiced 20 times in the office, alternating between the therapist present-ing the scene and the client doing it alone, and the client is asked to practice it at least 10 times a day outside the office.

A scene in which the drug itself is not reinforcing may be as follows:

Imagine that you're at a park with your friends and you decide to "shoot" up. You and your friends prepare the syringe and you inject the drug into your arm. But upon injecting the drug, you feel nothing. You get no "flash," no "high," no "rush," nothing. You feel no effects at all.

An example of a scene in which the client shoots up and gets no social reinforcement from his peers is:

Imagine that you're with some friends of yours in your apartment. You can hear your friends talk and you can feel the chair you're sitting on. You go into the kitchen and "shoot" up. You come back and tell them how great it feels. They look the other way. Suddenly they all get up to leave.

The Use of Covert Reinforcement in Increasing Incompatible Responses. Skinner (1969) reports that the most effective way to decrease a behavior is to use both punishment for the response you want to decrease and to reinforce incompatible responses. The use of covert reinforcement to increase incompatible responses can be combined with covert sensitization.

The procedure for covert reinforcement is the same as that described earlier, but scenes are used in which the client is tempted to take drugs and then decides not to. It is assumed that reinforcing the client for making such a decision will increase the probability of that decision occurring in the future.

One type of scene might involve deciding not to get a fix. An example is:

Imagine that you're driving in your car and you can feel the steering wheel in your hands; you can visualize the streets you're driving on. As you pass by the street your pusher lives on, the thought passes through your mind how good it would be to get a fix. But then you think to yourself, why do I want to ruin my life by taking that junk. Reinforcement. Imagine yourself eating a piece of chocolate cream pie. You can taste the whip cream and feel the creamy chocolate custard in your mouth. The graham cracker crust is just out of this world.

Another scene, an example which follows, is deciding not to take the drug and then doing something reinforcing, such as reading a book, going for a walk, or calling a friend.

Imagine that you're in your room and the thought passes through your mind how good it would be to have a fix. But then you think, that's a stupid thought. I should be doing something constructive instead. You go into the living room and pick up one of your favorite books and start reading it. Reinforcement. Imagine that you're listening to your favorite song on the radio. You can hear the beat and you feel your body swaying to the music. You feel good.

COVERT CONDITIONING IN TREATING DRUG ABUSE

While as previously stated there is ample evidence that covert conditioning is successful in modifying behavior, there have been few studies employing covert conditioning techniques with drug addiction. Gotestam and Melin (1974) treated four female hospitalized intravenous amphetamine addicts with covert extinction. The average age of the four subjects was 29 years; each subject had been addicted for an average of over 4 years. Treatment consisted of 15 trials of covert extinction per day for a period averaging around 2 weeks. A control group was not employed. After an average of around 1 week of treatment, all four subjects went AWOL and shot up. When they did inject the drug, they reported later that they were surprised to find that they had no "rush" or no "high." After subjects returned and communicated the lack of success of injection, investigators reported they could no longer get subjects for their study (personal communication, 1973). A 9-month follow-up indicated that only one subject had relapsed.

Wisocki (1973b) used covert conditioning techniques in the successful treatment of a heroin addiction of 3 years duration. The client was using an average of 20 bags per day and had been previously unsuccessfully involved in psychiatric, Synanon-type treatment, and twice a methadone treatment for his addiction. When he admitted himself for treatment, he stated that his past treatment experiences were poor, but that he thought he would take another chance.

The client was a 26-year-old male seen on an outpatient basis. Treatment for the addictive behavior included covert reinforcement and covert sensitization to decrease the consummatory behavior, and thought-stopping and relaxation were used to neutralize the antecedents to drug use. Three weeks and 4 days after treatment had started (the client had had two therapy sessions), the client injected himself with heroin and reported later that he felt immediately depressed.

After working on the addictive behavior, treatment was aimed at building up pro-social behaviors. The author noted that the pro-social behaviors took longer to treat than the addictive behavior. A 12-month follow-up indicated that the client had taken no heroin and had no desire to return to his old habits. He was married and working as a counselor for emotionally disturbed children. He reported liking his job and having an active social life.

Duehn and Shannon (1973) treated seven male adolescents, between 16 and 18 years old, with covert conditioning on LSD behavior. Besides having a history of LSD usage, they also took amphetamines and marijuana. All subjects volunteered for treatment and decided they wanted to use covert sensitization on LSD. They were all told they could drop out of treatment at any time, yet none did. Treatment was carried out in a group setting and consisted of relaxation training and covert sensitization with escape scenes.

The authors state that "in the second and subsequent sessions, all Ss felt nauseated during presentation of the aversive LSD scenes." Two subjects took LSD a few days following the initial covert sensitization session and reported "adverse effects." One subject was offered LSD two times and reported having stomach cramps and being nauseous each time he looked at an LSD tab.

At the end of treatment, two Ss were totally drug free, while the others reported using amphetamines and marijuana. Two of the Ss reported using the technique at home on other drugs. A 6-month follow-up of six of the subjects (one could not be located) indicated that none had taken LSD and all had no desire to even though they had been offered. An 18-month follow-up with the same six subjects indicated that they had still not taken LSD.

Steinfeld et al. (1972) also used group covert sensitization in treating eight male heroin addicts. All subjects were in prison and volunteered for treatment. Treatment consisted of eight covert sensitization sessions. Covert reinforcement was added onto the covert sensitization scene, where the subject was reinforced at the end of the scene for not shooting up. Thought-stopping and relaxation were also taught in conjunction with the covert conditioning.

Of the eight men, two have returned to jail. One hypothesized reason as to the two relapses is that the group scenes were not specific enough to the drug-taking behavior of these two subjects. The other six at the writing of this article are doing well, involved in school, working, not engaged in criminal activity, and not taking drugs.

A number of other studies have employed aversive imagery techniques similar to Cautela's covert sensitization. Anant (1968) reports the successful treatment of alcoholics and drug addicts. Of 26 subjects (only one was a drug addict) he reports that only one S dropped out before treatment was completed. Treatment for all the subjects showed no relapse at least 6 months after treatment. Some had not relapsed at the time the study was reported (26 months). Kolvin (1967) successfully used a form of aversive imagery with a 15-year-old male with a 7-year addiction to sniffing petrol. He would often pass out after sniffing, and the behavior would also result "In what can be described as expansive visual hallucinatory experiences in the form of cowboy pictures." His addiction was so bad that he once, in need of petrol, broke into a shed. The author expressed "grave doubts" at the start of treatment as to whether it would be successful.

Treatment consisted of 20 half-hour sessions of aversive imagery therapy. Sessions were held every day, except on weekends. A 13-month follow-up indicated that the subject had not sniffed petrol at all. The author also successfully used the technique with a 14-year-old fetishist. In both cases, there developed an aversion or a distaste for the behavior to be decreased.

A number of studies have employed covert conditioning techniques along with other techniques. Blanchard, Libet, and Young (in press) used covert sensitization along with apneic aversion in the treatment of a hydrocarbon inhalation addiction of 7 years duration. Treatment was successful.

O'Brien et al. (1972) used a combination of verbal and electrical aversion, relaxation, and systematic desensitization in treating two heroin addicts. Although treatment consisted of many behavioral techniques, the authors state that the verbal imagery aversion "produced a noticeable emotional impact on the patient." They also conclude from clinical observations of the subjects that the verbal imagery "played a strong role in the conditioning" and decreased the use of electric shock.

In a more recent report, O'Brien and Raynes (personal communication, 1973) combined electrical and verbal aversion along with other behavioral techniques in treating 20 drug addicts, 15 of whom were heroin addicts. The authors stated that after around 200 to 300 presentations of the aversive stimulus, the subjects had developed an indifference to drug related stimulus. Nineteen of the 20 subjects reported taking drugs during treatment. Almost all reported nervousness in the presence of and while injecting the drug. Although most reported neutrality and indifference to the drug (no rush), some reported having adverse effects. One subject thought that he had had a heart attack after injection and another reported severe headaches. A few subjects reported that the drug was as good as before.

A summary of both overt and covert studies is presented in Table 1.

DISCUSSION OF BEHAVIORAL APPROACHES TO DRUG TREATMENT

The covert conditioning techniques can have some advantages over the other behavioral techniques.

The Advantages of Covert Conditioning Over Other Aversive Techniques.

There appears to be one disadvantage with the chemical and electrical aversion therapy, and that is there is apt to be a high dropout rate. A few studies

Table 31.1. Drug Studies Employing Behavior Modification

Author and date	Sample size	Screening criteria	Drug treated	Treatment	Length of sessions	Average length of treatment	Success criteria	Treatment outcome
Anant, 1968	One	None stated	Tranquilizers	Relaxation and verbal aversion	Not stated	Not stated: approximately 4–8	Abstinence	Abstinence maintained at 3 month follow-up
Blanchard, Libet and Young, in press	One	None stated	Hydrocarbon inhalation	Covert sensitization and apneic aversion based on Anectine	Half hour	26 sessions (22 covert sensitization, 4 apneic aversion)	2 objective measures of consummatory behavior (''smell'' test and free access test)	Abstinence maintained at 7 month follow-up
Boudin, 1972	One	None stated	Amphetamines	Contingency contracting and self-administered shock	Not applicable	Three months	Fulfilling contract	Abstinence at 2 year follow-up
Boudin and Valentine, 1973	Not stated	Cooperative and follow contingency contract	Mostly heroin	Various combinations of in vivo aversion, contingency contracting, behavioral rehearsal, covert sensitization, and systematic desensitization	Not applicable	Not stated	Self-recorded data of covert and overt behavior	Not stated: one successful case report included
Duehn and Shannon, 1973	Seven	Volunteered	LSD	Relaxation and group covert sensitization	50–60 minutes	6 weeks (11 sessions)	Abstinence	Abstinence maintained at 18 month follow-up for 6 subjects; 7th couldn't be located
Gotestam and Melin, 1974	Four	inpatient on a ward, intravenously injecting amphetamines	Amphetamine	Covert extinction	20 minutes	2 weeks (2–3 sessions a day)	Abstinence	Abstinence maintained at 9 month follow-up for three subjects

Table 31.1. Drug Studies Employing Behavior Modification (continued)

Author and date	Sample size	Screening criteria	Drug treated	Treatment	Length of sessions	Average length of treatment	Success criteria	Treatment outcome
Gotestam, Melin and Dockens, 1972	18	Had to be on ward at least 1 day, and not psychotic	None	Detoxification, contingency contracting, and rehabilitation training	Not applicable	Not stated	Increase in behaviors conducive to management of ward	All four behaviors changed except one (staying in room)
Kolvin, 1967	One	None stated	Sniffing petrol	Relaxation and aversive imagery	Half hour	4 weeks (20 sessions)	Abstinence	Abstinence maintained at 13 month follow-up
Kraft, 1969a	One	None stated	Barbituates	Systematic desensitization	1 hour	8 months (72 sessions)	Abstinence	Abstinence at termination of treatment
Kraft, 1969a, 1970a, 1970b	Two	None stated	Drinamyl (desamyl)	Systematic desensitization	1 hour	4 months (36 sessions)	Abstinence	Abstinence maintained at 2 year follow-up
Lesser, 1967	One	None stated	Morphine	Relaxation, assertive training, and electrical aversion conditioning	1 hour	4½ Months (33 sessions)	Abstinence	Abstinence maintained at 10 month follow-up
Liberman, 1968	Two	None stated	Heroin	Aversion conditioning with apomorphine, social reinforcement for responses incompatible to taking drugs	1 hour	5 weeks (38 sessions) plus booster sessions	Decrease in urges and abstinence	One relapsed shortly after treatment; other abstained at 1 year follow-up
O'Brien and Raynes, 1973	20	None stated	Heroin (15 subjects), other drugs (5 subjects)	Various combinations of electrical and chemical aversion, relaxation, systematic desensitization, contingency contracting, family contracting, assertive training	Not stated	Of the 70% who completed treatment: 26 sessions	Self-rating scale of urges and abstinence	60% success. of those who completed treatment: 77% success. Abstinence maintained at follow-ups ranging from 1 to 2½ years

Table 31.1. Drug Studies Employing Behavior Modification (continued)

Author and date	Sample size	Screening criteria	Drug treated	Treatment	Length of sessions	Average length of treatment	Success criteria	Treatment outcome
O'Brien, Raynes and Patch, 1971	150	Proven narcotic addiction, residency in the immediate area	None	Premack principle	Not applicable	30 days hospitalization	Number of low frequency behaviors conducive to ward management	Increase from 20% (baseline) to above 80% while treatment was ongoing
O'Brien, Raynes and Patch, 1972	Two	Volunteered after detoxification	Heroin	Verbal and electrical aversion, relaxation, and systematic desensitization	Not stated	23 sessions	Self-rating scale of urges and abstinence	Abstinence maintained at 14 and 6 month follow-up
Raymond, 1964	One	None stated	Physeptone	Aversion conditioning with apomorphine	Not stated	17 days	Abstinence	Abstinence at 2 years follow-up
Steinfeld, Rautio, Egan and Rice, 1973	8	Imprisoned heroin addicts within a few months of release; and volunteered	Heroin	Relaxation, group covert sensitization and overt reinforcement, and thought stopping	Not stated	8 sessions	Abstinence and not involved in criminal activities	Six successful: 2 returned to jail at follow-up (length not stated
Wisocki, 1973	One	Willingness of client to cooperate	Heroin	Covert reinforcement covert sensitization, covert reinforcement sampling, thought stopping, and relaxation	Not stated	4 months (12 sessions)	Abstinence, positive thoughts and statements about himself, and engaging in prosocial behaviors	Abstinence at 12 months follow-up; working and married
Wolpe, 1965	One	None stated	Demand	Self-administered shock and assertive training	Not stated	4 months (8 sessions)	Urges and abstinence	Abstinence for 3 months; left treatment and returned to drugs

indicated that the dropout rate for covert conditioning is low (Anant, 1968) or nonexistant (Duehn and Shannon, 1973). You need certain equipment for chemical or electrical aversion, and it is often hard for the client to carry out treatment on his own. Two studies (Boudin, 1972; Wolpe, 1965) indicated that shock treatment had to be discontinued because the apparatus did not work consistently. Electrical or chemical aversion techniques cannot be as readily used as self-control techniques as the covert conditioning techniques. Whenever covert conditioning techniques are used, the rationale and procedure are carefully described and presented to the client. He is instructed how to employ the covert conditioning procedure after treatment is terminated if he finds he is about to or begins to engage in the maladaptive behavior.

Contingency Contracting

Although the two studies employing contingency contracting to decrease the consummatory behavior (Boudin, 1972; Boudin and Valentine, 1973) proved successful, they require a lot of time, energy, and money. The therapist was required to be on call 24 hours a day for the client to call him in case he had a desire to use the drug. Boudin and Valentine and Boudin also reported using aversion therapy combined with contingency contracting to decrease the behavior.

The Modification of Physiological Responses.

An interesting observation in these studies is that in a number of instances subjects reported that they did not feel a high or the enjoyable feelings when they tried to administer the drug to themselves after treatment. Lesser (1967), who successfully employed electrical aversion with one subject, quoted his subject as saying he didn't get the "good feeling" when using morphine after the eighth aversion session. Liberman (1968) reported that his subject, at his sixth apomorphine conditioning session, reported he felt nauseous as soon as he began injecting morphine. Similar observations have been made by investigators employing covert conditioning procedures. Gotestam and Melin (1974) reported that after covert extinction ranging from 100 to 200 trials, their four female subjects stated that after intravenously injecting amphetamine that they felt no rush or high from the drug. Duehn and Shannon (1973) indicated that two of their subjects reported "adverse effects" after taking LSD after the initial covert sensitization session. Wisocki's (1973b) client, after two treatment sessions, reported that he felt depressed when he injected heroin. O'Brien and Raynes (personal communication 1973) state a number of subjects in their study reported either no reinforcing or aversive effects while injecting themselves with heroin.

The above studies, in which conditioning procedures were employed, are somehow able to overcome the usual enjoyable physiological effects of drugs.

This appears to cut across different drugs and conditioning procedures. What appears especially surprising is the fact that the use of imagery procedures in covert conditioning were powerful enough to overcome the properties of drugs, such as elation, euphoria, rush, and high which maintain drug use.

Related literature gives supporting evidence that instructions to imagine certain sensations can alter autonomic processes. Barber and Hahn (1962) ran an experiment in which the subjects had to immerse their hands in near freezing water. They measured the intensity of pain by respiratory irregulatrities, heart rate, decrease in skin resistance, and an increase in muscle tension. In both a hypnotic and waking imagined group, the subjects were instructed that the stimulus would not hurt. Results indicated that those two groups, as compared to an uninstructed group, reported a decrease in pain experience. They also found a decrease in muscle tension and respiratory irregularities, but it was ineffective in modifying cardiac acceleration and drop in skin resistance. This is becuase these are autonomic responses and are not as subject to voluntary control. This study shows that you can bet a change in physiological responses and a decrease in pain as measured by self-reports as a function of the instructions given.

Barber et al. (in press) reviewed a number of studies which "suggest the possibility that many individuals might be able to produce localized changes in the temperature of their skin after they have received training in thinking and imagining that the skin is cold or warm" (Chap. 10). Lang (1969) states that reward and punishment and biofeedback training indicate that autonomic activity can be brought under control. He also asserts that evidence indicates that human subjects can develop considerable facility at controlling autonomic responses such as sweat gland activity, heart rate, and blood volume (p. 183). Schwartz and Shapiro (in press) have shown that by biofeedback training, subjects can learn to control their blood pressure.

The studies mentioned above employing conditioning procedures seem to be more successful if the clients report after injection that there is no enjoyable altered mood state.

Motivation

One factor that many investigators feel is necessary for successful treatments is high motivation. Most of the studies (Anant, 1968; Boudin and Valentine, 1973; Duehn and Shannon, 1973; Kraft, 1969a, 1969b, 1970a, 1970b; Lesser, 1967; Liberman; 1968; Gotestam and Melin, 1974; O'Brien and Raynes, 1973; Steinfeld et al., 1972; Wisocki, 1973b) stated that their subjects were either very motivated or volunteered for treatment. Two studies (Kraft, 1969a; Wisocki, 1973b) stated that their subjects showed motivation even though their therapist did not show optimism. Of course, there is no reason to assume that subjects receiving covert conditioning are more motivated than subjects receiving other treatment. In fact, in two studies (Boudin, 1972; Blanchard,

Libet and Young, in press) the authors indicated that either their subject was not optimistic or was "minimally" motivated for treatment. Both these studies were successful.

One of the problems in a discussion concerning the motivation is the use of the term motivation as a construct independently without operational criteria. In the senior author's experience, he judges the degree of motivation by the following criteria: (1) Verbal statements such as "I really want to get well," "I really want to kick the habit," "I am sick of this crap," "I want to stop taking drugs," "I really want treatment," and "I'll cooperate." (2) Nonverbal behaviors such as keeping appointments and making an effort to stay away from sources of drugs and peers who engage in drug-taking behavior. (3) Doing homework assignments such as keeping records, practicing relaxation, using thought stopping, and doing covert conditioning homework.

A scale can be devised in which the client can be rated on the above criteria (Table 2). One of the most important variables appears to be the degree to which the client participates in homework assignments. The least relevant variable appears to be the verbal behavior.

In our view, a behavior therapist should consider it unethical to treat any individual unless they want treatment as expressed by what appears to be sincere verbal statements.

Suggestions for Improvement

The covert conditioning studies reported thus far can be improved in a number of ways. (1) More controls are needed. (2) Urinalysis should be taken to determine if the subject's self-reports of drug behavior are correct. (3) The physiological responses to certain drugs should be quantified and measured before and after treatment to see if they are affected. (4) The dependent variables should be more adequately measured.

Training of Therapists Using Covert Conditioning

As with the use of any behavior therapy procedure, it is necessary for the therapist to have a general background and familiarity with learning theory and with a wide range of behavior modification procedures. From a clinical standpoint, the therapist should be experienced in doing a behavioral analysis and have specific experience with covert procedures under supervision.

It has been our experience that under supervision, after a behavioral analysis has been completed and particular covert conditioning scenes designed with a specific program of treatment, ward level personnel with minimal training can be utilized to present covert conditioning scenes. This enables the client to get more sessions than possible with the usual time restrictions of a trained and experienced single behavior therapist.

Table 31.2 Motivation for Behavior Change Scale (MBCS)

Date _____

Name _____

1. Frequency of verbal behavior indicating the client wants treatment:
   a. not at all (   )
   b. a little (   )
   c. a fair amount (   )
   d. much (   )
   e. very much (   )

2. Intensity of desire for treatment as expressed by verbal behavior:
   a. not at all eg. I really don't want to change. (   )
   b. a little intensity eg. I don't want to change but my (wife) (husband) (children) (parents) want me to so I might as well try. (   )
   c. a fair amount of intensity eg. I'm ambivalent about it, sometimes I want to stop (change) and sometimes I don't. (   )
   d. much intensity eg. I guess I really should change. (   )
   e. very much intensity eg. I really want to change, believe me. (   )

3. Number of appointments missed:
   a. cancels or fails to show up for appointments over 60% of the time (   )
   b. cancels or fails to show up for appointments around 40% to 60% of the time (   )
   c. cancels or fails to show up for appointments around 20% to 40% of the time (   )
   d. cancels or fails to show up for appointments around 10% to 20% of the time (   )
   e. cancels or fails to show up for appointments around 5% to 10% of the time (   )
   f. rarely and then with good reasons (   )

4. Record keeping:
   a. never keeps records as required (   )
   b. keeps records occasionally and omits some data (   )
   c. keeps records occasionally and includes all relevant data (   )
   d. keeps records consistently but omits some data (   )
   e. keeps records consistently and includes all relevant data (   )

5. Does homework assignments:
   a. not at all (   )
   b. occasionally and incomplete (   )
   c. regularly but does not complete assignment (   )
   d. regularly and completes assignment (   )

6. During the therapy session the client:
   a. refuses to answer any questions (   )
   b. refuses to answer some of the questions with evasion (   )
   c. tries to answer some questions without evasion (   )
   d. tries to answer most of the questions without evasion (   )
   e. answers all of the questions without evasion (   )

7. Pays attention (looks at therapist, answers questions promptly, follows directions easily, etc.):
   a. not at all (   )
   b. a little (   )
   c. a fair amount of the time (   )
   d. most of the time (   )
   e. all of the time (   )

Table 31.2 (continued)

8. Scheduling of appointments (assuming work or school schedule permits):
   a. is available only on a particular hour during the week ( )
   b. is available on either a particular morning, afternoon or evening ( )
   c. is available any time on a particular day ( )
   d. is available on any one of three days ( )
   e. is available any time the therapist has an opening ( )

The Attitude of Treatment Agents Toward Individuals Who Engage in Drug Abuse

From a behavioral point of view, drug abuse is considered a faulty habit like any other maladaptive behavior and is not considered to be a symptom of some emotional illness. The client is told that the misuse of drugs does not indicate a weak will, mental illness, a wish to slowly kill oneself, or moral degeneracy. He is told only that it is a behavior that can be changed if he wants to change it. The therapist indicates that in general it is probably a good idea to give up a drug habit because of expense, possible secondary reactions such as infections, and dependency on drugs as reinforcers or enriching one's reinforcement repertoire.

OUTLINE OF TREATMENT

Use of Other Procedures

A thorough treatment approach should include modification of antecedent conditions associated with drug-taking behavior. Techniques such as covert reinforcement, thought stopping, relaxation, and systematic desensitization should be used to neutralize the influence of the antecedent. Since by association, many previously neutral cues become attached to the behavior maintained by reinforcement and by the reinforcing effects of the drug itself (Cahoon and Crosby, 1972; Wikler, 1965), it is also necessary to focus directly on the addictive behavior itself by altering the consequences.

Thought stopping (Wolpe, 1969) can be used to decrease positive thoughts of drug use which act as cues for the drug taking behavior. The procedure consists of the client yelling stop to himself subvocally as soon as the thought arises. Since you cannot think of two things at the same time, saying the word "stop" reciprocally inhibits the maladaptive thought.

In the office, the client raises his right index finger and the therapist yells stop. The client is then instructed to do it on his own, alternating with the therapist. The client is told that whenever he has the thought, he should use the thought-stopping technique.

In the treatment of drug abuse, the client should use it on any positive thoughts about drugs, such as "Boy, it would be great to be high" or "It would be so easy to see——and get some stuff."

Relaxation could be taught as an incompatible response to anxiety, and can be used as a self-control technique (Cautela, 1969) whenever the client experiences anxiety and in particular situations that are followed by drug taking. Usually addicts have exhibited social anxiety and a low self-esteem. In the office, the use of assertive training is useful in relieving social anxiety and often results in an increase in self-esteem.

Other Training

A complete treatment program would have to provide the client with other reinforcers once the previously reinforcing drug behavior is modified. This would include working on educational, vocational, social, and recreational aspects of the client's life. The covert conditioning techniques can also be used for this purpose.

For example, if the client has a poor self-concept consisting of negative thoughts about himself, you can decrease the thoughts by using thought stopping and increase positive thoughts by using covert positive reinforcement. If he needs more social reinforcers, the therapist can teach him social behaviors. In, for example, teaching him to ask girls out, assertive training and covert positive reinforcement can be used. This would include teaching the client what to say, and covertly reinforcing him for practicing the behavior in imagination. If the client needs to lose weight, covert sensitization and covert reinforcement can be used.

The client may also need a new setting where his old behavior is not reinforced. This may include getting a new job. If the client reports anxiety about interviewing for jobs, covert reinforcement can be used to desensitize him to the situation.

It appears that from evidence available concerning behavioral treatment of drug addiction, and the success of various behavioral techniques in modifying behavior, that a useful model for treatment should contain the following elements:

1. A behavioral analysis of drug abuse which determines the antecedents and consequences of drug-taking behavior.

2. Modifying antecedent conditions by relaxation (Cautela, 1969; Wolpe, 1969), systematic desensitization (Cautela, 1969; Wolpe, 1969), assertive training (Salter, 1949; Lesser, 1967), and covert reinforcement (Cautela, 1970a).

3. Modification of the consequences by aversive conditioning, especially covert conditioning which renders itself useful as a self-control technique, and

the evidence presented thus far that the covert conditioning procedures appear to have validity. Consequences can also be modified by reinforcing responses antagonistic to drug-taking behavior such as the thought, "If I take the drug, I will screw up my life." The reinforcement of alternative responses such as listening to music, visiting a friend, or reading.

4. As indicated throughout the paper, a comprehensive treatment plan should involve the modification of responses in addition to drug-taking behavior. The behavioral techniques cited should be employed to enhance vocational and educational adjustment, increase social interaction that is reinforcing, change self-concepts (Krop et al., 1971, 1973), and improve sexual and marital adjustments.

REFERENCES

Ayllon, T., and Azrin, N. *The Token Economy.* New York: Appleton-Century-Crofts, 1968.

Anant, S. S. Treatment of alcoholics and drug addicts by verbal aversion techniques. *Intern. J. Addictions 3*: 381-388, 1968.

Ascher, L. M. Covert extinction: An Experimental test. Unpublished data, State University of New York, Fredonia, 1970.

Ashem, B., and Donner, L. Covert sensitization with alcoholics: A controlled replication. *Behav. Res. Therapy* 6: 7-12, 1968.

Barber, T. X., and Hahn, K. Physiological and subjective responses to pain producing stimulation under hypnotically suggested and waking-imagined analgesia. *J. Abnormal Soc. Psychol.* 65: 411-418, 1962.

Barber, T. X., Spanos, N. P., and Chaves, J. F. *"Hypnosis," Directed Imagining, and Human Capabilities.* New York: Pergamon, In press.

Barlow, D. H., Leitenberg, H., and Agras, W. S. Experimental control of sexual deviation through manipulation of the noxious scene in covert sensitization. *J. Abnormal Psychol. 72*, 596-601, 1969.

Barlow, D. H., Leitenberg, H., Agras, W. S., Callahan, E. J., and Moore, R. C. The contribution of therapeutic instruction to covert sensitization. *Behav. Res. Therapy 10*, 411-415, 1972.

Blanchard, E. B., and Draper, D. O. Treatment of a rodent phobia by covert reinforcement: A single subject experiment. *Behav. Therapy 4*, 559-564, 1973.

Blanchard, E. B., Libet, J. M., and Young, L. D. The use of apneic aversion and covert sensitization in the treatment of a hydrocarbon inhalation addiction: A case study. *J. Behav. Therapy Exp. Psychiat.* In press.

Boudin, H. M. Contingency contracting as a therapeutic tool in the deceleration of amphetamine use. *Behav. Therapy 3*, 604-608, 1972.

Boudin, H. M., and Valentine, V. E., III. Behavioral techniques as an alternative to methadone maintenance. Unpublished manuscript, University of Florida, 1973.

Cahoon, D., and Crosby, C. A learning approach to chronic drug use: Sources of reinforcement. *Behav. Therapy 3*, 64-73, 1972.

Callahan, E. J., and Leitenberg, H. Aversion therapy for sexual deviation: Contingent shock and covert sensitization. *J. Abnormal Psychol. 81*, 60-73, 1973.

Cautela, J. R. Treatment of compulsive behavior by covert sensitization. *Psychol. Rec. 16*, 33-41, 1966.

Cautela, J. R. Covert sensitization, *Psychol. Rep. 20*, 459-468, 1967.

Cautela, J. R. Behavior therapy and self-control: Techniques and implications. In C. M. Franks (ed.) *Behavior Therapy: Appraisal and Status*. New York: McGraw-Hill, 1969.

Cautela, J. R. Covert reinforcement. *Behav. Therapy 2*, 33-50, 1970a.

Cautela, J. R. The treatment of alcoholism by covert sensitization. *Psychotherapy 7*, 86-90, 1970b.

Cautela, J. R. Treatment of smoking by covert sensitization. *Psychol. Rep. 26*, 415-520, 1970c.

Cautela, J. R. Covert extinction. *Behav. Therapy 2*, 192-200, 1971.

Cautela, J. R. The treatment of over-eating by covert conditioning. *Psychotherapy 9*, 211-216, 1972.

Cautela, J. R. Covert processes and behavior modifications. *J. Nervous Mental Disease 157*, 27-36, 1973.

Cautela, J. R., and Kastenbaum, R. A reinforcement survey schedule for use in therapy, training and research. *Psychol. Rep. 20*, 1115-1130, 1967.

Cautela, J. R., Walsh, K., and Wish, P. The use of covert reinforcement in the modification of attitudes toward the mentally retarded. *J. Psychol. 77*, 257-260, 1971.

Cautela, J. R., Steffen, J., and Wish, P. Covert reinforcement: An experimental test. *J. Clin. Consult.* In press.

Curtis, R. H., and Presley, A. S. The extinction of homosexual behavior by covert sensitization: A case study. *Behav. Tes. Therapy 10*, 81-83, 1972.

Droppa, D. C. Behavioral treatment of drug addiction: A review and analysis. *Intern. J. Addictions 8* (1), 143-161, 1973.

Duehn, W. D., and Shannon, C. *Covert Sensitization in the Public High School: Short Term Group Treatment of Male Adolescent Drug Abusers*. Paper presented (revised version) at the 100th Annual Forum of the National Conference on Social Welfare, May 31, 1973, Atlantic City, New Jersey.

Flannery, R. B. A laboratory analogue of two covert reinforcement procedures. *J. Behav. Therapy Exp. Psychiat. 3*, 171-177, 1972.

Fleiger, D. L., and Zingle, H. W. *Covert Sensitization Treatment with Alcoholics*. Unpublished Doctoral Dissertation, University of Alberta, 1971.

Gotestam, K. G., and Melin, G. L. Covert extinction of amphetamine addiction. *Behav. Therapy 5*, 90-92, 1974.

Gotestam, K. G., Melin, G. L., and Dockens, W. S. *Behavioral Program for Intravenous Amphetamine Addicts*. Paper presented at International Symposium on Behavior Modification, October 4-6, 1972, Minneapolis, Minnesota.

Hunt, W. A., Barnett, L. W., and Branch, L. G. Relapse rates in addiction programs, *J. Clin. Consult. Psychol. 4*, 455-456, 1971.

Irey, P. A. *Covert Sensitization of Cigarette Smokers with High and Low Extraversion Scores*. Unpublished Masters Thesis, University of Southern Illinois at Carbondale, 1972.

Janda, L. H., and Rimm, D. C. Covert sensitization in the treatment of obesity. *J. Abnormal Psychol.* 80, 37-42, 1972.

Kolvin, I. "Aversive imagery" treatment in adolescents. *Behav. Res. Therapy 5*, 245-248, 1967.

Kraft, T. Successful treatment of a case of chronic barbituate addiction. *Brit. J. Addictions 64*, 115-120, 1969a.

Kraft, T. Treatment of drinamyl addiction. *Intern. J. Addictions 4*, 59-64, 1969b.

Kraft, T. Successful treatment of "drinamyl" addicts and associated personality changes. *Canad. Psychiat. Assoc. J. 15*, 223-227, 1970a.

Kraft, T. Treatment of drinamyl addiction. *J. Nervous Mental Disease 150*, 138-144, 1970b.

Krop, H., Calhoon, B., and Verrier, R. Modification of the "self-concept" of emotionally disturbed children by covert reinforcement. *Behav. Therapy 2*, 201-204, 1971.

Krop, H., Perez, F., and Beaudoin, C. Modification of "self-concept" of psychiatric patients by covert reinforcement. In R. D. Rubin, J. P. Brady, and J. D. Henderson (eds.) *Advances in Behavior Therapy*, Vol. 4. New York: Academic, 1973.

Krop, H., Messinger, J., and Reiner, C. Increasing eye contact by covert reinforcement. *Inter. Devel. In press.*

Lang, P. J. The mechanics of desensitization and the laboratory study of human fear. In C. M. Franks (ed.) *Behavior Therapy: Appraisal and Status.* New York: McGraw-Hill, 1969.

Lesser, E. Behavior therapy with a narcotics user: A case report. *Behav. Res. Therapy 5*, 251-252, 1967.

Liberman, R. Aversive conditioning of drug addicts: A pilot study. *Behav. Res. Therapy 6*, 229-231, 1968.

Manno, B., and Marston, A. R. Weight reduction as a function of negative reinforcement (sensitization) versus positive covert reinforcement. *Behav. Tes. Therapy 10*, 201-207, 1972.

Miller, P. M., and Hersen, M. *A Quantitative Measurement System for Alcoholism Treatment and Research.* Unpublished manuscript, Veterans Administration Center and University of Mississippi Medical Center, Jackson, Mississippi, 1972.

O'Brien, J. S., and Raynes, A. E. Unpublished data, Drug Detoxification Ward, Boston City Hospital. Personal communication, 1973.

O'Brien, J. S., Raynes, A. E., and Patch, V. D. An operant reinforcement system to improve ward behavior in inpatient drug addicts. *J. Behav. Therapy Exp. Psychiat. 2*, 239-242, 1971.

O'Brien, J. S., Raynes, A. E., and Patch, V. D. Treatment of heroin addiction with aversion therapy, relaxation training and systematic desensitization. *Behav. Res. Therapy 10*, 77-80, 1972.

Primo, R. V. *Covert Avoidance Learning: A Refined Covert Sensitization Method for the Modification of Smoking Behavior.* Unpublished Doctoral Dissertation, University of Pittsburgh, 1972.

Raymond, M. J. The treatment of addiction by conditioning with apomorphine. *Behav. Res. Therapy 1*, 287-291, 1964.

Sachs, L. B., and Ingram, G. L. Covert sensitization as a treatment for weight control. *Psychol. Rep. 30*, 971-974, 1972.

Salter, A. *Conditioned Reflex Therapy.* New York: Capricorn Books, 1949.

Schwartz, G. E., and Shapiro, D. Biofeedback and essential hypertension: Current findings and theoretical concerns. *Seminars in Psychiatry.* In press.

Segal, B., and Simms, J. Covert sensitization with a homosexual: A controlled replication. *J. Clin. Consult. 39*, 259-263, 1972.

Skinner, B. F. *Contingencies of Reinforcement.* New York: Appleton-Century-Crofts, 1969.

Steffen, J. *Covert Reinforcement with Schizophrenics.* Paper presented at the annual meeting of the Association for the Advancement of Behavior Therapy, Washington, D. C., 1971.

Steinfeld, G. J., Rautio, E. A., Egan, M., and Rice, A. H. *The Use of Covert Sensitization with Narcotic Addicts (Further Comments).* Unpublished manuscript, Federal Correctional Institution, Danbury, Connecticut, 1972.

Stuart, R. B. Behavioral control of over-eating. *Behav. Res. Therapy 5*, 357-365, 1967.

Wikler, A. Conditioning factors in opiate addiction and relapse. In D. M. Wilner and G. G. Kassebaum (eds.) *Narcotics.* New York: McGraw-Hill, 1965.

Wiscoki, P. A. A covert reinforcement program for the treatment of test anxiety: Brief report. *Behav. Therapy 4*, 264-266, 1973a.

Wisocki, P. A. The successful treatment of heroin addiction by covert conditioning techniques. *J. Behav. Therapy Exp. Psychiat, 4*, 55-61, 1973b.

Wolpe, J. Conditioned inhibition of craving in drug addiction: A pilot study. *Behav. Res. Therapy 2*, 285-288, 1965.

Wolpe, J. *The Practice of Behavior Therapy.* New York: Pergamon, 1969.

Chapter 32

Use of Covert Conditioning in the Behavioral Treatment of a Drug-Dependent College Dropout*

Raymond B. Flannery, Jr.†

Summary — A drug-dependent, college dropout was treated successfully with covert conditioning in a behaviorally oriented treatment program. The drug-taking behavior was not altered directly. Attention is drawn to these findings as well as to a proposed treatment program for heroin-addicted college dropouts.

Two problems of growing national importance for counseling and clinical psychologists in university clinics are the drug-dependent student (Eells, 1968) and the college dropout (Keniston, 1965). This article reports the application of a behavior modification treatment program for a drug-dependent college dropout.

CASE REPORT

History

Christine was a 20-year-old female, the eldest of five children, and a

*Reprinted with permission from the *Journal of Counseling Psychology*, 1972, 19, 547–550. © The American Psychological Association 1972.

†The author wishes to thank Joseph R. Cautela of Boston College for his consulting supervision in the case being reported.

self-defined member of the youth subculture. She referred herself to the clinic because of severe depression. The presenting problems were extensive. They included her withdrawal from college at the end of her second year (2.8 grade point average) because of its meaninglessness to her; continual family arguments; and interpersonal problems with her alcoholic, drug-abusing boyfriend with whom she lives on weekends were recurring difficulties. Somatization included persistent headaches and insomnia. To escape these tensions, the client used marijuana at least 2 times per day, 7 days a week and LSD usually twice a month. Her reactions to LSD ingestion were always terrifying. At the time of referral, she was still using LSD, and taking prescribed Darvon for her headaches.

The general consensus of the staff was that Christine needed either long-term individual analytically oriented therapy or a group therapy experience for drug abusers. At the time of referral, no such openings were available in the clinic's programs. The urgency of the client's distress required some form of immediate treatment. She was referred to me with the hope that a behavioral treatment program could reduce her anxiety until an opening occurred in one of the two previously mentioned treatment modes. While understanding the staff's choice of alternatives for the client's problems, I did not assume that a behavior modification approach to any of the presenting problems need necessarily be precluded. A 12-session contract was negotiated with the client.

METHOD

It was hypothesized that the use of drugs by the client in the present case appeared to be a learned, maladaptive response. It was hypothesized that teaching the client appropriate behaviors to deal with her several problems would eliminate her use of drugs. Accordingly, the use of drugs was never discussed by the therapist. In this way reinforcing attention was not given to the maladaptive behaviors (Krasner, 1962). All procedures were taught as self-control techniques (Cautela, 1969).

Procedure

Treatment began by teaching Christine the basic skills necessary for fielding questions and diplomatically asserting herself. The technique chosen was behavioral rehearsals (Lazarus, 1966). Various problems that the family needed to discuss (e.g., school withdrawal, her boyfriend) were rehearsed in the office with the therapist. The client then was instructed to spend 10 minutes each evening conversing with her family. The change was dramatic and in the expected direction within 2 weeks. Fewer arguments occurred and the family spent more time communicating.

The central assumptions the client made about herself were modified next. First, she was instructed to thought stop (Wolpe, 1958) about any negative self-referent statements she made to herself. Then, she was instructed in the use of coverant control therapy. This technique, introduced by Homme (1965) and supported by initial clinical findings (Johnson, 1971; Mahoney, 1971) consists of having the individual make positive self-statements and then reward himself for making those statements.

This procedure was adapted for Christine in the following manner. The therapist and the client carefully prepared four positive self-referent statements the client felt she could state honestly. These were written on cards and included that she was pretty, pleasant to be with, a good conversationalist in a group, and intellectually bright enough to succeed in college. The client was instructed to recite each of the four statements five times, and then to reward herself by reading any book she enjoyed for 15 minutes. Reading was chosen as a reinforcer because of its importance to academic achievement. This entire procedure was repeated three times per day. One week later, Christine announced that she had signed up for courses for the next semester.

The remaining treatment sessions were spent practicing behavioral rehearsals (Lazarus, 1966) in an attempt to solve Christine's problems in asserting herself at work and with her boyfriend. Reports from both Christine and her parents indicated significantly improved family communication, more self-assertive behaviors with her parents, peers, and her employer, little depression, no headaches, no insomnia, and no use of drugs. Therapy terminated after 12 sessions.

Two weeks later, Christine called and stated that her medically prescribed birth control method had failed and that she was pregnant. All previous tests for pregnancy before and during her treatment at the clinic had been negative. However, the client was 16 weeks pregnant. She and her parents had arranged for a legal, therapeutic interruption. Since severe depression had been one of her initial presenting problems, a second 12-session contract was negotiated.

Christine's therapeutic learning was evident during the interim hospitalization. She went through the saline-induced therapeutic interruption without incapacitating fear, enlisted the aid of her parents, and withstood the loss of her part-time job as well as the loss of emotional support from her boyfriend. Upon discharge from the hospital, she did in fact begin her course work and at no time did she revert to drug use or dependence.

The second 12-session treatment program began after hospitalization and dealth with two problems — Christine's therapeutic interruption and her indecision about leaving her male friend. Thought stopping (Wolpe, 1958) for visual images of the fetus (which she had actually seen) was immediately introduced, and the recurring image was eliminated permanently within 3 weeks.

Covert modeling (Cautela, 1971; Cautela, Flannery, & Hanley, 1971) and coverant control therapy (Homme, 1965) were chosen as procedures to deal with the approach-avoidance behavior toward her male friend.

Covert modeling is a procedure in which the therapist writes out a script

incorporating the selected behaviors to be emitted, the nature of the dis-
criminating stimuli, the contingencies of reinforcement, and the appropriate
affect for a specific environmental situation. The individual is instructed to
imagine a model performing the appropriate behaviors as the therapist reads
the script. Later, the person is asked to imagine himself emitting the same
behaviors.

Christine was instructed to imagine a college senior calmly making a
decision (any decision) about continuing a 4-year relationship with her boyfriend. The scene included the senior on a warm sunny day deciding not to be
distraught about reaching a decision. The model made her decision and calmly
laid down to rest on her bed and enjoyed the warmth of the sun steaming
through the window. The client was instructed to practice this scene at least 10
times per day. Two weeks later, she stated her desire to break off the relationship with her boyfriend.

Coverant control therapy was again introduced as outlined above. The
statements this time included that she would not be without a mate for life, that
she could complete her schooling even though she would see the former
boyfriend, and that she was a confident person because of her many assets. The
following week (Session 9) she returned and stated that she had left her male
friend and was living with two female peers. She remained in school, obtained
a part-time job, sought out new male friends, a continued to refrain from drugs.
Treatment was terminated after Session 9 at the client's request.

RESULTS

A 6-month follow-up of self-reports from both Christine and her parents
indicated that she had completed her course work with good grades, had dated
frequently, and had better family communication. No somatic complaints or
depression were reported, and Christine said she felt in control of her future for
the first time in her life. She had decided to take one semester off to work for a
veterinarian to see if she would like a career in veterinary medicine. This
interim evaluation of a career was a highly adaptive behavior and one recommended often by university counselors. This was a mature response and not a
maladaptive avoidance of school. Christine acknowledged the use of marijuana and LSD on four occasions for enjoyment in a peer-group setting. This
amount of drug usage appears to be an emerging norm (Barber, 1970, p. 81). In
the interim, her former boyfriend committed himself voluntarily to a hospital
for extended psychiatric care.

DISCUSSION

No case study can present conclusive evidence for the effects of differing treatment procedures on the observed outcome (Paul, 1969). Nevertheless, the rapid changes in the expected direction when coverant control therapy and covert modeling were introduced to Christine in an attempt to get her to return to college and make a decision about her boyfriend lends some support to the differential effectiveness of the procedures. The present findings are similar to previously reported clinical evidence for coverant control therapy (Homme, 1965; Johnson, 1971; Mahoney, 1971) and covert modeling (Flannery, 1972). As with previous research for coverant control therapy (Johnson, 1971), it was then necessary to teach the client new behavioral responses. However, it was most encouraging that the two pressing problems (college withdrawal and drug dependence) could be treated with such success in so short a time period (21 sessions).

While drug abuse was reduced, the present rationale of indirectly modifying drug behavior as causative in this reduction is more difficult to evaluate. Certainly, the client's spontaneous statements that she no longer needed drugs because she had learned alternative ways to solve problems during treatment tends to support this hypothesis. Christine's ability to assert herself with her friends and refuse drugs would also appear to support this reasoning. The lack of abnormal drug usage beyond conventional norms (Blum, 1971) after treatment suggests even further support. However, fortuitous life events (Wolpe, 1958) such as rooming out and having new dates may have augmented the treatment program. This was particularly possible during the follow-up period. Therefore, it might be beneficial for other college dropouts who use drugs as a way of reducing tension because of maladaptive coping behaviors to try such treatment as discussed here.

The question naturally arises as to whether this same form of treatment could be applied to heroin addicts. This treatment probably would not be effective because of the immediacy of the reinforcement. In cases such as these, it would appear that the maladaptive drug response itself would have to be extinguished. While Lesser (1967) and Wolpe (1965) have used faradic shock to modify this response, both Lesser (1969) and Wisocki (P. Wisocki, personal communication, May 1971) reported the successful application of covert conditioning techniques, particularly covert sensitization (Cautela, 1966) to maladaptive drug usage. One might conceptualize a covert conditioning treatment program for the college dropout addicted to heroin in the following manner. Covert sensitization would be used to modify the heroin-addicted behavior itself. Since what is learned in the drug state may not transfer to the nondrug state (Wisocki, 1970), covert sensitization might need to be employed before, during, and after withdrawal. Covert reinforcement (Cautela, 1970) might then be employed to modify attitudes toward college and educators. Coverant control therapy (Homme, 1965) could be introduced to increase the student's positive self-reference statements, and finally covert modeling (Cautela, 1971) could be applied to teach the student any behaviors necessary for successful adaptation to the classroom environment.

Two further points are of clinical importance. The first is the apparent value of teaching all procedures as self-control techniques (Cautela, 1969). The present client demonstrated highly adaptive behaviors to an entirely dissimilar problem (the abortion) under circumstances of severe stress for any woman. This finding has been noted previously (Flannery, 1972) and would suggest the important need for research in this area. Marston and Feldman (1970) have begun such experimental inquiry. Second, the question of ethics is raised at times regarding coverant control therapy. From my clinical experience, writing positive self-referent statements with the client is a practical necessity if the responses are to be meaningful to the client. For example, for one woman, a statement that she was a nice person was not acceptable since the word nice connoted adversive life experiences. Writing the statements with the client can insure his or her freedom of choice (Bandura, 1969, p. 84) and an efficacious treatment outcome.

The present data and similar research (Lesser, 1969; P. Wisocki, personal communication, May 1971) suggest that behavior modification treatment programs incorporating covert conditioning techniques may be applied successfully to the problem of drug abuse. These findings point to the need for controlled experimental research on this problem so that the practicing clinician can be assured of the internal and external validity of these covert procedures (Goldstein, Heller, & Sechrest, 1966, pp. 23–39).

REFERENCES

Bandura, A. *Principles of behavior modification.* New York: Holt, Rinehart & Winston, 1969.

Barber, T. *LSD, marijuana, yoga, and hypnosis.* Chicago: Aldine, 1970.

Blum, R. To wear a nostradamus hat: Drugs and America. *Journal of Social Issues,* 1971, **27**, 89–106.

Cautela, J. Treatment of compulsive behavior by covert sensitization. *Psychological Record,* 1966, **16**, 33–41.

Cautela, J. Behavior therapy and self-control: Techniques and implications. In C. M. Franks (Ed.), *Behavior therapy: Appraisal and status.* New York: McGraw-Hill, 1969.

Cautela, J. Covert reinforcement. *Behavior Therapy,* 1970, **1**, 33–50.

Cautela J. Covert modeling. Paper presented at the meeting of the Association for the Advancement of Behavior Therapy, Washington, D.C., September 1971.

Cautela, J., Flannery, R., Jr., & Hanley, S. Covert modeling: An experimental test. Unpublished manuscript, Boston College, 1971.

Eells, K. Marijuana and LSD: A survey of one college campus. *Journal of Counseling Psychology,* 1968, **15**, 459–467.

Flannery, R., Jr. The use of covert conditioning in the behavioral treatment of an agoraphobic woman. *Psychotherapy: Theory, Research, and Practice,* 1972, in press.

Goldstein, A., Heller, K., & Sechrest, L. *Psychotherapy and the psychology of behavior change.* New York: Wiley, 1966.

Homme, L. Control of coverants, the operants of the mind. *Psychological Record,* 1965, **15**, 501–511.

Johnson, W. Some applications of Homme's coverant control therapy: Two case reports. *Behavior Therapy,* 1971, **2**, 240–248.

Keniston, K. *The uncommitted.* New York: Harcourt, Brace & World, 1965.

Krasner, L. The therapist as a social reinforcement machine. In H. Strupp & L. Luborsky (Eds.), *Research in psychotherapy.* Washington, D.C.: American Psychological Association, 1962.

Lazarus, A. Behaviour rehearsal vs. non-directive therapy vs. advice in effecting behaviour change. *Behaviour Research and Therapy,* 1966, **4**, 209–212.

Lesser, E. Behavior therapy with a narcotics user: A case report. *Behavior Research and Therapy,* 1967, **5**, 251–252.

Lesser, E. A college senior. *Psychology Today,* 1969, **3**, 10.

Mahoney, M. The self-management of covert behavior: A case study. *Behavior Therapy,* 1971, **2**, 575–578.

Marston, A., & Feldman, S. Toward use of self-control in behavior modification. Paper presented at the meeting of the American Psychological Association, Miami Beach, September 1970.

Paul, G. Behavior modification research: Design and tactics. In C. M. Franks (Ed.), *Behavior therapy: Appraisal and status.* New York: McGraw-Hill, 1969.

Wisocki, P. The empirical evidence of covert sensitization in the treatment of alcoholism; An evaluation. Paper presented at the meeting of the Association for the Advancement of Behavior Therapy, Miami Beach, September 1970.

Wolpe, J. *Psychotherapy by reciprocal inhibition. Stanford: Stanford University Press, 1958.*

Wolpe, J. Conditioned inhibition of craving in drug addiction: A pilot experiment, *Behavior Research and Therapy,* 1965, **2**, 285–288.

Chapter 33

Sequential Phases of Covert Reinforcement and Covert Sensitization in the Treatment of Homosexuality*

Sherrill R. Kendrick and James P. McCullough

Summary — A two-phase therapy plan was used in the treatment of a 21-year-old male homosexual. Following a one week baseline period during which he counted the daily frequency of homosexual and heterosexual urges, homosexual fantasies were used for covert reinforcement of heterosexual urges. The second phase of treatment consisted of decreasing the daily frequency of homosexual urges by covert sensitization.

Covert reinforcement (Cautela, 1970) and covert sensitization (Cautela, 1967) provide the behavior therapist with an effective rationale and technique for treating certain homosexual behaviors. Homme (1965) expanded an earlier Skinnerian position by stating that the private world of the individual is not made of any different stuff than the world outside the skin; hence, "private behavioral events obey the same laws as non-private ones" (p. 501).

Premack (1959) demonstrated how the experimenter might use response frequency to identify potential reinforcers. A high frequency response can be a reinforcer of a lower frequency response. Homme derived from this idea his program of "coverant control". His central thesis is that the subject can

*Reprinted with permission from the *Journal of Behavior Therapy and Experimental Psychiatry*, 1972, *3*, 229–231. © Pergamon Press.

increase specific private behavior if reinforcing behavior occurs immediately following the occurrence of the private behavior. This principle was used in the treatment of an undergraduate male student who came to the clinic complaining of homosexual problems.

Case Background

S was a 21-yr-old white male who presented himself to The University Psychology Clinic because of homosexual problems, periodic episodes of depression and stuttering. The speech defect was judged to be mild and assertive training was successfully used to modify this behavior. Since S's depression appeared to be elicited by his sexual difficulties, it was felt that it could be resolved by dealing with the client's sexual habits.

S said that he had had about 15 homosexual encounters since the age of 17. He related a history of homosexual experiences which began in the second grade. He usually assumed the aggressor role. There had been no homosexual contacts since September, 1969. S stated that he was occasionally aroused by females and that he had had about 15 dates during the past 4 yr. He said that he wanted to achieve a heterosexual adjustment. We decided that even though his heterosexual responses were less frequent and less intense than the homosexual ones, they did provide a basis for shifting his primary sexual interest from males to females.

TREATMENT PROCEDURES AND OUTCOME

Formal treatment began on a once per week schedule in September, 1970. S was encouraged to increase the frequency of heterosexual contacts and to make sexual advances on dates. Part of each session was used as a sexual training period, and the client was given the opportunity to discuss his experiences on previous dates and to receive feedback from the therapist. He continued to date throughout the year though his heterosexual experiences stopped short of sexual intercourse.

A 7-day baseline period was established by having S count both his homosexual and heterosexual urges during his waking hours (Fig. 1). A sexual urge was defined as a thought plus a concomitant emotion. The client was given the Reinforcement Survey Schedule (Cautela and Kastenbaum, 1967). The fantasies judged by S to be the most vivid and pleasant were homosexual. Since the homosexual urges were more frequent than the heterosexual urges, the former might be used as a reinforcer to increase the frequency of the latter. We decided to use several homosexual fantasies of equal strength to reinforce heterosexual imagery following the covert reinforcement paradigm.

During phase 1, the client was instructed to imagine himself participating in a heterosexual activity and that contact was progressively becoming more explicitly sexual. When the heterosexual image became clear, S was told to visualize a homosexual image (the reinforcer). He was told to terminate the reinforcer when he signaled to the therapist that its image was clear. This sequence was repeated, at 1-min intervals, until five trials were completed. A set of five trials was given at the beginning and again at the end of each session. S practiced five times per day at home during this phase.

Following Cautela's program, S was shifted each week to an increasing ratio of heterosexual to homosexual images until a 5:1 ratio was achieved in the sixth week. Figure 1 shows the daily frequency of urges which occurred outside the therapy sessions throughout Phase 1 (days 8–42). S's average number of heterosexual urges per week increased to 31 during this phase. His heterosexual base rate was 21 per week.

Phase II of treatment began on Day 43 and continued for 14 days. Covert sensitization was used to decrease the frequency of homosexual urges. The homosexual fantasies were now paired with verbally induced nausea while the heterosexual imagery was reinforced by using highly reinforcing nonsexual imagery from the Reinforcement Survey Schedule. Five sensitization pairings and five covert reinforcement trials were administered during each therapy session; and the client also practiced the sensitization pairings 10 times daily at home. The increasing frequency of heterosexual urges and decrease of homosexual urges are illustrated in Fig. 1. (Four days of data relating to the homosexual urges were lost (days 46, 49, 51 and 52); but our impression was that the trend of the lost days was consistent with the recorded days during this period.) The average frequency of heterosexual urges per week was 30. For the first time, the frequency of homosexual urges was consistently below that of the heterosexual urges.

Two months and 3 months after treatment the patient was seen to evaluate

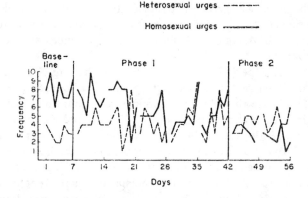

Fig. 33.1. The daily homosexual and heterosexual urge frequency compared across stages of treatment.

the effects of therapy. He reported that he had been dating one girl steadily. He also said that his homosexual urges were infrequent and much less intense than before treatment. He was encouraged at both sessions to employ covert reinforcement and covert sensitization procedures whenever he wished to modify the frequency and quality of his sexual urges. He stated he was doing so irregularly.

DISCUSSION

The present case study supports the view of Homme and Cautela that similar behavioral laws are operative in both covert and overt processes. Success attended the application of covert sensitization and covert reinforcement to the covert processes of the client. Homosexual imagery, used contingently as a reinforcer, increased the frequency of heterosexual behavior. During the fifth treatment week (days 29–35), S had a nocturnal emission that, for the first time in his life, solely involved heterosexual imagery. The dream content included sexual intercourse, producing in the client emotions he had never experienced in real life. This event served as an additional reinforcer to him and suggested to him that an internal change was actually occurring. The frequency of heterosexual contacts increased as treatment progressed. S dated more frequently and engaged in petting more often on dates. He also sought out and talked to more female friends on campus than he had done prior to treatment.

We were both convinced that the client's record keeping was as reliable as possible. He was a conscientious person who accepted the fact that accurate record keeping was an important part of his therapy.

The use of homosexual imagery to reinforce heterosexual imagery appears to be a useful therapeutic tool for subjects who are not actively engaged in overt homosexual behavior and who can to some extent be aroused by females.

REFERENCES

Cautela J. R. (1970) Covert reinforcement, *Behav. Therapy* 1, 33–49.
Cautela J. R. (1967) Covert sensitization, *Psychol. Rep.* 20, 459–468.
Cautela J. R. and Kastenbaum R. (1967) A reinforcement survey schedule for use in therapy, training and research, *Psychol. Rep.* 20, 1115–1130.
Homme L. E. (1965) Perspectives in psychology. XXIV. Control of coverants, the operants of the mind, *Psychol. Rec.* 15, 501–511.
Premack D. (1959) Toward empirical behavior laws: I. Positive reinforcement, *Psychol. Rev.* 66, 219–233.

Chapter 34

The Treatment of Over-Eating by Covert Conditioning*

Joseph R. Cautela

Summary — The paper presents a treatment procedure for the modification of over-eating behavior which punishes particular responses (using covert sensitization) and reinforces responses antagonistic to eating (using covert reinforcement). The application of other behavior modification techniques (e.g., relaxation, desensitization, stimulus control) to change behaviors thought to be related to maladaptive eating also is described. Results which suggest the efficacy of such approaches to the problem of over-eating are reviewed, and problems encountered in the use of covert conditioning techniques are discussed.

A major assumption of behavior theory is that behavior is influenced by the consequences that follow the behavior. Evidence (Skinner, 1969) indicates that if the frequency of a particular behavior is to be decreased, a combination of punishment for the behavior and reinforcement for antagonistic behavior is most effective.

It is the purpose of this paper to present a treatment procedure for the modification of eating behavior which punishes particular eating responses and reinforces responses antagonistic to eating. A number of studies (Ferster, et al., 1962; Meyer & Crisp, 1964; Harmatz & Lapuc, 1968; Moore & Crum, 1969; Upper & Newton, 1971) indicate that the manipulation of the consequences of eating can be successfully employed to reduce over-eating.

In the procedure to be described both the punishing stimulus and reinforcing stimulus are presented in imagination *via* instructions. The method presenting a punishing stimulus in imagination to decrease behavior is labeled covert sensitization (Cautela, 1966, 1967). The presentation of a reinforcing

---

*Reprinted with permission from *Psychotherapy: Theory, Research and Practice*, 1972, *9*, 211–216.

stimulus in imagination is designated as covert reinforcement (Cautela, 1970). A major assumption of this paper is that an aversive stimulus and a reinforcing stimulus presented in imagination *via* instructions have the same functional relationship to covert and overt behavior as externally presented aversive and reinforcing stimuli. The assumption that covert events obey the same laws as overt events has been held by learning theorists such as Pavlov (1955, p. 285), Skinner (1969, p. 242,) Kimble (1961), and Franks (1967). There is ample experimental evidence that both covert sensitization (Ashem & Donner, 1968; Barlow et al. 1969; Stuart, 1967; Viernstein, 1968; Wagner & Bragg, in press) and covert reinforcement (Cautela et al., in press; Cautela et al., 1971; Flannery, in press; Krop et al., 1971) are effective in the modification of behavior.

DESCRIPTION OF PROCEDURE

After the usual assessment procedure (Cautela, 1968), the client is given a weight questionnaire which is used to determine weight history and eating habits. The patient is also asked to write down everything he eats including the time and place and exact amount. He is also asked to indicate the amount of calories and grams of carbohydrates for each food item. Sometimes just recording eating behavior results in a loss of weight but in the author's experience the loss is only temporary and the client will usually gain weight unless covert sensitization is used.

Data are accumulated for two weeks. Meanwhile during the two sessions (the client is usually seen once a week), the client is tested for clarity of imagery, and the Fear Survey Schedule (Wolpe & Lang, 1964) and the Reinforcement Survey Schedule (Cautela & Kastenbaum, 1967) are administered to determine possible aversive and reinforcing situations that may be presented in imagination.

The client is told that over-eating is a habit which gives him pleasure. The habit consists of eating too much food and food containing more fuel than is necessary to maintain his normal activity. He is told that one way to reduce his food intake is to have him associate particular eating behaviors with something unpleasant and to reward him for not engaging in the maladaptive eating behavior. He is also told that this will be done by asking him to imagine certain unpleasant and pleasant scenes. The client is reassured that he will not develop a dislike for food in general but only for over-eating and eating particular kinds of foods. The client and therapist then agree on the desired loss of weight and keep charts on the progress of weight loss.

After the client turns in his eating habits data on the second week, the therapist circles with a pencil the eating behavior that has to be eliminated. This behavior includes:

(1) eating between meals

(2) eating foods with high caloric content

(3) eating too much food at one sitting (e.g. eating two four-ounce steaks or five lamb chops or too much bread).

The client is simply told that he is to stop engaging in these behaviors and to continue to accumulate the eating data. The client is also asked to weigh himself every day.

At the beginning of the fourth session, the therapist indicates to the patient where he has failed to eliminate the undesirable behavior. At this time, covert sensitization and covert reinforcement are applied to those situations in which he did not eliminate the maladaptive eating behavior.

The Application of Covert Sensitization

The following instructions concern the general applications of covert sensitization given to the client:

I am going to ask you to imagine this scene as vividly as you can. I do not want you to imagine that you are seeing yourself in these situations. I want you to imagine that you are actually in these situations. Do not only try to visualize the scenes, but try to feel, for example, the fork full of food in your hand, or the chair on which you are sitting. Actually smell the warm apple pie on the plate before you. Try to use all of your senses as if you were really there. The scenes I will pick are concerned with situations in which you are about to eat. It is very important that you try to visualize the scenes as clearly as possible and try to actually feel yourself in the situation.

If the client has eaten between meals he is presented with a scene similar to the following:

I want you to imagine that you are walking along the street and as you pass a candy counter, you stop and pick up a few candy bars. As you begin to open the wrapper of the first bar you get a very queasy feeling in the pit of your stomach. You start to feel weak, nauseous, and sick all over. As you raise the candy bar to your mouth, you feel a bitter liquid come up into your throat. You try to swallow it down and put the candy in your mouth. As soon as the candy reaches your lips, you puke. The vomit rushes out all over your hands, the candy, and down the front of your dress. The sidewalk is a mess and people stop to stare at you. Your eyes are burning, and slimy mucous continues to run down your chin and your neck. The sight of all the vomit makes you vomit even more until you can not vomit any more than a little trickle of watery substance. You feel so horrible and so sick, and so embarrassed. You turn and run away from all that mess and feel much better.

A typical covert sensitization scene for eating highly caloric foods is as follows:

I want you to imagine that you are at your dinner table and have just finished your first serving of steak. You reach across the table to get yourself another piece, and just as your hand reaches the plate, you feel a queasy, churning feeling in your stomach. You transfer the steak to your plate and just as you do a bitter spit comes up into your throat and mouth. You swallow it down and raise a piece of meat on your fork. Just as the fork reaches your lips, you puke all over your hand, all over the plate in front of you. The vomit goes all over the table and splashes on the people eating with you. They look at you horrified. You feel miserable, slimy and the sight of the vomit mixed with food particles spread all over the table makes you vomit even more and more. You hurry and get up from the table and rush out of the room and you feel better.

After presentation of each scene which applies to the client, he is questioned concerning the clarity of the scene and how much discomfort he felt. If the client reports that the scene was not clear or he could not get any discomfort from the scene, the scene is presented again in more detail. After the client reports that the scene is clear, he is asked to carefully imagine the scene by himself. Again he is questioned concerning the clarity and degree of discomfort. He is asked to keep practicing the scene until it is clear and discomfort is experienced.

In each session, the scenes are presented to the subject in which he gives in to the temptation to eat and vomits. Then the client presents the same scenes to himself.

Besides the above scenes in which the client gives in to temptation, ten escape (or self-control) scenes are presented in which the client is tempted to eat, feels nauseous, and then decides not to eat. A typical escape scene is:

I want you to imagine that you have just finished eating your meal and you decide to have some dessert. As soon as you make that decision you start to get a funny feeling in the pit of your stomach. You say, 'Oh, no. I will not eat dessert.' Then you immediately feel calm and comfortable.

As in the other scenes the client is asked to repeat the scene to himself. At the end of the session, the client is told to practice each scene performed in the office at least twice a day at his home. He is cautioned to make the scenes as clear as possible and to include a self-control scene with each failure scene.

The client is also instructed to say, "Stop!" to himself and to imagine he is vomiting on food whenever he is tempted to eat maladaptively in real life situations.

At each subsequent session, the client is weighed, and asked if he did all his homework. The therapist then goes over all the eating data from the previous week and covert sensitization is applied where necessary. At this time, daily calorie and carbohydrate maximums are determined and the client is told not to exceed the limit set.

The Application of Covert Reinforcement

Covert reinforcement is employed to increase the probability of behaviors antagonistic to over-eating.

Reinforcers are chosen from the Reinforcement Survey Schedule (RSS) and from questioning the client. The items are then tested for their reinforcing properties. The client is asked to close his eyes and imagine that he is receiving the stimulus, e.g., if the item selected is rock and roll music, the patient is instructed in the following manner:

Choose your favorite rock and roll song — one that you know quite well — and try to imagine that you really hear it. As soon as you feel that you can really hear it, signal me by raising your right index finger.

The client is then questioned about the clarity of the image. Practice receiving the reinforcer is continued until he can imagine it clearly and without any delay.

After a number of reinforcers have been chosen and tested by the client, it is explained to him that these certain items or activities that give him pleasure will be paired in imagination with the behaviors that he finds difficult to do (e.g., walking away from the table after a meal). He is then instructed as follows:

In a minute I am going to ask you to try to relax and close your eyes. Then I will describe a scene to you. When you can imagine the scene as clearly as possible, raise your right index finger. I will then say the word, 'reinforcement.' As soon as I say the word, 'reinforcement,' try to imagine the reinforcing scene we practiced before — the one about your swimming on a hot day, the feeling of the refreshing water, and feeling wonderful. As soon as the reinforcing scene is clear, raise your right index finger. Do you understand the instructions? Remember to try to imagine everything as vividly as possible, as if you were really there. All right, now close your eyes and try to relax.

After the patient has closed his eyes and appears comfortable, the therapist presents a scene such as this one:

You are sitting at home watching TV . . . you say to yourself, 'I think I'll have a piece of pie.' You get up to go to the pantry. Then you say, 'This is stupid. I don't want to be a fat pig.' (Reinforcement)

Other examples of covert reinforcement scenes are:

You are at home eating steak. You are just about to reach for your second piece and you stop and say to yourself, 'Who needs it, anyway?' (Reinforcement)

I want you to imagine that as you eat a dish of your favorite ice cream, you see it turn to fat on your arm. (Reinforcement)

Imagine that you have lost 50 pounds and you are standing naked in front of a mirror. You congratulate yourself for getting rid of all the flab. (Reinforcement)

As with the covert sensitization procedure, the client is asked to practice each scene twice a day at home. Sometimes covert reinforcement is combined with covert sensitization in the following ways:

(1) After the client has imagined himself vomiting, he tells himself that doing that (i.e. giving in to temptation) was stupid and that he will not do it again and administers a reinforcement to himself.

(2) The client imagines he is tempted to eat and feels a little nauseous but decides not to eat and feels better and administers a reinforcement to himself.

Other Procedures Combined with Covert Sensitization and Covert Reinforcement Relaxation

If anxiety appears to be an antecedent condition to eating, the client is taught to relax using a modified Jacobson (1938) procedure. He is taught to use relaxation as a self-control procedure (Cautela, 1969). He is taught to relax before he enters into what he feels will be an anxiety-provoking situation and after he has just experienced anxiety which may still persist in part. He is also instructed to relax and covertly reinforce himself for not eating if he feels anxious and is about to eat.

Desensitization

If it is clear that specific anxiety-provoking situations are antecedent to maladaptive eating, the client is desensitized (Wolpe, 1958) to the situation. Covert reinforcement can also be used to reduce anxiety in specific situations by reinforcing antagonistic responses.

Stimulus Control

The client is instructed to try to eat only in proper eating situations such as the kitchen or dining room. He is told not to eat in such situations as while watching TV or while reading since these situations may act as stimuli for eating. In Hullian terms, they may pick up secondary drive properties (Hull, 1952); or in operant terms, they may become discriminative stimuli (SD) for eating.

Covert Conditioning as a Self-Control Procedure

It is clear from the description of the homework assignments that the client learns to make responses that are antagonistic to eating. Also, before the client is discharged he is given a weight range (e.g. 160-165 lbs.). The client is instructed to weigh himself once a week and to apply the covert conditioning procedure whenever the maximum weight is reached. The procedure is again carefully explained for possible future use.

Length of Treatment

The length of treatment, of course, depends on the desired amount of weight loss. The client is usually seen once per week for a period of three months and then once every two weeks until the desired weight is reached. The average goal for weekly pound loss is two or three pounds.

RESULTS

Though the author has found the procedure outlined above quite effective, anecdotal results such as these are not sufficient evidence for the acceptance of the treatment procedure. The procedure outlined above is confounded by a number of interacting variables such as the behavior of the therapist which is not specified in the procedure. Also, a combination of procedures has been used. Questions arise such as — would desensitization or covert sensitization alone be sufficient to modify maladaptive eating behavior? Of course, the questions can be properly answered by experimental analysis. Although no experimentation has been completed investigating the efficacy of combining covert sensitization and covert reinforcement to the modification of eating behavior, the author is of the opinion that the procedures outlined deserve serious consideration for further investigation for the following reasons:

(1) Experimental studies indicate that covert sensitization is effective in modifying other approach behaviors such as alcoholism (Ashem & Donner, 1968), sexual deviation (Barlow et al., 1969), smoking (Wagner & Bragg, in press).

(2) Studies employing covert reinforcement (Cautela et al., in press; Cautela et al., 1971; Flannery, in press; Krop et al., 1971) indicate that it is a powerful procedure for the modification of behavior.

(3) In one study (Sachs et al., 1970) in which covert sensitization was compared to an operant self-control procedure in eliminating smoking behavior, covert sensitization appeared more effective.

The few studies investigating the efficacy of covert sensitization in the treatment of weight control generally report positive results. Stuart (1967) presented additional anecdotal evidence of the successful combination of covert sensitization with other operant self-control procedures in the elimination of over-eating.

Ashem et al., (1970) compared covert sensitization with an overt aversive stimulus in the treatment of over-eating. They concluded that:

> Results using covert sensitization with obesity appear good. There seems to be no need to use overt stimuli as adjuncts. Undoubtedly, results could be enhanced by conditioning a response incompatible with the compulsive eating response, once the covert sensitization has taken effect.

Sachs & Ingram (1972) found covert sensitization effective in reducing intake of selective foods.

An important question that needs experimental testing is whether the combination of covert sensitization and covert reinforcement is superfluous because maybe either of the procedures alone would be sufficient to eliminate a certain behavior. In the author's experience, the combination of both covert sensitization and covert reinforcement seems to hasten treatment and decrease the probability or relapse.

PROBLEMS ENCOUNTERED IN THE USE OF COVERT CONDITIONING

A number of factors have been found to hinder the successful application of covert conditioning. These factors do not preclude the use of covert conditioning since modification in procedure can usually eliminate or reduce the detrimental effects.

Poor Imagery

The inability to obtain clear imagery is reported by a few (about five percent) of the clients. They claim they cannot get sufficiently clear imagery whenever a scene is described. Usually poor imagery can be overcome by: describing scenes in more detail; emphasizing the sense modality that enables the client to get the clearest imagery; and having the client observe certain real life situations and then try to imagine them immediately after.

Ineffective Aversive Stimuli

Rarely a client will claim that even after very vivid and detailed description of the vomiting scenes, he never can feel nauseous or get any discomfort. For such clients, other possible aversive stimuli are chosen from the Fear Survey Schedule (FSS) or from the interview situation. One client was asked to imagine that the food was covered with worms just as she was about to eat. Another client was asked to imagine that the food turned to blubber as it was entering her body.

Incomplete Homework

Some clients report that they forget or are too busy to do the homework. It is again emphasized that homework will make treatment more effective thereby saving them time or money. Covert reinforcement is applied by having them imagine they are practicing the procedures at home and then a reinforcement is presented.

Health Problems

Contrary to what some colleagues have expected would occur, the clients treated by covert conditioning do not lose their taste for all food. They only lose the "urge" to eat in a maladaptive manner. The author also insists that every patient have a thorough physical examination before treatment is begun. This rarely has to be done, however, since by the time the clients come to the author for treatment, they have made many attempts to lose weight and have had physical examinations in the process.

SUMMARY

In summary, the covert conditioning procedure combines punishment in imagination for eating and reinforcement in imagination for responses antagonistic to eating. Often it is necessary to eliminate the drive component (anxiety) of the eating behavior. In such cases, procedures such as desensitization and relaxation are also employed.

Thus far, there have been no reported adverse effects such as *anorexia nervosa* or physical complaints. The data supporting the general effectiveness of covert sensitization and covert reinforcement as applied to other maladaptive behaviors, the author's experience with the techniques, and all the reports of colleagues warrant serious consideration of the procedures described in this paper. However, hardcore experimental investigations are still needed.

REFERENCES

Ashem, B., & Donner, L. Covert sensitization with alcoholics: A controlled replication. *Behavior Research and Therapy,* 1968, **6**, 7–12.

Ashem, B., Poser, E., & Trudall, P. The use of covert sensitization in the treatment of over-eating. Paper presented at the Association for the Advancement of Behavior Therapy, Miami, September, 1970.

Barlow, D. H., Leitenberg, H., & Agras, W. S. Experimental control of sexual deviation through manipulation of the noxious scene in covert sensitization. *Journal of Abnormal Psychology,* 1969, **5**, 596–601.

Cautela, J. R. The treatment of compulsive behavior by covert sensitization. *Psychological Record,* 1966, **16**, 33–41.

Cautela, J. R. Covert sensitization. *Psychological Record,* 1967, **20**, 459–468.

Cautela, J. R. Behavior therapy and need for behavioral assessment. *Psychotherapy: Theory, Research and Practice,* 1968, **5** (3), 175–179.

Cautela, J. R. Behavior therapy and self-control: Techniques and implications. In C. Franks (Ed.), *Behavior Therapy: Appraisal and Status.* New York: McGraw-Hill, 1969, 323–340.

Cautela, J. R. Covert reinforcement. *Behavior Therapy,* 1970, **1**, 33–50.

Cautela, J. R., & Kastenbaum, R. A reinforcement survey schedule for use in therapy and research. *Psychological Reports,* 1967, **20**, 115–130.

Cautela, J. R., Walsh, K., & Wish, P. The use of covert reinforcement to modify attitudes toward the mentally retarded. *Journal of Psychology,* 1971, **77**, 257–260.

Cautela, J. R., Steffen, J., & Wish, P. An experimental test or covert reinforcement. *Journal of Clinical and Consulting Psychology,* in press.

Ferster, C. B., Nurnberger, J. I., & Levitt, E. B. The control of eating. *Journal of Mathetics,* 1962, **1**, 87–109.

Flannery, R. An investigation of differential effectiveness of office vs *in vivo* therapy of a simple phobia: an outcome study. *Behavior Therapy and Experimental Psychiatry,* in press.

Franks, C. Reflections upon the treatment of sexual disorders by the behavioral clinicians: an historical comparison with the treatment of the alcoholic. *Journal of Sex Research,* 1967, **3**, 212–222.

Harmatz, M. G. & Lapuc, P. Behavior modification of over-eating in a psychiatric population. *Journal of Consulting and Clinical Psychology,* 1968, **32**, 583-587.

Hull, C. *A behavior system.* New Haven: Yale University Press, 1952.

Jacobson, E. *Progressive relaxation.* Chicago: University of Chicago Press, 1938.

Kimble, G. A. *Hilgard & Marquis' Conditioning and Learning.* New York: Appleton-Century-Crofts, 1961.

Krop, H., Calhoon, B., & Verrier, R. Modification of the "self-concept" of emotionally disturbed children by covert reinforcement. *Behavior Therapy,* 1971, **2**, 201–204.

Meyer, V., & Crisp, A. H. Aversion therapy in two cases of obesity. *Behavior Research and Therapy,* 1964, **2**, 143–147.

Moore, C. W., & Crum, B. C. Weight reduction in chronic schizophrenia by means of operant conditioning procedures: a core study. *Behavior Research and Therapy,* 1969, **7**, 129–131.

Pavlov, I. P. *Selected works.* Translated by S. Belsky, J. Gibbons (Ed.). Moscow: Foreign Languages Publishing House, 1955.

Sachs, L. B., Bean, H., & Morrow, J. E. Comparison of smoking treatments. *Behavior Therapy,* 1970, **1**, 465–472.

Sachs, L. B., & Ingram, G. L. Covert sensitization as a treatment for weight control. *Psychological Reports,* 1972, **30**, 971–974.

Skinner. B. F. *Contingencies of reinforcement.* New York: Appleton-Century-Crofts, 1969.

Stuart, R. Behavioral control of over-eating. *Behavioral Research and Therapy,* 1967, **5**, 357–365.

Upper, D., & Newton, J. G. A weight reduction program for schizophrenic patients on a token economy unit: Two case studies. *Journal of Behavior Therapy and Experimental Psychiatry,* 1971, **2**, 113–115.

Viernstein, L. Evaluation of therapeutic techniques of covert sensitization. Unpublished data, Queens College, Charlottesville, North Carolina, 1968.

Wagner, M. K., & Bragg, R. A. Comparing behavior modification methods for habit decrement — smoking, *Journal of Consulting and Clinical Psychology,* in press.

Wolpe, J. *Psychotherapy by reciprocal inhibition.* Stanford: Stanford University Press, 1958.

Wolpe, J., & Lang, P. J. A fear survey schedule for use in behavior therapy. *Behavior Research and Therapy,* 1964, **2**, 27–30.

Chapter 35

Covert Conditioning in the Behavioral Treatment of an Agoraphobic*

Raymond B. Flannery, Jr.†

Summary — The paper describes the extension of covert conditioning procedures, which have been shown in experimental studies to be effective means of changing maladaptive behaviors, to a clinical case of severe, complex agoraphobia. The application of covert reinforcement and covert modeling in significantly reducing severe agoraphobic behavior is outlined, and methodological considerations in the implementation of covert conditioning techniques are discussed.

A number of studies have demonstrated the effectiveness of covert conditioning procedures in changing maladaptive behaviors (Cautela, 1970, 1971; Cautela et al., 1970; Cautela & Wisocki, 1969; Krop et al., 1971; Steffen, 1971). Since the author was an experimenter in two such studies (Cautela, et al., 1971; Flannery, 1970), he sought to extend these laboratory findings in a clinic setting to a case of severe, complex agoraphobia.

CASE REPORT

History

Mrs. J. Was a 46-year-old, white, Roman Catholic. She was married to a chronic alcoholic and was the mother of five adolescents. Raised in the

---

*Reprinted with permission from *Psychotherapy: Theory, Research and Practice*, 1972, 9, 217-220.
†The author wishes to gratefully acknowledge the consulting supervision of Dr. J. R. Cautela, Boston College, on the present case report.

Midwest, the client was molested sexually by her father many times, beginning at age five. When Mrs. J. told her mother of this, the mother was placed in a mental institution after attempting to stab the client's father with a pair of scissors. Mrs. J. then went to live with an aunt and uncle. However, the uncle continued the molesting until the client ran away at age 18. After settling on the East Coast and working successfully as a secretary, the client desired human companionship. This led her to have what she called ''extra-marital affairs,'' which meant dating married men, but not having sexual relations with them. Her guilt feelings over this led her to avoid elevators, subways, buses, and finally her place of work, lest she have an ''affair.'' Her marriage at age 25 abated the problem somewhat; but, within two years, she was again fearful of being alone on public conveyances. Further, she was now afraid of being alone both on the street and even in her own home. Twenty-one years later, Mrs. J. would go nowhere without one of the children.

She was referred to the author as a case of last resort. Previous treatment had included three years of weekly group therapy, and four years of weekly individual therapy, but her phobias proved resistant to change. The presenting problems were the transportation/agoraphobia of 23 years, an obsessional fear of going insane, and hallucinations of the world going dark. Her pretreatment Fear Survey Schedule score (Wolpe, & Lang, 1964) was 264. She was taking prescripted Miltown PRN, and would only come to the clinic by taxi with two children.

Method and Results

The treatment program consisted of 29 sessions of one hour and a quarter each. The first session included a naturalistic explanation (Wolpe, 1958) for the reported hallucinatory phenomenon of darkness. It was pointed out that in her anxiety the client probably hyperventilated, and might also be closing her eyes unintentionally. This phenomenon which had occurred three to five times in the previous five years has not recurred since this explanation was given, and the client's daily anticipatory anxiety over the possibility of this event has been eliminated.

After being taught muscle relaxation (Wolpe & Lazarus, 1966) as a self-control procedure, she was instructed to thought stop (Wolpe, 1958) to her obsessional response of going insane, a response which the baseline frequency indicated happened five times per week. This response was eliminated in six weeks (after a duration of 36 years), and has not recurred since.

In session seven, the client chose the transportation stimuli of the agoraphobia as the most pressing problem to be dealt with. A 20-step, spatial-temporal hierarchy was constructed of the client's riding a bus alone from her home to the clinic. Since self-reports and careful behavioral assessment (Cautela, 1968) revealed Mrs. J. to be afraid of the dissolution of her marriage (Goldstein, 1970), the thematic issue of not having to have an ''affair'' was included in the hierarchy in an attempt to augment stimulus generalization.

Covert reinforcement (Cautela, 1970) was chosen as a new technique with which to approach this problem. In this operant procedure, the reinforcing stimulus is presented in imagination. Usually, the client chooses reinforcers from the Reinforcement Survey Schedule (Cautela & Kastenbaum, 1967), and practices imagining them clearly and vividly. When the person has learned this, he is instructed to pair the reinforcing scene with the word "reinforcement." Then, when the individual emits the response to be increased, the therapist says the word "reinforcement," and the client shifts to imagining the reinforcing stimulus.

This procedure was adapted to Mrs. J.'s problem in the following manner. Based on her general level of fear, the extent of the generalization gradient, and the *in vivo* avoidance of buses for 15 years, a decision was made to present both the responses to be increased (the steps of the hierarchy) and the reinforcing stimuli in imagination. Mrs. J. would imagine one of the 20 steps of the hierarchy, the therapist would say "reinforcement," and the client would shift to imagining one of her reinforcing scenes. This procedure was practiced during treatment and between sessions for the next five weeks (each of the 20 steps of the hierarchy was practiced three times a day). The client successfully rode the bus alone to the clinic for session 12.

When this behavioral response chain was adequately maintained, the therapist hypothesized that an *in vivo* approach to riding the subways, the next stimulus of the transportation avoidance gradient, might facilitate new learning. It was suggested to Mrs. J. that she consider actually riding the subway with the therapist and covertly reinforcing herself after each stop. She returned to the next treatment session visibly shaken, and reported realizing for the first time in her life a fear of being mutilated, particularly stabbed. The client stated that, two days after the suggestion of the *in vivo* program, she was thinking of waiting on the platform for the subway car, and suddenly became aware of the fear of being mutilated not only on the subway or the street, but even in her own home. She could not account for this lack of awareness in her previous seven years of treatment.

A new behavioral analysis of the fear of being mutilated revealed the need to learn several skills including calling for help, enjoying an event without anticipatory fears, and feeling secure in the darkness. As the client was in acute distress, vicarious learning by modeling (Bandura, 1969) appeared indicated. Since Mrs. J. asked to begin with her fear of being mutilated at home during the night, practical considerations precluded overt modeling. Thus, Covert Modeling (Cautela, 1971) was introduced. In this procedure the therapist writes a script for a given problem which incorporates the selected adaptive behaviors, the correct discriminative stimuli, the contingencies of reinforcement, and the appropriate affect for a given situation. The client is instructed to imagine a model performing the appropriate behaviors as the therapist reads them from the script. When the individual can do this clearly, he is then instructed to imagine himself as the model engaging in exactly the same behaviors.

This technique was adapted for Mrs. J. by writing a scene in which she imagined a woman her own age enjoying television at home alone, calmly putting out the lights at bedtime since she knew she could call for help, and falling into a restful sleep. Mrs. J. was instructed to covertly model this scene 30 times each day. She reported one week later that she had no fear of being home alone, no fear of mutilation in her own home, no problems in sleeping, and no further use of Miltown. In addition, she spontaneously reported a dream in which she spoke up to her father (now deceased) about his immoral behavior when she was a youngster.

In the remaining sessions, the client demonstrated her newly learned ability to change her own behaviors. For example, she wrote her own covertly modeled script for going to the beauty parlor, and then actually had her first permanent in many years. She began to spontaneously create her own *in vivo* programs such as incrementally reinforcing herself in imagery for traveling to different parts of the city, and actually observing women in supermarkets to see how they managed environmental events. After spending two sessions discussing her relationship with her husband and the possibility of a divorce, she terminated with the feeling that she had mastered a basic set of skills she could apply to future problems.

At the end of treatment, Mrs. J.'s Fear Survey Schedule score was 183; she could walk the streets alone or remain at home relaxed; she continued to ride the bus and stated she would master the subway at her own pace. She was considering part-time employment, and thinking through her marital problems in a composed manner. A four-month follow-up indicated that these treatment gains had been maintained. In addition, the client had had to face exploratory surgery for a possible cancer malignancy and hysterectomy, and had been able to draw up her own covert modeling sequence for the hospitalization.

DISCUSSION

In a single case study no definitive statements can be made about the effectiveness of differing procedures on observed treatment outcome (Paul, 1969). However, there appears to be some presumptive evidence for the contributing effectiveness of both the covert reinforcement (Cautela, 1970) and the covert modeling (Cautela, 1971) procedures in the present case. The client's severe agoraphobic behavior, resistant through seven years of treatment, changed dramatically in the expected direction when these procedures were introduced for the fear of buses, and fear of mutilation respectively. The case report can serve as an important source of hypotheses for further evaluation (Lazarus & Davison, 1971). The present study included such clinical findings suggestive of further research.

The first was the use of the actual fear stimulus which laboratory data

(Cautela et al., 1971; Flannery, 1970) suggested facilitated learning. These findings cannot be extrapolated isomorphically to the severely incapacitated clinic patient. The general level of stress, the number and extent of presenting problems, and the impracticalities of the natural environment may not only preclude presenting the actual stimulus, but may point to the obvious advantages of covert techniques. As a case in point, an *in vivo* modeling of being home alone at night was partially precluded because the stimuli in the client's home had adversive properties of long duration, and because she was too embarrassed to observe a live model. Here, the covert modeling technique provided a necessary alternative for new learning. Further, it should be noted that, while the client at first rejected the use of actual stimuli, she spontaneously used actual stimuli towards the end of treatment. This change may have resulted from a general reduction in fear, the contingent reinforcement of successful progress *per se* (Wolpe & Flood, 1970), or boredom with imagery. In any case, these differing findings suggest the need for flexibility by the clinician adapting behavioral techniques in a community mental health center.

Another clinical finding in this case was the importance of teaching all techniques as self-control procedures (Cautela, 1969). Not only did the client apply her knowledge to recurring problems; but emitted a most adaptive set of behaviors when faced with a serious crisis (surgery). This high degree of transfer of training in a stressful and highly dissimilar situation suggests the need for further research into the general nature of the self-control process (Marston & Feldman, 1970). A related finding specific to the present case was the problem presented by the rapidity of treatment gains made by this client. When treatment was under control of the therapist, thought-stopping was employed to eliminate the fear of failure of maintaining behavioral goals. However, as the client progressed, social reinforcement came from many sources, and the thought of failing was more difficult to extinguish. The client chose to live with this subjective fear, and continue her overt behavioral changes. Two variables appeared important here. The first was the importance of action as a valued belief by the ethnic group to which Mrs. J. belonged (Spiegel, 1959). The second was that the poor social reinforcement standards (Baron, 1966) of people in low-income communities may augment the fear of failure when successful gains have been made. That the interaction effect of these two variables may necessitate the adaptation of behavior modification techniques for this population in a community setting is currently being investigated by the author.

A third finding from this study suggesting the need for further experimental study is the effect of imagery on cognition. The client's sudden awareness of her fear of being physically mutilated after completion of the covert reinforcement procedure (Cautela, 1970) is a finding highly similar to those reported by Cautela (1965) for Systematic Desensitization (Wolpe, 1958). It may well be that the client becomes relaxed enough to perceive antecedent-consequent relationships which were formerly avoided because of the intense anxiety associated with them. Also the client's spontaneous report of her dream of assertive behavior to her father after completing the covert modeling procedure (Cautela, 1971) is akin to that reported by Bergin (1970) following desensitization. Both of these findings suggest the importance of cognitive variables in behavior modification procedures (Beck, 1970; Bergin, 1970).

REFERENCES

Bandura, A. *Principles of behavior modification.* New York: Holt, Rinehart, and Winston, 1969.

Baron, R. Social reinforcement effects as a function of social reinforcement history. *Psychological Review*, 1966, 6, 529-539.

Beck, A. Cognitive therapy: Nature and relation to behavior therapy. *Behavior Therapy*, 1970, 1, 184-200.

Bergin, A. Cognitive therapy and behavior therapy: Foci for a multidimensional approach to treatment. *Behavior Therapy*, 1970, 1, 205-212.

Cautela, J. Desensitization and insight. *Behavior Research and Therapy*, 1965, 3, 59-64.

Cautela, J. Behavior therapy and the need for behavioral assessment. *Psychotherapy: Theory, Research and Practice*, 1968, 5(3), 175-179.

Cautela, J. Behavior therapy and self-control: Techniques and implication. In C. M. Franks (Ed.), *Behavior therapy: Appraisal and status.* New York: McGraw-Hill, 1969.

Cautela, J. Covert reinforcement. *Behavior Therapy*, 1970, 1, 33-50.

Cautela, J. Covert modeling. Paper presented at the Association for the Advancement of Behavior Therapy, Washington, D.C., September, 1971.

Cautela, J., Flannery, R., Jr., & Hanley, S. Covert modeling: An experimental test. Unpublished data, Boston College, 1971.

Cautela, J., & Kastenbaum, R. A reinforcement survey schedule for use in therapy, training, and research. *Psychological Reports*, 1967, 20 1115-1130.

Cautela, J., Walsh, K., & Wish, P. The use of covert reinforcement to modify attitudes toward retardates. *Journal of Social Psychology*, 1970, in press.

Cautela, J., & Wisocki, P. The use of imagery in the modification of attidues toward the elderly: A preliminary report. *Journal of Psychology*, 1969, 73, 193-199.

Flannery, R., Jr. The use of actual and imagined fear stimuli in the behavior modification of a simple fear with covert reinforcement. Unpublished doctoral dissertation, University of Windsor, 1970.

Goldstein, A. Case conference: Some aspects of agoraphobia. *Journal of Behavior Therapy and Experimental Psychiatry*, 1970, 1, 305-313.

Goldstein, A., Heller, K., & Sechrest, L. *Psychotherapy and the psychology of behavior change.* New York: John Wiley, 1966.

Krop, H., Calhoon, B., & Verrier, R. Modification of the "self-concept" of emotionally disturbed children by covert reinforcement. *Behavioral Therapy*, 1971, 2, 201-204.

Lazarus, A., & Davison, G. Clinical innovations in research and practice. In A. Bergin, & S. Garfield (Eds.), *Handbook of psychotherapy and behavior change.*

New York: John Wiley, 1971.

Marston, A., & Feldman, S. Toward use of self-control in behavior modification. Paper presented at the American Psychological Association, Miami Beach, September, 1970.

Paul, G. Outcome of systematic desensitization, I: background procedures, and uncontrolled reports of individual treatment. In C. M. Franks (Ed.), *Behavior therapy: Appraisal and status*. New York: McGraw-Hill, 1969.

Spiegel, J. Some cultural aspects of transference and countertransfer:. In J. Masserman (Ed.), *Individual and familial dynamics*. New York: Grune and Stratton, 1959.

Steffen, J. Effects of covert reinforcement upon hospitalized schizophrenics. Paper presented at the Eastern Psychological Association, New York City, April, 1971.

Wolpe, J. *Psychotherapy by reciprocal inhibition*. Stanford, Ca.: Stanford University Press, 1958.

Wolpe, J., & Flood, J. The effect of relaxation on the galvanic skin response to repeated phobic stimuli in ascending order. *Journal of Behavior Therapy and Experimental Psychiatry*, 1970, 1, 195-200.

Wolpe, J., & Lang, P. A fear survey schedule for use in behavior therapy, *Behavior Research and Therapy*, 1964, 2, 27-30.

Wolpe, J., & Lazarus, A. *Behavior therapy techniques*. New York: Pergamon Press, 1966.

Chapter 36

The Use of Covert Conditioning in Modifying Pain Behavior*

Joseph R. Cautela

Summary — The covert conditioning procedure has been successfully employed to modify a wide range of behaviors. There is both anecdotal and experimental evidence that cognitive strategies can modify pain responses. The rationale and description of the application of covert conditioning to modify pain responses are given. A case is presented to illustrate how covert conditioning can be combined with other procedures to modify pain. Cautions and implications of the procedures are discussed.

There are a number of reasons to pursue research in investigating the relationship of psychological variables and pain.

(1) There are some pain responses whose etiology seems to be mainly psychological.

(2) Psychological factors influence the pain threshold.

(3) Reliance on the use of drugs can sometimes cause addiction and other side effects.

(4) Sometimes pain is intractable to all physical therapy, including drugs and surgery.

(5) Pain can lead to aversive social consequences.

Since the sensation of pain must always be a response to some antecedent, it is not too far-fetched to consider it subject to the same influences as other responses, in being affected by learning and other variables.

We shall consider two aspects of the pain experience; the conceptualization of pain, and the development of procedures to eliminate or alleviate it.

*Reprinted with permission from the *Journal of Behavior Therapy and Experimental Psychiatry*, 1977, 8, 45-52.

THE CONCEPTUALIZATION OF PAIN

In this paper pain is conceptualized as a response with one or more of the following characteristics: verbal report of pain; behavioral expressions such as moaning, groaning, grimacing; and avoidance of stimuli considered noxious or defined by the client as noxious. One might also include autonomic behavior such as increased respiration, heart rate, GSR, and so forth but these responses are also concomitants of other kinds of reported arousals.

The pain response has two other important features: (1) It is affected by the quality of other subjective experiences that can be labelled on an unpleasant-pleasant dimension, i.e. if an individual is anxious (unpleasant state) the pain threshold will be lowered and is apt to be labelled as more intense than if an individual is experiencing a state he labels as pleasurable. (Beecher 1969; Melzack 1961); (2) The pain response can be sometimes brought under operant control (Fordyce et al., 1973; Levendusky and Pankratz 1975).

PROCEDURES TO MODIFY PAIN

The procedures to be described are designed to modify the antecedents or the consequences of a pain response, or to interrupt the behavior itself. As indicated above there is some evidence that distraction, relaxation, imagining a pleasant scene and operant manipulation can modify pain behavior. The main components of the treatment package here proposed are thought stopping, relaxation, imagining a pleasant scene and operant manipulation by covert and overt consequences. The procedure is based on the covert conditioning assumptions (Cautela, 1973) and the anecdotal and experimental evidence reported by various investigators. There is some evidence that covert conditioning is effective in modifying behavior (Cautela, 1973; Kazdin, 1973a; 1973b; 1974a; 1974b).

Rationale for Procedures

Thought stopping has a distractive component as well as whatever inhibiting effect is associated with the word "stop". The distractive component can have a counterconditioning effect by eliciting a new response in the presence of the overt and covert stimuli that elicit the maladaptive pain response.

Similarly, a distractive *relaxation* has component, i.e. attending to the muscles to relax them, besides in and of itself reducing any pain due to muscle tension or anxiety (Bobey and Davidson, 1970).

The primary rationale for the use of *covert reinforcement* is to increase the probability that if one feels pain one will say "Stop!", then relax. Covert reinforcement is also used to dissociate certain activities and the pain response. This is done by asking the client to imagine the situation in which he usually experiences pain, but this time he feels no pain and is completely relaxed. Then he imagines a pleasant scene (reinforcement). Two other components of the procedure could also produce pain reduction. The reinforcing scene imagined might reciprocally inhibit the pain response; and thinking of a pleasant scene has distracting counterconditioning potentialities.

Experimental Evidence

Scott and Leonard (Note 1) compared covert reinforcement with other procedures for reducing pain threshold. The threshold for cold pain was obtained for male and female subjects by having them immerse one hand in ice water before and after one of four experimental treatments. The treatments were: (1) the covert positive reinforcement procedure (reinterpreting the sensations in a manner incompatible with the experience of the pain and then imagining a pleasant, ''reinforcing'' image), (2) a reinterpretation strategy only, (3) leading the group to expect pain reduction on the posttest and (4) a control group. In the covert reinforcement group the pain threshold rose above that of the control group, while in the groups given instructions to expect pain reduction or cognitive reinterpretation it did not.

Description of the Procedure

As in the attempt to modify any other behavior, a behavioral analysis is performed in a manner described elsewhere (Cautela, 1968). The client is also given the Pain Survey Schedule presented in Table 1.

Table 36.1 Pain Survey Schedule

1. When did you first notice your pain? _____

2. Where was it? _____

3. What did you do about it? _____

4. Has your pain been off and on over the months or years? _____
Yes _____No_____. If yes, describe its development. _____
_____
_____

5. Where do you feel pain now? _____
_____

6. What do you think is the cause of your pain? _____

7. Is your _____pain with you all the time? Yes _____
No _____

8. Does your pain spread? Yes _____ No _____ Where? _____

9. Where does your pain seem to settle? _____

Table 36.1 (continued)

10. How long does the pain take to become its worst? _____

11. How long does the pain usually last? _____

12. How would you rate your pain? Mild _____ Fairly severe _____ Severe _____

13. If you were to rate the worse pain you have as 100%, how would you describe your pain on a scale from 0-100%?

   a. Dull _____%

   b. Sharp _____%

   c. Piercing _____%

   d. Deep _____%

   e. Crushing _____%

   f. Throbbing _____%

   g. Steady _____%

   h. Burning _____%

   i. Prickling _____%

   j. Shooting _____%

   k. Stabbing _____%

   l. Boring _____%

   m. Numb _____%

   n. Dead _____%

   o. Tingling _____%

   p. Pins and Needles _____%

   q. Bursting _____%

   r. Tender to the touch _____%

14. Is pain accompanied by:

   a. Vomiting: Yes_____ No _____

   b. Nausea: Yes_____ No_____

   c. Dizziness: Yes _____ No_____

   d. Feeling faint: Yes_____ No_____

   e. Fear: Yes_____ No_____

   f. Rapid breathing: Yes_____ No_____

   g. Sweating: Yes_____ No_____

   h. Blurred vision: Yes_____ No_____

   i. Feeling flushed: Yes_____ No_____

   j. Heart beating fast: Yes_____ No_____

   k. Heart beating loud: Yes_____ No_____

15. What times does it become worse?

	Yes	No
a. When you wake up	_____	_____
b. From breakfast to lunch	_____	_____
c. From lunch to supper	_____	_____
d. From supper to bedtime	_____	_____
e. While trying to sleep at night	_____	_____

16. Do you have warning signs that the pain is coming? Yes_____ No_____ If yes, what are they? _____

17. If you were to rate the worst pain you have as 100%, how would you rate the pain from 0 to 100% in the following situations?

   a. Getting out of bed_____%

   b. Standing up after being seated_____%

   c. Lifting_____%

   d. Working_____%

   e. Walking_____%

   f. Sitting_____%

   g. Standing_____%

   h. Coughing_____%

   i. Sneezing_____%

   j. Urinating_____%

   k. Defecating_____%

   l. Moving the part that bothers you if it is a part that can be moved_____%

   m. Running_____%

   n. Leaning over_____%

   o. Other exertion_____%

Table 36.1 (continued)

18. How much does pain interfere with the following activities from 0 to 100% where 100% means you cannot do it at all because of the pain.

    a. While trying to fall asleep at night_____%

    b. While trying to sleep during the night_____%

    c. leaving the house_____%

    d. Your sexual activities_____%

    e. Enjoying your family_____%

    f. Enjoying yourself in hobbies or relaxation_____%

19. How would you rate your pain (0-100%) in the following situations?

    a. Watching T.V._____%   h. Being alone_____%

    b. Reading_____%   i. Feeling lonely_____%

    c. Watching movies_____%   j. Being anxious_____%

    d. Watching sports_____%   k. Being bored_____%

    e. Socializing with friends_____%   l. Being busy_____%

    f. Socializing with strangers_____%   m. Being happy_____%

    g. Arguing with someone_____%

20. How many times a day do you think of pain? 0-5_____, 5-10_____, 10-20_____, 20-40_____, 40+_____.

21. What medication(s) have you received before now?

Medication	How long did you take it	How effective was it?
_____	_____	_____
_____	_____	_____
_____	_____	_____

22. What medication are you taking now?

    a. _____   dosage _____   times a day _____

    b. _____   dosage _____   times a day _____

    c. _____   dosage _____   times a day _____

23. How well does the pain medication work? _____

24. What other medication do you take?

    a. _____   dosage _____   times a day _____

    b. _____   dosage _____   times a day _____

25. What do you do besides taking pain medication to relieve pain? _____

26. Does drinking coffee, alcohol, or other beverages tend to bring on or affect the pain? Yes_____ No_____. If other beverages are involved, what are they? _____

27. Does any type of food seem to bring on or affect the pain? Yes_____ No_____. If yes, what? _____

28. What other factors seem to bring on or are associated with pain? _____

29. What do your relatives or friends do when you complain of pain? _____

Table 36.1 (continued)

30. If you get rid of pain how would your life change? _____

_____

_____

31. Comments: _____

_____

Thereafter he is given the following rationale:

You can consider pain a psychological response. This is true whether it is caused by some obvious organic factor such as a wound, a disease such as arthritis, or tension. There is some recent experimental evidence to indicate that pain can be manipulated by certain psychological techniques. Also, it has been my experience that it is possible to reduce or eliminate pain by some behavior therapy procedures that we will use. The treatment requires a lot of cooperation on your part as well as my teaching you the techniques.

Treatment Procedure

The client is told to yell, "Stop, relax" and then imagine a reinforcing scene every time he feels pain or the pain becomes more intense. He is told to continue this three part sequence until the pain subsides or is eliminated. Situations in which the pain occurs or is exacerbated are determined. Covert positive reinforcement is applied to these situations by having the client imagine he is in these situations and feels very comfortable and free from pain, and then he reinforces himself covertly. For example, the client who reports he feels cramps when he wakes up in the morning is asked to imagine he wakes up feeling fine, comfortable and with no cramps, and then to imagine a pleasant scene. If at any time during the day or evening pain occurs or becomes more intense, the client is to imagine the situation again, but this time with no pain and with a reinforcing scene to follow. He is asked to do this five times for each pain event before retiring for the evening. As part of the therapeutic strategy, he is instructed not to complain about pain to anyone. Also, significant others are asked to ignore the client every time he complains of pain. If their cooperation is not obtained, the covert extinction procedure is employed (Cautela, 1971), by which the client is asked to imagine that he is complaining of pain to someone but that that individual completely ignores him. If the pain is usually localized in a particular area of the body, he is especially trained to relax that part particularly intensely.

CASE ILLUSTRATION

Case history

The client was a 37-yr-old married female with three children. She was referred for therapy for treatment of depression and, as she stated, "To do something about the damned arthritis" which was causing her great pain. She reported that when she was anxious, she could "feel anxiety" and pain in her knees and toes. She had undergone psychotherapy for 5 yr without apparent alleviation of her depression or arthritic symptoms.

At the time of referral, the client was taking six eight-hour aspirins and 50 mg of Mercaptopurine daily, as well as Tofranil 150 mg a day for her depression. Her previous treatment for arthritis included: Indocin (3 months), Plaquenil (6 months), and gold salts (2 yr).

In 1972 she was diagnosed as having psoriatic arthritis. Since then her condition worsened until at the time of referral she had generalized pain over most of her body, especially severe in her knees and toes and slightly less in the wrists. At times the pain became so severe that help was required to get in and out of chairs. Crutches were recommended when her knees were highly inflamed and the pain was intolerable. Finally, in situations requiring considerable walking, she used a wheel chair. For the last 3 yr, each knee was drained of between 50 and 70 cc of sinovial fluid almost twice every month. One toe in her left foot and two toes on her right foot had become fused.

Treatment

We agreed to attend first to her pain since it was aversive and incapacitating, and also seemed to me to be a contributing factor to the "depression". The usual rationale was presented to the client. She was also told of the possible reinforcement of her pain behavior by the attention she received from her husband and children following her complaining, because the behavioral analysis revealed that she constantly complained to her family about her condition.

She was given the following treatment procedures:

(1) She was taught relaxation as a self-control procedure (Cautela, 1969) to reduce general stress and to reduce the pain.

(2) She was told to shout "stop" to herself, relax all over with special emphasis on her wrists, knees, and toes, and then to imagine a pleasant scene whenever she became especially aware of pain and when there was an exacerbation of it.

(3) She was taught to use covert reinforcement (Cautela, 1970) to reduce pain in the situations such as getting in and out of chairs, walking, writing, typing, turning door knobs, and unscrewing lids. The scenes involved imagining that she was in one of these situations, but experiencing no pain and then imagining a reinforcing scene. She was asked to do this five times daily for each situation experienced.

(4) She was told not to complain to anyone about her pain experience.

(5) Her husband and children were asked to ignore her whenever she complained.

Results

The client's husband and children cooperated and did not respond when she complained. She complained twice the first week and then never again. She reported that after one week, the pain was minimal. After 3 weeks, she reported no pain in her knees and feet. Scenes were continued every day for three more weeks. Occasionally she experienced pain in her wrists after writing a great deal (she was taking three undergraduate courses each semester), but reported that the pain was relieved through the use of scenes. The gains have been maintained for 8 months. At the time of this report, she and her husband are still being seen weekly for marital counseling. She no longer finds reason to take Tofranil.

DISCUSSION

Since this is an anecdotal report, it is not presented as evidence for the efficacy of the procedure. It is a description of how the procedure can be utilized in clinical practice. The procedure could have been coincidentally applied at the beginning of spontaneous remission due to other factors. Also, the medication could have become effective.

Although causal inferences concerning the procedures cannot be drawn, the procedures can be conceptualized as operating to alter pain behavior. Analyzing the results from the theoretical model proposed in this paper, thought stopping had the effect of presenting an incompatible response to the pain response. Relaxation served a similar function. There is some evidence that arthritic individuals respond to stress by contraction of the muscles that control the tendons across the joints (Engel, et al., 1971, pp. 349-375). If it is assumed that some of the arthritic pain is due to the tightening of the muscles across the tendons that control the joints, relaxation might reciprocally inhibit the pain response, through the development of an incompatible response. The covert reinforcement procedure was intended to reinforce the functional relationship between the pain response, saying "Stop", and relaxing. Since the reinforcement imagined was pleasant, it could have also acted to reciprocally inhibit the pain response. Finally, thought stopping, relaxation, and covert positive reinforcement could have all been distracting stimuli. The decrease in the reinforcement of complaining behavior could have extinguished not only the overt complaining behavior but also the covert pain response. This is consistent with the covert conditioning model that covert behavior influences overt behavior. It is quite likely that when one complains about the behavior, there is some accompanying imagery that also gets reinforced. Another factor complicating its interpretation of results is the possibility that the ignoring alone (Fordyce et al., 1973) could account for the results.

Another factor that could also account for these results and the effectiveness of covert positive reinforcement in dealing with pain is that the covert reinforcement procedure involves a cognitive rehearsal. Cognitive rehearsal has been found to modify pain behavior (Bobey and Davidson, 1970). One could hypothesize that the effectiveness of cognitive rehearsal is due to decreasing uncertainty and increasing familiarity. There is some evidence to support the hypothesis (Jones, Bantler and Petry, 1966; Neufeld and Davidson, 1971).

As in any beginning theoretical model the assumptions should be investigated rigorously and evidence accumulated to determine the efficacy of the methodology. The attempt of this paper was to provide a theoretical model and methodology that can be investigated and modified so that more tools will be available to modify pain behavior. It is not the contention of this paper that covert conditioning can generally be used alone as the main therapeutic approach. Often it is necessary to use drugs, increase the general level of reinforcement and use other behavioral procedures such as relaxation and contingency management.

REFERENCE NOTE

Scott D. S. and Leonard C. F. (1974). The modification of pain threshold by the covert reinforcement procedure and a cognitive strategy. Unpublished manuscript. Boston College.

REFERENCES

Beecher H. K. (1969). Anxiety and pain. *J. Am. Med. Ass. 209*, 1080.

Bobey M. J. and Davidson P. O. (1970). Psychological factors affecting pain tolerance, *J. Psychosom. Res. 14*, 371-376.

Cautela J. R. (1969). *Behavior Therapy and Self-Control: Techniques and Implications*. (Ed. by Franks C. M.), Behavior Therapy: Appraisal and Status, McGraw-Hill, New York.

Cautela J. R. (1968). Behavior therapy and the need for behavioral assessment. *Psychother.: Theory, Res., Practice 5*, 175-9.

Cautela J. R. (1970). Covert reinforcement, *Behav. Therapy, 1*, 35-50.

Cautela J. R. (1971). Covert extinction, *Behav. Therapy. 2*, 192-200.

Cautela J. R. (1973). Covert processes and behavior modification. *J. Nerv. Ment. Dis. 157*, 27-36.

Engel B. T., Shapiro D., Benson H., Slucki H., Whatmore G. B., Harris A. H. and Vachon, L. (1971). The use of biofeedback training in enabling patients to control autonomic function, *Mental Health Progress Reports* (Ed. by Sengal J.) *5*, 349-375.

Fordyce W. E., Fowler R. S., Lehmann J. F., DeLateur B., Sand P. and Treischmann R. (1973). Operant conditioning in the treatment of chronic pain, *Arch. Phys. Med. Rehabil. 54*, 399-408.

Jones A., Bantler P. M. and Petry G. (1966). The reduction of uncertainty concerning future pain. *J. Abnorm. Psychol. 71*, 87-94.

Kazdin A. E. (1973a). Covert modeling and the reduction of avoidance behavior, *J.*

Abnor. Psychol. 81, 87-95 (a).

Kazdin A. E. (1973b). Effects of covert modeling and reinforcement on assertive behavior, *Proceedings of the 81st Annual Convention of the American Psychological Association, Montreal, Canada,* (Vol. 1), pp. 537-538(b).

Kazdin A. E. (1974a). Covert modeling, model similarity and reduction of avoidance behavior, *Behav. Therapy, 5*, 325-340(a).

Kazdin A. E. (1974b). Effects of covert modeling and model reinforcement on assertive behavior, *J. Abnorm. Psychol. 84*, 240-252(b).

Levendusky R. and Pankratz L. (1975). Self-control techniques as an alternative to pain medication. *J. Abnorm. Psychol. 84*, 165-8.

Melzack R. (1961). The perception of pain. *Scientific American.* February, Reprint 457. California: W. H. Freeman and Co.

Neufeld R. W. J. and Davidson P. O. (1971). The effects of vicarious and cognitive rehearsal on pain tolerance, *J. Psychosom. Res. 15*, 329-335.

Name Index

Subject Index

Achievement Anxiety Test, 99, 100, 101, 103

Agoraphobia, treatment of, 358-364

Alcoholism, treatment of, 8, 9, 11, 35-36, 40, 41, 247-250

Amphetamine addiction. *See* Drug abuse, treatment of

Anorexia nervosa, 356

Approach behavior test, 107, 108

Assertiveness training, 4, 33, 221, 228-229, 295, 300, 316

Assessment. *See* Behavioral analysis and assessment

Aversion-relief therapy, 33

Aversive conditioning, 40-41, 43-44, 52-53, 63, 182, 257-258, 284, 292, 295, 310-311, 316, 323, 327

Behavioral alcohol interview questionnaire, 248

Behavioral analysis and assessment, 4, 53, 59, 64, 164, 296-297, 360

Behavioral Avoidance Test, 122, 123

Behavioral processes, classification of, 19-20

Behavioral rehearsal, 290, 339

Behavioral role-playing test, 232, 233, 237-238

Behaviorism, 17-19

Biofeedback, 328

Chronic pain. *See* Pain, treatment of

Cigarette smoking. *See* Smoking, treatment of

Cognitive behavior modification, 3, 4, 20

Conflict Resolution Inventory, 224, 232, 233, 236, 237, 241

Contracting, 288, 291, 316, 327

Coverant control therapy, 339-341, 344-345

Covert conditioning
  general assumptions underlying, 21-22
  general rationale for, 4

Covert extinction
  description of, 9-10, 164-167
  difficulties with, 10
  experimental evidence on, 10
  learning theory basis for, 167-168
  possible problems with, 168-169
  used in combination with other procedures, 169-170

Covert modeling
  advantages of, 12
  description of, 11-12, 190-191
  experimental evidence on, 12, 25, 27, 191-192

Covert negative reinforcement
  choice of aversive stimulus for, 7, 139
  compared to ''anxiety-relief'' conditioning, 143-144
  description of, 7-8, 138-141
  experimental evidence on, 8, 141-142, 146-152
  practical considerations, 142-143

Covert positive reinforcement
  compared to systematic desensitization, 97-104
  description of, 5-6, 71-74, 87, 118-119
  experimental evidence on, 6-7, 24-27, 87-88, 117-134
  parameters of, 79-81
  possible problems with, 81

Covert reinforcement sampling, 288

Covert response cost
  compared to overt response cost, 266
  description of, 10-11, 260-262
  difficulties with, 11
  experimental evidence on, 11, 264
  typical examples of use of, 263-264
  used in combination with other procedures, 265-266

About the Contributors

Dr. Dennis Upper is coordinator of the Behavior Therapy Unit at the Veterans Administration Medical Center in Brockton, Massachusetts, and Instructor in Psychology in the Psychiatry Department of the Harvard Medical School. He graduated from Yale University and received his Ph.D. from Case Western Reserve University in 1969. A prolific researcher and writer, Dr. Upper has authored or edited many articles, chapters, and books on behavior therapy, including *Perspectives in Behavior Therapy* and the *Behavioral Group Therapy: An Annual Review* series. He was awarded the Diploma in Clinical Psychology of the American Board of Professional Psychology (ABPP) in 1978.

Joseph R. Cautela is a professor of Psychology at Boston College, and director of the Behavior Modification Program. He is past-president of the Association for the Advancement of the Behavior Therapies. He has been a visiting professor at the Max Planck Institute in Munich. Author of two books and over ninety articles in the field of behavior therapy, he is most well-known for his original work in the development of the covert conditioning model.

W. Stewart Agras: Stanford University, Department of Psychiatry and Behavioral Sciences, Stanford, California 94305

L. Michael Ascher: Eastern Pennsylvania Psychiatric Institute, Behavior Therapy Unit, Psychiatry Department, Henry Avenue, Pennsylvania 19129

David H. Barlow: Brown University/Butler Hospital, 345 Blackstone Boulevard, Providence, Rhode Island 02906

Mary Grace Baron: Behavioral Development Center, 80 Mt. Hope Avenue, Providence, Rhode Island 02906

Edward B. Blanchard: State University of New York-Albany, Department of Psychology, Albany, New York 12222

Douglas O. Draper: Clinical Psychology and Psychiatry Associates, Suite 234, Highland Village, Jackson, Mississippi 39211

Raymond B. Flannery, Jr.: Somerville Mental Health Center, Somerville, Massachusetts 02144

John P. Galassi: University of North Carolina at Chapel Hill, Counseling Psychology, School of Education, Peabody Hall 037A, Chapel Hill, North Carolina 27574

Louis Gershman: Villanova University, Villanova, Pennsylvania 19085

Kinloch Gill, Jr.: Region VI Mental Health Center, P.O. Box 1505, Greenwood, Mississippi 38930

K. Gunnar Gotestam: University of Trondheim, Ostmarka Hospital, P.O. Box 3008, N-7001 Trondheim, Norway

Stephen Hanley: 195 Willow Street, West Roxbury, Massachusetts 02132

Linda R. Hay: Brown University/Butler Hospital, 345 Blackstone Boulevard, Providence, Rhode Island 02906

William M. Hay: Brown University/Butler Hospital, Division Psychiatry and Human Behavior, Providence, Rhode Island 02906

Ronald C. Hughes: Denton County Mental Health Unit, 319 E. Oak, Denton, Texas 76201

Alan E. Kazdin: Pennsylvania State University, Department of Psychology, University Park, Pennsylvania 16802

Sherrill R. Kendrick: Pan American University, Medical Center, 1111 North 10th Street, McAllen, Texas 78501

Marion P. Kostka: West Virginia University, Student Counseling Service, Morgantown, West Virginia 26506

James R. Lane III: Regional Mental Health Complex, P.O. Box 1567, Harksville, Mississippi 39759

Harold Leitenberg: University of Vermont, Psychology Department, Burlington, Vermont 05401

James P. McCullough: Virginia Commonwealth University, Psychology Department, 800 W. Franklin St., Richmond, Virginia 23284

Lennart Melin: University of Uppsala, Department of Applied Psychology, P.O. Box 468, S-751 06 Uppsala, Sweden

Rosemery O. Nelson: University of North Carolina at Greensboro, Psychology Department, Greensboro, North Carolina 27412

Michael J. Paquin: University of Western Ontario, Psychology Department, London, Canada N6A 5C2

Susan L. Reese: University of Arizona, Health Science Center, 2631 East 20th Street, Tucson, Arizona 85716

Ted L. Rosenthal: Memphis State University, Department of Psychology, Memphis, Tennessee 38152

Anne K. Rosenstiel: Duke University, Department of Psychology, Durham, North Carolina 27706

Donald S. Scott: University of Carolina at Chapel Hill, Pain Clinic, Dental Research Center, Chapel Hill, North Carolina 27514

John J. Steffen: University of Cincinnati, Department of Psychology, Cincinnati, Ohio 45221

Thomas R. Tondo: Hamden Mental Health Service, 3000 Dixwell Avenue, Hamden, Connecticut 06518

Patricia A. Wisocki: University of Massachusetts, Psychology Department, Amherst, Massachusetts 01003

Pergamon General Psychology Series

Editors: Arnold P. Goldstein, Syracuse University
Leonard Krasner, SUNY, Stony Brook

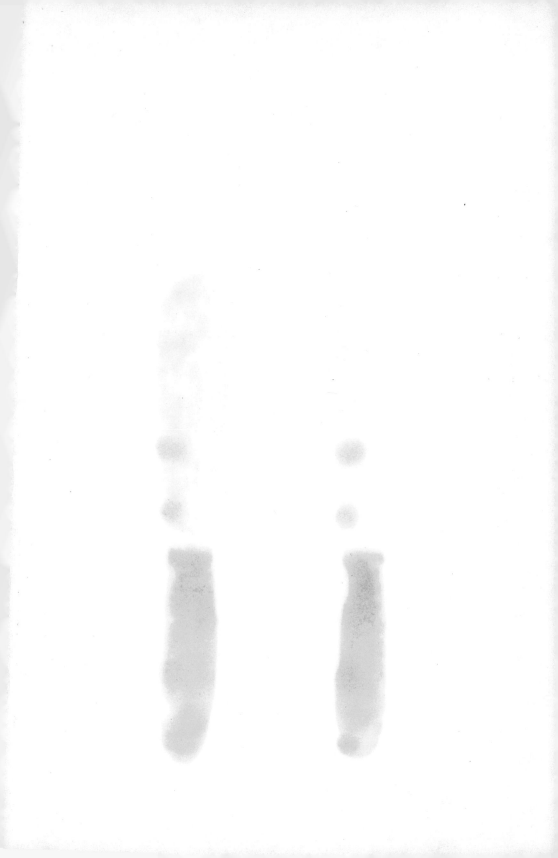